THE LAW OF THEFT

THE LAW OF THEFT

FOURTH EDITION

J. C. SMITH, Q.C., LL.D., F.B.A.
Honorary Bencher of Lincoln's Inn;
Honorary Fellow of Downing College,
Cambridge;
Professor of Common Law
and Head of the
Department of Law
University of Nottingham

LONDON
BUTTERWORTHS
1979

ENGLAND:	BUTTERWORTH & CO. (PUBLISHERS) LTD.
	LONDON: 88 Kingsway, WC2B 6AB
AUSTRALIA:	BUTTERWORTHS PTY. LTD.
	SYDNEY: 586 Pacific Highway,
	Chatswood, NSW 2067
	Also at Melbourne, Brisbane, Adelaide and Perth
CANADA:	BUTTERWORTH & CO. (CANADA) LTD.
	TORONTO: 2265 Midland Avenue,
	Scarborough, M1P 4S1
NEW ZEALAND:	BUTTERWORTHS OF NEW ZEALAND LTD.
	WELLINGTON: 77-85 Customhouse Quay
SOUTH AFRICA:	BUTTERWORTH & CO. (SOUTH AFRICA) (PTY.) LTD.
	DURBAN: 152-154 Gale Street
USA:	BUTTERWORTH & CO. (PUBLISHERS) INC.
	BOSTON: 10 Tower Office Park, Woburn, Mass. 01801

©

Butterworth & Co. (Publishers) Ltd.
1979

ISBN Casebound: 0 406 37906 8
Limp: 0 406 37907 6

Printed in Great Britain by.
Billing & Sons Limited,
Guildford, London and Worcester

PREFACE

The reason for the appearance of this fourth edition so soon after the third is the passing of the Theft Act 1978. An analysis of the provisions of this Act has been incorporated into the text. Sections 1 and 2 take their place as offences of obtaining by deception in the chapter devoted to that subject while the new offence created by section 3, making off without payment, is considered in a short new chapter. The Act of 1978 is printed after that of 1968 in the Appendix. The nine pages of discussion in the third edition of the three lines of the repealed section 16(2)(a) have been eliminated.

In the short period since the last edition, there has been a considerable amount of case law and this has been incorporated into the text. The problems to which stealing in supermarkets have given rise are considered in a short new section and the discussion of attempts to steal has been expanded. In this connection, the problems created by the notorious case of *Husseyn* (1978) 67 Cr. App. R. 131 remain unresolved at the time of going to press but it is understood that the Court of Appeal will shortly have an opportunity to reconsider the matter and it is to be hoped that the law will be put on a more rational basis before the book appears.

Since the third edition a major examination of the law of theft has appeared in Professor Glanville Williams's *Textbook of Criminal Law*. Neither time nor space has permitted a full consideration of the many original points made by Professor Williams but reference has been made to some of these.

Once again I have to record my grateful thanks to Mrs. Diane Bailey for invaluable assistance in the reading of the proofs.

I have endeavoured to state the law as at June 1, 1979.

J. C. Smith

CONTENTS

CHAPTER I

INTRODUCTION

CHAPTER II

STEALING UNDER THE THEFT ACT

vii

Contents

CHAPTER V

MAKING OFF WITHOUT PAYMENT

Contents

CHAPTER XIV
ENFORCEMENT AND PROCEDURE

Contents

APPENDIX

THE THEFT ACT 1968

THE THEFT ACT 1978

(For a detailed list of contents of the Acts see page xv below.)

INDEX

TABLE OF STATUTES

References to "*Statutes*" are to Halsbury's Statutes (Third Edition) showing the volume and page at which the annotated text of the Act will be found. All references are to paragraph numbers. For the Theft Acts 1968 and 1978 see the Appendix where the full text of each Act is set out with cross-references following the principal sections indicating where those sections are discussed in the narrative part of the book.

TABLE OF CASES

NOTE. **Cases are listed under the name of the accused whenever the usual method of citation would cause them to be preceded by the abbreviation "R. *v.*" signifying that the prosecution was undertaken by the Crown.**

PARA.

PARA.

M

PARA.

O

Oddy, [1974] 2 All E.R. 666; [1974] 1 W.L.R. 1212; 138 J.P. 515; 118 Sol. Jo. 329;
    59 Cr. App. Rep. 66, C.A.; 14(2) Digest (Reissue) 862   450
Ohlson v. Hylton, [1975] 2 All E.R. 490; [1975] 1 W.L.R. 724; 139 J.P. 531; 119 Sol.
    Jo. 255; 15 Digest (Reissue) 903   370
Ord v. Ord, [1923] 2 K.B. 432; [1923] All E.R. Rep. 206; 92 L.J.K.B. 859; 129 L.T.
    605; 39 T.L.R. 437; 21 Digest (Repl.) 198   173
Overington, [1978] Crim. L.R. 692   389
Oxford v. Moss, [1979] Crim. L.R. 119   100

P

Palmer v. R., [1971] A.C. 814; [1971] 1 All E.R. 1077; [1971] 2 W.L.R. 831; 115 Sol.
    Jo. 264; 55 Cr. App. Rep. 223, P.C.; 15 Digest (Reissue) 1171   311
Parker (1910), 74 J.P. 208; 15 Digest (Reissue) 1496 .. .. 181, 206
Parker, [1969] 2 Q.B. 248; [1969] 2 All E.R. 15; [1969] 2 W.L.R. 1063; 133 J.P. 343;
    113 Sol. Jo. 186; 53 Cr. App. Rep. 289, C.A.; 14(1) Digest (Reissue) 415   53
Parker, [1970] 2 All E.R. 458; [1970] 1 W.L.R. 1003; 134 J.P. 497; 114 Sol. Jo. 396,
    C.A.; 14(2) Digest (Reissue) 672 .. .. 440, 441, 447
Parkes, [1973] Crim. L.R. 358   317
Parkes, [1974] Crim. L.R. 320   317
Partington v. Williams (1976), 120 Sol. Jo. 80; 62 Cr. App. Rep. 220, C.A.; 14(1) Digest
    (Reissue) 113   52
Patterson, [1962] 2 Q.B. 429; [1962] 1 All E.R. 340; [1962] 2 W.L.R. 496; 126 J.P.
    126; 106 Sol. Jo. 156; 46 Cr. App. Rep. 106, C.C.A.; 15 Digest (Reissue) 1360 ..   378
Pear (1779), 1 Leach 212; 15 Digest (Reissue) 1268   37
Pearce, [1961] Crim. L.R. 122, C.C.A.   282
Pearce, [1973] Crim. L.R. 321   284
Peart, [1970] 2 Q.B. 672; [1970] 2 All E.R. 823; [1970] 3 W.L.R. 63; 134 J.P. 547; 114
    Sol. Jo. 418; [1970] R.T.R. 376; C.A.; Digest Cont. Vol. C, p. 263   287
Peirce v. London Horse and Carriage Repository, [1922] W.N. 170, C.A.   397
Percy Dalton (London) Ltd. *See* Dalton (Percy) (London) Ltd.
Perkins (1852), 2 Den. 459; 21 L.J.M.C. 152; 16 J.P. 406; 16 Jur. 481; 5 Cox C.C. 554;
    15 Digest (Reissue) 1371   418
Petch (1878), 38 L.T. 788; 42 J.P. 694; 14 Cox C.C. 116; 15 Digest (Reissue) 1247 ..   94
Peter Jackson Pty., Ltd. v. Consolidated Insurance of Australia, Ltd. *See* Jackson
    (Peter) Pty., Ltd. v. Consolidated Insurance of Australia, Ltd.
Pettingall v. Pettingall (1842), 11 L.J.Ch. 176; 8(2) Digest (Reissue) 299   64
Pharmaceutical Society of Great Britain v. Boots Cash Chemists (Southern), Ltd.,
    [1953] 1 Q.B. 401; [1953] 1 All E.R. 482; [1953] 2 W.L.R. 427; 117 J.P. 132; 97
    Sol. Jo. 149, C.A.; 12 Digest (Reissue) 86   42
Phetheon (1840), 9 C. & P. 552; 15 Digest (Reissue) 1288   133
Phillips and Strong (1801), 2 East P.C. 662; 15 Digest (Reissue) 1287   134
Pierre, [1963] Crim. L.R. 513   369
Pilgram v. Rice-Smith, [1977] 2 All E.R. 658; [1977] 1 W.L.R. 671; 121 Sol. Jo. 333;
    15 Digest (Reissue) 1263 .. .. 40, 41, 102
Pitchley (1973), 57 Cr. App. Rep. 30; [1972] Crim. L.R. 705, C.A.; 15 Digest (Reissue)
    1362 .. .. 382, 400, 416
Pitham and Hehl (1976), 65 Cr. App. Rep. 45, C.A. 20, 23, 40, 48, 52, 382, 419
Porter, [1976] Crim. L.R. 58   389
Potger (1970), 114 Sol. Jo. 906; 55 Cr. App. Rep. 42, C.A.; 14(2) Digest (Reissue) 804 181,
    184, 220
Powell v. MacRae, [1977] Crim. L.R. 571   72
Practice Note, [1971] 3 All E.R. 829, C.A.   433

Q

Quigley v. Stokes, [1977] 2 All E.R. 317; [1977] 1 W.L.R. 434; 121 Sol. Jo. 224; 64
    Cr. App. Rep. 198; [1977] R.T.R. 333; [1977] Crim. L.R. 282   450

R

Ragg (1860), Bell, C.C. 208, 214; 29 L.J.M.C. 86; 1 L.T. 337; 24 J.P. 85; 6 Jur. N.S. 178;
    8 W.R. 193; 8 Cox C.C. 262; 15 Digest (Reissue) 1413   180
Rao, [1975] Crim. L.R. 451   116
Rashid, [1977] 2 All E.R. 237; [1977] 1 W.L.R. 298; 120 Sol. Jo. 856; [1977] Crim.
    L.R. 237, C.A.; 15 Digest (Reissue) 1348 .. .. 166, 377

xxvi

xxvii

PARA.

ABBREVIATIONS

The following are the abbreviations used for the principal text-books and other materials cited in this book. References are to the latest editions, as shown below, unless it is specifically stated otherwise. The particulars of other works referred to in the text are set out in the relevant footnotes.

Archbold	*Criminal Pleading, Evidence and Practice*, by John Frederick Archbold. 39th ed. (1976) by S. Mitchell
Blackstone, *Commentaries*, I	*Commentaries on the laws of England*, by Sir William Blackstone, Vol. 1 (4 Vols.). 17th ed. (1830) by E. Christian
C.L.J.	Cambridge Law Journal
C.L.R.C.	Criminal Law Revision Committee
East, 1P.C.	*Pleas of the Crown*, by E. H. East, Vol. 1 [2 Vols.] (1803)
Eighth Report, Cmnd. 2977	Criminal Law Revision Committee, Eighth Report, "Theft and Related Offences." (1966) Cmnd. 2977
Griew	*The Theft Acts* 1968 and 1978. 3rd ed. (1978) by Edward Griew
Hale, 1P.C.	*The History of the Pleas of the Crown*, by Sir Matthew Hale, Vol. 1 [2 Vols.] (1736)
Hawkins, 1P.C.	*Pleas of the Crown*, by W. Hawkins, Vol. 1 [2 Vols.] (1916)
J.Cr.L.	Journal of Criminal Law (English)
Kenny, *Outlines*	*Outlines of Criminal Law*, by C. S. Kenny. 19th ed. (1965) by J. W. C. Turner
L.Q.R.	Law Quarterly Review
M.L.R.	Modern Law Review
N.L.J.	New Law Journal
Russell	*Crime*, by Sir W. O. Russell. 12th ed. (1964) by J. W. C. Turner [2 Vols.]
SHC	*Criminal Law: Cases and Materials*, by J. C. Smith and Brian Hogan, (1975)
Smith and Hogan	*Criminal Law*, by J. C. Smith and Brian Hogan (4th ed. 1978)
Thirteenth Report, Cmnd. 6733	Criminal Law Revision Committee, Thirteenth Report, "Section 16 of the Theft Act 1968." (1977) Cmnd. 6733
Williams, C.L.G.P.	*Criminal Law: The General Part*, by Glanville L. Williams, (2nd ed., 1961)
Williams, T.B.C.L.	*Textbook of Criminal Law*, by Glanville L. Williams (1978)

CHAPTER I

INTRODUCTION

[1] Until 1968 the English law of stealing developed in a piecemeal and haphazard fashion over several centuries. The common law began with a very elementary and crude notion of stealing which covered only the most obvious and direct deprivations by one person of property which was in the possession of another. As the inadequacies of the law were exposed by the ingenuity of rogues, so the courts and, later, Parliament extended the law to punish more sophisticated forms of dishonesty. The courts generally achieved their purpose by extending the ambit of the original crime of larceny by means of fictions and strained interpretations of the concepts which constitute the definition of that crime—particularly the concept of possession. Parliament's method was to create a new crime to supplement the old.

[2] In one way or another most varieties of dishonest appropriation of the property of another were brought within the ambit of the criminal law and, with one or two exceptions, the gaps through which the dishonest might slip were narrow and did not present a serious problem. But this was at the price of tolerating an immensely and unnecessarily complicated structure, full of difficult distinctions of a purely technical character and bristling with traps for the judges, magistrates, prosecutors and police who had to administer the law.

[3] The Theft Act 1968, which was based largely on the Eighth Report of the Criminal Law Revision Committee[1] (hereafter "CLRC"), swept all this away and gave us a completely fresh start with a new definition of theft which embraces all—or virtually all—of the kinds of dishonest conduct which came within the definitions of the old crime of larceny (in all its multifarious forms), embezzlement and fraudulent conversion. This was, in itself, an immense simplification, for the boundaries between these offences were difficult to draw precisely and, right up to the time of their repeal, were the subject of controversy. With the repeal of the old law, the fictions and strained interpretations also pass into legal history.

---

[1] Cmnd 2977, "Theft and Related Offences".

---

[4] It would be dangerously misleading to suggest, however, that the law of stealing is, or can ever be made childishly simple. Stealing consists in interference with other persons' rights in property, their rights of ownership, whether legal or equitable, their possession and control over chattels and things in action—intangible property. These rights are regulated by the civil law and, in an advanced society, their structure is inevitably complicated. This is something of which the reformer of the criminal law must take account in the legislation which he proposes, but which he cannot alter. The concepts of the

1

civil law must be utilised in the definition of the crime. Moreover, while many borderlines are eliminated by the use of a broadly based definition of theft, there must always remain the borderline between interferences with another's property which are criminal and those which are not. It is difficult to define this line in the first place and whatever definition is adopted will lead to difficulties of interpretation. One section of the Act—s. 16, which was introduced while the bill was passing through Parliament—proved to be so obscure and unsatisfactory that as early as 1972 it was referred to the CLRC for re-consideration. On the recommendation of the Committee, part of the section (s. 16 (1) (a)) was repealed and replaced by the Theft Act 1978.

[5] The old law of stealing was contained in the Larceny Acts of 1861 and 1916. These Acts contained the vice generally to be found in nineteenth and early twentieth century criminal statutes—the creation of a multitude of separate crimes to provide an aggravated punishment because of the presence of a single circumstance of aggravation. Simple larceny was punishable with five years' imprisonment, but there were many types of stealing with greater or less penalties according to the nature of the property stolen, the place where it was stolen and the relationship between the thief and the owner. The fact that the subject of the larceny was a will, title deeds or a mail-bag was a sufficient circumstance of aggravation to raise the maximum to life. Other single circumstances which allowed of an enhanced punishment were that the larceny was of cattle or goods in the process of manufacture, from the person, from a ship, by a clerk or servant, or by a tenant or lodger. On the other hand, lesser punishments were provided, for example, if the larceny was of ore from a mine or of a dog. Any court in sentencing a thief today will take account, in determining the sentence, of very many factors in addition to such single elements of aggravation or mitigation—indeed it is very unlikely that the factors enumerated will be the most important in the court's decision.

[6] In place of all these aggravated forms of larceny we now have the single offence of theft with a single penalty. As the definition comprehends within it offences which were formerly punishable with imprisonment for life and for fourteen years, it was inevitable that the maximum penalty provided should be more than the five years available for simple larceny. The ten year maximum which is provided by the 1968 Act[1] should, in accordance with general principles,[2] be reserved for the worst conceivable case of theft; and sentences in other cases should be proportionately lower.

---

[1] Section 7.
[2] *Edwards* (1910), 5 Cr. App. Rep. 229; *Austin*, [1961] Crim. L.R. 416; *Da Silva*, [1964] Crim. L.R. 68. Where the maximum is low the rule is less strictly applied; *Ambler*, [1976] Crim. L.R. 266.

1   THE INTERPRETATION OF THE THEFT ACT[1]

[7] The 1968 Act represents an almost completely fresh start, and its words should be interpreted in their natural meaning to produce sensible results,[2] without harking back unnecessarily to the concepts of the common law.

"It is expressed in simple language as used and understood by ordinary literate men and women. It avoids so far as possible those terms of art which have acquired a special meaning understood only by lawyers in which many of the penal enactments which it supersedes were couched."[3]

Very little attention was paid to the actual words of the Larceny Act 1916, for the courts constantly had recourse to the common law and assumed that the Act was intended to preserve it, even when the wording was somewhat difficult to reconcile with this view. The definition of larceny in the 1916 Act was a new statutory definition, but it did not purport to do more than codify the common law. There is therefore a fundamental difference between the Act of 1916 and those of 1968 and 1978. The Theft Acts enact, for the most part, completely new law. Only in a limited number of cases is it necessary or desirable to resort to earlier case law. When the 1968 bill was before the House of Lords, Lord Wilberforce introduced an amendment[4] to the effect that it should not be permissible "to refer to any decisions of any Courts prior to the passing of this Act, other than decisions in general terms dealing with the interpretation of Statutes". It is submitted that this amendment was wisely withdrawn. Such a rule might be workable in some statutes but only if they were drafted with such a rule of interpretation in mind, which the Theft Acts were not. In this field, moreover, it would simply not be possible to dispense with the previous case-law altogether. The Theft Acts assume the existence of the whole law of property much of which is to be found only in decided cases; and any such Act must surely make a similar assumption. The Acts include expressions like "tenancy", "proprietary right or interest", "trust", and many other terms describing concepts of the civil law which it would be quite impracticable to spell out in an Act concerned with theft. The court can be informed as to the circumstances in which a person is "under an obligation to make restoration" of property, its proceeds or its value,[5] only by reference to the law of contract and quasi-contract which is embodied in case-law.

---

[1] See R. Brazier, "The Theft Act: Three Principles of Interpretation", [1974] Crim. L.R. 701.
[2] *Baxter,* [1971] 2 All E.R. 359 at 362, *per* Sachs, L.J.
[3] *Treacy* v. *D.P.P.,* [1971] A.C. 537 at 565; [1971] 1 All E.R. 110 at 124, *per* Lord Diplock.
[4] Parl. Debates, Official Report (H.L.), Vol. 290, col. 897.
[5] Section 5 (4), below, para [74].

---

[8] No doubt Lord Wilberforce had in mind, not the civil law, but the old cases on the criminal law of larceny and related offences with all their technicalities. Most of these cases are now irrelevant because the criminal concepts employed in the Act are new. Where the interpretation of the Act requires an answer to some question of civil law—for example, when the ownership in property passes—it is particularly undesirable that resort should be had[1] to those cases in which the concepts of the civil law were distorted in order to force a case within the confines of one of the old offences. Where, however, the Act incorporates the substance of the provisions of earlier statutes—as, for example, with the amended version of taking motor vehicles[2]—it is surely undesirable that the courts should have to go back to square one and reconsider points of construction previously settled, with perhaps different and not necessarily better results. Again, where terms with a well-settled meaning under the Larceny Acts have been used in a similar

context in the Theft Act, it would seem desirable—and certainly in accord with the intention of the framers of the Act—that those concepts should be given their well-settled meaning. Examples are the use of the word "menaces" in blackmail[3] and "receives" in handling stolen goods.[4]

---

[1] As occurred in *Gilks*, [1972] 3 All E.R. 280; SHC 549 below, para **[79]**, where *Middleton* (1873), L.R. 2 C.C.R. 38 was applied and extended. See [1972] Crim. L.R. 586–590.
[2] Section 12, below, para. **[279]**.
[3] Section 21, below, para. **[300]**.
[4] Section 22, below, para. **[379]**.

---

[9] The old law is also relevant as an aid to construction insofar as its inadequacies illuminate the mischief at which the Act is aimed and in that it may persuade the court that Parliament could not have intended to legalise conduct which it thinks ought to be criminal and which was criminal under the old law.[1] On the other hand, the courts should "... shun the temptation which sometimes presses on the mind of the judiciary, to suppose that because a particular course of conduct ... was anti-social and undesirable, it can necessarily be fitted into some convenient criminal pigeon-hole." And where an act was an offence under a provision repealed by the Theft Act, "it does not follow that there is necessarily a convenient alternative criminal pigeon-hole provided which fits the facts under the provisions of the 1968 Act".[2] In the following pages, some old cases are referred to, but it will be noted that they are cited, not as authorities, but as illustrations of actual situations which have caused difficulty in the past, in order to demonstrate how the Act deals, or does not deal with those situations for the future.

---

[1] *Treacy* v. *D.P.P.*, [1971] A.C. at 557–558; [1971] 1 All E.R. at 118, *per* Lord Hodson.
[2] *Charles*, [1976] 1 All E.R. 659, at 666 *per* Bridge, L.J.

---

[10] Lord Wilberforce's amendment would also have provided that the 1968 Act should be interpreted "according to the plain and natural meaning of the words used, read in the context of the Act as a whole, and given a fair, large and liberal construction." It is submitted that the Acts should be interpreted according to the plain and natural meaning of the words used (if they have one) except where it appears that the word has a technical meaning which, in the context, it is intended to bear. Thus, if the word "menaces" were given its plain and natural meaning, it might be held to be confined to threats of violence and the like. This would result in a drastic narrowing of the offence of blackmail and would plainly defeat the intention of Parliament. The word should be given the extended meaning which, in this context, it has long borne in the law.

[11] No one could object to the words of the Acts being given a "fair" construction but the other expressions used in the amendment, "large and liberal", are of much more doubtful import. They suggest that the Acts should be given an extensive meaning, so as to prohibit acts not clearly within their terms. It is submitted that the Act should not be so interpreted. There is much to be said for ignoring the rule (only applied spasmodically and inconsistently) that penal statutes should be strictly construed; but this is achieved by giving words their plain and natural meaning and adopting the "fair" interpretation—"fair", that is, to both sides. It is not desirable that the courts should go to the other extreme and extend the meaning of penal provisions by a "large and liberal" construction. The principle, *nulla poena sine lege*, is of as great importance today as ever it was.

The most striking feature of the interpretation of the Act in practice has been the tendency of the courts to leave the meaning of words and phrases to be determined by the jury as "a question of fact". This is a most regrettable abdication of judicial responsibility which can lead only to uncertainty and inconsistency in the application of the law.[1]

---

[1] See *Feely*, [1973] 1 Q.B. 530; [1973] 1 All E.R. 341 below, para [**116**]; *Hale*, (C.A., No. 5908/A/77, 28 Nov. 78), below, para [**146**]; *Hayes* (1977), 64 Cr. App. Rep. 82, below, para. [**67**]; *Dawson*, [1976] Crim. L.R. 692, below, para. [**140**]; *Reader* (1978), 66 Cr. App. Rep. 33, below, para. [**423**]; Elliott, "Law and Fact in Theft Act Cases" [1976] Crim. L.R. 707.

---

2 THE LAW OF STEALING UNDER THE LARCENY ACTS

[**12**] A very brief résumé of the position before the 1968 Act will assist the understanding of some of its provisions. There existed the following crimes:

A. SIMPLE LARCENY

(i) Simple larceny was most commonly committed where D by a trespass took possession of goods which were in the possession or custody of P without P's consent. It was from this notion that the common law began. The concept of "taking" was expanded by the courts until, in the 1916 consolidation, it was defined to include:

"obtaining the possession—
(*a*) by any trick;
(*b*) by intimidation;
(*c*) under a mistake on the part of the owner with knowledge on the part of the taker that possession has been so obtained;
(*d*) by finding, where at the time of the finding the finder believes that the owner can be discovered by taking reasonable steps".[1]

It was essential in all these forms of larceny that, as well as a taking there should be a "carrying away" and the Act provided:

"the expression 'carries away' includes any removal of anything from the place which it occupies, but in the case of a thing attached, only if it has been completely detached."[2]

(ii) At common law a possessor could not steal but legislation from 1857 onwards made it larceny for a bailee to misappropriate the bailed goods and the 1916 Act provided:

"... a person may be guilty of stealing any such thing notwithstanding that he has lawful possession thereof, if, being a bailee or part owner thereof, he fraudulently converts the same to his own use or the use of any person other than the owner."[3]

Here a physical "taking and carrying away" was unnecessary. It was enough, for example, that D should have contracted to sell goods bailed to him, without laying hands on them at all. Though larceny was commonly (and, in general, accurately) described as an offence against possession, larceny by a bailee was plainly an offence by a possessor against ownership.

[1] Larceny Act 1916, s. 1 (2) (i).
[2] *Ibid.*, s. 1 (2) (ii).
[3] *Ibid.*, s. 1 (1), proviso.

B. LARCENY BY A SERVANT

[13] Where a master entrusted his servant with goods it was held at an early stage in the development of the common law that possession remained in the master and the servant merely had custody so that a misappropriation of the goods by the servant amounted to larceny. This was an aggravated form of larceny under s. 17 (1) (*a*) of the 1916 Act.

C. EMBEZZLEMENT

[14] The position was different where the servant received goods from a third party to transmit to the possession of the master. Here the servant was held to acquire possession and therefore to be incapable of larceny at common law. He was, no doubt, a bailee; but, in 1799, before legislation dealt with bailees generally, Parliament created the offence of embezzlement to deal with the particular case here discussed. The distinction between embezzlement and larceny by a servant was a subtle one. If D received money for his master and put it straight into his pocket this was embezzlement; but if he put the money into his master's till and then took it out again this was larceny since putting the money into the till reduced it into the possession of the master. Like larceny by a servant, embezzlement was punishable with fourteen years imprisonment.[1]

[1] *Ibid.*, s. 17 (1) (*b*).

D. FRAUDULENT CONVERSION

[15] By a series of statutes from 1812 onwards the offence known as fraudulent conversion was created and extended. By s. 20 of the 1916 Act it was provided that anyone who had been entrusted or become entrusted[1] with property for various purposes or had received property for or on account of another should, if he converted the property, be guilty of a misdemeanour, punishable with seven years' imprisonment. On the face of it, the definition of this offence comprehended within it larceny by a bailee, larceny by a clerk or servant and embezzlement. It also clearly applied to another category of persons—those who had been entrusted not merely with the possession but with the ownership of the property.

[1] *Grubb*, [1915] 2 K.B. 683.

E. OBTAINING BY FALSE PRETENCES

[16] Where D by a false statement induced P to transfer to him possession of the goods with intent to appropriate them, this was larceny by a trick at common law. Where D by a false pretence induced P to transfer to him *ownership* of the goods with intent to appropriate them, this was no offence at common law but was made a misdemeanour by statute in 1757; and, by s. 32 of the 1916 Act, it was an offence punishable with five years' imprisonment. The distinction between larceny by a trick and obtaining by false pretences was a fine one and a fruitful source of difficulties. As an example, if D by false pretences induced P to let him have goods on hire purchase intending to appropriate them, this was larceny by a trick since the property did not pass; but if he induced him to let him have the same goods on credit-sale terms, this was obtaining by false pretences, since the property did pass.

CHAPTER II

STEALING UNDER THE THEFT ACT

[17] Section 1 (1) of the Theft Act 1968 provides:

"A person is guilty of theft if he dishonestly appropriates property belonging to another with the intention of permanently depriving the other of it; and 'thief' and 'steal' shall be construed accordingly."

1 THE ACTUS REUS OF THEFT

[18] The *actus reus*, then, consists simply in the *appropriation of property belonging to another*. The two questions which require detailed consideration are, What is an appropriation? and, When does property belong to another?

A. APPROPRIATION

[19] By s. 3 (1) of the Act,

"Any assumption by a person of the rights of an owner amounts to an appropriation, and this includes, where he has come by the property (innocently or not) without stealing it, any later assumption of a right to it by keeping or dealing with it as owner."

[20] This is a "partial definition ... which is included partly to indicate that this is the familiar concept of conversion ...".[1] "Conversion" is the name of a tort about which there is a great deal of complicated law; and conversion was the principal ingredient of the former offences of larceny by a bailee and fraudulent conversion. The Committee thought that "conversion" and "appropriation" had the same meaning, but preferred "appropriation" on the valid ground that, in ordinary usage, it more aptly describes the kind of acts it is intended to cover.[2] Though the civil and criminal cases on "conversion" may occasionally be useful in elucidating the meaning of "appropriation" it is clear that they are not binding. It has been argued that no act should be held to amount to theft unless it is unlawful in the civil law.[3] This opinion has not yet been accepted by the courts and it has been said by the Court of Appeal that an act may constitute an appropriation though it does not amount to the tort of conversion.[4] Where the civil law gives a positive right, the exercise of that right certainly cannot properly be held to amount to a criminal offence. To do so would be, in effect, to alter the civil law. On the other hand, the mere fact that P has no civil remedy should not inhibit the court from finding that D has stolen P's property if the definition of theft is satisfied.[5] For example, if D dishonestly invited E to offer to buy P's property, D may not yet be guilty of any civil wrong against P but it would be strange to say that the civil law gave

8

D a "right" to do such an act; and it is submitted that, if the words of s. 1 fit D's act, he should be convicted of theft.[6]

---

[1] *Eighth Report*, Cmnd. 2977, para. 34.
[2] *Ibid.*, para. 35.
[3] Williams, "Theft, Consent and Illegality", 1977 Crim. L.R. 127; *TBCL* 770–773.
[4] *Bonner*, [1970] 2 All E.R. 97; SHC 482 below, para. [63]. The law of tort has since been amended by the Torts (Interference with Goods) Act 1977, s. 10.
[5] Cf. below, paras. [79], [105]–[106] and [120] and Smith, "*Civil Law Concepts in the Criminal Law*", [1972B] C.L.J. 197.
[6] Cf. *Pitham and Hehl* (1976), 65 Cr. App. Rep. 45, below, para. [23]. The position was the same under the Larceny Acts: *Rogers* v. *Arnott*, [1960] 2 Q.B. 244; [1960] 2 All E.R. 417.

---

[21] The adoption of appropriation as the act constituting the offence gets rid of the necessity for both a trespassory "taking" and a "carrying away" as constituents of stealing. These elements were never necessary in larceny as a bailee or in fraudulent conversion but they (and more particularly the former) led to endless complication in simple larceny. The law is freed from its involvement with the difficult and controversial concept of possession since it is only in the rarest cases that it is now necessary to prove that infringement of the possession of another which was an essential constituent of all instances of larceny except larceny by a bailee.

(a) Appropriation by taking possession

[22] The most obvious examples of appropriation are the typical thefts where D takes possession of P's property. He picks a watch from P's pocket, takes a briefcase from his car or money from his safe. He takes tools or materials belonging to and in the possession of his employer from his place of work. He takes goods from the counter of a shop, and puts them into his pocket, intending to slip out without paying. In each case he has assumed one of the basic rights of the owner, the right to possess, and, if he has done so with the dishonest intention of permanently depriving the owner of it, he is guilty of theft.

Clearly the full crime may now be committed at an earlier stage than formerly. Acts which were only attempted larceny constitute theft. If D only grasps the watch in P's pocket without succeeding in moving it, this amounts to an assumption of ownership and therefore an appropriation. More doubtful is the case where D puts his hand into the pocket, or in the direction of the pocket with intent to steal the watch. This may be only an attempt, or, possibly an act of preparation.[1]

---

[1] Below, para. [52].

(b) Appropriation by one already in possession

[23] It is very common for one person, D, to be in possession of property which belongs to another, P. Clearly P retains some of the rights of an owner which may be dishonestly assumed by D. The commonest examples are bailments, where P, the bailor, has entrusted D, the bailee, with possession for some limited purpose—he has loaned D a book, hired a car to him, let him have a television on hire-purchase or pledged his watch to him as security for a loan. If, in any of these cases, D destroys the property or gives it away or sells

it to another, he does something which only the owner, P, can lawfully do and he has assumed P's rights. Even if D has only gone so far as to offer to sell the thing, he has assumed a right which only the owner has and it seems clear that he is guilty of theft.[1] Probably even an invitation to E to make an offer to buy the thing is an assumption of the rights of an owner—it is certainly something that only P can lawfully do—but a charge of theft might fail on the ground that D's intention to deprive P was apparently conditional; E's offer might not be big enough.[2] A mere decision by D to sell P's property would not be enough. A decision to assume P's rights is not an assumption of them. Appropriation requires an act. The act must be one which D is not authorised by the terms of the bailment to do—otherwise he is only exercising his own rights and not assuming those of P. So, if he drives the car he has hired to E's house, he has not yet committed theft even if he intends dishonestly to offer to sell the car to E. This is no more than an act of preparation.[3]

---

[1] *Pitham and Hehl* (1976), 65 Cr. App. Rep. 45. Though there is a complete theft at the instant the offer is made, it does not necessarily follow that the theft does not continue for some time thereafter. Below, para. [48].

[2] *Cf. Husseyn* (1978), 67 Cr. App. Rep. 131, below, para. [124]. It is submitted that this ought to be theft.

[3] But cf. the argument in *Rogers* v. *Arnott*, [1960] 2 Q.B. 244; [1960] 2 All E.R. 417 (D.C.). "Once the defendant decided to keep the appointment to sell the tape recorder, and certainly once he had put it into the car, he committed an act of conversion" (Basil Wigoder). The decision was that the offence of larceny was complete when the bailee of the tape recorder offered to sell it.

[24] A person may come into possession of the property of another in ways other than bailment and the same principles apply. Any possible doubts are dispelled by the provision that appropriation includes—

> "... where he has come by the property (innocently or not) without stealing it, any later assumption of a right to it by keeping or dealing with it as owner."[1]

To the reader unfamiliar with the law of larceny, this provision probably seems quite unnecessary. Its purpose was to make quite clear that the law of theft is not governed by the rule of larceny that, except in the case of a bailee, the intention to steal must exist at the moment of taking possession. It is now entirely clear that the following acts amount to theft.

(i) D receives stolen property. He intends to restore it to the true owner or the police. Later he changes his mind and conceals the thing, intending to deprive the owner permanently of it.[2]

(ii) D, a lorry driver, receives a number of sacks of pig-meal into his employer's lorry for carriage from A to B. When he arrives, D discovers that ten sacks too many have been loaded. He appropriates them.[3]

In these two examples, D did not assume *all* the rights of the owner when he first received the property; he intended to hold it for another. When he later assumed the entire rights of the owner he committed theft. The same principle applies, however, where D intends innocently to assume the entire ownership at the start. For example:

(iii) D finds a banknote in the highway. There appears to be no reasonable means of ascertaining the owner and D decides to keep it for himself. This is no offence—D has "come by the property ... innocently." Two days later, being still in possession of it, he discovers that P is the owner and then uses the note for his own purposes.[4]

(iv) In the dark P hands a coin to D. Both believe it to be a shilling. In fact it is a sovereign. Some time later, D discovers it is a sovereign and spends it.[5] (It is assumed that the property in the sovereign does not pass in this situation. If this assumption is wrong, D will not escape liability, but it will then be necessary to rely on s. 5 (4).)[6]

(v) D is handed his workmate's pay packet by mistake. When he has been in possession of it for some hours he discovers that it contains more than he is entitled to and appropriates the money.[7]

In cases (iii), (iv) and (v), it may be argued that, since D intended to assume all the rights of an owner when he first took the thing, there is no room for any "later assumption of a right to it"; that one cannot assume what one has already assumed. It is submitted however that the words "*later* assumption" pre-suppose an earlier assumption; and that the later assumption envisaged may be an exercise of rights which have been assumed on "coming by" the thing in question. The contrary view would be disastrous for, it should be noted, s. 5 (4)[8] does no more than vest a fictitious property in the prosecutor and leaves open the necessity for an appropriation.

[1] Section 3 (1).
[2] *Cf. Matthews* (1873), 28 L.T. 645.
[3] *Cf. Russell* v. *Smith*, [1958] 1 Q.B. 27; [1957] 2 All E.R. 796.
[4] *Cf. Thurborn* (1849), 1 Den. 397; *Thompson* v. *Nixon*, [1966] 1 Q.B. 103; [1965] 2 All E.R. 741.
[5] *Cf. Ashwell* (1885), 16 Q.B.D. 190; below, paras. [47] and [75].
[6] Below, para. [74].
[7] *Cf. Flowers* (1886), 16 Q.B.D. 643.
[8] Below, para. [74].

[25] In the above cases the original possession was innocent. The same result follows where it is not:

D has left his flock of sheep for the night on P's farm. When he drives the flock away next morning it has been joined, without his knowledge, by one of P's sheep. When D discovers the additional sheep he appropriates it.[1] Whether D came by the sheep innocently or by the tort of trespass, he is guilty of theft at the moment of appropriation.

D, in a drunken frolic, takes P's bicycle. He has no intent to steal at that time. When he becomes sober he appropriates it.[2]

[1] *Cf. Riley* (1853), Dears. 149.
[2] *Ruse* v. *Read*, [1949] 1 K.B. 377; [1949] 1 All E.R. 398; *cf. Kindon* (1957), 41 Cr. App. Rep. 208.

(c) Appropriation without taking by persons not in possession

[26] The 1968 Act made an important extension of criminal liability in that the rules which were previously applicable only in the case of bailees[1] are now of general application. The effect of this may be illustrated by the case of *Bloxham*.[2] There D not only offered, but actually contracted to sell and received the price for a refrigerator belonging to the Urban District Council which employed him; and yet was held to be not guilty of an attempt to commit larceny on the ground that he had never done any act which was sufficiently

proximate to the complete crime—a striking contrast with the result in *Rogers v. Arnott*.[3] D was plainly not a bailee of the refrigerator nor, so far as appears, did he even have custody of it. It was presumably simply standing on the premises of his employer. He was not guilty of attempted larceny because:

> "The very essence of the offence of larceny is the asportation, and if the appellant had done anything which could amount to an attempt to take and carry away the refrigerator, he would of course have been guilty of the offence with which he was charged. But the fact is that he took no step whatever connected either immediately or remotely with taking and carrying away this refrigerator."[4]

[1] And possibly servants in custody of their masters' goods—but this was doubtful [1961] Crim. L.R. 448–451.
[2] (1943), 29 Cr. App. Rep. 37.
[3] Above, para. [23], footnote 3.
[4] *Per* Tucker, J., (1943), 29 Cr. App. Rep. at 39.

[27] If Bloxham had in fact intended to deliver the refrigerator there is no doubt that under the new law he would be guilty, not merely of an attempt, but of the full offence of theft. The crime would be complete when he offered to sell. The absence of any attempt at asportation would be quite irrelevant and it would also be immaterial that there was little or no chance of his carrying the enterprise through to a successful conclusion.

Bloxham probably never had any intention of delivering the refrigerator. This appears, at first sight, to be fatal to a charge of theft since it negatives "the intention of permanently depriving." However, s. 6 (1) provides that this requirement is satisfied by an intention "to treat the thing as his own to dispose of", even where the rogue does not mean "the other permanently to lose the thing itself." Bloxham appears to have treated the refrigerator as his own to dispose of, and so to be guilty of theft. Griew[1] objects to this conclusion on two grounds: (i) that there is no appropriation. "D's reference to the property is a mere device to support the deception practised on his purchaser. If D and E are not in the presence of any property when they conclude their bargain, it would seem to be all one whether the property referred to is actual or fictitious." Griew does not shrink from the corollary to this argument, that a bailee "who uses his possession *merely* as a device to defraud a dupe will not appropriate—save in a rare case such as that where the victim acquires title by the transaction, as on a contract to sell specific goods in market overt." It is submitted, however, that there is no valid ground for a distinction based on the presence of the property—and the property *was* present in *Bloxham*; that the case of fictitious property is plainly distinguishable; and that theft never did and does not depend on whether the true owner has been deprived of his title. In such a case, D causes the buyer to have a *bona fide* claim of right to the true owner's property. That claim may be easy to resist or it may be difficult,[2] but, in either event, it seems not unreasonable to describe the creation of it as an appropriation. (ii) In the last resort, Griew would be prepared to argue that "to dispose of" in s. 6 (1) should be construed narrowly, so as not to apply in this situation. But that subsection is undoubtedly intended to apply to the case

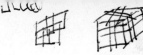

where D purports to sell P's own property to P. Is there any less "a disposition" when he purports to sell P another's property?

If the words of the Act appear, as they do, to make a person like Bloxham guilty of theft,[3] there is no reason to strain to exclude him from liability; but it would certainly be preferable to charge the accused with obtaining the money by deception and so avoid any of the difficulties discussed above. Cases are however conceivable where a charge of obtaining by deception will not lie; for example, D has a claim of right to the money which he obtains from E,[4] though not to the property of P which he purports to sell to E.

---

[1] Griew, 2–42 and 2–61.

[2] In *Bloxham*, the buyer might have claimed that she had a title on the ground of D's ostensible authority to sell.

[3] There is one other, rather technical objection which might be valid. A stolen article ceases to be "stolen" on being restored to the true owner: s. 24 (3). How then can it be stolen if it never leaves his possession? It may be that s. 24 (3) only applies where the stolen thing has in fact left the owner's possession. If D has ostensible but no actual authority to sell P's property which is in P's possession and he dishonestly sells it to E, D is surely guilty of theft immediately, even before E exercises his right to remove the property from P's possession. If D has stolen the thing, it is difficult to see that it is not stolen goods.

[4] Below, para. [**183**].

(d) Appropriation and the consent of the owner

[28] It was an essential constituent of larceny at common law and under the Larceny Acts that the taking be "without the consent of the owner." Those words do not appear in the definition of theft and the section is not to be construed as though it contained those words.[1] Suppose then, that P's employee, E, is incited by D to collaborate in stealing P's property. E reports the matter to P who instructs E to appear to fall in with the scheme and to hand the property to D in order to entrap him. E does so. Clearly P does not intend to part with his ownership in the property nor does D suppose that P intends to make him the owner. The property continues to belong to P, D is dishonestly appropriating property which he knows to belong to another and he is guilty of theft. This, however, does not mean that the consent of the owner is never relevant. It may be relevant to the questions, (i) whether there is dishonesty; (ii) whether the property belongs to another and (iii) whether there is an appropriation.

---

[1] *Lawrence v. Metropolitan Police Commissioner*, [1972] A.C. 626; [1971] 2 All E.R. 1253; SHC 505, below, para. [**34**].

Consent and dishonesty

[29] Where the owner consents to his entire interest passing to D and D knows this there is no theft because D is not dishonest. Even if P does not in fact consent, D is not dishonest if he appropriates the property in the belief that he would have P's consent if P knew of the appropriation and the circumstances of it: s. 2 (1) (*b*).

Consent and ownership[1]

[30] If P's consent is effective to transfer P's entire proprietary interest to D before D does any act capable of amounting to an appropriation, D cannot be guilty of theft because the property does not belong to another. It makes no difference that D is dishonest. For example, D "appropriates" a fountain pen which he believes P has left on D's desk by mistake. In fact P put the pen there intending to make D a gift and by this delivery made D the owner of the pen. D is guilty neither of theft nor of an attempt to steal. Where D honestly fills his tank at a self-service petrol station and then dishonestly decides to drive off without paying, he commits no theft.[2] The owner has consented to D's acquiring the entire proprietary interest in the petrol and it no longer belongs to another. It is the same as where a customer in a restaurant honestly consumes a meal and then dishonestly leaves without paying. Clearly, he does not steal the food.[3] These acts are offences of making off without payment under 1978, s. 3.[4]

---

[1] See Russell Heaton, "Belonging to Another," [1973] Crim. L.R. 736,
[2] *Greenberg*, [1972] Crim. L.R. 331 (Judge Friend); *Edwards* v. *Ddin*, [1976] 3 All E.R. 705; D.C.
[3] *Corcoran* v. *Whent*, [1977] Crim. L.R. 52, D.C. D had arrived home before he formed the dishonest intention; but it makes no difference to the result. The food was incapable of being stolen as soon as it was consumed.
[4] Below, para. [242].

Consent and appropriation[1]

[31] This is more controversial. The question is whether D commits an appropriation when he does no more than he is authorised to do by the owner, but he does so with a dishonest intention. Three decisions of the Court of Appeal hold that there is no appropriation in these circumstances. In *Meech*[2] P who had obtained a cheque by a forged instrument, asked D to cash the cheque for him and D agreed to do so. D paid the cheque into his own account, his bank being unwilling for him to cash it until it had been cleared. D then discovered for the first time the dishonest origin of the cheque and resolved to deprive P of the proceeds. He agreed with E and F to take the money after he had withdrawn it to a pre-arranged destination where, to explain to P the loss of the money, they would stage a fake robbery and divide the money between them. D, E and F were charged with theft and it was argued on behalf of E and F that D had appropriated the proceeds of the cheque when he drew the money from the bank and that E and F were liable to be convicted, if at all, only of handling with which they were not charged.[3] The court held that though the money was withdrawn with a dishonest intention, it was not appropriated until it was divided at the scene of the fake robbery.

In *Skipp*[4] D, posing as a genuine haulage contractor, obtained instructions to collect three loads from different places in London and deliver them to customers in Leicester. It was argued that a single count for theft of all the goods was bad for duplicity in that there were three separate appropriations. It was held that, though D may have had a dishonest intention permanently to deprive the owner at the time he received each load, he had done nothing inconsistent with the rights of the owner by loading the goods and probably until he diverted the goods from their proper destination.[5]

In *Hircock*[6] D obtained possession of a car under a hire-purchase agreement by deception. Later he dishonestly sold the car. It was held that he was guilty of obtaining by deception contrary to s. 15 when he got possession of the car and of theft when he sold it. It is implicit in this decision that D did not steal the car when he first "came by" it though he intended permanently to deprive the owner at that time. By signing the hire-purchase agreement, he acknow-ledged that he was not the owner and so long as he retained the car he was doing what he was authorised by the hire-purchase agreement to do. His later assumption of a right to it by selling could only be theft if he had come by the property without stealing it.

These decisions raise fundamental questions about the nature of "appro-priation." They suggest that "helping oneself" to the property of another is an essential characteristic, that a man does not "assume" the right of an owner if the owner confers those rights on him; and that, notwithstanding the fact that the words "without the consent of the owner" are neither expressed nor implied in the Act,[7] "appropriation" implies something done without the owner's authority. This is far from being an unreasonable interpretation of the words "appropriation"[8] and "assumption"; but there remains an element of doubt whether it is consistent with the decision of the House of Lords in *Lawrence*. It is submitted, however, that the better view is that *Skipp, Meech* and *Hircock* in this respect are rightly decided and that *Lawrence* is distinguishable.

[1] Williams, "Theft, Consent and Illegality," [1977] Crim. L.R. 127, 205 and 327.
[2] [1974] Q.B. 549; [1973] 3 All E.R. 939; SHC 501.
[3] Were they not, in any event, accessories to D's theft? If not, did they not steal, as well as handle, the money when it was divided? Below, para. [45].
[4] [1975] Crim. L.R. 114.
[5] If *Skipp* is rightly decided, the law of theft, surprisingly, is somewhat narrower than the law of larceny. D would have been guilty of larceny by a trick on each of the occasions when he collected a load. This case would also establish an important distinction between theft and obtaining by deception. Assuming that there was a sufficient deception, an offence was committed under s. 15 as soon as possession of each load was obtained. It was on that occasion and on that occasion only that there was an obtaining and it was accompanied by a dishonest intention permanently to deprive. Thus there were three separate offences under s. 15. The goods so obtained either continued to be the property of the original owners or became the property of the consignee so that they were still property belonging to another, capable of being dishonestly appropriated with the continuing intention permanently to deprive, when Skipp made off with the whole load.
[6] (1978), 67 Cr. App. Rep. 278; [1979] Crim. L.R. 184 and commentary and 192.
[7] *Lawrence,* below, para. [34].
[8] *Cf. Peter Jackson Pty., Ltd.* v. *Consolidated Insurance of Australia, Ltd.,* [1975] V.R. 781 (larceny—clerk given money to take to bank—money received with the intent to steal—no "appropriation" until he did something inconsistent with the terms of his custody).

[32] If this is correct it follows that a customer taking goods from the shelf in a supermarket and putting them into the wire basket provided cannot yet be guilty of theft, however dishonest his intention may be. He is only doing what the owner of the goods invites him to do. Where, however, he conceals the goods in his own shopping bag, he exceeds the authority given to him by the owner and may be guilty of theft.[1]

A more difficult problem is that of the customer at the self-service petrol station who fills his tank, not intending to pay and drives off without doing so. If, by driving into the garage like an honest customer who intends to pay, he induced the attendant, P, to operate a switch by means of which he was enabled to take the petrol, he might be convicted of obtaining it by deception. But, if his conduct did not cause P to do anything,[2] that offence is not committed. In filling his tank he has, at first sight, done no more than he is invited to do; and, if so, he has acquired both ownership and possession of the petrol and cannot thereafter steal.[3] The answer to this argument might be that the owner is making an offer to sell petrol and that the offer is addressed only to persons who intend to pay. If the service station displayed a prominent notice, "For sale to members of the A.A. only," a non-member who filled his tank would clearly do so without the authority of the owner. Can it be doubted that the owner in fact intended to sell only to persons who intend to pay and that everyone knows this? A persuasive analogy is that of a newsvendor who leaves a pile of newspapers and a moneybox in a street. It would be remarkable if a man who dishonestly took a newspaper without paying for it were not a thief. It is submitted that he is a thief because the newsvendor's offer is addressed only to persons who intend to pay, or have paid for a newspaper; and that the self-service petrol case is the same in principle. Why then does this principle not apply in the supermarket case discussed above? The proprietor of the supermarket intends his goods to be handled only by honest customers. However, the dishonest customer, wheeling the goods in the trolley provided, is behaving as one who intends to buy and is thus acknowledging the ownership of the shopkeeper. The taker of the newspaper and the petrol, on the other hand, purport to assume full rights of ownership to the exclusion of the entire interest of the true owner. Their act is fairly described as an appropriation. That of the customer in the supermarket is not.

---

[1] This may be the explanation of *McPherson*, [1973] Crim. L.R. 191.
[2] Below, para. [**154**].
[3] In *McHugh* (1976), 64 Cr. App. Rep. 92, C.A., it was assumed without discussion that the motorist who dishonestly fills his tank at a self-service station steals the petrol.

(e) *Appropriation of property obtained by deception*

[33] There is unhappily a good deal of uncertainty as to the proper interpretation of s. 1 where property has been obtained from another by a trick or deception. This uncertainty need cause no practical difficulty, however, if the advice given below is followed.

The problem springs from the existence of the two following situations:

(i) D, by deception, causes P to transfer possession or custody of property to D, ownership remaining in P. D dishonestly intends to, and does, assume the rights of the owner, P, over the property.

(ii) D, by deception, causes P to transfer his entire interest in property to D. D dishonestly intends to, and does acquire those entire rights.

Case (i) was formerly the crime of larceny by a trick, case (ii) the crime of obtaining by false pretences.[1] The distinction between the two was exceedingly troublesome and one of the objects of the Theft Act was to eliminate these difficulties. Consequently, s. 15, obtaining property by deception, is so drafted that it undoubtedly covers both situations and, if the charge is brought under that section, the distinction is quite immaterial. The golden rule for prosecutors, therefore is:

Whenever D has obtained property from P by any kind of trick or deception, he should be charged under s. 15 (1) and not under s. 1.

There is no doubt that it was the intention of the CLRC that, while s. 15

should cover both cases (i) and (ii), s. 1 (1) should cover only case (i). They stated[2] that ("to the regret of some members") they gave up the idea of extending the offence of theft to cover cases of obtaining by false pretences under the Larceny Act 1916.

> "Obtaining by false pretences is ordinarily thought of as different from theft, because in the former the *owner in fact consents to part with his ownership*, a bogus beggar is regarded as a rogue but not as a thief, and so are his less petty counterparts. To create a new offence of theft to include conduct which ordinary people would find it difficult to regard as theft would be a mistake."

It may of course be perfectly proper for the court to put on the Act an interpretation different from that intended by the framers of it. The question is one of the proper interpretation of the words enacted by Parliament and it could be that the Act does what the Committee thought was not practicable and what they did not intend it to do. It is submitted, however, that the right interpretation of the Act is that intended by the Committee.

---

[1] Above, para. [16].
[2] *Eighth Report*, Cmnd. 2977, para. 38.

---

[34] The present uncertainty arises because it has been suggested that s. 1 (1) also covers both situations. Two separate grounds have been advanced for this view:

(i) That this is the natural meaning of the words of s. 1 (1).

(ii) That this is the effect of s. 5 (4). This argument is considered below, para. [78].

The first argument is to be found in the judgment of the Court of Appeal in *Lawrence.*[1] The court took the view that the former distinction depended on the presence in the Larceny Act of the words, "without the consent of the owner," and, as these words do not appear in the definition of theft, the distinction is gone; all cases of obtaining by deception, contrary to s. 15, are also theft.[2] This argument, however, appears to give insufficient weight to the notion of "appropriation" and to the words, "property *belonging to another.*" Suppose that D writes to P falsely representing that he urgently needs a bottle of brandy for the medical treatment of his sick mother. P calls at D's house in his absence and leaves the brandy. He intends to and does make D the entire owner of it. D is detained and does not get his hands on the brandy until a week later. Can it really be said that he has appropriated property *belonging to another*? Before he does anything which could be described as an appropriation he has acquired the entire proprietary interest in the bottle. The case is clearly covered by s. 15 but not by the natural meaning of the words of s. 1. More usually, the alleged appropriation will approximate more closely in time to P's act of divesting himself of his proprietary interest. D makes the false pretence in P's presence and P takes the bottle and hands it over to D. The gift is complete only on delivery so that D's alleged appropriation is coincident with his acquisition of the entire proprietary interest. It is much more arguable that this is covered by

s. 1, but it is thought that a better view is that it is not really distinguishable from the case first put.

---

[1] [1971] 1 Q.B. 373; [1970] 3 All E.R. 933 at 935; SHC 505. See comment at [1971] Crim. L.R. 51.

[2] An exception to this would be an obtaining by deception of land, which cannot be the subject of theft.

---

[35] The facts of *Lawrence* were that P, an Italian with very little English, on arriving in London on a first visit to England, went up to D, a taxi driver, and showed D an address to which he wished to be carried. D said it was very far and expensive. P got into the taxi and tendered £1. D said it was not enough. P's wallet was still open and D took from it a further £1 note and a £5 note. He drove P to the address and gave him no change. The correct fare was about 10s. 6d. D was convicted of stealing "the approximate sum of £6." The Court of Appeal thought that this was a case which might have been obtaining by false pretences, not larceny by a trick under the old law, but, for the reasons discussed above, upheld the conviction. Leave was given to appeal to the House of Lords, their Lordships being asked (i) whether s. 1 (1) should be construed as though it contained the words "without the consent of the owner" and (ii) whether s. 1 (1) and s. 15 (1) were mutually exclusive.[1] The answer to both these questions was obviously in the negative, and, understandably, Viscount Dilhorne expressed surprise that leave had been given.[2] It was argued that D had not appropriated property belonging to another. Viscount Dilhorne pointed out[3] that s. 15 (1) also contains the words "belonging to another" and added:

> " 'Belonging to another' in s. 1 and s. 15 (1) in my view signifies no more than that, at the time of the appropriation or the obtaining, the property belonged to another ... The short answer to this contention on behalf of the appellant is that the money in the wallet which he appropriated belonged to another, to [P]."

---

[1] *Lawrence* v. *Metropolis, Police Commissioner*, [1972] A.C. 626; [1971] 2 All E.R. 1253; SHC 505.

[2] For a suggestion as to the questions which *ought* to have been asked, see [1971] Crim. L.R. 53.

[3] [1972] A.C. at 632.

---

[36] It is therefore certainly arguable that *Lawrence* decides that theft may be committed where ownership passes simultaneously with the alleged appropriation. It should be noted however:

  (i) that the House thought that the evidence fell far short of establishing that P consented to the taking of the £6.[1]
  (ii) That D in fact took the money out of P's possession, so that it was unlike the typical case of obtaining by deception where P delivers the property to D. There was no doubt that "the money in the wallet" belonged to P; and the House had no doubt that D's taking it was an "assumption of ownership." It is by no means so clear where P delivers the property to D.
  (iii) That the House recognised that some cases come only within s. 1 (1) and others only within s. 15 (1). It is unlikely that the House had in mind cases of obtaining land by deception (which come only within

15 (1)). They may have had in mind cases where there is an appreciable interval between the passing of the ownership and the appropriation; but that is not clear.

Where P actually delivers property to D, intending to make D owner of it, D's receipt would not seem to be properly described as an "appropriation" or an "assumption" of the rights of an owner. The characteristic of "helping oneself" to another's property[2] is lacking. Where an uncle hands a £5 note to a nephew on his birthday, it would be an abuse of language to say that the nephew "appropriated" the note or "assumed the rights of an owner" over it. And that is what is involved in the broad interpretation of *Lawrence*. *Lawrence* is certainly distinguishable. He helped himself to the notes. If P authorised him to take money from the wallet, his authority was to take whatever was the proper fare to his destination. If express authority had been given to take the fare from P's wallet in P's absence the taking of £6 would clearly have been unauthorised and theft. The position would seem to be the same if the wallet had been handed to D with authority to take the fare. P's apparent assent to the taking of money suggests that the act was authorised, but the other construction is not impossible. Professor Williams disagrees.[3] But he also writes concerning the £1 note tendered by P: "He intended to receive change if any was due and change was due. It is not unreasonable to construe his intention to pass the property as subject to an implied condition which was not fulfilled so that the property did not pass."[4] This may be accepted but what then is the difference between tendering the note and tendering the walletful of notes? They seem to be exactly the same. The conclusion that Lawrence did not get the property in the note that was handed to him and did get the property in the notes which he took is remarkable. A better view would be that he got the property in neither.

It is submitted, therefore, that the decision of the House should not be interpreted as going beyond the peculiar facts of the case; that *Meech* and *Skipp* are correct in their interpretation of "appropriation;" and that there is no appropriation of property belonging to another where D is given the entire proprietary interest of the other. The matter is, however, clearly not settled and it is necessary to bear in mind that the view of the Court of Appeal in *Lawrence* may yet be held to be correct.[5]

---

[1] It was not, however, for D to "establish" that fact but only to raise a doubt.
[2] Above, para. [31].
[3] [1977] Crim. L.R. at p. 208, footnote 11.
[4] *TBCL* 764–765.
[5] The trial judge in *Gilks*, [1972] 3 All E.R. 280; SHC 549, below, para. [74] adopted the *Lawrence* (C.A.) approach and so avoided the difficult problems of the passing of ownership.

---

[37] If the views of the Court of Appeal in *Lawrence* are correct, much of the discussion in the following pages of this chapter is affected. Where this is so it is pointed out that the propositions in the text are subject to "the *Lawrence*, (C.A.) principle". This principle is assumed to be:

D appropriates property belonging to P when, with P's consent, he receives P's entire proprietary interest in the property.

The following cases, which gave difficulty under the old law, are discussed subject to the *Lawrence*, C.A., principle. If that principle is correct, there is little doubt that *all* the cases amount to theft.

In the classic case[1] of larceny by a trick, D dishonestly obtained the hire of a horse from P by pretending that he wanted to ride it to Sutton. He then rode the horse to Smithfield Market and sold it. He was held to be guilty of larceny as soon as he took possession. Clearly D would be guilty of theft under the Act at the latest when he offered the horse for sale and probably as soon as he diverted from the route to Sutton. According to *Meech, Skipp* and *Hircock*, however, there was no appropriation at the moment when he took possession of the horse, since he was entitled to do this under the terms of the bailment—which is only voidable and not void. According to *Lawrence*, C.A., he would be guilty when he received the horse. He was certainly guilty of obtaining by deception at that moment; and this would be the most suitable charge.

---

[1] *Pear* (1779), 1 Leach 212.

---

[38] In the case just considered there was no doubt that it was the property of another that was appropriated. There were other cases under the old law, however, where it is very difficult to see how this could be so. A case in point is *Buckmaster*.[1] D, a bookmaker, took bets from P and, while the race was being run, left the course. The horse backed by P won the race. It was held that D was fraudulent from the start and therefore guilty of larceny by a trick. This case has been criticised on the ground that the property in the money must have passed to D.[2] Of course the criminal court held that it did not; but it is to be hoped that the construction of the 1968 Act will not be marred by such strained decisions which are quite irreconcilable, not only with well-established civil law, but also[3] with the experience of ordinary men. Of course the backer intends to part with his ownership in the money—he can have no complaint if he sees the bookmaker take the note handed to him and spend it on beer. Subject to the *Lawrence*, C.A.,[4] principle, the welshing bookmaker does not appropriate the property of another and is therefore not guilty of theft. He may, however, be guilty of criminal deception.[5]

All the observations here made on *Buckmaster* are equally applicable to *Russett*[6]—P agrees to buy a horse from D for £23, pays £8 and agrees to pay the balance on delivery of the horse. D, as he all along intended, absconds with the money and never delivers the horse.

---

[1] (1887), 20 Q.B.D. 182.
[2] Kenny, 264–265; Russell, 935–938; Smith and Hogan (1st ed.), 352, n. 15.
[3] See Russell, p. 937.
[4] Above, para. [37].
[5] This question is discussed, below, para. [166].
[6] [1892] 2 Q.B. 312.

(f) Appropriation in Supermarkets

[39] Stealing in supermarkets has raised so many problems that it deserves special consideration. The difficulty is to determine when the contract is made and when ownership in the goods passes to the customer. Once he has both ownership and possession he cannot thereafter steal.[1] Ownership *may* pass

under a contract for the sale of goods as soon as the contract is made and before the price has been paid.[2] Whether or not it does so pass in any particular case is, however, a question of intention; and it has been held that, in a sale in a supermarket, it is presumed that the ownership in the goods is not intended to pass until the goods are paid for.[3] This presumption has been held to be applicable, not only to the ordinary case where the customer collects the goods and tenders them to the cashier, but also to the case where the goods were weighed, bagged, priced and handed by an assistant to a customer, D, who, instead of tendering them to the cashier, dishonestly removed them from the store. It is possible that the contract of sale was made with the assistant but whether it was so or not was immaterial. The ownership had not passed and D was guilty of theft: *Davies* v. *Leighton.*[4] In *Davies* v. *Leighton* the court thought it might have been different if the assistant had been in a managerial capacity. But, even if it had been intended that the ownership in the goods should pass immediately to D, and therefore did pass to him, it is inconceivable that the manager would have intended to give up the seller's lien—i.e., his right to retain possession until the payment of the price. The customer would have only custody of the goods in his hands, until he paid the price, possession continuing in the seller,[5] to whom the property would still therefore "belong": s. 5 (1).

---

[1] But he may be guilty of making off without payment, contrary to 1978, s. 3. See below, paras. **[242]–[249]**.
[2] Sale of Goods Act 1893, s. 18, rule 1.
[3] *Martin* v. *Puttick*, [1968] 2 Q.B. 82; [1967] 1 All E.R. 899, D.C.; *Lacis* v. *Cashmarts*, [1969] 2 Q.B. 400, D.C.
[4] [1978] Crim. L.R. 575, D.C., and commentary.
[5] *Cf. Chisser* (1678), T. Raym. 275; 3 Salk. 194.

[40] Where, in collusion with a customer, a dishonest cashier undervalues the goods tendered by ringing up a price below the authorised price, the parties are guilty of theft: *Bhachu.*[1] The court thought that the appropriation was committed by the customer when she put the goods in the basket and wheeled them out of the shop. It seems however that the cashier dishonestly appropriated the goods when she sold them at an undervalue.[2] If so, according to *Pitham*,[3] the customer might have been convicted of handling as well as theft.

---

[1] (1976), 65 Cr. App. Rep. 261, C.A.
[2] *Pilgram* v. *Rice-Smith*, [1977] 2 All E.R. 658, D.C.
[3] (1976), 65 Cr. App. Rep. 45, C.A. above, para. **[23]**.

[41] A different problem arises where the goods are dishonestly underpriced by an assistant in the body of the shop and then tendered by the customer to the cashier who in good faith demands the false marked price. In *Pilgram* v. *Rice-Smith* the court assumed that, but for the fraud, the contract of sale would have been concluded between the assistant and the customer. They held, however, that this apparent contract was a nullity because the assistant had no authority to sell except at the authorised price. The purported sale was therefore theft of the goods. The decision has been criticised on the ground that the ordinary rule, namely that the contract is made at the cash desk and not before, was applicable so that the court was proceeding on a false assumption.[1]

However even if there was not even the semblance of a contract of sale until the customer reached the cash desk, it is possible that the underpricing of the goods by the assistant was a sufficient assumption of ownership to amount to theft. On the other hand, since it was the intention of the parties that the customer should carry the goods to the cash desk and offer to buy them, thus acknowledging the rights of the owner and behaving not as owner but as customer, it may be argued that the underpricing was not an assumption of ownership but only a preparatory act. When the customer tendered the goods she deceived the cashier as to the true price and obtained the goods by deception.

---

[1] See 93 L.Q.R. 497.

---

[42] A modern problem which has not yet been the subject of any reported decision in a higher court[1] but which is known to have arisen on more than one occasion is as follows:

Two pieces of meat in a supermarket bear price tickets of £2 and £1 respectively. D takes the £2 ticket, puts it in his pocket and attaches the £1 ticket to the £2 piece of meat which he then tenders at the cash desk. It cannot be said that D has yet appropriated the property (except in the £1 ticket) for he has not assumed the rights of an owner. When he tenders the meat, he is offering to buy it[2] which is an act inconsistent with present ownership and thus not an appropriation. If the cashier were to ask D for £1 and, on receiving it, allow him to take away the meat, it is submitted that this would clearly be obtaining by deception and not theft except under the *Lawrence* (C.A.) principle. D's offer to buy that particular piece of meat has been accepted and a contract (though voidable for fraud) has vested the property in the meat in D.[3] The position would be different if D had induced in P a mistake as to the identity of the subject-matter. In *Bramley*[4] D, having loaded his cart with coal in P's yard, covered it with slack and, on being asked by the weighing machine operator what he had in the cart, replied, "Slack" and was charged accordingly. It was held that he was guilty of larceny and he would now be guilty of theft of the coal as well as of obtaining it by deception since a contract is negatived—it is void, and not merely voidable—where the parties do not intend to contract for the same commercial commodity.[5]

---

[1] For a discussion of a case in a magistrates' court see (1961), 25 J. Cr. L. 168.
[2] *Pharmaceutical Society* v. *Boots (Cash Chemists), Ltd.*, [1953] 1 Q.B. 401; [1953] 1 All E.R. 482.
[3] It is submitted that D is not under an obligation to make restoration within s. 5 (4): below, paras. **[80]**–**[81]**.
[4] (1861), Le. & Ca. 21.
[5] *Scriven Brothers, Ltd* v. *Hindley*, [1913] 3 K.B. 564 (hemp and tow).

(g) Appropriation of property obtained by intimidation

[43] The Larceny Act 1916 specifically[1] provided that obtaining possession of goods by intimidation was a sufficient taking. There is no corresponding provision in the Theft Act, but its absence must not be taken to show that such conduct was not intended to be covered.[2] Theft may be committed by intimidation falling short of force or threats of force and so not amounting to robbery. In *Bruce*³ D generated such an "atmosphere of menace" that P was frightened into parting with his money. A verdict of not guilty of robbery and guilty of theft was legitimate. The question in each case is: Was this an appropriation by D of property belonging to another? If the effect of the intimidation is such that property does not pass from P to D then D is clearly guilty of theft. If property does pass, then it is submitted that he cannot be so guilty. This is so even though the transaction may be rendered voidable by the intimidation. If, however, the *Lawrence* C.A. principle is correct and D is guilty of theft when he receives the ownership in property under a transaction voidable for fraud, there is no reason why it should not equally be theft to receive the ownership in property under a transaction voidable for intimidation.

To determine whether property passes we must turn to the civil law. The great weight of authority there is to the effect that transactions induced by duress are merely voidable and not void.⁴ If D says to P "Your money or your life" and P hands over his money in order to preserve his life, no one will doubt that this is stealing and indeed robbery; and this can be technically justified by the fact that sparing P's life was no consideration for P's giving up his money. The "contract" was void for lack of consideration, even if it were not void for duress; and, plainly, no gift was intended. The decision in *McGrath*⁵ could be similarly justified under the new law. D and his accomplices asserted that P had bid twenty-six shillings for some cloth at an auction sale and refused to let her leave the room until she had paid. She paid because she was frightened. D was convicted of larceny. It is submitted that he would be guilty of theft. P had in fact made no bid and D's assertion that she had made a contract, when he knew she had not, clearly could not constitute a contract, even a voidable one, for there was not even the outward appearance of a contract. Similarly with *Lovell.*⁶ D ground some knives for P. The ordinary charge would have been one shilling and threepence. D demanded five shillings and sixpence and by threats induced P to pay. The threats did not induce a contract—the contract was already made—they induced the payment of a sum to which—as the jury's verdict of guilty of larceny showed—D knew very well he was not entitled. And, clearly, no gift was intended. He would be guilty of theft.

---

¹ Section 1 (2) (i), above, para. [12].
² *Cf. Bonner*, para. [63].
³ [1975] 3 All E.R. 277, C.A.
⁴ *Whelpdale's Case* (1604), 5 Co. Rep. 119a; 2 Co. Inst. 583; *Barton* v. *Armstrong*, [1976] A.C. 104; [1975] 2 All E.R. 465, at 474, 475 (P.C.); Leake on *Contract*, 63; Pollock, *Contracts* (12th ed.), 472; Chitty, *Contracts* § 341: Cheshire and Fifoot, *Law of Contract* (9th ed.), 285; Treitel, *Law of Contract* (4th ed.), 270. See D. J. Lanham, "Duress and Void Contracts" (1966), 29 M.L.R. 615.
⁵ (1869), L.R. 1 C.C.R. 205.
⁶ (1881), 8 Q.B.D. 185.

---

[44] Suppose, however, that D offers to buy P's car for an absurdly small sum and induces P to accept his offer by threatening to beat or imprison him if he does not do so. If the civil law authorities are correct in asserting that duress makes the contract voidable only, the car becomes D's as soon as it is delivered to him and, subject to the *Lawrence*, C.A., principle,¹ it is difficult to see how he can be guilty of theft. But although the civil authorities are so nearly unanimous, they are not really strong; for the cases are few and far between and in the great majority of them the result would have been the same whether the transaction was void or voidable. It is, moreover, difficult to see how the term "voidable" can properly be applied to this situation. A transaction between A and B is voidable when it is liable to be set aside on A's bringing it to the notice of B that he wishes to avoid the transaction. But where D has got property from P by duress (unlike fraud), he knows very well from the start that P wishes to avoid the transaction. In the case put at the beginning of this paragraph, D would probably expect P to go to the police as soon as he was free from the threat. Yet a voidable transaction which is avoided *ab initio* is indistinguishable from one which is void. Such a case, it is submitted, is rightly treated as void. Moreover, the authorities on robbery and on s. 30 of the Larceny Act 1916[2] are difficult to support except on the basis that at least some sorts of duress and intimidation make transactions void.

It should finally be noted that these difficulties might be overcome by charging blackmail under s. 21, where it would seem to be immaterial whether the transaction be void or voidable provided only that the demand be "unwarranted".

---

[1] Above, para. **[37]**.
[2] *Cf.* A. Hooper, "Larceny by Intimidation", [1965] Crim. L.R. 532, and 592.

(h) *Appropriation by a handler of stolen goods*[1]

[45] The wide definition of theft means that almost every person who would have been a receiver of stolen goods under the old law and almost everyone who is a "handler" under the new law will be guilty of theft. Dishonest handling of stolen goods will normally amount to an appropriation of property belonging to another and will generally be done with the intention of permanently depriving the other of his property. Where the evidence shows that property has been stolen and that D has come by it dishonestly and intends to keep it, the right course is to convict him of theft if there is a doubt whether he received the goods from an earlier thief or was himself the original thief.[2]

---

[1] See A. T. H. Smith, "Theft and/or Handling", [1977] Crim. L.R. 517.
[2] *Stapylton* v. *O'Callaghan*, [1973] 2 All E.R. 782; [1974] Crim. L.R. 64 and commentary; SHC 594. *Cf. Dolan* (1975), 62 Cr. App. Rep. 36; [1976] Crim. L.R. 145.

(i) *Appropriation by a purchaser in good faith of stolen goods*

[46] Section 3 (2) creates an exception to the general rule that appropriation of the property of another is theft. It provides:

> "Where property or a right or interest in property is or purports to be transferred for value to a person acting in good faith, no later assumption by him of rights which he believed himself to be acquiring shall, by reason of any defect in the transferor's title, amount to theft of the property".

This is designed to except from the law of theft the case where D purchases goods in good faith and for value and then later discovers that the seller had no title and that the goods still belong to a third party, P. P may simply have lost the goods or they may have been stolen from him. Having paid for the goods,

D may well, in many cases, be innocent of any crime simply on the ground that he believes he has a right to keep them and is thus not dishonest. But suppose he is enough of a lawyer to appreciate that the goods are not his but P's: he is still not guilty—while he may have *mens rea*, the subsection makes it clear that there is no *actus reus*. The result is otherwise, however, if D has not given value, as where he received the property as a gift. If, for example, C purchases the property in good faith from the thief and gives it to D who later discovers the truth and decides to keep it, D is guilty.

The protection afforded by s. 3 (2) is limited. D may with impunity keep the goods or give them away to an innocent donee. If, however, he sells the goods to an innocent buyer he will probably be guilty of obtaining the price by the implied deception that he is entitled to sell the goods. If he sells or gives the thing to one who knows it is the property of a third party, the recipient will be guilty of theft (and possibly of handling) and D, it seems, of abetting him. Section 3 (2) does not seem wide enough to exempt him from liability for abetting theft or handling by another of the property.[1]

If D assumes rights over and above those which he believed himself to be acquiring, he may be guilty of theft. If C finds goods in such circumstances that he reasonably believes the owner cannot be discovered by taking reasonable steps, and sells the goods to D who knows these facts, D is aware that he is acquiring only the rights of a finder. If, then, D subsequently discovers who the owner is, a later assumption of a right to keep the thing is the *actus reus* of theft.

---

[1] *Cf. Sockett* (1908), 1 Cr. App. Rep. 101; and see *Beasley*, [1971] Crim. L.R. 298.

---

[47] It should be noted that there is no similar exemption for the *handler* of stolen goods which have been bought in good faith. Suppose D enters into a contract to buy a picture hanging in a gallery, delivery to be made at the end of the exhibition. Unknown to D, the picture has been stolen. Before the end of the exhibition, he discovers the truth, but dishonestly takes delivery of the picture. He is not guilty of theft (s. 3 (2)) but is apparently guilty of handling the picture by receiving it knowing it to be stolen, contrary to s. 22.[1] Section 3 (2) would not exempt Ashwell.[2] He took the coin in good faith and for value (his promise to repay) and later (it is arguable) assumed rights of ownership which he believed himself to be acquiring when he received the coin; but his guilt would arise, not from any defect in the transferor's title, for there was none, but from a defect in his own title.

---

[1] Below, para. [421].
[2] Above, para. [24], and below, para. [75].

B. TO WHAT EXTENT IS APPROPRIATION A CONTINUING ACT?[1]

[48] There are three possible views about the nature of appropriation.

  (i) That it continues so long as the thief continues to exert the right of an owner over the property.

"Appropriation" is somewhat similar to the *contrectatio* of the Roman

Dutch law of theft, and South African courts have held that this makes theft a "continuing" crime:

> "... the theft continues so long as the stolen property is in the possession of the thief or of some person who was a party to the theft or of some person acting on behalf of or even, possibly, in the interests of the original thief or party to the theft."[2]

It is clear that appropriation under the Theft Act does not continue to this extent. That much is implicit in ss. 3 (1), 8 and 22 of the Act. Section 3 (1)[3] applies only when D has come by the property *without stealing it*. This implies that where he has come by the property through stealing it later assumptions of a right to it by keeping or dealing with it as owner do not amount to appropriation.[4] The requirement of s. 22[5] that the handling must be otherwise than in the course of the stealing would have a negligible application if the thief were necessarily still in the course of stealing when he handed the goods over to a receiver.

In *Meech*,[6] the court appears to have assumed that if (contrary to the actual decision) D had appropriated the money when he drew it from the bank, the theft would have been over and done with by the time D had taken the money to the agreed rendezvous so that E and F could not be abettors in such a theft.

   (ii) The second view is that appropriation is an instantaneous act, not continuing beyond the instant at which it is done.

This view might be thought to receive some support from *Pitham and Hehl.*[7] D1 stole P's property by inviting D2 to buy it. D2 did so and received it. It was held that the receiving was not in the course of the stealing. The appropriation was complete at the instant the invitation was given. The court, however, did not exclude the possibility of appropriation continuing in other circumstances, and the case may perhaps be explained as one in which the court thought that D1 had done everything he was going to do in relation to the property.

   (iii) The third view is that, while theft is committed at the instant that D does any act amounting to an assumption of the rights of an owner, appropriation continues for the duration of the "transaction" of which it forms part.

If D enters a house and seizes a jewellery box with theftuous intent, no doubt he is guilty of theft as soon as he does so, but the theft continues while he is in the course of removing it from the premises. This was the view taken in *Hale*[8] where the court held that, as a matter of common sense, D was in the course of committing theft for the purposes of s. 8 and that it was for the jury to decide whether or not the act of appropriation was finished. This is the view which is to be preferred though, for the sake of consistency, it is to be hoped that the courts will lay down principles for the guidance of juries.

---

[1] See *Williams*, [1978] Crim. L.R. 69; *Tunkel*,[1978] Crim. L.R. 313.
[2] *Attia*, [1937] T.P.D. 102 and 106. See Hunt, *South African Criminal Law and Procedure*, II, 603.
[3] Above, para. [24].
[4] *Cf. Hircock* (1978), 67 Cr. App. Rep. 278; [1979] Crim. L.R. 184 and commentary; above, para. [31]. It is different where rights are assumed, abandoned and resumed. Where D steals property but leaves it on the owner's premises because his van will not go, his later removal of it may amount to a second theft: *Starling*, [1969] Crim. L.R. 556, C.A. (Larceny).

[5] Below, paras. [379] and [417]–[418].
[6] Above, para. [31]. *Cf.* paras. [417]–[419], below.
[7] (1976), 65 C. App. Rep. 45, C.A.
[8] (C.A., No. 5908/A/77, 28 Nov. 78).

[49] What is the position if D steals property abroad, brings it to this country and exercises proprietary rights over it here? Mere possession in England of property stolen abroad is no longer an offence,[1] though handling it, contrary to s. 22, is. If D brings the stolen goods into England for the benefit of another,[2] then he might be convicted of handling in England. Whether he could be convicted of theft depends on whether "stealing" in the phrase "without stealing it" in s. 3 (1)[3] means "theft indictable in England" or "stealing by the law of the place where the act was done". If the former, then D might be convicted of theft in England but, if the latter, not. Probably the latter is correct. Section 24, though not directly applicable, suggests that theft abroad, though not indictable in England, is regarded as "stealing" for the purposes of the Act.

[1] Below, para. [387].
[2] Below, para. [420]. Cf. *Figures*, [1976] Crim. L.R. 744 (Mr. Recorder Waud).
[3] Above, para. [24].

C. INTENTION AN ESSENTIAL ELEMENT OF APPROPRIATION

[50] "Appropriation" is being discussed as the principal constituent of the *actus reus* of theft; but the traditional (and useful) analysis of the crime into *actus reus* and *mens rea* must not be allowed to obscure the fact that it is impossible to determine whether there has been an appropriation without having regard to the intention with which an act was done. Even if there had been no express provision requiring an intent permanently to deprive, such an intent would probably have been implicit in the notion of appropriation. This may be illustrated by the case of *Holloway*.[1] D broke into the warehouse of his employer, P, and took a number of dressed skins. It was his intention to produce the skins to P's foreman and pretend that he had done the work of dressing them and thereby to get paid for them. He was acquitted of larceny on the ground that he had no intent permanently to deprive P of the skins. On the same ground he would not be guilty of theft; but he would surely also be innocent of the new crime on the more fundamental ground that he had never appropriated the goods since he did not assume the rights of an owner but intended to act only as the employee—which he was—handling his employer's goods.

[1] (1849), 1 Den. 370; below, para. [122].

D. ACT OR OMISSION AN ESSENTIAL ELEMENT OF APPROPRIATION

[51] It seems probable that some act or omission is required to constitute an appropriation and that a mere decision in D's mind to assume the rights of an owner is not enough.[1] Appropriation can be performed by omission as well as by act. This seems to be implicit in the provision in s. 3 (1) that a person may appropriate by "keeping ... as owner" property which he has come by innocently. "Keeping" would not seem necessarily to involve doing any act but

to be satisfied by D's omission, with the appropriate intent, to divest himself of possession.

If D's seven-year-old child brings home P's tricycle and D, knowing that the child has come by it unlawfully, does nothing about it,[2] intending that P shall be permanently deprived of the tricycle, it is submitted that this would be theft by D. This might be regarded as an assumption of ownership through the innocent agency of the child who, no doubt, would continue to act as owner. If D were to say to his wife, "Let Richard keep it," this, it is thought, would probably be sufficient assumption of ownership. Even where D does nothing at all, as where sheep stray from P's land on to D's and he simply allows them to remain there,[3] he ought to be guilty if it can be proved that he omitted to act with the appropriate intent. In such circumstances it may, however, be difficult or impossible to prove any such intention and the charge will then fail, not merely on the ground of lack of *mens rea*, but because there was no appropriation.

---

[1] Above, para. **[23]**.
[2] *Cf. Walters v. Lunt*, [1951] 2 All E.R. 645.
[3] *Cf. Thomas* (1953), 37 Cr. App. Rep. 169.

E. ATTEMPTED THEFT

[52] An attempt to assume the rights of an owner is an attempt to steal. The fact that D will be held fully to have assumed the rights of an owner at an early stage in a transaction—for example where he has invited a third party to buy P's property[1]—means that there will often be little scope for an offence of attempt. D's first dishonest act will be the complete crime.[2]

For instance, an attempt to make an offer—D puts into the post an offer to sell P's tape-recorder which never arrives—appears to be no less an assumption of ownership than a complete offer. More doubtful, perhaps, is the case where D has merely written the letter making the offer and it is still lying on his desk. But if this is not an assumption of ownership it is probably not an attempt to assume ownership either, but a mere act of preparation. The scope for attempt is further reduced by the strict interpretation of intention to steal. D may dishonestly pick up P's property to decide if it is worth having. Since this is not treated as an intention to steal[3] D can be convicted neither of stealing nor of an attempt; and, once he has made up his mind to have the thing, he will be guilty of the full offence. Where, however, D is attempting to pick up P's property, having made up his mind to have it, then it may be that he has attempted to assume but not yet assumed the rights of an owner and so may properly be convicted of attempted theft.

Where D tries to steal property from a particular place which is empty, for example, a particular pocket or wallet or car, he may not be convicted of an attempt to steal.[4] The impossibility of completing the theft is a defence. The onus is on the prosecution to prove that there was something in the place to be stolen and, in the absence of such evidence, the pocket, etc. must be considered empty.[5] If D is looking for money and nothing else, a pocket, etc., will be empty for this purpose though it contains articles other than money. According to some of the Law Lords in *D.P.P.* v. *Nock*,[6] it is different if D is going on from place to place—pocket to pocket, wallet to wallet or car to car, as the case may be. In that case, though the place (or places) he has tried is empty, he might be convicted "under an indictment drafted in suitably broad terms"[7] of attempting to steal. It is a strange concept. D is to be convicted, apparently, of attempting to steal from some unascertainable pocket containing money carried by some unascertainable person at some unascertainable place and time in the future. The dicta have not yet been put to the test and, if and when they are, it is submitted that they should be found wanting. A better solution would be the rejection of the holding in *Haughton v. Smith*[4] that there can be no attempt to steal from a particular empty place. These remarks were held to be part of the *ratio decidendi* in *Partington v. Williams* but this deserves reconsideration, particularly since the House of Lords in *Nock* recognises that the result "seems to offend common sense and common justice".[8]

[1] *Cf. Pitham and Hehl* (1976), 65 Cr. App. Rep. 45, above para. [23].
[2] *Cf.* the argument in *Rogers v. Arnott*, [1960] 2 Q.B. at 246–247.
[3] *Husseyn* (1978), 67 Cr. App. Rep. 131, below, para. [124].
[4] *Haughton v. Smith*, [1975] A.C. 476; [1973] 3 All E.R. 1109, followed in *Partington v. Williams* (1975), 62 Cr. App. Rep. 220, D.C., criticised [1977] Crim. L.R. 609.
[5] But there may be an evidential burden on the defendant: *Bennett* (1979) 68 Cr. App. Rep. 168.
[6] [1978] A.C. 979; [1978] 2 All E.R. 654; [1978] Crim. L.R. 483 and commentary.
[7] [1978] 2 All E.R. at p. 657, *per* Lord Diplock.
[8] *Per* Lord Diplock at p. 657.

F. PROPERTY "BELONGING TO ANOTHER"

[53] Theft can be committed only in respect of a specific item of property[1] and it is essential that that property should belong to another. "Belonging to another" is however widely defined to include almost any legally recognised interest in property. By s. 5 (1) of the Act:

> "Property shall be regarded as belonging to any person having possession or control of it, or having in it any proprietary right or interest (not being an equitable interest arising only from an agreement to transfer or grant an interest)."

[1] It is unnecessary for the prosecution to prove that D stole the whole of the property mentioned in the information or indictment, but the sentence should relate only to property proved to have been stolen: *Parker*, [1969] 2 Q.B. 248, [1969] 2 All E.R. 15; *Machent v. Quinn*, [1970] 2 All E.R. 255. *Cf. Levene v. Pearcey*, [1976] Crim. L.R. 63, below, para. [189], footnote 1.

[54] Almost anything can be owned, but one exception appears to be a human corpse. There could be no larceny of a corpse at common law.[1] This was not simply a rule of the criminal law (like the rule that dogs could not be stolen) which has died with larceny. It seems to be a rule of the law of property to which we must have recourse in interpreting s. 5 (1). Thus a civil action for conversion will not lie in respect of a human corpse.[2] No one can have any proprietary right or interest in it. But Kenny points out[3] that:

> "It is not entirely certain whether the rule must be taken to be 'once a corpse, always a corpse'; if so the protection of the criminal law would perhaps not extend even to skeletons and similar anatomical preparations on which great labour has been expended or to ethnological collections of skulls and mummies—a conclusion which does not seem reasonable."

It has been held in Australia that a proprietary interest in a corpse could be acquired by one who expended time and skill on it with a view to its preservation on scientific or other grounds.[2] It seems certain that tissue removed from a corpse for the purpose of a transplant would be held to be in the possession of a surgeon.[4]

Fluids taken from the living body are property. So a motorist has been convicted of stealing a specimen of his own urine provided by him for analysis.[5] The same rule should clearly apply to a blood sample.[6]

It is probable that parts of the living body may be stolen from the living person. Thus, a magistrates' court has held a man guilty of larceny when he cut some hair from a girl's head without her consent:[7] and this seems entirely reasonable. It would be extraordinary if a woman did not own her own hair!

[1] *Handyside*, 2 East P.C. 652; *Sharpe* (1857), Dears. & B. 160. See A. T. H. Smith, "Stealing the Body and its Parts", [1976] Crim. L.R. 622. For other offences which might be committed, see Williams, *TBCL*, 679–680.
[2] *Doodeward* v. *Spence* (1907), 9 S.R. (N.S.W.) 107.
[3] *Outlines of Criminal Law* (19th ed.), 294.
[4] Cf. Human Tissue Act 1961.
[5] *Welsh*, [1974] R.T.R. 478, C.A.
[6] Cf. *Rothery*, [1976] R.T.R. 550, C.A.
[7] (1960), *Times*, 22 December.

[55] A person in possession of land has sufficient possession or control of articles in or on the land, even if he is unaware that they are there, at least if he intends to exclude trespassers from entering and taking any such thing.[1] A trespasser on a golf course was convicted of stealing from the secretary and members of the golf club balls which had been lost by their owners while playing. He was not guilty of stealing from the owners unless he believed that they could be discovered by taking reasonable steps; but he certainly knew of the interest of the club in excluding him as a "pilferer" of lost balls.[2] Possibly a finder who was not trespassing—a visitor playing a round of golf or a person crossing the course under a public right of way—would have a better right than the club to the ball. If so, (and it is a question of civil law) it is submitted that he could not be guilty of theft.

[1] *Woodman*, [1974] Q.B. 754; [1974] 2 All E.R. 955; SHC 492.
[2] *Hibbert* v. *McKiernan*, [1948] 2 K.B. 142; [1948] 1 All E.R. 860 discussed in [1972B] C.L.J. at pp. 213–215.

[56] If the property belongs to no one, it cannot be stolen. If property is abandoned there can be no theft of it. Whether an owner has abandoned his property or not is a question of the intention evinced by him in disposing of his property. If he intends to exclude others from it, he does not abandon it, though it may be clear that he intends to make no further use of it himself. So it will be theft for D to appropriate diseased carcasses which P has buried on his land.[1] A householder does not abandon goods which he puts in his dustbin. *Prima facie*, he intends the goods for the local authority which collects the refuse, so that a dustman may be guilty of theft if he appropriates the goods knowing that he is not entitled to do so.[2] A person who loses property does not necessarily abandon it because he abandons the search for it.[3] The test is whether P has evinced an intention to relinquish his entire interest in the property, without conferring an interest on anyone else. Of course, if D mistakenly believes that P has abandoned his interest in the property, D's appropriation cannot be theft, whether his belief be reasonable or unreasonable, because he is not dishonest.[4]

If the prosecution are unable to establish the identity of the owner, a charge of stealing from a person unknown should lie.[5] It will be necessary to prove that the accused knew, or believed that by taking reasonable steps he could find out, who was the owner.[6] A mis-statement of the owner is not a material averment if the accused is not prejudiced thereby.[7]

---

[1] *Edwards* (1877), 13 Cox C.C. 384.
[2] *Williams* v. *Phillips* (1957), 41 Cr. App. Rep. 5, D.C.
[3] Cf. *Hibbert* v. *McKiernan*, [1948] 2 K.B. 142, D.C.
[4] Below, para. [**109**]; *Ellerman's Wilson Line, Ltd.* v. *Webster*, [1952] 1 Lloyds Rep. 179 (D.C.).
[5] Cf. *Gregory*, [1972] 2 All E.R. 861, below, para. [**405**] (handling stolen goods belonging to a person unknown).
[6] See s. 2 (1) (c), below, p. 235.
[7] *Etim* v. *Hatfield*, [1975] Crim. L.R. 234, below, para. [**156**].

(a) Ownership, possession and control

[57] Since the law protects all interests in property, it is clear that a person with a greater interest in a specific chattel can be guilty of theft from a person with a lesser interest in the same chattel. As was the case with larceny,[1] an owner in the strict sense can be guilty of stealing his own property from one who has mere possession or custody of it. For example, D pledges his watch with P as security for a loan but takes it back again without repaying P and without his consent. This is an appropriation by D of property which belongs to P for the purposes of the section. The position is precisely the same where D bids for a car at an auction, it is knocked down to him and he then takes the car without paying the auctioneer, P, and without his (P's) consent.[2] The car became D's property on the fall of the hammer but P retained his seller's lien for the price and D has therefore appropriated P's property. If in either of these examples possession was obtained by deception, it would be prudent to rely on s. 15 (1) and not on s. 1 (1), in case *Meech, Skipp* and *Hircock*[3] were preferred to *Lawrence* (C.A.).

---

[1] Cf. *Rose* v. *Matt*, [1951] 1 K.B. 810, D.C.
[2] Cf. *Dennant* v. *Skinner*, [1948] 2 K.B. 164 (Hallett, J.).
[3] Above, para. [**31**].

---

[58] The owner may steal from his bailee at will. Though he has a right to terminate the bailment at any time, he will be guilty of theft if he simply dishonestly appropriates the bailed chattel. It is only in exceptional cases that the problem will arise, because it will usually be clear that the bailor had a claim of right to recover possession. In *Turner* (*No.* 2),[1] however, D, who had delivered his car to P to be repaired, took it back, dishonestly intending not to pay for the repairs which P had carried out. In truth, P probably was not a mere bailee at will, having a lien on the car. But the judge directed the jury that they were not concerned with liens and so the Court of Appeal had to decide the appeal on the basis that there was no lien. An argument that P's possession as a bailee at will was insufficient, was rejected. The court said

there was no ground for qualifying the words "possession or control" in any way.

It looks a little odd that, where D has a better right to possession than P, he can nevertheless commit theft by the exercise (however dishonestly) of that "right." It might have been thought that a thing does *not* belong to a possessor, P, as against D who has an immediate right to take possession from him. Possibly *Turner* (*No.* 2) may be explained by holding that a bailor has no right, even in the civil law, to take back the chattel bailed, without notice to the bailee at will.

Suppose D's car is stolen by P, and D later finds the car standing outside P's house (or the house of a *bona fide* purchaser, P). D has, of course, a right to take it back. But suppose he does not know this, and thinks that a court order is necessary to enable him lawfully to resume possession. Believing that he has no right in law to do so (i.e. dishonestly), he takes the car. According to *Turner* (*No.* 2), he is guilty of theft. If he were convicted and the court asked to exercise its power to order the car to be restored to the person entitled to it,[2] the incongruous result would be that the car should be given to the convicted thief, who was and always had been the person entitled to it. Perhaps the decision in *Turner* (*No.* 2) would not be pressed so far.[3]

---

[1] [1971] 2 All E.R. 441; [1971] Crim. L.R. 373; SHC 494, discussed in [1972B] C.L.J. at pp. 215–217.

[2] See s. 28 (1), below, para. **[437]**.

[3] *Meredith*, [1973] Crim. L.R. 253; SHC 496 (Judge Da Cunha) seems inconsistent but right in principle (no theft of impounded car from police because police had no right to retain it).

---

[59] Similar problems arise where D retains possession as well as ownership and P has that lower interest which is described as "control" in the Act. D, an employer, entrusts his employee, P, with goods for use in the course of his employment. D continues both to own and to possess the goods; but, if he dishonestly deprives P of control, he may, to the same extent as the bailor at will, be guilty of theft. It was larceny at common law for a master who had entrusted money to his servant to re-take it, intending to charge the hundred for an alleged theft. So if today an employer takes his own property from the custody of his servant, intending to claim against his insurers for its loss, he might be held to have stolen it. The more natural charge would be under s. 15; but he might not have reached the stage of an attempt to obtain by deception.

[60] Where the property belongs to more than one person, as may easily occur under s. 5 (1), and D appropriates it for himself, it follows that he may be convicted of stealing it from any one of the persons to whom it belongs. P lets a lawn-mower on hire to Q who hands it over to his servant, R, to mow the lawn. P remains the owner, Q remains in possession as bailee and R has control. If D now appropriates the lawn-mower for himself, he commits theft from all three of them. If, in order to appropriate the lawn-mower, he uses force on R, he commits robbery from P, Q and R.[1]

---

[1] See s. 8 of the Act. At common law, it would have been robbery only from R, and similarly under the Larceny Acts. *Cf. Harding* (1929), 21 Cr. App. Rep. 166.

(b) Equitable interests

[61] It is clear that equitable as well as legal interests are protected. If T, a trustee, holds a painting on trust for P, and D appropriates it, this is theft not only from the legal owner, T, but also from the equitable owner, P. Equally, if T appropriates the picture it will be theft by him from P.

Excluded from the protection of the law is "an equitable interest arising only from an agreement to transfer or grant an interest". If D, the owner of land, enters into a specifically enforceable contract to sell it to P, an equitable interest in the land passes to P, and D is, in some respects, a trustee of the property for P. If D were to sell the land to a third party, it might have been held, but for the provision under consideration, that this was theft of the land under s. 4 (2) (a).[1] If, after D has contracted to sell to P, a third party, E, enters on the land and appropriates something forming part of the land by severing it, this will be theft from D but, because of the provision under consideration, it will not be theft from P. An equitable interest similarly passes to the buyer under a specifically enforceable agreement to buy shares. The seller who dishonestly re-sells is protected.[2] It does not follow that the buyer's contractual right is not a thing in action capable of being stolen.[3]

---

[1] Below, para. [79].
[2] Gower, *Modern Company Law* (3rd ed.), 395, n. 25.
[3] See [1979] Crim. L.R. 220 at pp. 224–5.

---

[62] A contract for the sale of goods may be a sale or an agreement to sell. If it is a sale, the legal interest passes to the buyer and a re-sale by the seller who remains in possession may thus constitute theft from the buyer.[1] If however, it is an *agreement* to sell, the buyer usually acquires neither a legal, nor (since contracts for the sale of goods are generally not specifically enforceable) an equitable interest,[2] so the provision will not generally be required in such cases. It may be, however, that in the exceptional case where a contract for the sale of goods is specifically enforceable, an equitable interest does pass to the buyer before the legal ownership does so. Again, it is clear that there can be no theft from the buyer. The reason for this provision probably is that an action for breach of contract is a sufficient sanction against a person who, having contracted to sell to X, re-sells in breach of contract to Y. Such conduct is, perhaps, not generally thought to be more reprehensible than other breaches of contract. It is probably incidental that an appropriation by a third party is not a theft from the buyer; but this is not serious since it is inevitably a theft from the seller.

---

[1] See below, para. [106].
[2] *Re Wait*, [1927] 1 Ch. 606.

(c) Co-owners and partners

[63] D and P are co-owners of a car. D sells the car without P's consent. Since P has a proprietary right in the car, it belongs to him under s. 5 (1). The position is precisely the same where a partner dishonestly appropriates the partnership property. Whether or not his conduct constitutes the tort of conversion, it is theft.[1]

33

(d) Trustee and beneficiary

Conversion by a trustee was a special offence under s. 21 of the Larceny Act 1916. Now it is ordinary theft. The beneficiary, by definition, has a proprietary interest in the trust property and any act of appropriation of it by the trustee is theft.

The restrictions on the prosecution of trustees which existed in the Larceny Act, have been repealed.

Section 5 (2) provides:

> "Where property is subject to a trust, the persons to whom it belongs shall be regarded as including any person having a right to enforce the trust, and an intention to defeat the trust shall be regarded accordingly as an intention to deprive of the property any person having that right."

Where the trust is a charitable one, its object is to effect some purpose beneficial to the public, rather than to benefit particular individuals. Such trusts are enforceable by the Attorney-General, and an appropriation of the trust property by a charitable trustee will, accordingly, be regarded as theft from that officer.

---

[1] *Bonner*, [1970] 2 All E.R. 97, SHC 482. The Torts (Interference with Goods) Act 1977, s. 10, amends the law of conversion.

---

[64] Trusts for the purpose of erecting or maintaining monuments[1] or maintaining animals[2] have been held valid, though unenforceable for lack of a human beneficiary or a charitable intent. If the trustee of such a trust were to appropriate the funds for himself it would seem clear that he would commit theft from anyone who was entitled to the residue. It would be no defence that he believed the residuary legatee to be undiscoverable: s. 2 (1) (c). If the trustee were himself entitled to the residue, he could not commit theft, since he would be, in effect, the absolute and exclusive owner of the property.

---

[1] *Trimmer* v. *Danby* (1856), 25 L.J. Ch. 424; *Re Hooper*, [1932] 1 Ch. 38.
[2] *Pettingall* v. *Pettingall* (1842), 11 L.J. Ch. 176; *Re Dean* (1889), 41 Ch. D. 552.

(e) P's right that D shall retain and deal with property

[65] There are other cases which would have amounted to fraudulent conversion under the old law where D is an owner but where there is only doubtfully a proprietary right or interest in P. These are brought within the scope of theft by s. 5 (3):

> "Where a person receives property from or on account of another, and is under an obligation to the other to retain and deal with that property or its proceeds in a particular way, the property or proceeds shall be regarded (as against him) as belonging to the other."

It will be noticed that the obligation must be to deal with *that property* in a particular way. Therefore the appropriation of an advance payment for work to be done by D will be theft only if the money was given with an obligation to use it for a specific purpose. In this respect, the Act seems to reproduce the old law of fraudulent conversion.[1] Suppose, for example, D agrees to paint P's house for £50 and simply asks for "an advance payment of £10." If he appropriates the £10 to his own use this will not be theft for P has no proprietary right or interest in it nor is D under any obligation to deal with *that* property in any particular way.

The result should be different where D agrees to paint P's house and asks for £10 *to buy the paint* which he will use on the job. If he appropriates the £10, it is submitted that this now will be theft.[2] Similar situations arise where D employs P and requires him to deposit a sum of money as security for his honesty. If the terms of the arrangement are that D can do what he likes with the money then D cannot steal it[3] but if, as is more likely, D has agreed to retain the money, as by depositing it at a bank,[4] then it is capable of being stolen.

Similarly where D is a debt-collector who is required by the terms of his contract to hand over the money he collects, less a certain percentage, to the creditors: if he is under an obligation to keep in existence a separate fund, then the money he receives is capable of being stolen.[5] If however, the arrangement with the creditors is such that D is merely their debtor to the extent of the debts collected, less commission, the money he receives from the debtors is his and he is under no obligation to deal with *that* money in a particular way. It is a question of the construction of the contract between the debt-collector and the creditors. Where D, an insurance agent, failed to account for money which he had collected from clients the judge ruled that there was no case to answer; he was under no duty to keep the money in a separate fund and was merely a debtor to the insurance companies.[6]

---

[1] See [1961] Crim. L.R. 741 at 797.
[2] *Cf. Jones* (1948), 33 Cr. App. Rep. 11; *Bryce* (1955), 40 Cr. App. Rep. 62; *Hughes*, [1956] Crim. L.R. 835.
[3] As in *Hotine* (1904), 68 J.P. 143.
[4] As in *Smith*, [1924] 2 K.B. 194.
[5] *Lord* (1905), 69 J.P. 467.
[6] *Robertson*, [1977] Crim. L.R. 629 (Judge Rubin, Q.C.).

---

[66] A travel agent who receives money from clients to pay for travel arrangements is under an obligation to provide tickets, etc., but not necessarily under an obligation to retain and deal with the money in a particular way. In *Hall*[1] the agent paid the money into his firm's general trading account—a fact which was not decisive since it did not affect any interest his clients might have in the money[2]—and applied it in the firm's business. The firm failed and the clients received neither tickets nor the return of their money. Not a penny remained. In the absence of evidence of a special arrangement imposing an obligation on the agent it was held that he was not guilty of stealing from the clients. If he was entitled to use the money for the general purposes of the firm's business, he committed no theft from the clients even if he was completely profligate in its expenditure or had spent it all at the races.[3] The court stressed the need for a careful direction where s. 5 (3) is relied on. If the arrangement is wholly in writing, the judge should direct the jury as a matter of law whether it creates an "obligation"; but if it is wholly or partly oral, the court thought, the judge should direct them that "if they find certain facts proved, it would be open to them to find that an 'obligation' within s. 5 (3) had

been undertaken."⁴ "Obligation" means legal obligation.⁵ Whether a legal obligation arises on given facts is a question of law. It should therefore be for the judge to direct the jury that, if they find certain facts, they *must* decide that there is an obligation; and that if they find that the requisite facts do not exist, they must not so decide.

¹ [1973] Q.B. 126; [1972] 2 All E.R. 1009; [1972] Crim. L.R. 453 and commentary.
² *Yule*, [1964], 1 Q.B. 5; [1963] 2 All E.R. 780.
³ In the latter case it might have been theft from his partners.
⁴ [1973] Q.B. at 132; [1972] 2 All E.R. at 1012–1013.
⁵ *Gilks*, [1972] 3 All E.R. 280; SHC 549 (s. 5 (4)); *Meech*, [1974] Q.B. 549; [1973] 3 All E.R. 939; SHC 501; above, para. **[31]**; *Wakeman* v. *Farrar*, [1974] Crim. L.R. 136, D.C.

[67] *Hayes*,¹ however, contradicts these principles. The question was whether a deposit paid by a purchaser to an estate agent "belonged to" the vendor or the purchaser so as to be capable of being stolen by the estate agent. The Court of Appeal held that the judge was wrong to rule that there was an obligation. They agreed that there was an obligation in the civil law but said that was not the question. It should have been left to the jury to say whether there was an obligation within the meaning of s. 5 (3). By what criteria are the jury to decide whether there is an obligation? They can only proceed on the basis that they, laymen, think there ought to be an obligation. The decision is thus inconsistent with the cases which hold that "obligation" means legal obligation. Legal obligations to retain and deal with property exist only in the civil law. It is submitted that whether particular facts create a legal obligation is a question of law for the judge.

¹ (1977), 64 Cr. App. Rep. 82; [1977] Crim. L.R. 691.

[68] In *Cullen*¹ P gave his mistress, D, £20 to buy food for their consumption and to pay certain debts. She spent the money on herself. The Court of Appeal held that this was a plain case of theft, rejecting D's argument that it was a domestic transaction not intended to create, and so not creating, legal relations.² The court does not seem to have answered a serious argument. If the civil courts would not regard it as even a breach of contract for a wife to spend the housekeeping money on a new hat, the criminal courts should not regard it as theft.

¹ Unreported, No. 968/C/74 of 1974; SHC 500.
² *Balfour* v. *Balfour*, [1919] 2 K.B. 571 was relied on.

[69] It is submitted that a person cannot be under a legal obligation to "retain and deal" unless a failure to retain and deal would involve him in civil liability to some third person—the victim of the alleged theft. That obligation must have been in existence at the moment of the appropriation. Property is regarded as belonging to P where D "receives property from [P] ... and *is* under an obligation" to P. If D receives property from P with an obligation at the moment of receipt but the obligation is later terminated the property ceases to "belong" to P from that moment. It is thereafter no longer possible for D to appropriate property "belonging to P". In determining whether there was an obligation at the relevant time, the court must have regard to all the material facts which are proved to have existed at that time. A case which is difficult to reconcile with these principles is *Meech*, the facts of which have been given above."[1] The court held that the proceeds of the cheque "belonged to" P only through the operation of s. 5 (3). It had been argued that P was under no obligation to D because D had obtained the cheque by forgery. The court held that D assumed an obligation when he received the cheque because he was ignorant of its dishonest origin; that the cheque therefore belonged to P and that it did not cease to belong to him when D learned the truth about its origin, even (apparently) if the effect was that D was no longer under any obligation.

> "The fact that on the true facts if known [P] might not and indeed would not subsequently have been permitted to enforce that obligation in a civil court does not prevent that 'obligation' on [D] having arisen. The argument confuses the creation of the obligation with the subsequent discharge of that obligation either by performance or otherwise. That the obligation might have become impossible of performance by [D] or of enforcement by [P] on grounds of illegality or for reasons of public policy is irrelevant. The opening words of section 5 (3) clearly look to the creation of, or the acceptance of the obligation by the bailee and not to the time of performance by him of the obligation so created and accepted by him."[2]

It is submitted that if, in the light of all the proved facts, P would have had no civil claim to the cheque or its proceeds, s. 5 (3) was inapplicable. It is agreed that, where reliance is placed on s. 5 (3), it must be proved that D knew of the facts which gave rise to the obligation (and probably that there was an obligation, mistake of civil law being a defence here). But, while this is necessary, it is not enough. There must also be an *actus reus* as well as *mens rea*. The section says "*is* under an obligation", not "*believes* he is under an obligation".

---

[1] Para. [31]. See commentary, [1973] Crim. L.R. 772.
[2] [1974] Q.B. at p. 554; [1973] 3 All E.R. at p. 942; SHC at 502.

---

[70] Because of these difficulties, it is advisable to rely on s. 5 (3) only where it is necessary to do so. Many situations which are within s. 5 (3) are also within s. 5 (1). Virtually every case of theft by a bailee falls within the words of s. 5 (3), but it is certainly unnecessary to rely on them. The bailor continues to be the "owner"—in the strict sense of the word—of the bailed property, so that it plainly belongs to him under s. 5 (1). Because the bailor has a proprietary right, no question whether there is any "obligation" arises. In such a case it would be no answer that the bailor had obtained the property by deception and might have difficulty in suing for it. It was clear at common law, and is clear under the Theft Act, that property may be stolen from a person who has himself stolen it from a third person. The law protects the possession even of a thief against one who would dishonestly dispossess him. *A fortiori*, D may be convicted of stealing from P property which P has obtained by deception from a third person. P will usually have not merely possession of the property obtained, but also ownership, at least until the third person takes steps to avoid the transaction under which the property was obtained. Thus in *Meech*

P was probably the owner of the cheque which he had obtained by a forged instrument from the hire-purchase company. If the cheque had been stolen from him, there would have been no difficulty. The problem arose because there was no evidence of dishonest appropriation until after D had paid the cheque into his bank. The question was whether P could follow his interest into the proceeds. It is submitted that P could have done so under the principle of *Taylor* v. *Plumer*;[1] where an agent converts his principal's property into another form (even wrongfully) the property in the changed form continues to belong to the principal. Since the court held that the money withdrawn by D was the proceeds of P's cheque,[2] the money belonged to P and it was unnecessary to rely on s. 5 (3).

---

[1] (1815) 3 M. & S. 562. Below, para. [401].
[2] This conclusion may, however, be questionable on the facts since P's "money" became mixed with D's money in D's bank account. See *Re J. Leslie Engineers Co. Ltd.*, [1976] 2 All E.R. 85 at 89–91 (Oliver, J.).

---

[71] Where reliance is placed on s. 5 (3) the property is regarded as belonging to another only "as against him", that is, the person owing the obligation. If, therefore, in *Meech* the property belonged to P only by virtue of s. 5 (3), E and F who dishonestly appropriated part of the proceeds of the cheque could not commit theft from P except as aiders and abettors of D. Only D had assumed an obligation to P. If the argument that D's theft was over and done with had been accepted, they could not have been guilty of theft at all but only of handling. If, however, P retained a proprietary interest in the proceeds then D and E were guilty of an independent theft.

[72] Where D is indebted to P but no obligation attaches to any particular money, s. 5 (3) is inapplicable. Where D, a turnstile operator, was improperly given £2 to admit to Wembley Stadium a person who had no ticket, it was held that D had not stolen the £2 from his employer, P: the bribe did not belong to the employer.[1] Yet there is no doubt that P could have recovered £2 from D. It seems that D and P were debtor and creditor. This is in accordance with the decision of the (civil) Court of Appeal in *Lister & Co.* v. *Stubbs*.[2] Some doubt has been cast on that decision. If it were held to be wrongly decided and that the bribe is held on a constructive trust for the employer, then the result in the criminal law would be different. It would not be necessary to rely on s. 5 (3), for the property would belong to P under s. 5 (1) and (2).

---

[1] *Powell* v. *MacRae*, [1977] Crim. L.R. 571, D.C.
[2] (1890), 45 Ch. D. 1. See also *Cullum* (1873), L.R. 2 C.C.R. 28; Eighth Report, Cmnd. 2977, para. 38; Williams, *TBCL*, 720–723, A. T. H. Smith, "Constructive Trusts in the Law of Theft", [1977] Crim. L.R. 395. J. C. Smith, [1979] Crim. L.R. at pp. 225–6.

---

[73] A similar problem arises where D makes a secret profit by a wrongful use of his employer's property. It is often said that a person in a fiduciary position who makes a secret profit is a constructive trustee of the profit. If D really is a trustee[1] the profit belongs to P and D (if he is dishonest) steals it by retaining it as if it were his own. There is, however, a vital distinction between a duty to hold specific property on trust and a duty to account. In *Tarling* v. *Singapore Republic Government*[2] a majority of the House of Lords decided

that evidence of an agreement by company directors to acquire and retain a secret profit for which they were accountable to the shareholders was not evidence of an agreement to defraud. Lord Wilberforce said that "the making of a secret profit is no criminal offence, whatever other epithet may be appropriate".

---

[1] It is a matter of some doubt. It has been said that in none of the cases in which a fiduciary has been held liable to account for profits did the question arise whether the defendant was a trustee as opposed to being merely accountable: Hanbury and Maudsley, *Modern Equity* (10th ed. 314).
[2] (1978), Times, 20 April; [1978] Crim. L.R. 490; not fully reported. Discussed, [1979] Crim. L.R. 220.

(f) An obligation to make restoration of property

[74] Suppose that D acquires possession of property by another's mistake and is liable (a question of civil law) to account to P for the value of the property so obtained. The ownership in the property may pass to D, or it may remain in P, depending on the character of the mistake. If the ownership remains in P, then, under the rules already discussed, D may steal the property: but if the ownership passes to D then P retains no proprietary right or interest and (subject to the *Lawrence* (C.A.) principle[1]) D can commit no offence under the provisions so far discussed. Such a case is, however, covered by s. 5 (4) which provides:

> "Where a person gets property by another's mistake, and is under an obligation to make restoration (in whole or in part) of the property or its proceeds or of the value thereof, then to the extent of that obligation the property or proceeds shall be regarded (as against him) as belonging to the person entitled to restoration, and an intention not to make restoration shall be regarded accordingly as an intention to deprive that person of the property or proceeds."

---

[1] Above, para. [37].

---

[75] This provision is obviously apt to cover such a case as *Ashwell*.[1]

P, in the dark, gave D a sovereign in mistake for a shilling. When, some time later, D discovered that he had a sovereign and not a shilling, he at once decided to keep it for himself. Likewise with the case of *Middleton*:[2]

P, a post office clerk, referred to the wrong letter of advice and handed to D, a depositor in the Post Office Savings Bank, a sum which ought to have gone to another depositor. D took it, knowing that it was a much larger sum than he was entitled to.

In neither of these cases, however, is s. 5 (4) strictly necessary. In *Ashwell*, it was implicit in the decision (and rightly so) that no property in the sovereign passed to D (a sovereign is necessarily a different coin from a shilling—it was a mistake of identity)—so D today would be guilty of appropriating property belonging to another under s. 1 (1) and s. 3 (1) of the Act.[3] The basis of *Middleton* too was that no property in the money passed to D because of a mistake as to the identity either of the deposit or of the depositor. If, however, *Ashwell* and *Middleton* should have been wrongly decided (because the property did pass)—and both have been criticised[4]—s. 5 (4) makes it quite clear that under the Act, persons who act as they did should nevertheless be convicted. Even if the property in the money did pass to D in each of those cases, it is clear that D would be under an obligation to make restoration, if not of the actual property or its proceeds, at least of its value; and therefore the property would be treated as belonging to P. The only slight distinction is this: Middleton received £8 16s. 10d. and was convicted of stealing that sum—rightly on the basis of mistake of identity. He was, however entitled to 10s. and, if the property had passed, he would under the Act be guilty of stealing only £8 6s. 10d.—the amount which he was bound to restore.

---

[1] (1885), 16 Q.B.D. 190.
[2] (1873), L.R. 2 C.C.R. 38.
[3] Above, paras. **[17]**–**[19]**.
[4] Russell, 970–974, 979–982, 1553–1574.

---

[76] The real object of s. 5 (4) however (or, at least of that part of it which deals with the value of the goods) is to get rid of the decision in *Moynes* v. *Coopper*.[1] D, a labourer, had received most of his week's wages in advance from his employer. It was the employer's intention to tell the wages clerk to deduct the amount of the advance when paying D at the end of the week. He forgot to do so. The clerk therefore gave D a packet containing the full amount of his wages. D did not discover this until he arrived home when he opened the envelope and, knowing he was not entitled to it, decided to keep the whole sum. The divisional court dismissed the prosecutor's appeal on the ground that D had no larcenous intent at the time of taking as required by the Larceny Act 1916. This is no longer a problem: see s. 3 (1). The Court of Quarter Sessions (chairman, Mr. Thesiger, Q.C.), however, had acquitted Moynes on the more fundamental grounds that (*a*) D received ownership in the money and (*b*) D took the money with the consent of the owner. These were valid grounds.[2] The wages clerk, no doubt, had a general authority to pay each workman the weekly wage due to him. You do not revoke your agent's authority by deciding to do so and then forgetting about it. When the clerk handed the wages packet to D it seems clear that he transferred to him both ownership and possession in the money. In that case, it was quite impossible for D to be guilty of larceny of the money and it was really irrelevant (as Mr. Thesiger decided) whether D decided to keep the money for himself at the wages table, or later when he got home. No one else had any legal interest in the money—D was merely under a quasi-contractual obligation to repay to his employer an equivalent sum. He was in fact merely a particular kind of debtor. On such an analysis, there is a good deal to be said in favour of Moynes's acquittal; but few cases have attracted so much adverse criticism and it is hardly surprising that it was thought necessary to bring this case within the new law of theft; and s. 5 (4) (and particularly the words "or the value thereof") does so. Though the money would still be D's, a notional property in it would be vested in P for the purposes of this Act; and D's intention not to repay would be regarded as an intention to deprive P of the money.

---

[1] [1956] 1 Q.B. 439; [1956] 1 All E.R. 450, criticised in [1956] Crim. L.R. 516.
[2] This is implicitly recognised by the Act which, by s. 5 (4), circumvents ground (*b*). Ground (*a*) has become irrelevant with the disappearance of trespass as a constituent of stealing.

[77] There remains the necessity for an appropriation—it will be noted that s. 5 (4) does not itself create any offence—and this must be an appropriation of the property which was given by mistake or its proceeds. Suppose that Moynes had given his pay packet to E without opening it and been informed later of how much it contained. His resolution not to make repayment would not make him guilty of any offence, for there would be no appropriation. It would be otherwise if E repaid him the sum by which the actual contents of the packet exceeded the supposed contents and D retained that. He would then have appropriated the proceeds. Suppose that D had opened the packet and, forgetting for the moment about his "sub.", bought a bicycle with the money. Since he was under an obligation to make restoration of the value, it would seem that the bicycle would be deemed to belong to his employer. Suppose D then realised the mistake had been made: any act of appropriation of the bicycle would seem to make him guilty of an *actus reus*—but dishonesty might be hard to establish in such a case.

If Moynes, not appreciating the mistake, had spent the whole of the contents of the wages packet on beer which was consumed by himself and his workmates, he could not thereafter be guilty of any offence. After learning of the mistake, the intention not to restore would provide *mens rea* but there would be nothing which could be the subject of an appropriation. He would be simply a recalcitrant debtor.

[78] Plainly, s. 5 (4) extends the scope of stealing. Bringing Moynes within the net inevitably involves bringing in a number of others whose activities have not generally been thought of as criminal. For example, P pays money to D under the mistaken belief that the property of D has been lost through a peril insured against. D receives the money under the same belief.[1] Or P pays money to D under a contract for the sale of a fishery. In fact the fishery already belongs to P.[2] In both these cases, D discovers the truth and resolves not to make restoration. In legal analysis, D's situation is indistinguishable from that of Moynes: he has received money under a mistake and is under an obligation to make restoration of the value thereof. Plainly, then, the money (notionally) belongs to P in both these cases and (if D's resolution not to repay can be regarded as dishonest) D is guilty of theft if he appropriates the money or the proceeds (e.g. the Rolls Royce which he has bought with it). Only if the money cannot be traced into some property in his possession will he be exempt. Whether such cases are wisely brought within the net of theft is questionable but it is the inevitable result of covering the *Moynes* situation. The difficulty is, essentially, one of making a thief of a particular kind of debtor when debtors generally cannot steal. And it can involve the criminal law in some of the finest distinctions drawn in the civil law. Suppose that P wishes to terminate the employment of his servant, D. Both P and D believe that a binding contract of service exists between them and P pays D £30,000 to be released from his obligation to continue to employ D. The parties then discover that P could (and, had he known the truth, would) have dismissed D without paying him a penny, since D had committed breaches of contract which were unknown to P and not present to D's mind when he accepted the £30,000. D then appropriates the £30,000. If, as the Court of Appeal held,[3] D was under an obligation to restore the value of £30,000, this would be the *actus reus* of theft

by D; but as the House of Lords held[4] that there was no such obligation, it is
no offence. It may be that all of the cases discussed in this paragraph would
founder from the inability to prove a dishonest intention; yet these recipients of
money are, in law, in no different situation from Moynes himself.

---

[1] *Cf. Norwich Union, Fire Insurance Society, Ltd.* v. *Price*, [1934] A.C. 455.
[2] *Cooper* v. *Phibbs* (1867), L.R. 2 H.L. 149. It is assumed for the purpose of this example that the
contract was void.
[3] *Lever Brothers, Ltd.* v. *Bell*, [1931] 1 K.B. 557. The Court of Appeal thought the contract was
void.
[4] *Bell* v. *Lever Brothers, Ltd.*, [1932] A.C. 161.

(g) The meaning of "obligation"

[79] The word "obligation", in s. 5 (4) means a legal obligation.[1] It was so
held in *Gilks*.[2] D placed bets including one on a horse, Fighting Scot. Fighting
Scot was unplaced and the race was won by Fighting Taffy. Because of a
mistake on the part of the clerk in the betting shop, D was paid as if he had
backed the winning horse and received £117.25 instead of £10.62 to which he
was entitled. D took the money, knowing that he was being overpaid. The trial
judge ruled that "at the moment the money passed, it was money belonging to
another." This appears to be an application of the *Lawrence*, C.A.,[3] principle
and, if that principle is right, there can be no quarrel with that ruling.[4] In case
his first ruling was wrong, however, the judge went on to consider s. 5 (4) and
ruled that it was applicable if D was under an "obligation", even though it was
not a legal obligation, to repay. The Court of Appeal decided that the latter
ruling was wrong: "obligation" cannot be construed as meaning a moral or
social obligation as distinct from a legal one. The court interpreted the judge's
first ruling as meaning that "the property in the £106.63 *never* passed to the
appellant;" and they held that the ruling, so interpreted, was right.

The difficulty over s. 5 (4) arises because of the decision of the Court of
Appeal in the civil case of *Morgan* v. *Ashcroft*.[5] It was there held that, (i)
since the Gaming Act 1845 makes wagering transactions void, the court could
not examine the state of accounts between a bookmaker and his client and (ii)
that money paid under a mistake is recoverable only if the mistake was as to a
fact which, if true, would have made the payer legally liable to pay. For both
these reasons an overpayment by a bookmaker was held to be irrecoverable.
Gilks, therefore, was under no legal obligation to repay the money.

It is of interest to note that where a bet is placed with the "Tote" this
problem does not arise. Such a bet is not a wager, since the Tote can neither
win nor lose. The bet is an enforceable contract.[6] An overpaid investor is no
doubt under an obligation to repay.

The decision of the court in *Gilks* that the ownership never passed was based
on the decision in *Middleton*, one of the most dubious and hotly debated
decisions on the old law of larceny. It is regrettable that recourse should be had
to such a case in interpreting the Theft Act; but, even if *Middleton* was rightly
decided, its ratio was inapplicable to the facts of *Gilks*. It turned on the fact
that the court held that there was a mistake of identity, either the identity of
the payee or the identity of the Post Office deposit which was being repaid. In
Gilks there was no question of any such mistake. The clerk intended to pay the
sum of money which he handed over to Gilks and to no one else. It is difficult

to suppose that the bookmaker (or the plaintiff in *Morgan* v. *Ashcroft*) could have successfully sued for conversion of the money. It is submitted that there is no doubt that the ownership in money does pass in these circumstances and that *Gilks* is wrongly decided. It may seem a deplorable result; but, while *Morgan* v. *Ashcroft* stands, Gilks was doing no more than retaining money which he was entitled in law to retain. If so, however dishonest he may have been, it would be wrong to convict him of theft.[7] He could have resisted a restitution order under s. 28 of the Act on the ground that *Morgan* v. *Ashcroft* is direct authority that the bookmaker was not a "a person entitled to recover" the money. A person should not be held guilty of stealing property when he has a better right to it than anyone else. The defect in the law, if there is one, is with the decision in *Morgan* v. *Ashcroft*.

The legal obligation must be to "*make restoration* of the property or its proceeds or of the value thereof". An obligation to pay the price for goods sold is not an obligation "to make restoration". So if P sells goods to D for £10 and, by mistake, sends a bill for £5, D does not steal if he dishonestly pays £5 and keeps the goods.[8]

---

[1] But cf. *Hayes*, [1977] Crim. L.R. 691, above, para. [67].
[2] [1972] 3 All E.R. 280, C.A.; [1972] Crim. L.R. 585 and commentary; SHC 549.
[3] Above, para. [37].
[4] But the facts provide another argument against the principle. It suggests that a man might steal property which, when stolen, is entirely his.
[5] [1938] 1 K.B. 49; [1937] 3 All E.R. 97.
[6] *Tote Investors, Ltd.* v. *Smoker*, [1968] 1 Q.B. 509; [1967] 3 All E.R. 242, C.A.
[7] See commentary, [1972] Crim. L.R. at 588–589 and [1972B] C.L.J. at p. 202.
[8] See discussion of *Lacis* v. *Cashmarts*, [1969] 2 Q.B. 400, at 411, [1972B] C.L.J. at p. 204.

(h) A right to rescind is not property

[80] Where D gets property from P by deception he gets it "by another's mistake". If P is not deceived, the offence is not committed. All cases of obtaining by deception contrary to s. 15 (1)[1] are thus cases in which D gets property by another's mistake. This is the second ground on which it has been argued[2] that almost all cases falling within s. 15 are theft contrary to s. 1 (1). Even if the *Lawrence*, C.A., principle[3] is invalid, the same result may follow through s. 5 (4). This was plainly not intended by the CLRC, and, since it would have the effect of making s. 15 substantially redundant, it may be argued that it was not the intention of Parliament either. The question is whether D, having obtained property by deception, is under an obligation to make restoration of the property or its proceeds or its value. In most cases there will be a voidable contract between P and D.

A voidable contract has all the effects of a perfect contract until it is avoided by rescission. Generally, P can avoid only by giving notice to D of his intention to do so. When the right to rescind has lapsed, as it does if it is not exercised promptly, it is indistinguishable from a perfect contract. Until that occurs P certainly has the power to subject D to an obligation to make restoration, but that is not the same thing as a present obligation. The Act says "is", not "may be", under an obligation. D is under no obligation to repay until P does a positive act, which he may never do, or may not do until it is too late to be legally effective.[4]

Until the voidable contract is avoided it would seem that D is under no obligation to make restoration to P. If that is correct, D's retaining or dealing with the property cannot amount to theft. He is not appropriating property belonging to P since, under the voidable contract, the property has passed to D and it is his own property that he is retaining or dealing with; nor is the property to "be regarded as" belonging to P under s. 5 (4) since D is under no obligation to make restoration. Where a legal transaction other than a contract is induced by deception,—for example, a gift—it is presumably again voidable, and the same considerations apply.

---

[1] Below, para. [188].
[2] See Roy Stuart, "Law Reform and Reform of the Law of Theft" (1967), 30 M.L.R. 609.
[3] Above, para. [37].
[4] See the criticism of this argument by P. Glazebrook in 10 J.S.P.T.L. (N.S.) 299 at 300. Mr. Glazebrook argues that there is a quasi-contractual action to recover property obtained by fraud which is unaffected by the victim's ability to rescind the contract. *Sed qu.* A quasi-contractual action will not lie while there exists an inconsistent contract.

---

[81] There are cases of obtaining by deception, however, where the deception induces a mere payment or transfer of property, unaccompanied by any new voidable transaction. This occurs where the payment is made supposedly in pursuance of an existing valid transaction. This is the situation in the example based on *Norwich Union* v. *Price*.[1] The mistake led to no new legal transaction but to a payment supposedly in pursuance of an existing insurance contract. It is thought that, in these circumstances, P has an immediate right to repayment; there is no transaction to be set aside.[2] Suppose then that P's mistake had been induced by D's deception. D would, of course, be guilty of an offence under s. 15, but he would also, it would seem, be guilty of theft by virtue of s. 5 (4).

Again if, for example, Moynes had induced the pay clerk's mistake by telling him that he had not received an advance payment, he would still be guilty of theft, as well as of obtaining by deception. Thus the question is not whether or not there was any deception. It is: Was the mistake (whether induced by deception or not) such that D was, there and then, under an obligation to repay? If so, it is theft. Otherwise, it is not.

---

[1] [1934] A.C. 455., above, para. [78], footnote 1.
[2] The statute of limitations would begin to run against P immediately; whereas, in the case of the voidable transaction, it would run only from the time when the transaction was avoided.

---

[82] Where there is a voidable contract or other transaction and P has avoided it, the matter is entirely different. The property now does belong to P and D's keeping it or dealing with it as owner is an appropriation of property belonging to another. There is no need to rely on s. 5 (4) to vest a fictitious property in P since he is now once again the owner under the civil law.

If, as will usually be the case, D has put it out of P's power to communicate his intention to rescind, P may rescind the contract by overt acts falling short of communication.[1] D may therefore commit the *actus reus* of theft by retaining or dealing with the property even though he does not know that the contract has been rescinded. Has he the necessary *mens rea* in such a case? Of course, he is dishonest throughout and undoubtedly intends to deprive P permanently of his property. The difficulty is that he does not know of the facts which, in law, give P property in the goods. It is submitted that D has a sufficient *mens rea*. Unless he happens to be a lawyer or a law student he will not appreciate the niceties of the problem discussed in this paragraph or the nature of P's interest. If he were asked to whom the property belonged, however, and he were to answer truthfully, he would probably say that it belonged to P. The fact probably is that D intends to deprive P of his interest in it, whatever that interest may be. This should be enough.

---

[1] *Car and Universal Finance Co., Ltd.* v. *Caldwell*, [1965] 1 Q.B. 525; [1964] 1 All E.R. 290.

G. WHAT CAN BE STOLEN

[83] Stealing is the dishonest appropriation of property and, by s. 4 (1):

> " 'Property' includes money and all other property, real or personal, including things in action and other intangible property."

It should be noted at once that this definition is highly qualified, so far as land and wild creatures are concerned, by subsections (2), (3) and (4) of s. 4.[1] Under the old law, there could be no theft of land, things in action or other intangible property or wild creatures while at large. The point about the first two cases was that there could be no taking and carrying away. Land was regarded as an immovable and things in action had no physical existence. The difficulty with wild creatures at large was that they had no owner. Each of these items requires separate consideration.

---

[1] Below, paras. [84], [93] and [95].

(a) Land

[84] Now that the requirement of taking and carrying away has disappeared from the law, the technical obstacle to land being the subject of theft has disappeared. Land was formerly a possible subject of fraudulent conversion[1] and, since fraudulent conversion has now been swallowed by theft, it was essential that land should, in some circumstances at least, be stealable. It would have been possible to leave s. 4 (1) unqualified and a perfectly workable law would have resulted. The Committee, for reasons of policy, decided against this course. Section 4 (2) provides:

> "A person cannot steal land, or things forming part of land and severed from it by him or by his directions, except in the following cases, that is to say—
> (a) when he is a trustee or personal representative, or is authorised by power of attorney, or as liquidator of a company, or otherwise, to sell or dispose of land belonging to another, and he appropriates the land or anything forming part of it by dealing with it in breach of the confidence reposed in him; or
> (b) when he is not in possession of the land and appropriates anything forming part of the land by severing it or causing it to be severed, or after it has been severed; or

(c) when, being in possession of the land under a tenancy, he appropriates the whole or part of any fixture or structure let to be used with the land.

For purposes of this subsection 'land' does not include incorporeal hereditaments; 'tenancy' means a tenancy for years or any less periods and includes an agreement for such a tenancy, but a person who after the end of a tenancy remains in possession as statutory tenant or otherwise is to be treated as having possession under the tenancy, and 'let' shall be construed accordingly."

It may be helpful to spell out the possible liability of the various categories of persons in detail.

---

[1] Above, para. [15].

(i) Trustees, personal representatives, and others authorised to dispose of land belonging to another

[85] Any of these persons may steal the land or anything forming part of it by dealing with it in breach of the confidence reposed in him. So if he sells or gives away the land or any fixture or structure forming part of it, he commits theft.

(ii) Other persons not in possession

[86] Such a person may steal only by severing, or causing to be severed, or obtaining severance of the thing in question. A purported sale by such a person of the land would not be theft. An attempt to sever, as by starting to dig out a sapling, is an assumption which is not a sufficient appropriation, though no doubt an attempt to steal.

The rule formerly was that a person could not be convicted of stealing anything which he had severed from the realty (subject to specific statutory exceptions) unless he first abandoned and then re-took possession. Under the Act the general rule is that a person who is not in possession of land can steal fixtures, growing things and even the substance of the land itself, if, in each case, he first severs it from the realty. The following acts, which would not (or may not) have been larceny under the old law, are theft under the new:

D enters upon land in the possession of P and (i) demolishes a brick wall and carries away the bricks; (ii) removes a stone statue fixed in the land; (iii) digs sand from a sand pit and takes it away; (iv) cuts grass growing on the land[1] and at once loads it onto a cart to drive away; (v) takes away P's farm gate.[2]

Outside the law of theft remains the case where D appropriates land without severing it as where he moves his boundary fence so as to incorporate a strip of P's land into his own.[3]

---

[1] *Cf. Foley* (1889), 17 Cox C.C. 142.
[2] *Cf. Skujins*, [1956] Crim. L.R. 266.
[3] The arguments for and against making land the subject of theft are summarised in *Eighth Report*, Cmnd. 2977 at pp. 21–22.

(iii) Other persons in possession as tenants

[87] If a tenant removes a fixture—for example a washbasin or fire-place—he may be guilty of stealing it. Likewise if he removes any struc-ture—for example a shed or greenhouse which is fixed to the land. If the structure is resting on its own weight and not a fixture then it is, of course, stealable under the general rule and there is no need to rely on s. 4 (2) (c). But the tenant will not be guilty if he digs soil or sand from the land and appropriates that. This exemption applies only to the person in possession of the land. If his wife or a member of the family were to dig and sell sand, it would seem that s. 4 (2) (b) would be applicable and theft would be com-mitted. In such a case, there is some authority for suggesting that the husband could be convicted as an aider and abettor.[1] If the husband were the principal in the act it is possible that anyone assisting him might be held liable as an aider and abettor, even though he could not himself be convicted.[2]

Unlike s. 4 (2) (b), 4 (2) (c) does not require that the thing be severed. It appears then that if the tenant contracted to sell the unsevered fireplace in his house he would be guilty of theft, even where there was no intention to sever it, as where it is sold to the tenant's successor in the tenancy. If the tenant purports to sell the land he commits no offence and a purported sale of an ordinary house would be indistinguishable from a sale of the land. The house could hardly be held to be a "structure let to be used with the land". The phrase implies that the structure is of an ancillary nature.

---

[1] *Sockett* (1908), 1 Cr. App. Rep. 101.
[2] *Cf. Bourne* (1952), 36 Cr. App. Rep. 125; *Cogan and Leak*, [1976] Q.B. 217; [1975] 2 All E.R. 1059; Smith and Hogan, 132–136.

(iv) Other persons in possession otherwise than as tenants

[88] A person may be in possession of a land as a licensee.[1] Curiously, he is not within the terms of s. 4 (2) (c) and so is incapable of stealing the land or anything forming part of it. He thus commits no offence if he dishonestly appropriates fixtures or digs sand or ore from the land. This appears to be an oversight in the Act. He of course may be guilty of stealing structures not forming part of the land.

---

[1] *Errington* v. *Errington and Woods*, [1952] 1 K.B. 290; [1952] 1 All E.R. 149; See Cheshire, *Modern Law of Real Property* (11th ed.), 458, 570–573; and Megarry and Wade (4th ed.), 619–620.

---

[89] It may still occasionally be important to determine whether a particular article forms part of the land. Generally appropriation will involve severance, so non-possessors will be caught by s. 4 (2) (b) while tenants are caught by s. 4 (2) (c). But if a licensee in possession appropriates a structure, it is vital to know whether it forms part of the land. This is a question of the law of land and the answer depends on the degree of annexation and the object of annexation. The chattel must be actually fixed to the land, not for its more convenient use as a chattel, but for the more convenient use of the land.

[90] Incorporeal hereditaments[1] are now stealable. The most important of these are easements, profits and rents. The main purpose of the provision would

seem to be to cover the theft of a rent-charge. No doubt this was the subject of fraudulent conversion under the old law, and called for a provision of this kind. But instances of theft of the other interests can only be extremely rare. For example, P has a right of way over O's land—an easement. D executes a deed purporting to relieve O's land of the burden of the easement. Or D, a tenant of P's land, purporting to be the freeholder, allows O, the adjoining landowner to erect a building which will necessarily obstruct the flow of light to windows on P's land which have an easement of light. These acts seem to be appropriations of the easement which, if done with the necessary *mens rea* will amount to theft. The most obvious instances will be those where a trustee or personal representative disposes of an easement, profit or rent for his own benefit. These cases are not covered by s. 4 (2) (*a*) but incorporeal hereditaments can be stolen by persons generally.

It will be noted that these examples relate to existing incorporeal hereditaments. Dishonestly to purport to *create* an easement in the land of another would not seem to amount to an offence unless it is done by one of the persons mentions in 4 (2) (*a*). In the latter case, such an act would seem to amount to "dealing with the land in breach of the confidence reposed in him".

[1] See Cheshire, *Modern Law of Real Property* (11th ed.), 111–112.

[91] The fact that D's efforts to dispose of an interest in P's land in these cases would be ineffective to do so would not seem to affect the result in the criminal law. When a bailee of goods purports to sell the goods, he is unable (in general) to pass a good title; yet it cannot be doubted that his purporting to do so amounts to an appropriation of the goods. The same is now true of a person who has no proprietary or possessory interest of any sort in the goods. The position must be the same in the case of a purported disposal of an interest in land.[1]

It may be added that where the person purporting to dispose of the interest in land has done so for reward, the simpler and more appropriate course will be to charge him with obtaining or attempting to obtain by deception from the person from whom he seeks the reward. Where D purports to dispose of the interest as a gift, however, the only possible charge will be one of stealing the interest; but such cases are likely to be extremely rare.

[1] The problem of "intention permanently to deprive" is the same as that discussed in connection with *Bloxham*, above, para. [26].

[92] A rather strange anomaly resulting from the exception of incorporeal hereditaments is that if D, not being one of the persons mentioned in 4 (2) (*a*), purports to dispose of the whole of P's interest in the land (for example, the fee simple) he will not commit theft (though he might be guilty of obtaining the price of the land by deception); whereas if, as in the examples given, he purports to dispose of a comparatively small part of P's interest he will be guilty of theft.

(b) Exception of things growing wild

[93] Things growing wild on land undoubtedly fall within the definition of

property in the Act and, but for an exception, could be stolen by a person not in possession of land if he severed and appropriated them. Section 4(3), however, provides:

"A person who picks mushrooms growing wild on any land, or who picks flowers, fruit or foliage from a plant growing wild on any land, does not (although not in possession of the land) steal what he picks, unless he does it for reward or for sale or other commercial purpose.

For purposes of this subsection 'mushroom' includes any fungus, and 'plant' includes any shrub or tree."

The effect is in general to exempt things growing wild from the law of theft. It will be theft however if:

(i) (Except in the case of a mushroom) D removes the whole plant. For example, he pulls out a primrose or a sapling by the roots. This is not picking *from a plant* and so is not within the exception.

(ii) D removes the plant or part of it by an act which cannot be described as "picking". For example, he saws off the top of a Christmas tree growing wild on P's land, or cuts the grass growing wild on P's land with a reaper or a scythe.

(iii) D picks mushrooms or wild flowers, fruit or foliage, for a commercial purpose—for example, mushrooms for sale in his shop or holly to sell from door to door at Christmas. The provision is no doubt intended to be used against depredation on a fairly large scale but it would seem to cover such cases as where D, a schoolboy, picks mushrooms intending to sell them to his mother or the neighbours. It is possible, however, that such a single isolated case might be held not to fall within the law as not being a "commercial" purpose—for it will be noted that the wording of the subsection requires that sale, as well as other purposes, be "commercial". It might be argued that this requires that D, to some extent, must be making a business of dealing in the things in question.[1]

It will, of course, be theft to pick a single *cultivated* flower, wherever it is growing.

---

[1] But cf. Williams, *TBCL*, 683 footnote 1.

(c) Wild creatures

[94] The distinction between wild creatures (*ferae naturae*) and tame creatures (*mansuetae naturae*) is a matter of common law.[1] Some tame animals, like dogs and cats, could not be stolen at common law; but now, all tame animals may be stolen. Wild creatures could not, while at large, be stolen at common law or under the Larceny Acts because no one had any property in them until they were taken or killed. The owner of the land on which they happened to be had an exclusive right to take them which was protected by the criminal law relating to poaching but was not protected by the heavier guns of larceny.

When the wild creature was killed or taken, the property in it vested in the owner of the land on which this was done,[2] but the thing was now in the possession of the taker who could not therefore steal it. If, however, he abandoned the thing on P's land, then possession of it vested in P and a

49

subsequent removal of it by D was larceny. Difficult questions could arise whether D had abandoned the creature or not. If he put rabbits into bags or bundles and hid them in a ditch on P's land, he retained possession so that it was no larceny if he returned later and appropriated them;[3] whereas if he merely left the things lying on the surface of the land, this might well have constituted abandonment of the thing.[4]

Though this result was rightly criticised, it was the logical consequence of the rule of the civil law which provided that the thing was owned by no one until it was taken. Had no special provisions been made in the Theft Act for wild animals they could probably have been stolen by virtue of s. 3 (1): though there would have been no appropriation at the instant of taking (because the thing was no one's property) any subsequent assumption of ownership (as by carrying the thing away) would have been theft from the owner of the land on which it was taken.

---

[1] See East, 2 P.C. 607; Russell, 2, 903.
[2] *Blades* v. *Higgs* (1865), 11 H.L. Cas. 621.
[3] *Townley* (1871), L.R. 1 C.C.R. 315; *Petch* (1878), 14 Cox C.C. 116.
[4] Cf. *Foley* (1889), 17 Cox C.C. 142.

---

[95] For reasons of policy, it was decided that it was undesirable to turn poaching generally into theft; and accordingly, s. 4 (4) provides:

> "Wild creatures, tamed or untamed, shall be regarded as property; but a person cannot steal a wild creature not tamed nor ordinarily kept in captivity, or the carcase of any such creature, unless either it has been reduced into possession by or on behalf of another person and possession of it has not since been lost or abandoned, or another person is in course of reducing it into possession."

The effect of s. 4 (4) is that wild creatures cannot be stolen, except in the following cases:

(i) The creature is tamed or ordinarily kept in captivity. For example, P's tame jackdaw, the mink which he keeps in cages, the animals in Whipsnade Zoo. The eagle which escaped some time ago from London Zoo could be stolen while at large, because it was *ordinarily* kept in capitivity. (This phrase seems clearly to refer to the specific animal and not to the species of animal.[1]) Animals like bees or pigeons which roam freely are sufficiently reduced into possession if they have acquired a habit of returning to their home (*animus revertendi*).[2] Possession is not lost because they are flying at a distance. If bees swarm, the common law rule is that the owner retains his possession only so long as he can keep them in sight and follow them. Possession is lost even though they are in sight if they have swarmed on land where he cannot lawfully follow.[3] A person who then takes them, or destroys them does not commit theft or criminal damage. Bees could not be said to be "tamed" or "ordinarily kept in captivity".

(ii) The creature has been reduced into and remains in the possession of another person or is in the course of being so reduced.[4] For example, P, a poacher, takes or is in course of taking a rabbit on O's land. This is not an offence under the Act. D takes the rabbit from P. This is theft by D from both P and O.

Except in these two cases, wild creatures cannot be stolen; so it will not be theft to take mussels from a mussel bed on an area of the foreshore which belongs to P and which P has tended in order to maintain and improve it.[5]

---

[1] In *Nye* v. *Niblett*, [1918] 1 K.B. 23, it was held that the words of s. 41 of the Malicious Damage Act 1861 (now repealed, see Criminal Damage Act 1971) "... being ordinarily kept ... for any domestic purpose" referred to the species of animal; but Darling, J. thought the section also protected a particular animal which was kept for a domestic purpose though the class to which it belonged was not so ordinarily kept. In the present section, however, the interpretation actually adopted in *Nye* v. *Niblett* is untenable. Even though the great majority of animals of a particular wild species are ordinarily kept in captivity, a particular wild animal of that species which is and always has been in fact at large, can hardly be stolen.
[2] Blackstone, *Commentaries*, 2, 392–3.
[3] *Kearry* v. *Pattinson*, [1939] 1 K.B. 471; [1939] 1 All E.R. 65, C.A.
[4] Section 4 (4).
[5] *Howlett and Howlett*, [1968] Crim. L.R. 222.

---

[96] The effect is that the poacher who reduces game into possession, abandons it and later resumes possession (so that he was guilty, under the old law, of larceny from the owner of land) no longer commits any offence of theft. The creature has not been reduced into possession by or on behalf of another person. The landowner may have acquired possession when the game was left on his land[1] but it can hardly be said that the reduction into possession was by him or on his behalf. Clearly, this slight narrowing of the law of stealing is of no great significance.

---

[1] *Hibbert* v. *McKiernan*, [1948] 2 K.B. 142; [1948] 1 All E.R. 860; above, para. [52].

---

[97] If the creature, having been reduced into possession, escapes again (and it is not a creature ordinarily kept in captivity) it cannot be stolen since possession of it has been lost. A more difficult case is that where the possession of the *carcase* of the creature is lost. P, a housewife, buys a pheasant and loses it from her shopping basket on the way home. D picks it up and reads her name and address on the wrapping but determines to keep it for himself. If possession of the pheasant has been lost then D is not guilty and we have a curious case of a particular kind of chattel where there can be no stealing by finding. It is very arguable, however, that even in this case, theft is committed, for the old law of larceny by finding must have proceeded on the assumption that even the person who had lost goods retained possession of them—otherwise there would not have been that trespass which was an essential element of larceny at common law.[1] If that argument is correct, however, then there is another rather anomalous distinction between the loss of a dead wild creature and the loss of a live one—for the Act clearly contemplates that it is possible to lose possession of a wild creature and, even if this is inapplicable to the carcase, it must apply at least to the living animal. This is one of very few instances where possession is important under the Act and, significantly, it presents problems.

---

[1] "It appears clear on the old authorities that every person who takes a thing upon a finding is civilly a trespasser, except in the one case of a person who finding a thing when it is really lost takes it 'in charity to save for its owner' ": Pollock and Wright on *Possession in the Common Law*, 171.

(i) Poaching

[98] Poaching may amount to an offence under a variety of enactments—the Night Poaching Act 1828, the Game Act 1831 as amended by the Game Laws Amendment Act 1960, and the Poaching Prevention Act 1862. In addition certain provisions relating to the poaching of deer and fish were dealt with in the Larceny Act 1861 and, in view of the decision to repeal the whole of that Act, these are reproduced in the Second Schedule to the Act (below) in a simplified form and with revised maximum penalties. These provisions have been put in the Schedule rather than in the body of the Act to avoid giving the impression that they are intended to be a permanent part of the law of theft.[1] The CLRC has suggested that there should be a review of the whole law of poaching followed by comprehensive legislation which would repeal the Second Schedule.[2]

---

[1] *Eighth Report,* Cmnd. 2977, para. 53.
[2] *Ibid.*

(ii) Criminal Damage

[99] The Criminal Damage Act 1971 defines "property" in such a way as to exclude those wild creatures and those growing things which cannot be stolen; so the provisions of the Theft Act cannot be circumvented by a charge of criminal damage.

(d) Things in action

[100] A thing in action is property which does not exist in a physical state but which may be vindicated by a legal action. Examples are a debt, shares in a company, a copyright or a trade mark. The Patents Act 1977, s. 30 declares that a patent or an application for a patent is not a thing in action but is personal property so it is clearly "other intangible property" and is capable of being stolen. An invention for which no patent has been granted or applied for is clearly another form of intangible property,[1] whether or not it is a thing in action. Confidential information is not property so an undergraduate who unlawfully acquires and reads or makes a copy of an examination question paper may not be convicted of stealing intangible property, namely confidential information belonging to the University.[2] It follows that the wrongful acquisition and use of trade secrets is not theft.[3] In practice relatively small numbers of cases of theft of things in action might be expected to arise and the great majority of these will be cases of misappropriation by trustees, personal representatives and others. The following cases will amount to theft:

D purports to sell the copyright in a book owned by P to O. This is theft of the copyright from P.

D, being in possession of P's books of account which show a credit balance, purports to assign the debts to O. This is theft from P of the book debts.

D purports to sell the right to use a trade mark owned by P to O. This is theft from P of the trade mark.

It might be objected that these cases will amount to theft only if D believes he has the power (but not the right) to dispose of the thing in action. Otherwise, it may be said, he has no intention permanently to deprive the owner of it. This is the same argument as that considered above in relation to *Bloxham*[4] and the same answers apply. In each of these cases—as in the examples put concerning land—it would generally be simpler and more appropriate to charge D with obtaining by deception from O. There will be cases where D obtains nothing and a charge of theft may be appropriate and useful. For example:

D, a company secretary, receives signed but otherwise blank cheques from his employers to pay the company's creditors. He uses them to pay debts of his own.[5] This is theft from the company not only of the cheque forms but of the amount by which the company's credit balance is diminished.[6] D assumes the rights of the owner of the debt owed by the bank to the company and intends to deprive the company and does deprive it, of part of the debt. On the discovery of the forgery, the bank may be obliged to restore the balance. If D knows this, does he have an intent *permanently* to deprive? Probably yes, because the thing in action is like money or other fungibles—what is restored is a different "thing". Alternatively, reliance might be placed on s. 6 (1).[7]

---

[1] See Patents Act 1977, s. 7 (2) (*b*).
[2] *Oxford* v. *Moss*, [1979] Crim. L.R. 119. But might he have been convicted of stealing the question paper on the ground that the "virtue" had gone out of it when he put it back? Below, para. **[128]**–**[131]** and commentary at [1979] Crim. L.R. 120.
[3] Griew, 2–14, 2–54; Williams, *TBCL* 688–689, 722–723.
[4] Above, para. **[26]**.
[5] *Cf. Davenport*, [1954] 1 All E.R. 602.
[6] In *Davenport*, D was in fact convicted of larceny of the money which was the proceeds of the cheques. His conviction was quashed. Lord Goddard, C.J. said: "I think the fallacy that led to this charge of stealing money was this. It was thought that, because the master's account had been debited, that was enough to make a theft, but, although we talk about people having money in the bank, the only person who has money in the bank is the banker. If I pay money into my bank, either by paying cash or a cheque, the money at once becomes the property of the banker. The relationship between banker and customer is that of debtor and creditor." A conviction for theft could be upheld under the Theft Act since it is now possible to steal a debt.
[7] *Cf.* Griew, 2–11.

---

[101] It is thought that theft would not be committed by a mere breach of copyright. If D, in writing a book, were to copy out large sections of another book in which P owned the copyright, this would be a breach of copyright but it would not be theft. It is submitted that it would not amount to an appropriation of the copyright; and, in any event, there would seem to be no evidence in such a case of an intent to deprive P permanently of his property. It would be more analogous to making a merely temporary use of another's chattel.

(e) The necessity for specific property

[102] The necessity for the existence of some specific property has been insisted upon more than once in the above pages. This necessity, while not expressed in the Act, is really self-evident since there can be no appropriation unless there exists some thing to be appropriated. A resolution by D not to repay a debt he owes to P cannot be regarded as an appropriation because there is nothing to appropriate.[1]

It is not necessary that the property be "specific" in the sense in which that term is used in the Sale of Goods Act 1893.[2] It would be enough under the Theft Act that D had appropriated an unascertained part of an ascertained whole though such property would not be "specific" for the purposes of the Sale of Goods Act. If D is charged with stealing five out of a consignment of ten tins and it emerges at the trial that he was guilty of stealing all ten, he may be convicted of stealing the five.[3] Conversely, if he is charged with stealing ten tins and it emerges that he stole only five of them, he may be convicted of stealing the five. It is not an objection that it is impossible to point to the five which have been stolen. In *Tideswell*[4] P's servant, E, weighed a quantity of ashes into trucks for D, but entered a less quantity in P's books and charged D for that less quantity. It was held that D was guilty of larceny of the balance of the ashes over those for which he had paid. D's contract with P was not to buy the whole bulk of the ashes at so much per ton, but only to buy such as he might want at that price. The court took the view that E had no authority to pass the property except in those ashes for which he charged; that the balance therefore remained P's property, and it was immaterial that it was not distinguishable from the bulk.[5] It is submitted that this is theft under the Theft Act. Indeed, it would be more accurate in such a case to charge D with theft of the whole; for it is difficult to see how property passes in any of the ashes since "Where there is a contract for the sale of unascertained goods no property in the goods is transferred to the buyer unless and until the goods are ascertained."[6] The goods appear never to have been ascertained in that case.[7] On the other hand, it may be said that, while there is an appropriation of the whole quantity (an *actus reus*), D has a claim of right in respect of the quantity for which he has paid or agreed to pay. Such reasoning was not, however, used in *Middleton*[8] where D was convicted of stealing the whole sum of money although he was entitled to a less sum.

---

[1] It should be noted that this is not an appropriation of the debt—a thing in action—because it is not an assumption of ownership of it. That would occur if E purported to assign P's debt to another.

[2] Section 62.

[3] *Cf. Pilgram v. Rice-Smith*, [1977] 2 All E.R. 658, above, para. **[41]**.

[4] [1905] 2 K.B. 273.

[5] In *Lacis* v. *Cashmarts*, [1969] 2 Q.B. 400 at 411 (discussed in [1972B] C.L.J. at 204–208), the divisional court thought it an unavoidable and apparently fatal difficulty on a larceny charge that it was impossible to distinguish the goods alleged to be stolen from other goods lawfully taken. The court thought there would be no difficulty under the Theft Act. It is thought that it is as much, or as little, a difficulty for theft as for larceny; and that it is not a real difficulty in either case. The court seems to have overlooked *Tideswell*. Difficulties do arise, of course, if there is a charge of handling and the stolen goods cannot be identified.

[6] Sale of Goods Act 1893, s. 6.

[7] *Cf. Re Wait*, [1927] 1 Ch. 606.

[8] (1873) L.R. 2 C.C.R. 38.

---

[103] A more intractable problem than that of *Tideswell* is presented by *Tomlin*.[1] D was the manager of P's shoe shop. Between stocktakings in March, 1953 and September, 1953 goods to the value of £420 had gone from the shop without the proceeds of sale being accounted for. D's conviction for embezzlement of that sum was upheld. The court[2] rejected the argument that there could be no conviction for embezzling a general deficiency and that embezzlement of specific sums on specific dates must be proved. Clearly in cases of this kind it is virtually impossible to prove that D took the money for a particular pair of shoes and put it straight into his pocket; and it is submitted that the defence that there can be no theft of a general deficiency would fail under the Theft Act. D has not in fact appropriated "a deficiency"; he has appropriated a sum of money, no doubt on a number of different occasions, but between specific dates. Thus far *Tomlin* should present no problems; but a further point which was not argued is not easily solved. On the evidence it is very difficult to see how the jury could have been satisfied beyond reasonable doubt that D took money and not shoes.[3] If D has appropriated shoes, it is difficult to see how he can properly be convicted on an indictment alleging that he stole money, even to the same value. If the jury are satisfied that he took the shoes or the money it may well be that, in practice, they will convict him of stealing the money if that is what he is charged with and they think it the more likely event; but strictly speaking, they ought not to do so unless satisfied beyond reasonable doubt; and, if the defence is raised, it would seem that the judge would be bound so to direct the jury.

[1] [1954] 2 Q.B. 274; [1954] 2 All E.R. 272.
[2] Following *Balls* (1871), L.R. 1 C.C.R. 328.
[3] Or that he took the money before he put it into the till (embezzlement) and not after (larceny). As both types of appropriation are now theft, this problem need not be pursued.

[104] There are other instances of dishonest profit-making which may be morally indistinguishable from theft but which are not punishable under the Act because of absence of an appropriation of any specific thing. Where, for example, an employer withholds part of his servant's wages as a contribution to a pension fund and dishonestly omits to make that contribution. The employer may now be guilty of inducing the employee by deception to forgo payment of the portion of his wages, contrary to 1978, s. 2 (1) (*b*).[1] In the particular case where an employer fails to pay any contribution which he is liable to pay under the National Insurance Act 1946, he commits an offence punishable on summary conviction with a fine not exceeding £50. Finally, there is the example discussed *obiter* in *Tideswell*:

> "Suppose the owner of a flock of sheep were to offer to sell, and a purchaser agreed to buy, the whole flock at so much a head, the owner leaving it to his bailiff to count the sheep and ascertain the exact number of the flock, and subsequently the purchaser were to fraudulently arrange with the bailiff that whereas there were in fact thirty sheep they should be counted as twenty-five and the purchaser should be charged with twenty-five only, there would be no larceny, because the property would have passed to the purchaser before the fraudulent agreement was entered into."[2]

If the property in the whole flock had passed, then it might be argued that there was no appropriation of "property belonging to another". Apart from the *Lawrence* (C.A.) principle,[3] however, it might be answered that the owner retained his lien for the unpaid part of the true price, and that the bailiff appropriated it by delivering the sheep. Whether the property would have passed before the appropriation is, however, less clear than the learned judges appear to have thought; for, under the Sale of Goods Act 1893, s. 18, rule 3, where

> "the seller is bound to weigh, measure, test, or *do some other act or thing* with reference to the goods for the purpose of ascertaining the price, the

property does not pass until such thing be done, and the buyer has notice thereof."

If the bailiff agreed to deliver the whole flock of sheep before he counted them the agreement would be a sufficient act of appropriation of P's property.[4]

When the bailiff accounted to the owner for the price of 25 sheep, he would be guilty of dishonestly inducing him by deception to forgo payment for the other five, contrary to 1978, s. 2 (1) (*b*);[5] and he and the purchaser would be guilty of a conspiracy to defraud.[6]

---

[1] Below, para. [**238**].
[2] *Per* Lord Alverstone, C.J., [1905] 2 K.B. at 277; see to the same effect, Channell, J., *ibid.* at 279.
[3] Above, para. [**37**].
[4] *Cf. Rogers* v. *Arnott*, above, para. [**23**].
[5] Below, para. [**238**].
[6] Smith and Hogan, 232.

H. APPROPRIATIONS OF THE PROPERTY OF ANOTHER AUTHORISED BY THE CIVIL LAW

[**105**] There are many cases where the civil law authorises D to appropriate P's property with the intention of permanently depriving P of it.[1] If, in such a case, D is aware of the law, then it is obvious that he is not acting dishonestly and he commits no offence. Suppose, however, that D is unaware of the civil law which authorises him to act as he does and proceeds in a furtive manner evincing a dishonest intention. He now falls literally within the terms of the Act (for it contains no such expression as "unlawfully"[2]) and nothing is expressed which could save him from conviction from theft. It is submitted, however, that it would be ludicrous to convict P where the civil law gave him express authority to do what he did and that the Act should be interpreted so as to exclude such cases.

---

[1] E.g., A sale of uncollected goods under Schedule 1 of the Torts (Interference with Goods) Act 1977.
[2] Rightly, because there are cases which are and must be crimes under the Theft Act which do not amount to civil wrongs. The dishonest receiver of goods obtained by deception gets a title (though a voidable one) and commits no civil wrong; yet none would deny that his act should be a crime.

[**106**] A mere liberty or power must, however, be distinguished from an express authority or right in the strict sense. D has a liberty under the civil law to do an act if the performance of that act does not amount to a civil wrong. There is no reason why the criminal law should not curtail such liberties in appropriate cases, and the Theft Act has done so in the case of a co-owner who dishonestly appropriates the joint property;[1] and where D has the power to pass a good title, he may nevertheless in some cases be properly convicted of theft when he does so. For instance, the mercantile agent who is in possession of goods with the consent of the owner passes a good title if he sells to a *bona fide* purchaser, even though he does so dishonestly and in breach of the arrangement made with the owner.[2] This is clearly theft by the mercantile agent. The distinction between power and right appears in s. 48 of the Sale of

Goods Act 1893 and it is instructive to consider the effect of the Theft Act upon the situations there envisaged. By subsections (1) and (2):

"(1) Subject to the provisions of this section, a contract of sale is not rescinded by the mere exercise by an unpaid seller of his right of lien or retention or stoppage in transitu.

"(2) Where an unpaid seller who has exercised his right of lien or retention or stoppage in transitu re-sells the goods, the buyer acquires a good title thereto as against the original buyer."

The unpaid seller who re-sells after the property has passed has clearly appropriated the property of another (the first buyer) and commits the *actus reus* of theft although in doing so he passes a good title to the second buyer. It is unlikely that he could be convicted in most cases, for it would be difficult to prove dishonesty where no part of the price had been paid. But a seller is unpaid[3] until he receives the *whole* price, and a seller would certainly be dishonest if, having received 90 per cent of the price, he were to re-sell the goods, intending not to repay. This subsection gives the seller a mere power, not a right. The re-sale is a wrongful one and the first buyer, if he were to tender the price, could sue in conversion. There seems to be no reason why this should not be a crime. A quite different situation is created by subsection (3):

"Where the goods are of a perishable nature, or where the unpaid seller gives notice to the buyer of his intention to re-sell, and the buyer does not within a reasonable time pay or tender the price, the unpaid seller may re-sell the goods and recover from the original buyer damages for any loss occasioned by his breach of contract."

Though it is now established that the re-sale rescinds the contract and terminates the first buyer's property in the goods, the goods belong to the first buyer up to the amount of sale. It would be intolerable that the law should say, at one and the same time, that "the unpaid seller may re-sell the goods" and that he is guilty of theft if he does this, not knowing that the law permits him to do so. He is not guilty.[4] The position is the same under subsection (4):

"Where the seller expressly reserves the right of re-sale in case the buyer should make default, and on the buyer making default, re-sells the goods, the original contract of sale is thereby rescinded, but without prejudice to any claim the seller may have for damages."

---

[1] *Bonner*, above, para. [63], and *Turner* (*No.* 2), above, para. [58].
[2] Factors Act 1889, s. 2 (1).
[3] Sale of Goods Act 1893, s. 38.
[4] *R. V. Ward, Ltd.* v. *Bignall*, [1967] 1 Q.B. 534; [1967] 2 All E.R. 449, C.A.

2 THE MENS REA OF THEFT

[107] The changes made by the Act in the *mens rea* of theft are certainly much less significant than the fundamental reforms of the *actus reus*. The characteristics of the old law were:

(i) The stealing need not be done *lucri causa*, that is, it was unnecessary to prove that D intended to make any kind of profit for himself or another.

(ii) It must be done "fraudulently" and

(iii) without a claim of right made in good faith; and

(iv) with intent permanently to deprive the owner of his property.

[108] These characteristics are broadly preserved. They must be proved by the Crown. Inferences may be drawn from D's conduct but it is plain, and must be made plain to a jury, that the question is as to the state of D's mind.[1] By s. 1 (2):

> "It is immaterial whether the appropriation is made with a view to gain, or is made for the thief's own benefit."

Thus if D takes P's letters and puts them down a lavatory[2] or backs P's horse down a mine shaft[3] he is guilty of theft notwithstanding the fact that he intends only loss to P and no gain to himself or anyone else. It might be thought that these instances could safely and more appropriately have been left to other branches of the criminal law—that of criminal damage to property for instance. But there are possible cases where there is no such damage or destruction of the thing as would found a charge under another Act. For example, D takes P's diamond and flings it into a deep pond. The diamond lies unharmed in the pond and a prosecution for criminal damage would fail. It seems clearly right that D should be guilty of theft.

---

[1] *Ingram*, [1975] Crim. L.R. 457, C.A. (defence of absent-minded taking to charge of shop-lifting).

[2] *Cf. Wynn* (1887), 16 Cox C.C. 231.

[3] *Cf. Cabbage* (1815), Russ. & Ry. 292.

A. DISHONESTY WHERE SECTION 2 APPLIES

[109] By s. 2 of the Act:

> "(1) A person's appropriation of property belonging to another is not to be regarded as dishonest—
>
> (a) if he appropriates the property in the belief that he has in law the right to deprive the other of it, on behalf of himself or of a third person; or
>
> (b) if he appropriates the property in the belief that he would have the other's consent if the other knew of the appropriation and the circumstances of it; or
>
> (c) (except where the property came to him as trustee or personal representative) if he appropriates the property in the belief that the person to whom the property belongs cannot be discovered by taking reasonable steps.
>
> (2) A person's appropriation of property belonging to another may be dishonest notwithstanding that he is willing to pay for the property."

(a) Belief in the right to deprive

[110] D is not dishonest if he believes, whether reasonably or not, that he

58

has the legal right[1] to do the act which is alleged to constitute an appropriation of the property of another. This is in accordance with the old law of larceny. In spite of the courts' general insistence on reasonableness when defences of "mistake" were raised, it never seems to have been doubted that a claim of right afforded a defence, even though it was manifestly unreasonable.[2]

The onus is clearly on the Crown to prove a dishonest intention and, therefore, if the jury are of the opinion that it is reasonably possible that D believed that he had the right to do what he did, they should acquit.

---

[1] It is irrelevant that no such right exists in law. A dictum to the contrary in *Gott* v. *Measures*, [1948] 1 K.B. 234; [1947] 2 All E.R. 609, is irreconcilable with the decision in *Bernhard* (below).
[2] *Bernhard*, [1938] 2 K.B. 264; below, para. **[311]**.

---

[111] The Act refers specifically to a right *in law*. This does not *necessarily* exclude a belief in a merely moral right.[1] The common law, that taking another's property is not justifiable, even where it is necessary to avoid starvation,[2] suggests that even the strongest moral claim to deprive another is not enough; but, if it is now a jury question, there is no *law* to this effect and a jury would be likely to find that a truly starving person was not dishonest.[3]

It is made clear that a belief in the legal right of another will negative dishonesty, just as it amounted to a claim of right under the law of larceny.[4] If D, acting for the benefit of E, were to take property from P, wrongly but honestly believing that E was entitled to it, he would clearly not be guilty of theft.

---

[1] A belief in a moral right was not a defence to larceny: *Harris* v. *Harrison*, [1963] Crim. L.R. 497, (D.C.). *Cf.* Williams, *C.L.G.P.*, 322.
[2] Hale, 1 P.C. 54; *Dudley and Stephens* (1884), 14 Q.B.D. 273; *Southwark London Borough Council* v. *Williams*, [1971] Ch. 734 at 744.
[3] *Cf. Close*, [1977] Crim. L.R. 107 (Employee paying employer's debt in kind by taking employer's property without consent apparently held not to be dishonest by jury).
[4] *Williams*, [1962] Crim. L.R. 111.

(b) Belief that the person to whom the property belongs cannot be discovered by taking reasonable steps

[112] Though the Act makes no reference to finding, this is obviously intended to preserve the substance of the common law[1] rule relating to finding. The finder who appropriates property commits the *actus reus* of theft (assuming that the property does belong to someone and has not been abandoned) but is not dishonest unless he believes the owner can be discovered by taking reasonable steps. Even if the finder knows who the owner is, he may not be dishonest if he believes that the property cannot be returned except by taking wholly unreasonable steps. P inadvertently leaves a cigar in D's house and flies to his home in New Zealand. D finds the cigar and smokes it. Even if D does not believe that P would have consented to his smoking the cigar, it is submitted that D is not dishonest.

The important change in the law of finding made by the Act has already been dealt with.[2] At common law, if D's finding were innocent (either because he did not believe that the owner could be discovered by taking reasonable steps or because he intended to return the thing to the owner when he took it) no subsequent dishonest appropriation of the thing could make him guilty of larceny; but now, in such a case, he will be guilty of theft by virtue of s. 3 (1).[3]

It should be stressed that the question is one of D's actual belief, not whether it is a reasonable belief. If D, wrongly and unreasonably, supposed that the only way in which he could locate the owner of property he had found, would be to insert a full page advertisement in *The Times*, he would have to be acquitted unless that course were a reasonable one to take, which would depend upon the value of the property and all the surrounding circumstances.

---

[1] *Thurborn* (1849), 1 Den. 387.
[2] Above, para. [**24**].
[3] Above, para. [**19**].

---

[113] While this provision is intended mainly for the case of finding it is not confined to that case and there are other instances where it would be useful. Suppose that P arranges with D that D shall gratuitously store P's furniture in D's house. P leaves the town and D loses touch with him. Some years later D, needing the space in his house and being unable to locate P, sells the furniture.[1] This is undoubtedly an appropriation of the property of another and D is civilly liable to P in conversion; but he appears to be saved from any possibility of conviction of theft by s. 2 (1) (c).[2] Though the purchase money probably belongs to P,[3] D's immunity under the Act must extend to the proceeds of sale.

---

[1] *Cf. Sachs* v. *Miklos*, [1948] 2 K.B. 23; [1948] 1 All E.R. 67; *Munro* v. *Willmott*, [1949] 1 K.B. 295; [1948] 2 All E.R. 983.
[2] The bailee who disposes of uncollected goods under Schedule 1 of the Torts (Interference with Goods) Act 1977 will not usually be able to rely on this provision, for he will know where the owner is; but since he is "entitled ... to sell the goods", it is submitted that there is no *actus reus*. See above, para. [**105**].
[3] In equity, if not in law: *Taylor* v. *Plumer* (1815), 3 M. & S. 562 discussed by Goode, (1976) 92 L.Q.R. 360, 376 and by Khurshid and Matthews, (1979) 95 L.Q.R. 79. See also Williams, *TBCL*, 713, footnote 2 and 715, footnote 6.

---

[114] Where the property came to D as a trustee or personal representative and he appropriates it, he *may* be dishonest even though he believes that the person to whom the property belongs cannot be discovered by taking reasonable steps. The point seems to be that the trustee or personal representative can never be personally entitled to the property (unless it is specifically so provided by the trust instrument or the will) for, if the beneficiaries are extinct or undiscoverable, the Crown will be entitled to the beneficial interest as *bona vacantia*. If the trustee or personal representative appropriates the property to his own use, honestly believing that he is entitled to do so, then it is submitted that he must be acquitted. But if he knows that he has no right to do this and that the property in the last resort belongs to the Crown, he commits theft, from the beneficiaries if they are in fact discoverable and, if not, from the Crown.

(c) Dishonest appropriation, notwithstanding payment

[115] Section 2 (2) is intended to deal with the kind of situation where D takes bottles of milk from P's doorstep but leaves the full price there. Certainly D has no claim of right and he intends to deprive P permanently of his

property. Doubts had, however, arisen as to whether this was dishonest.[1] This
subsection resolves them. The mere fact of payment does not negative
dishonesty but the jury are entitled to take into account all the circumstances
and these may be such that even an intention to pay for property, let alone
actual payment,[2] may negative dishonesty. The fact of payment may be cogent
evidence where D's defence is that he believed P would have consented. D takes
milk bottles from P's unattended milk-cart and leaves the price. He says that
he assumed that P would have been very happy to sell him the milk had he
been there, but that he had not time to wait for P to return. If D is
believed—and the fact of repayment would be persuasive evidence—it would
seem that he has no dishonest intent.[3]

---

[1] *Cf.* Hawkins, 1 P.C. c. 34, s. 7; Blackstone, *Commentaries* IV, 243; Russell, 855–856.
[2] *Boggeln* v. *Williams*, [1978] 2 All E.R. 1061, below, para. [**117**].
[3] Section 2 (1) (*b*), above, para. [**109**].

B. DISHONESTY WHERE SECTION 2 DOES NOT APPLY

[116] Section 2 describes three situations which do not amount to dishonesty
and one situation which may. It does not tell us anything positive about
dishonesty. Yet dishonesty is an essential ingredient of theft and the jury must
be reminded in every case that they must be satisfied that the accused acted
dishonestly. It has been held by the Court of Appeal in *Feely*[1] that it is for the
jury in each case to decide, not only what the accused person's state of mind
was, but also (subject to s. 2) whether that state of mind is to be categorised as
dishonest.

> "Jurors, when deciding whether an appropriation was dishonest can be
> reasonably expected to, and should, apply the current standards of
> ordinary decent people. In their own lives they have to decide what is and
> what is not dishonest. We can see no reason why, when in a jury box, they
> should require the help of a judge to tell them what amounts to
> dishonesty."

The court was much influenced by the decision of the House of Lords in
Brutus v. *Cozens*[2] that the meaning of an ordinary word of the English
language is not a question of law for the judge but one of fact for the jury.
They thought that "dishonesty" is such a word, whereas "fraudulently", the
word used in the Larceny Acts, was a technical word with a special meaning.
This view derives some support from the opinion of the Committee:[3]

> " 'Dishonestly' seems to us a better word than 'fraudulently'. The
> question 'Was this dishonest?' is easier for a jury to answer than the
> question 'Was this fraudulent?' 'Dishonesty' is something which laymen
> can easily recognise when they see it, whereas 'fraud' may seem to involve
> technicalities which have to be explained by a lawyer."

This seems to be too optimistic a view of the abilities of the layman to
recognise dishonesty. Judges have held differing views about whether particular conduct should be stigmatised as dishonest;[4] and it would be surprising
indeed if laymen were more consistent. A difficulty about the *Feely* approach

is that juries—and magistrates—are likely to give different answers on facts which are indistinguishable.

Feely was concerned with a common situation. An employee, charged with theft of his employer's money, said that when he took the money he intended to repay it and had reasonable grounds for believing and did believe that he would be able to do so. The judge told the jury:

> "... even if he were prepared to pay back the following day and even if he were a millionaire, it makes no defence in law to this offence ..."

In so ruling, the judge was following a decision of the Court of Appeal in a similar situation under the Larceny Act.[5] It was held that this was a misdirection and *Feely's* conviction must be quashed. It should have been left to the jury to say whether the accused's state of mind amounted to dishonesty.

It is submitted that standards of honesty should be laid down by the law, not left to the vagaries of jury decision. This is particularly so in a commonly recurring situation such as that in *Feely*. If a jury return to court and say: "We find that D took his employer's money; he knew he was forbidden to do so; he intended to repay it before his employer missed it and he knew he had sufficient resources to do so. Was this dishonesty?", the judge can only answer: "That is for you to decide. Apply your own standards. The law has nothing to say on the matter." This seems wrong.

---

[1] [1973] Q.B. 530; [1973] 1 All E.R. 341; [1973] Crim. L.R. 193 and commentary; SHC 509. See Griew, *Dishonesty and the Jury* (Leicester U.P., 1974).
[2] [1973] A.C. 854; [1972] 2 All E.R. 1297.
[3] *Eighth Report*, para. 39.
[4] *Cf. Sinclair* v. *Neighbour*, [1967] 2 Q.B. 279; [1966] 3 All E.R. 988.
[5] *Cockburn*, [1968] 1 All E.R. 466, criticised in the second edition of this work, para. [123]. *Cf. Rao*, [1975] Crim. L.R. 451.

---

[117] Accepting *Feely* as the present law, it does not follow that the jury or magistrates will always have an unfettered discretion. The usual judicial controls over the finding of facts will apply. The jury may not find to be dishonest a state of mind which, in the view of the judge, no reasonable man could properly so describe; and—it is submitted—they must find a state of mind to be dishonest if no reasonable man, in the view of the judge, could fail so to find. The effect of *Feely* depends very greatly on the extent to which the judges are prepared to exert their powers of control. The present trend is to give the jury a very free hand.[1]

On the facts of *Feely*, it must be taken that a reasonable jury could go either way. If, however, Robin Hood were to tell the court that he took P's money to give it to Q because P is very rich and Q is very poor and he, Robin, does not consider that to be dishonest, is the judge really to leave it to the jury to say whether Robin's state of mind is dishonest or not? This example may not appear so fanciful when it is recalled that there are many people who think it right to go to extreme lengths to raise money for political causes in which they believe. If *Feely* leaves too much to the jury, two later cases go even further. In *Gilks*,[2] D agreed that it would be dishonest if his grocer gave him too much change and he kept it but he said bookmakers are "a race apart" and there was nothing dishonest about keeping the over-payment in the case.[3] The judge invited the jury to "try and place yourselves in [D's] position at that time and answer the question whether in your view he thought he was acting dishonestly;" and the Court of Appeal thought this a proper and sufficient direction, agreeing apparently that the prosecution had not established dishonesty if D did have the belief he claimed to have. This goes beyond *Feely* in that it applies the accused's own standards and not "the current standards of ordinary decent people;" and it goes too far. It might have been hoped that this departure from *Feely* was an oversight but in *Boggeln* v. *Williams*[4] the court expressly rejected an argument that a man's belief as to his own honesty was irrelevant and held that, on the contrary, it was crucial. D, whose electricity had been cut off, reconnected the supply through the meter. He knew the electricity board did not consent to his doing so, but he notified them and believed, not unreasonably, that he would be able to pay at the due time. It was held that the crucial question was whether the defendant believed that his conduct was honest.

It may be that, on any test, Williams would have been found not to be dishonest; but it is easy to envisage cases in which the defendant's standards of honesty fall far below those of the community generally. If such a person is to be acquitted of dishonesty, it is indeed a case of "Everyman his own legislator." It is submitted that the law should take a firm stand in such cases. It is the business of the law to establish standards. If a belief that bookmakers are "fair game" is to be allowed as a defence it will not be long before bookmakers *are* fair game; yet the bookmakers are as much entitled to the protection of the law for their property as anyone else. The danger does not stop there. A belief has sometimes prevailed in the army and other large organisations that it is "all right" to take small items of property belonging to the organisation. Such a belief by D does not necessarily amount to a defence under *Feely* for the jury may well be satisfied that, by the "current standards of ordinary decent people," this is dishonest but under *Boggeln* v. *Williams* D must be acquitted unless the prosecution can prove that *he* did not hold the belief. It is submitted, however, that it would be preferable if the judge could direct the jury that the pilferer was acting dishonestly, certainly where, as will usually be the case, he knows that he has no right in law to take the property.

---

[1] See below, para. [184]. Cf. *D.P.P.* v. *Stonehouse,*[1977] 2 All E.R. 909; [1977] Crim. L.R. 544 and commentary.
[2] Above, para. [79], [1972] 3 All E.R. at 283; SHC at 516.
[3] Gilks, of course, knew nothing of *Morgan* v. *Ashcroft* and had no belief in any right in law to keep the money, even if in truth he had such a right.
[4] [1978] 2 All E.R. 1061; [1978] Crim. L.R. 242 and commentary.

C. THE INTENTION OF PERMANENTLY DEPRIVING THE OTHER

[118] The Theft Act preserves the rule of the common law and of the Larceny Act 1916 that appropriating the property of another with the intention of depriving him only temporarily of it is not stealing.[1] English law, in general, recognises no *furtum usus*—the stealing of the use or enjoyment of a chattel or other property. This is subject to two exceptions which are considered below. The first exception concerns the removal of articles from places open to the public[2] and is a creation of the 1968 Act. The second exception, in so far as it relates to motor vehicles, has existed in the Road Traffic Acts since 1935, but

the extension to other "conveyances" is new.[3] Outside these cases the law seems to remain substantially unchanged; so that, if D takes P's horse without authority and rides it for an afternoon, a week or a month, he commits no offence under the Act and, probably, no offence against the criminal law (though a civil trespass) if he has an intention to return the horse at the end of this period.

[1] *Warner* (1970), 55 Cr. App. Rep. 93; SHC 517.
[2] Section 11, below, para. [**281**].
[3] Section 12, below, para. [**279**].

(a) Deprivation of persons with limited interests

[**119**] Theft may be committed against a person having possession or control of property or having any proprietary right or interest in it.[1] The element of permanence relates to the deprivation of P, not to the proposed benefit to D. It would seem clear, therefore, that where P has an interest less than full ownership, an intention by D to deprive him of the whole of that interest, whatever it might be, is sufficient. If, as D knows, P has hired a car from Q for a month, and D takes it, intending to return it to Q after the month has expired, this must be theft from P, for he is permanently deprived of his whole interest in the property, but it is not theft from Q for he, plainly, is not permanently deprived. It should be stressed that the question is always one of intention; so if, in the above example, D, when he took the car, believed P to be the owner, he would apparently not commit theft even though P was, in fact, deprived of his whole interest.

This is capable of producing rather odd results where the interest of the person deprived is a very small one. O writes a letter and gives it to P to deliver by hand to Q. D intercepts P and takes the letter from him. Having read it, he delivers it (as he always intended) to Q. This appears to be theft of the letter from P (though not from O or Q) since P is permanently deprived of his possession or control of it. If the letter is taken by force or threat of force, it will be robbery from P.

[1] Section 5 (1), above, para. [**53**].

(b) Disposition of property as one's own

[**120**] There is no comprehensive definition of "intention of permanently depriving" in the Act, but s. 6 "gives illustrations, as it were, of what can amount to the dishonest intention demanded by section 1 (1). But it is a misconception to interpret it as watering down section 1."[1] Section 6 (1) provides:

> "A person appropriating property belonging to another without meaning the other permanently to lose the thing itself is nevertheless to be regarded as having the intention of permanently depriving the other of it if his intention is to treat the thing as his own to dispose of regardless of the other's rights, and a borrowing or lending of it may amount to so treating it if, but only if, the borrowing or lending is for a period and in circumstances making it equivalent to an outright taking or disposal."

It seems clear that this is intended to affirm the common law rule that where D appropriates P's property with the intention that P shall have it back again only by paying for it, D has a sufficient intent permanently to deprive. For example, D takes P's £1 note and tenders it to P, asking if he can give change for it. Where D, the servant of P, a tallow-chandler, with an accomplice who purported to be E's servant, took fat from P's store room and offered it to P for sale as the property of E, D was guilty of larceny of the fat.[2] If D had alleged that the property was his own, he would have come squarely within the words of s. 6 (1)—his intention would have been to treat the thing *as his own* to dispose of regardless of the other's rights. On the actual facts, D and his accomplice treated the thing as the property of another which they had power to dispose of regardless of P's rights. Since s. 6 does not lay down an exclusive definition of the intention required, it is submitted that this would undoubtedly be theft within the Act; it is not distinguishable in principle from the case which is specifically dealt with in s. 6 (1).

Another type of case which would be covered by s. 6 (1) is that where D appropriates P's property, sells it to O, and then tells P where his property is to be found, knowing that P will be able to assert his proprietary rights against O and recover the property.

---

[1] *Warner* (above, para. [118], footnote 1) at 97, *per* Edmund Davies, L.J.
[2] *Hall* (1849), 1 Den. 381.

---

[121] In all of these examples D has probably committed an offence of obtaining property (the price) by deception contrary to s. 15 (1) and the simplest course might be to charge that offence. If, however, D were to appropriate P's property and offer it to P in return for something other than property or a pecuniary advantage—for example, an office or appointment of some kind—theft would be the only charge (unless the offer amounted to an offence of corruption). There might seem to be no difference in principle if D offered P P's own property as a gift. D, by purporting to be the owner, treats the thing as his own to dispose of regardless of P's rights; and to deceive P into supposing that he is receiving a gift is evidently dishonest. It would, however, be remarkable that one should evince an intention to deprive another permanently of his property by *giving* that property back to him; and it may be that the courts will think it proper to draw the line at the case where D asks for consideration for the return to P of P's own property. In this case, it may be said that there is a real, though conditional, intention to deprive—P may refuse to pay the price—which is lacking in the case of an outright gift.

[122] It has been submitted above[1] that on the facts of *Holloway*[2] there would be no theft under the Act, because there is no appropriation. Even if this is wrong, it would seem that a prosecution would fail because of the lack of evidence of intent permanently to deprive. Holloway did not intend to treat the skins as his own, or as the property of P to be disposed of regardless of P's rights; he intended to treat them as P's property and he did not intend to "dispose" of them.

---

[1] See para. [50].
[2] (1848), 1 Den. 370.

(c) Conditional intention to deprive

[123] In *Easom*,[1] the Court of Appeal said that "a conditional appropriation will not do." The difficulty of supporting this proposition is that all intention is conditional, even though the condition be unexpressed and not present to the mind of the person at that time. In *Easom* D picked up a woman's handbag in a cinema, rummaged through the contents and put it back having taken nothing. The handbag was attached by a thread to a policewoman's wrist. D's conviction for stealing the handbag and the specified contents—tissues, cosmetics, etc.—was quashed because there was no intention permanently to deprive. Consequently, he was not guilty of attempting to steal the handbag, or the specified contents either. The court said, "if a dishonest postal-sorter picks up a pile of letters intending to steal any which are registered, but, on finding that none of them are, replaces them, he has stolen nothing."[2] As the chattels were rejected as soon as they were identified, it may be better to say that there was no appropriation, not even a conditional one.

---

[1] [1971] 2 Q.B. 315 at 319; [1971] 2 All E.R. 945 at 947; SHC 324.
[2] Under the law existing at that time, the dishonest sorter might have been convicted of an *attempt* to steal *registered* letters; and Easom might have been convicted of an attempt to steal the *money* for which he was undoubtedly looking. A conviction for attempt would now be possible in neither case: *Haughton* v. *Smith*, [1975] A.C. 476; [1973] 3 All E.R. 1109; SHC 311.

---

[124] In *Husseyn*[1] DD opened the door of a van in which there was a holdall containing valuable sub-aqua equipment. They were charged with attempted theft of the equipment The judge directed the jury that they could convict if DD were about to look into the holdall and, if its contents were valuable, to steal it. The Court of Appeal, following *Easom*, held that this was a misdirection: "it cannot be said that one who has it in mind to steal only if what he finds is worth stealing has a present intention to steal." This ruling creates difficulties in the law of burglary[2] and of loitering with intent to steal[3] because most persons charged with these crimes enter or loiter intending to steal, not some specific thing, but anything they find which they think is worth stealing. Though *Husseyn* is supported by other decisions in the Court of Appeal[4] and the opinion has been expressed in the House of Lords[5] that it was rightly decided, it is submitted that it is inconsistent with the basis on which the law of burglary has always been administered—namely, that an intention to appropriate anything which D thinks to be worth taking *is* an intention to steal.[6] The Theft Act 1968 made no change in this respect and centuries of common law practice should be preferred to these decisions in which the courts failed to observe that what they said about intention to steal was inconsistent with the established law of burglary. No distinction can properly be made between intent to steal in burglary and loitering on the one hand and stealing or attempting to steal on the other.

---

[1] (1978), 67 Cr. App. Rep. 131; [1978] Crim. L.R. 219 and commentary; discussed at [1978] Crim. L.R. 444 and 644 and followed in *Bozickovic*, [1978] Crim. L.R. 686 (Mr. Recorder McAulay), below, para. **[359]**.
[2] S. 9 (2) (a) of the Act is rendered practically a dead letter: See *Bozickovic* below, para. **[359]**.
[3] Cf. *Lyons* v. *Owen*, [1963] Crim. L.R. 123; (1962), Times, 16 November.
[4] *Easom*, above and *Hector* (1978), 67 Cr. App. Rep. 224.
[5] *D.P.P.* v. *Nock*, [1978] A.C. 979; [1978] 2 All E.R. 654.
[6] Moreover, in other contexts the courts have commonly construed intention to include

conditional intention. See *Bentham*, [1973] 1 Q.B. 357; [1972] 3 All E.R. 271; *Buckingham* (1976), 63 Cr. App. Rep. 159; *Becerra and Cooper* (1975), 62 Cr. App. Rep. 212; Archbold (39th ed.) 8th Supplement, para. 1441f.

[125] It is submitted that in a case such as *Husseyn* the true position is that, where D's act is sufficiently proximate to be an attempt (as the court held it to be), D is guilty of an attempt to steal if there is something in the car (or building) which he would have stolen if he had found it. The qualification is necessary because of the decision in *Haughton* v. *Smith*;[1] if there is nothing in the place which D would have taken it is, in effect, an empty place. He must then be acquitted of an attempt, not because he has no intention to steal but because there is no *actus reus*. In *Husseyn* it is possible that D would not have wanted the sub-aqua equipment but, if the holdall had been full of used £5 notes and the jury had been satisfied that D would, if he had not been interrupted, have immediately stolen them, surely he should be convicted of attempting to commit the theft he was *in fact* on the point of committing. If there is nothing in the place in question that D would, on inspection, have stolen, he cannot, so long as *Haughton* v. *Smith* stands, be convicted of attempted theft; but, in truth, he has an intention to steal and, if the place is a building or an "inhabited"[2] vehicle, he should be guilty of burglary.

[1] Above, para. **[52]**.
[2] Below, para. **[354]**.

[126] It is submitted that the better view is that an assumption of ownership, which is conditional because there is an intent to deprive only in a certain event, is theft. For example, D takes P's ring intending to keep it if the stone is a diamond, but otherwise to return it. He takes it to a jeweller who says the stone is paste. D returns the ring to P. It is submitted that he committed theft when he took the ring. The fact that he returned it is relevant only to sentence. The case put in *Easom* of the postal-sorter may be distinguishable on the ground that he was authorised to sort through the letters; but if he had taken them home intending to keep any one which was registered, it would seem to be the same as the case of the ring.

A similar problem may arise where D takes the property of P, intending to claim a reward from P for finding it. If he intends to return the property in any event and hopes to receive the reward, he is not guilty of stealing though he is attempting to obtain property by deception, contrary to s. 15 (1). But if he intends to retain the property *unless* he receives the reward, he seems to be in substantially the same situation as the taker who *sells* the property back to the owner. It might be said, however, that in this example, the taker is not treating the property *as his own*. There are two possible answers to this; the assertion of a better right to possession might be regarded as treating the property as one's own; or, s. 6 not providing an exclusive definition, this might be regarded as an analogous case falling within the same general principle.

[127] It is submitted that, on a similar basis, there is no reason why there should not be a conviction for theft in a case like that of the taker of the Goya from the National Gallery: "I will return the picture when £X is paid to charity". Substantially, the taker is offering to sell the thing back and his case is, in principle, the same as those contemplated by s. 6 (1). Nor should it make any difference that the price demanded is something other than money. "I will return the picture when E (who is imprisoned) is given a free pardon"—this should be sufficient evidence of an intent permanently to deprive.

The general principle might be that it is sufficient that there is an intention that P shall not have the property back unless some consideration is supplied by him or another; or, more generally still, unless some condition is satisfied.

(d) Borrowing or lending

[128] Unlawful borrowing is generally not theft because the borrower, by definition, intends to return the thing. If the borrowing "is for a period and in circumstances making it equivalent to an outright taking ...", however, the borrower may be regarded as having the intention of depriving the owner permanently. This is a rather puzzling provision, because it would seem, *prima facie*, that borrowing cannot be an "outright taking". Clearly, however, this part of the subsection is intended to do something and, therefore, certain borrowings are to be treated as the equivalent of outright takings. Once this is accepted, it is not difficult to divine the kind of borrowings which are intended to be covered: they are those where the taker intends not to return the thing until the virtue is gone out of it. D takes P's dry battery, intending to return it to P when it is exhausted; or P's season ticket, intending to return it to P when the season is over. Similar in principle are those cases where D intends to return the thing only when it is completely changed in substance; D, being employed by P to melt pig iron, takes an axle belonging to P and melts it down in order to increase his output and, consequently, his earnings;[1] or D wrongfully feeds his employer's oats to his employer's horses.[2] Likewise where D takes possession of P's horse, intending to kill it and leave him the carcase[3]—though, plainly, theft is not the most appropriate charge.

---

[1] *Richards* (1844), 1 Car. & Kir. 532.
[2] *Morfit* (1816), Russ. & Ry. 307.
[3] Cf. *Cabbage* (1815), Russ. & Ry. 292; in that case he may in fact have been deprived of the carcase.

---

[129] The difficulty has been raised in connection with the theft of cheques that, if they are cashed as the thief presumably intends, they will be returned in due course to the bank of the drawer. How can the thief be said to intend to deprive him permanently of the cheque? The answer given by the court in *Duru*[1] was twofold. (i) That P was permanently deprived of the thing in action represented by the cheque; and (ii) that the cheque, as a piece of paper, changed its character completely once it was paid, "because then it receives a rubber stamp on it saying it has been paid and it ceases to be a thing in action, or at any rate it ceases to be, in its substance, the same thing as it was before: that is, an instrument on which payment falls to be made." The first reason is a good one only where the cheque is drawn by another in favour of P—a cheque on which he might have sued and therefore a thing in action belonging to him. Where, however, as in *Duru*, P himself drew the cheque in favour of D or another (being induced so to do by deception) the thing in action never belonged to anyone except the person in whose favour it was drawn. A thing is a thing in action because there is a right to sue on it; and such a right never belonged to P.[2] P could not be deprived, permanently or otherwise, of something he never owned. The second reason, however, seems a good one; the cancelled cheque which is returned to the drawer might be thought of as different in substance from the thing with which he parted as the carcase from the living horse, or the axle from the pig iron to which it is reduced. The same arguments might be invoked where D appropriates a ticket belonging to British Rail. He intends to return a cancelled ticket, a substantially different thing. There is an alternative explanation for these cases. D intends the owner of the cheque or the ticket to have it back only by paying for it—in the case of the cheque, by the money or credit which P's bank gives to D; in the case of the ticket, by rendering services. The cases are indistinguishable in principle from *Hall*,[3] which appears to be confirmed by s. 6 (1). This explanation has the advantage that it extends to things which are intended to be returned (but only for value) in an unchanged form. For example, D takes milk tokens from a dairy intending to return them in exchange for milk; or, possibly, gaming chips from the proprietor of a gaming club, intending to return them in exchange for the right to play.[4] In all these cases there is probably a conditional intention permanently to deprive in the literal sense. The cheque, ticket, tokens and chips will probably not be returned at all if the taker realises that he is not going to receive the value they represent.

[1] [1973] 3 All E.R. 715; SHC 519; [1973] Crim. L.R. 701 (sub nom. *Asghar*) and commentary. See also *Wakeman* v. *Farrar*, [1974] Crim. L.R. 136.
[2] See further, below, para. [205].
[3] Above, para. [120].
[4] *Cf.* correspondence in [1976] Crim. L.R. 329.

[130] The cases considered above are examples of situations where the property has been entirely deprived of an essential characteristic, which has been described as its "virtue". But what if the virtue has not been entirely eliminated—but very nearly? D takes P's season ticket for Nottingham Forest's matches intending to return it to him in time for the last match of the season. Is this an "outright taking" so as to amount to theft of the ticket? If it is, is it theft if D intends to return the ticket in time for two matches?—or three, four, five or six—where should the line be drawn? The difficulty of drawing a line suggests that it should not be theft of the ticket unless D intends to keep it until it has lost *all* its virtue.[1] This means, of course, that if D takes P's car and keeps it for ten years, he will not be guilty of theft if, when, as he intended all along, he returns it to P, it is still a roadworthy vehicle, though the proportion of its original value which it retains is very small. If it can no longer be described as a car, but is scrap metal, then, if D intended to return it in this state, he has stolen it.

[1] The difficulty might satisfactorily be overcome in this particular case by holding that the right to see each match is a separate thing in action, of which P is permanently deprived once that match is over.

[131] The provision regarding lending appears to contemplate the situation where D is in possession or control of the property and he lends it to another. If D knows that the effect is that P will never get the property back again, he clearly has an intent permanently to deprive. Similarly if D knows that, when P

gets the property back again, the virtue will have gone out of it, this is equivalent to an outright disposal. The examples of the dry battery, season ticket, etc.[1] are applicable here, though they seem less likely to arise in the context of lending than of borrowing.

---

[1] Above, para. [128].

(e) Parting with property under a condition as to its return

[132] Section 6 (2) provides:

> "Without prejudice to the generality of subsection (1) above, where a person, having possession or control (lawfully or not) of property belonging to another, parts with the property under a condition as to its return which he may not be able to perform, this (if done for purposes of his own and without the other's authority) amounts to treating the property as his own to dispose of regardless of the other's rights."

This is clearly intended to deal with the kind of case which gave difficulty under the old law, where D, being in possession or control of P's goods, pawns them. If D had no intention of ever redeeming the goods, there was no problem—he was guilty of larceny and he would now clearly be guilty of theft, apart from s. 6 (2). But what if D does intend to redeem? The answer now is that if he knows that he may not be able to do so, he is guilty of theft. The subsection does not seem to permit of a distinction between the case where D knows that the chances of his being able to redeem are slight and the case where he believes the chances are high; in either case, the condition is one which he knows he *may not* be able to perform.

[133] The common law cases suggested that it was theft, notwithstanding an intention to redeem, if the pawner had no reasonable prospects of being able to do so.[1] It is submitted, however, that the question under the Theft Act is a purely subjective one: D must *intend* to dispose of the property regardless of the other's rights, and s. 6 (2) merely describes what he must intend. If then D is in fact *convinced*, however unreasonably, that he will be able to redeem the property, he does not come within the terms of s. 6 (2) because he does not intend *to dispose of it under a condition which he may not be able to perform*.

This is not necessarily conclusive, however, for subsection (2) is without prejudice to the generality of subsection (1); and it might reasonably be argued that even the pawner who is convinced of his power to redeem intends to treat the thing as his own to dispose of, regardless of the other's rights. This would be equally true if the pawner in fact had power to redeem; and, since pawning is not "lending", there is no need to prove that it was equivalent to an outright disposal. The difficulty about this interpretation is that it makes it very difficult to see why s. 6 (2) is there at all; if D's disposition of property under a condition which he *is* able to perform is theft under sub-section (1), why refer specifically to the case of a condition which he may not be able to perform? On the whole it would seem that the better approach is to hold that one who is certain of his ability to redeem does not have an intent permanently to deprive. Such a person, in some circumstances, may well be found by the jury not to be dishonest.[2] For example D, a tenant for a year of a furnished house, being temporarily short of money, pawns the landlord's clock, knowing that he will certainly be able and intending to redeem it before the year expires. A prosecution for theft of the clock should fail on the grounds both that he is not dishonest and that he has no intent permanently to deprive. The case might formerly have been dealt with as one of unlawful pawning.[3]

[1] *Phetheon* (1840), 9 C. & P. 552; *Medland* (1851), 5 Cox C.C. 292. *Trebilcock* (1858), Dears. & B. 453 and *Wynn* (1887), 16 Cox C.C. 231 are inconclusive.
[2] Above, para. [122].
[3] Pawnbrokers Act 1872, s. 33 is repealed from 1 August 1977, and not replaced by the Consumer Credit Act 1974.

(f) Abandonment of property

[134] Early nineteenth century cases on the taking of horses decided that there was no intent permanently to deprive, although D turned the horse loose some considerable distance from the place where he took it.[1] In the conditions of those times it might be supposed that D must have known that there was a substantial risk that P would not get his property back. This lenient attitude may be contrasted with that adopted in the pawning cases[2] and the right course would seem to be to attach no importance to these old decisions in the interpretation of the Theft Act.

The case where the property is abandoned is not within s. 6 (2) for D does not part with the property under a condition. He might, however, be regarded as having an intention to treat the thing as his own to dispose of regardless of the other's rights. If D borrows the thing and then leaves it where he knows the owner or someone on his behalf will certainly find it, he clearly does not have an intent permanently to deprive. But if he abandons the thing in circumstances such that he knows that it is quite uncertain whether the owner will ever get it back or not, then it would not be unreasonable to hold that he has an intention to treat the thing as his own to dispose of regardless of the other's rights. By analogy to the pawning case discussed above, it would seem that it should be immaterial whether D believes that the chances of P's getting the property back are large or small; it is sufficient that he intends to risk the loss of P's property. Suppose, for example, that D, being caught in the rain when leaving a restaurant in London, takes an umbrella to shelter him on his way to the station and abandons it in the train on his arrival at Nottingham. He should be guilty of theft.

[1] *Phillips and Strong* (1801), 2 East P.C. 662; *Crump* (1825), 1 C. & P. 658; *Addis* (1844), 1 Cox C.C. 78.
[2] Above, para. [133].

CHAPTER III

ROBBERY

[135] Robbery was a common law offence and was never defined in the Larceny Acts. A definition is now contained in s. 8 (1) of the Theft Act:

"A person is guilty of robbery if he steals, and immediately before or at the time of doing so, and in order to do so, he uses force on any person or puts or seeks to put any person in fear of being then and there subjected to force."

A. ROBBERY NOW A SINGLE OFFENCE

[136] Under the Larceny Act 1916, s. 23, there was a distinction between simple robbery, punishable with a maximum sentence of fourteen years, and robbery with violence and aggravated robbery, punishable with life imprisonment. No such distinction is drawn in the Theft Act. There is a single offence, punishable under s. 8 (2) with life imprisonment. This is in accordance with the general policy of the Act against creating separate offences depending on a single aggravating factor. The fact that force has actually been used as distinct from merely threatened may be a reason for imposing an increased punishment; but this fact alone could hardly justify a difference in the maximum between fourteen years and life. The threat may actually be the more serious factor—a threat to murder being, surely, a factor of greater aggravation than the use of a small amount of force.

[137] Assault with intent to rob formerly carried a maximum of only five years but now, under s. 8 (2) of the Theft Act, it is equated with actual robbery and carries life imprisonment. Assault with intent to rob will usually amount to an attempt to rob which would have been punishable with imprisonment at the discretion of the court at common law, so this is a less far-reaching change than might appear; and it is not unreasonable that the maximum should be the same, for the fact that the offence was never consummated may not detract in any way from its seriousness.

B. ROBBERY AN AGGRAVATED FORM OF THEFT

[138] Robbery under the Theft Act is essentially an aggravated form of stealing—the only one of many aggravated thefts to survive the repeal of the Larceny Acts. Proof of the commission of theft is essential to secure a conviction for robbery just as, at common law, the commission of larceny had to be proved. So it is not robbery if D has a claim of right to the property which he takes by force even if he knew he had no right to use force.[1] The extended definition of theft makes robbery a potentially wider crime than at common law, but in practice this is likely to be of small importance since the occasions on which force is used or threatened in committing acts which amounted to the old crimes of embezzlement and fraudulent conversion must be very few indeed.

---

[1] *Skivington,* [1968] 1 Q.B. 166; [1967] 1 All E.R. 483. *Robinson,* [1977] Crim. L.R. 173.

[139] Under the old law, it was necessary to prove that there had been a taking and carrying away—that the robber had got possession of the property stolen and moved it[1]. This is no longer necessary. It is sufficient to show that there has been an appropriation[2] of the property of another by force or threat of force. Taking hold of the property with the intention of appropriating it would be enough, whereas under the old law this might have constituted only an attempt. If D by threats of force induced P to lay down property with the intention of taking it up;[3] or if he snatched at a lady's earring but failed to detach it from her ear[4] the robbery, it is thought, would be complete. If D were pursuing P with intent to take his purse by force and P were to throw away the purse in order to escape,[5] this would not be theft until D did some act to appropriate the purse; but, even before he did so, he would be guilty of attempted robbery, for his pursuit of P would be a sufficiently proximate act; and he might also be guilty of an assault with intent to rob.

---

[1] *Cf.* Hale, 1 P.C. 533.
[2] See above, para. [**19**].
[3] *Cf. Farrell* (1787), 1 Leach 322 n. (robbery held not complete).
[4] *Cf. Lapier* (1784), 1 Leach 320 (held robbery, because the earring *was* detached).
[5] *Cf.* Hale, 1 P.C. 533.

C. USE OR THREAT OF FORCE

[140] The aggravating factor is the use, or the threat of the use, of force against the person. The term "force" has been preferred to "violence" which was used in the Larceny Act 1916 to designate an aggravated form of robbery. Though the difference, if any, between the words is an elusive one, it is probable that "force" is a slightly wider term. Thus it might be argued that simply to hold a person down is not violence but it certainly involves the use of force against the person. Force denotes any exercise of physical strength against another whereas violence seems to signify a dynamic exercise of strength as by striking a blow. In *Dawson*[1] it was held that, where D nudges P so as to cause him to lose his balance and enable D to steal, it is a question of fact for the jury whether the nudge amounts to "force". It is submitted that it would be better if the law gave an answer to the question—preferably in the affirmative.

---

[1] [1976] Crim. L.R. 692, C.A. and commentary.

[141] The force must be used or threatened *in order to steal*[1]. So, if D is attempting to commit rape on P and she offers him money to desist, which he takes, he is not guilty of robbery (even assuming that there is theft of the money) whether he in fact desists, or continues and completes the rape.[2] Similarly if D knocks P down out of revenge or spite and, having done so, decides to take, and does take, P's watch, he does not commit robbery. Such cases can, however, be adequately dealt with by charging rape or an offence under the Offences against the Person Act 1861, as well as theft.

[1] *Shendley*, [1970] Crim. L.R. 49, C.A. If the jury are satisfied that D stole, but not satisfied that he used force for the purpose of stealing, they should acquit of robbery and convict of theft.
[2] *Cf. Blackham* (1787), 2 East P.C. 711.

[142] It is now clear that only force or threats of force *to the person* will suffice. This narrows the common law offence in some respects. Threats to damage property[1] or to accuse P of an unnatural offence[2] which would found an indictment for robbery at common law are no longer enough. Such cases are, however, properly dealt with as blackmail under s. 21.

[1] *Simons* (1773), 2 East P.C. 731; *Astley* (1792), 2 East P.C. 729.
[2] *Donnally* (1779), 2 East P.C. 715; *Pollock and Divers*, [1967] 2 Q.B. 195; [1966] 2 All E.R. 97.

[143] Force directed purely to gaining possession of the property stolen is probably not sufficient unless D knows that the use of such force must affect P's person or cause P to fear that his person will be affected. Thus force used to detach P's watch chain from his waistcoat pocket is not, in itself, sufficient. The force is directed at the watch chain not at P's person.[1] The bag-snatcher is not necessarily or even usually guilty of robbery. If, however, P retains or recovers a grasp on his property and D overcomes this by the use of force then, it is submitted, the crime has become robbery. Likewise where, though P makes no resistance, D realises he must cause injury to P if he is to secure the property, and continues to do so; as where he drags on P's earring knowing that this will tear her pierced ear.[2]

[1] *Cf. Gnosil* (1824), 1 C. & P. 304.
[2] *Lapier* (1784), 1 Leach 320.

[144] Though the Act omits the word "wilfully", which was included in the draft bill proposed by the Criminal Law Revision Committee,[1] it is submitted that the force or threat must be used intentionally or at least recklessly; so that for D accidentally to cause P to fall and injure himself while picking his pocket or accidentally to cut him while slitting his pocket to get his money would not be robbery.

[1] Eighth *Report*, Cmnd. 2977, at p. 102.

D. IMMEDIATELY BEFORE OR AT THE TIME OF STEALING

[145] The force or threat must be used immediately before or at the time of stealing, and, in the case of a threat, it must be of force "then and there". Thus there can be no robbery or attempted robbery by letter or telephone, except in the most unlikely circumstances—for example, D telephones P that if P does not hand over certain property to E (D's innocent agent who has called at P's house) D will detonate an explosive charge under P's house. Where the threats seek to secure a transfer of property at some time in the future the proper charge would be blackmail, contrary to s. 21.

[146] To use force when a theft has been, but is no longer being, committed—for example, in order to escape—does not constitute robbery. This raises the question which arises in other contexts under the 1968 Act of how long a theft continues.[1] It is submitted that this question should receive a uniform answer in these different contexts. In the context of robbery, *Hale*[2] decides that, where D has assumed the ownership of goods in a house, the "time of" stealing is still continuing while he is removing the goods from the premises so that he is guilty of robbery if he uses force to get away with the goods. Whether he is guilty of robbery if he uses force when running down the garden path or driving off in the getaway car are, it seems, questions which the court will leave to the jury[3] which renders speculation fruitless; but there must come a point when no reasonable jury could find the thief to be still in the course of stealing and this must surely be not later than the time when the expedition is complete.

---

[1] Above, para. **[48]**, below, para. **[417]**.
[2] C.A., No. 5908/A/77, 28 Nov. 78.
[3] *Hale, supra.*

---

[147] Where an act of force has occurred after the theft is over, it would, of course, be proper to charge D both with theft and with the appropriate crime under the Offences against the Person Act 1861.[1] Where a mere threat has been used after the theft is over this will generally not constitute a separate offence unless it is a threat to kill[2] because a threat to do some lesser degree of harm is not an offence unless it amounts to an assault.[3]

---

[1] Offences against the Person Act 1861, s. 16.
[2] Offences against the Person Act 1861, s. 16, as amended by the Criminal Law Act 1977, Schedule 12. See Smith and Hogan 332.
[3] See Smith and Hogan 350.

E. FORCE OR THREAT AGAINST A THIRD PERSON

[148] It is clear that under the Theft Act, force used against *any person* will constitute robbery only if it is used in order to commit theft. Similarly a threat to use force against any person aimed at putting that person in fear of being then and there subjected to force is enough. So if D, being about to commit theft from P, is interrupted by a passer-by, Q, and repels Q's attempt to interfere, either by actual force or the threat to use force, he is guilty of robbery if he completes the theft. It is immaterial that no force or threat is used against P from whom the theft is committed. It would seem that in such a case the indictment would properly allege robbery from P, for clearly there was no robbery from Q.

[149] The case put above may be an extension of the common law of robbery; but there is another respect in which the Act may have narrowed the law. Suppose that D threatens P that, if P will not hand over certain property to D, D will use force on Q. This was probably robbery at common law.[1] It is difficult if not impossible, however, to bring such a case within the words of the Act since D does not seek to put any person in fear of being then and there subjected to force in order to commit theft. He does not put P in such fear because the threat is to use force on Q. He does not put Q in fear because the threat is not addressed to him. Such cases should again be treated as blackmail contrary to s. 21.

---

¹ *Reane* (1794), 2 East P.C. 734 at 735–736, *per* Eyre, C.B., *obiter.*

---

[150] It might be different in the example put in the previous paragraph if the threat were addressed to Q as well as to P or overheard by Q. If it were D's object to cause Q to intercede with P to hand over the property, so as to save himself from D's threatened force, this would be robbery.

[151] At common law, the theft had to be from the person or in the presence of the victim. In *Smith* v. *Desmond and Hall*¹ the House of Lords, reversing the Court of Criminal Appeal,² put a wide interpretation upon this rule, holding that it was satisfied if the force or threat of force was used on a person who had the property to be stolen in his immediate personal care and protection. D was therefore guilty of robbery when he overpowered a nightwatchman and a maintenance engineer in a bakery and then broke into a cash office some distance away and stole from a safe. Though the victims did not have the key to the office or the safe they were in the building to guard its contents which were, therefore, in their immediate personal care and protection.

---

¹ [1965] A.C. 960; [1965] 1 All E.R. 976.
² [1964] 3 All E.R. 587.

---

[152] Such a case is obviously within the terms of the Theft Act. Indeed, it follows from what has been said above that there is no longer any necessity to prove that the property was in the care and protection of the victim of the force or threat. It is enough that the force or threat was directed against any person so that, if in *Smith* v. *Desmond and Hall* the persons overpowered had been mere passers-by who happened to have interfered with D's plans, this would be enough under the Theft Act, though not at common law.

CHAPTER IV

CRIMINAL DECEPTION

[153] The Theft Acts create a number of offences of dishonestly getting something by deception. They are:

1. Obtaining property: 1968, s. 15.
2. Obtaining a pecuniary advantage: 1968, s. 16.
3. Procuring the execution of a valuable security: 1968, s. 20 (2).
4. Obtaining services: 1978, s. 1.
5. Securing the remission of a liability: 1978, s. 2 (1) (a).
6. Inducing a creditor to wait for or to forgo payment: 1978, s. 2 (1) (b).
7. Obtaining an exemption from or abatement of liability: 1978, s. 2 (1) (c).

Though the Acts use four verbs, "obtain", "procure", "secure" and "induce", the offences all contain a common element in that D must achieve the proscribed result by deception. It is convenient to consider this and the other elements common to all these offences together. The word "obtain" is used, for this purpose, to include the other three verbs. The common elements are:
1. The meaning of "obtaining *by* deception";
2. The meaning of *"any deception"*;
3. The meaning of "dishonestly".

A. THE COMMON ELEMENTS IN OBTAINING OFFENCES

(a) *Obtaining* by *deception*

[154] The obtaining must be *by* deception. It must be proved[1] that the false statement actually deceived P and caused him to do whatever is the act appropriate to the offence charged. So if P knows that the statement is false,[2] or if, though he does not know the statement to be false, he would have acted in the same way even if he had known it;[3] or if he does not rely on the false statement but arrives at the same erroneous conclusion from his own observation or some other source,[4] or, of course, if he does not read or hear the false statement, D is not guilty of obtaining. In each of these cases, however, D may be convicted of an *attempt* to obtain by deception.[5] The onus is on the prosecution to prove that the representation operated on P's mind. The normal way of proving this must be by calling P.[6] Like any other allegation, however, this may be proved by inference from other facts without direct evidence.[7]

---

[1] See *Agbim*, [1979] Crim. L.R. 171, and commentary.
[2] *Ady* (1835), 7 C. & P. 140; *Mills* (1857), Dears. & B. 205; *Hensler* (1870), 11 Cox C.C. 570; *Light* (1915), 11 Cr. App. Rep. 111.
[3] *Edwards*, [1978] Crim. L.R. 49. See commentary at p. 50.

77

4 *Roebuck* (1856), Dears. & B. 24. *Cf.* the similar principle which applies to misrepresentation in relation to the law of contract: *Attwood* v. *Small* (1838), 6 Cl. & Fin. 232; *Smith* v. *Chadwick* (1884), 9 App. Cas. 187s.
5 *Hensler* (1870), 11 Cox C.C. 570.
6 *Laverty*, [1970] 3 All E.R. 432; *Tirado* (1974), 59 Cr. App. Rep. 80 at 87.
7 *Tirado* (above) at 87.

[155] A case that is difficult to reconcile with these principles is *Sullivan*.[1] D represented that he was the "actual maker" of dartboards. The representation was untrue and it was held that he was guilty of obtaining by false pretences from customers who sent him the price of a board although they said in evidence that they parted with their money "because I wanted a dartboard." No one said that he paid because he thought D was the "actual maker." The court apparently thought that there could be no other conceivable reason for their doing so. This seems doubtful. As Sullivan was unknown to them, it probably mattered not at all whether he was the actual maker, so long as he supplied a dartboard.

In *Laverty*[2], a case under s. 15, D changed the registration number-plates and chassis number-plate of a car and sold it to P. It was held that this constituted a representation by conduct that the car was the original car to which these numbers had been assigned; but D's conviction for obtaining the price of the car by deception from P was quashed on the ground that it was not proved that the deception operated on P's mind. There was no direct evidence to that effect—P said he bought the car because he thought D was the owner—and it was not a necessary inference[3].

1 (1945), 30 Cr. App. Rep. 132.
2 [1970] 3 All E.R. 432.
3 If the only flaw in the prosecution's case was that the representation did not influence P, it would have been in order for the court to substitute a conviction for an attempt. They did not do so, possibly because there was also insufficient evidence that D intended by this representation to deceive P into buying the car. The purpose of changing the plates may well have been, not to deceive the buyer, but to deceive the police, the true owner and anyone else who might identify the vehicle. It would seem that the prosecution would have been on stronger ground had they alleged that D had made a representation by conduct that he had a right to sell the car.

[156] In *Etim* v. *Hatfield*[1] where D produced to a post office clerk a false declaration that he was entitled to supplementary benefit and was granted £10.60, but no post office employee gave evidence, it was held that D was rightly convicted because there was no conceivable reason for the payment other than the false statement. In *Laverty*, the court stated that the principle in *Sullivan* should not be extended; but *Sullivan* was followed and *Laverty* distinguished in *Etim* v. *Hatfield*. *Etim's* case is defensible as one where it was a *necessary* inference that P acted on the representation; but such a conclusion is hard to justify in the case of *Sullivan*. Equally difficult to reconcile with principle and more significant is *D.P.P.* v. *Ray*.[2] D, having consumed a meal in a restaurant, dishonestly decided to leave without paying, waited until the waiter went out of the room and then ran off. The House of Lords, Lords Reid and Hodson dissenting, held that the waiter was induced to leave the room by D's implied and continuing representation that he was an honest customer intending to pay his bill. It does not appear that the waiter was ever called in evidence; and it would seem, on the facts, very far indeed from being a necessary inference that the waiter acted on the alleged representation. A doubtful application of a fundamental principle, even by the House of Lords, does not, however, impair the validity of the principle itself; and it remains necessary in every case to prove beyond reasonable doubt that P was deceived by, and acted upon, the representation.

---

[1] [1975] Crim. L.R. 234.
[2] [1974] A.C. 370; [1973] 3 All E.R. 131; [1974] Crim. L.R. 181 (see commentary); SHC 527. The prosecution was brought under 1968, s. 16 (2) (a) which has now been repealed but the case remains an authority on this point.

---

[157] (i) *Obtaining and cheque cards.*—The principle has created problems where goods or a pecuniary advantage are obtained by one who dishonestly uses a cheque and a cheque card. When a cheque is tendered in payment there is an implied representation that the facts are such that, as far as can reasonably be foreseen, the cheque will be honoured on presentation.[1] When D tenders a cheque card, this representation will usually be true although D has no money in the account and no authority to overdraw. The card contains an undertaking by the bank that the cheque will be honoured, provided only that the conditions on the card are fulfilled. The conditions may be fulfilled even though D's account is overdrawn or has been closed. The undertaking becomes a contract with the recipient of the cheque, Q, that it will be met. Q will usually accept the cheque and supply the goods, the pecuniary advantage or the service because the cheque is backed by a cheque card and the conditions on the card are fulfilled—and for no other reason. He will neither know nor care whether the drawer has the right to draw on his bank for the amount or whether he is entitled to use the card. Q will get his money whether the drawer is acting in accordance with his contract with the bank or not—and that is all he will be concerned with. This is neither immoral nor unreasonable. The whole object of the cheque card is to dispense the tradesman from concerning himself with the relationship between the drawer and his bank. The tradesman is perfectly entitled to take advantage of the facility which the bankers offer him.

---

[1] Below, para. **[166]**.

---

[158] In *Charles*[1] D obtained gaming chips at a gaming club by the use of cheques and a cheque card, knowing that his account was overdrawn and that he had no authority to overdraw. He was convicted of obtaining a pecuniary advantage by deception, namely increased borrowing by way of overdraft, by the deception that he was entitled and authorised to use the card. The manager, Q, said "If there is a cheque card we make no inquiries as to [D's] credit-worthiness, or as to the state of his account with the bank. All this is irrelevant unless the club has knowledge that he has no funds, or the club has knowledge that he has no authority to overdraw."[2] Notwithstanding this forthright statement (and others) the House of Lords held that there was evidence that Q had been induced to give the gaming chips by an implied representation that he was entitled and authorised to use the cheque card.[3]

In the light of the evidence quoted, this finding seems, with respect, to be almost perverse; but it means that *Charles* is a very special case with limited effect. The vast majority of cheques backed by cheque cards are undoubtedly accepted by shop assistants whose *only* concern is whether the conditions on the card are fulfilled.[4] What then is the position in the ordinary case? Presumably, like the manager in *Charles*, Q would not accept the cheque if he actually *knew* that D had no authority to use the card and was doing so in fraud of the bank—if he did accept it he might be held to have conspired to defraud the bank. The question, in general terms, is then: "Is Q's act obtained by deception where Q does not care whether the statement in question is true, or false, but he would not have acted had he known the statement to be false?" An affirmative answer to this question would require an extension of the notion of deception beyond the actual decision in *Charles* or any other case.

---

[1] *Metropolitan Police Commissioner* v. *Charles*, [1977] A.C. 177; [1976] 3 All E.R. 112.
[2] See [1976] 1 All E.R. at pp. 663–664.
[3] The holding that there is an implied representation of authority to use the card is suspect. If the relationship between D and his bank is irrelevant, as it surely is, why should D be taken to be saying anything about his authority? If Q actually asks him, D can answer, "It is none of your business—you are only concerned with the conditions on the card." Representations, like terms in contracts, should only be implied under the compulsion of necessity.
[4] [1977] Crim. L.R. 620–621.

---

[159] (ii) *Obtaining and machines.*—"To deceive is ... to induce a man to believe that a thing is true which is false, and which the person practising the deceit knows or believes to be false".[1] Deceit can be practised only on a human mind.[2] Where D obtains property or a pecuniary advantage as the result of some dishonest practice on a machine, without the intervention of a human mind, he cannot be guilty of an obtaining offence. It was held to be larceny (and, implicitly, not obtaining) to get cigarettes from a machine by using a brass disc instead of a coin.[3] The owner of the machine intends to pass ownership and possession of the goods to anyone who inserts the proper coin.[4] There is no difference, so far as the law of theft is concerned, between operating the machine by the use of a foreign coin and causing it to disgorge its contents by the use of a screwdriver. If a tradesman makes a dishonest claim on the appropriate form for the repayment of VAT input tax and the claim, without being read by anyone, is fed into a computer which automatically produces a cheque for the sum claimed, this may be regarded as indistinguishable from obtaining the cigarettes by the foreign coin. The clerks who feed the document into the machine and put the cheque in the envelope are innocent agents—like an eight-year old child, told to put the foreign coin in the machine and bring home the cigarettes.

There is a similar problem where the machine does not produce goods but provides a service.[5] If the service is dishonestly obtained without deceiving a human being, there can be no obtaining offence.[6] If D, by using a foreign coin, operates the washing machine in P's launderette, he is not guilty of obtaining the service by deception but may be convicted of the offence of abstracting electricity and possibly of making off without payment contrary to 1978, s. 3 (1).[7]

---

[1] *Re London and Globe Finance Corporation*, [1903] 1 Ch. 728 at 732; [1900–3] All E.R. Rep. 891 at 893.
[2] See (1972) Law Soc. Gaz. 576 and Law Commission Working Paper No. 56, p. 51.
[3] *Hands* (1887), 16 Cox C.C. 188. Cf. *Cooper and Miles*, [1979] Crim. L.R. 42 (Judge Woods).

⁴ *Cf.* the example of the newsvendor, above, para. **[32]**.
⁵ Below, para. **[219]**.
⁶ Below, para. **[245]**.
⁷ Below, para. **[242]**.

[160] (iii) *Obtaining too remote from deception.*—The same problems of remoteness arise as under the old law of false pretences. If D induces P to accept bets on credit by falsely representing that he is acting on behalf of a number of other persons, money paid by P to D on D's bet proving successful is not obtained by deception; the effective cause of D's receiving the money is not the deception, but the fact of having backed a winning horse.¹ It is an offence under s. 16 (2)(e) of the 1968 Act.² An offence is committed under s. 15 (1) where D, an athlete, by deception procures a longer start in a race than he is entitled to and, consequently, wins the prize. Here the start is an effective cause of his winning the race and so the prize.³ If, however, the deception merely gains D admission to the race, without any start or other advantage, it may well be that there is no offence under this section.⁴

Another case where D's deception is too remote is that where he obtains an appointment by deception and then receives wages or a salary; the money is held to be paid in respect of services rendered and not because of the misrepresentation.⁵ This case, however, is specifically dealt with by s. 16⁶. D might possibly be convicted under s. 15 where he procures a higher salary because of some special qualification which he falsely pretends he has. Suppose that a higher salary scale is payable to a person with a second class honours degree. D, who got a third, says he got a second and is paid accordingly. Here it is arguable that the deception is the direct and effective cause of his obtaining the additional money, and that an offence against s. 15 (1) is, therefore, committed.⁷

¹ *Clucas*, [1949] 2 K.B. 226; [1949] 2 All E.R. 40. As there were two accused in that case, they were convicted of a conspiracy to defraud. If there were only one, it would be necessary to rely on s. 16.
² Below, para. **[210]** and **[215]**.
³ *Button*, [1900] 2 Q.B. 597; *Dickenson*, Russell, 1186; *contra, Larner* (1880), 14 Cox C.C. 497. But suppose D's deception procures him an additional two yards start and he wins by five yards? It may be said that the deception was not an effective cause because he would have won anyway. It might be answered that the psychological effect of the long start was a contributory factor; but this could hardly be proved beyond reasonable doubt.
⁴ A start was obtained in each of the cases cited in footnote 3 above.
⁵ *Lewis* (1922), Somerset Assizes, *per* Rowlatt, J.; Russell, at 1186n. In such a case, the nature of the scheme is such that the deception can never be sufficiently proximate. Contrast the cases where D is interrupted or desists before a scheme which would constitute the complete crime if carried out, but has not been advanced beyond the steps of preparation and become an attempt: *Robinson*, [1915] 2 K.B. 342; *Comer v. Bloomfield* (1970), 55 Cr. App. Rep. 305.
⁶ Below, paras. **[210]** and **[215]**.
⁷ *Cf. Levene* v. *Pearcey*, [1976] Crim. L.R. 63 and commentary thereon (taxi-driver obtaining excessive fare by telling passenger normal route blocked).

(b) Any deception

[161] By s. 15 (4):

"For purposes of this section 'deception' means any deception (whether deliberate or reckless) by words or conduct as to fact or as to law, including a deception as to the present intentions of the person using the deception or any other person."

The definition in 1968, s. 15 (4) applies to 1968, ss. 15, 16 and 22 (2) and to 1978, ss. 1 and 2.

[162] (i) *Proof of falsity.*—It must be proved that D made a false statement.[1] If his statement was true he cannot be guilty of the offence or of an attempt to commit it, even though he believed it to be false and was completely dishonest.[2] Where this rule requires the prosecution to prove a negative and the affirmative fact which, if it exists, will establish the truth of the statement, is within the knowledge of the accused, there may be an onus on him, not to *prove* anything, but at least to introduce some evidence of the affirmative fact. In *Mandry and Wooster*[3] street traders selling scent for 25p. said "You can go down the road and buy it for 2 guineas in the big stores". The police checked on certain stores but it was admitted in cross-examination that they had not been to Selfridges. It was held that it was not improper for the judge to point out that it was impossible for the police to go to every shop in London and that "if the defence knew of their own knowledge of anywhere it could be bought at that price ... they were perfectly entitled to call evidence." Since no evidence was called to show that the perfume was on sale at Selfridges or anywhere else, the convictions were upheld.

---

[1] Cf. *Banaster*, [1970] R.T.R. 113.
[2] *Deller* (1952), 36 Cr. App. Rep. 184, C.C.A. *Cf. Edwards*, [1978] Crim. L.R. 49 and commentary thereon. *Haughton* v. *Smith*, [1975] A.C. 476; above, para. **[52]**, [1975] 3 All E.R. 1109.
[3] [1973] 3 All E.R. 996.

---

[163] (ii) *Deliberate or reckless.*—A deception is deliberate if D knows his statement is false and will or may be accepted as true by P. It is reckless if he is aware that it may be true or false and will or may be accepted as true by P. Carelessness or negligence is not enough.[1] As in the civil law of deceit, it is sufficient that D makes a statement which he knows to be false or does not believe to be true.[2] The fact that a reasonable man in the circumstances would have known that the statement was, or might be, false, is evidence that D knew it was or might be false; but it is not conclusive and must be taken into account with any other relevant evidence, including D's own statement, that he believed it to be true. If the jury think that D, however unreasonably, may have believed his statement to be true, then they must acquit.

If then D says to P, "This watch chain is solid gold", not knowing whether it is solid gold or not and, either not caring a jot whether the statement is true or false or hoping that the statement will turn out to be true, he is guilty of an offence under s. 15 (1) if the statement turns out to be untrue and, in consequence, P is induced to pay money for the chain.

---

[1] *Staines* (1974), 60 Cr. App. Rep. 160, C.A.
[2] *Derry* v. *Peek* (1889), 14 App. Cas. 337.

---

[164] (iii) *By words or conduct.*—These words make it clear that all the cases within the old law of false pretences are covered. Though reported examples of false pretences by conduct were far from numerous, it was universally accepted that such a pretence was enough. The stock example is the case of *Barnard*[1] where D went into an Oxford shop wearing a fellow-commoner's cap and gown. He induced the shop-keeper to sell him goods on credit by an express representation that he was a fellow-commoner; but Bolland, B. said, *obiter*, that he would still have been guilty even if he had said nothing. In an Australian case, the wearing of a badge was held to be a false pretence when it indicated that the wearer was entitled to take bets on a racecourse.[2]

---

[1] (1837), 7 C. & P. 784.
[2] *Robinson* (1884), 10 V.L.R. (L) 131.

---

[165] Positive steps taken by a seller to conceal from a buyer defects in the goods may amount to fraud in the civil law and would seem to be capable of being deception under the Theft Acts. If P inspected the goods and, because of the concealment, failed to detect the fault, the offence would be complete. If P omitted to inspect the goods and so was not deceived,[1] D would be guilty of an attempt. The vendor of a house who papers over the cracks would seem to be in exactly the same position and a strict application of the law might interfere with some well-established practices which perhaps ought to be discouraged. It is thought that these cases were, in any event, within the old law relating to false pretences. To display a picture with a collection belonging to a particular seller may amount to fraud and seems to be capable of being a deception, if it is known that the price will be enhanced by the fact that the picture appears to belong to that collection.[2]

It has been held to be fraud in the civil law for the seller of a ship to remove her from the ways where she lay dry and where it might be seen that the bottom was eaten and her keel broken, and to keep her afloat so that these defects were concealed by the water.[3] This would seem to amount to deception. Suppose, however, that the ship was already in the water before any sale was in prospect. Would it be an offence for the seller to leave her there when viewed by the buyer and say nothing about the defects? It would seem not; there are no "words or conduct" here and presumably the seller would not even be civilly liable in such a case.

---

[1] *Cf. Horsfall v. Thomas* (1862), 1 H. & C. 90. D, being employed by P to make a steel gun, drove a metal plug into the breach end of the chamber to conceal the fact that the metal was all soft and spongy. It was held that the concealment did not invalidate the contract, since it did not affect the mind of the buyer.
[2] *Cf. Hill v. Gray* (1816), 1 Stark. 434, a doubtful decision, since it is not clear that the seller induced the buyer's mistake.
[3] *Schneider v. Heath* (1813), 3 Camp. 506, approved by the Court of Appeal in *Ward v. Hobbs* (1877), 3 Q.B.D. 150 at 162.

---

[166] (iv) *Deception by implied statement.*—The most difficult question is as to how far statements should be held to be implied in words or conduct. It is established that one who enters a restaurant and orders a meal impliedly represents that he intends to pay for the meal before leaving[1] and probably also represents, in the absence of an agreement for credit, that he has the money to pay.[2] A person who registers as a guest in a hotel represents that he intends to pay the bill at the end of his stay.[3] A wine waiter employed at a hotel impliedly represents that the wine he offers is his employer's, not his own.[4] A motor trader who states that the mileage shown on the odometer of a second-hand car "may not be correct" represents that he does not know it to be incorrect.[5] A bookmaker, it is submitted, represents, when he takes a bet, that he intends to pay if the horse backed wins.[6] One who takes a taxi represents that he intends to pay, and has the means of paying, at the end of the ride.[7] These are all representations of present fact. In *Charles*[8] Viscount Dilhorne (with whose speech three judges agreed) said that, "until the enactment of the Theft Act 1968", it was necessary to prove a false pretence of an existing fact, as if the Act changed that rule. It did not. All that the Act did[9] was to declare that one particular type of existing fact which was not a sufficient false pretence before the Act, namely the "present intentions" of the accused or any other person, should be treated like other representations of fact (or law).

From *Hazelton* (1874)[10] until *Metropolitan Police Commissioner* v. *Charles* (1976)[11] it was thought to be settled law that a person tendering a cheque impliedly makes three representations: (i) that he has an account on which the cheque is drawn; (ii) that he has authority to draw on the bank for that amount; and (iii) that the cheque as drawn is a valid order for that amount. In *Charles* the House of Lords cast doubt on the second of these representations[12] saying that in substance there is only one representation—that the facts are such that, as far as can reasonably be foreseen, the cheque will be honoured on presentment. If D in fact has no account, the prosecutor can hardly go wrong by relying on representation (i) above, but it would be wise to avoid (ii). Viscount Dilhorne thought[13] that the only representation to be implied on drawing a cheque is that it will be honoured on presentment. This is the language of promises about the future but such a promise is incapable of amounting to a deception.[14] The promise may imply a belief on D's part and, though the Act speaks only of "present intentions", it is submitted that belief is so inseparably linked with intention that the same principle must apply. Lords Diplock[15] and Edmund-Davies[16] made it clear that they regarded implied representations of fact as necessary. If D knows the cheque will not be met, or may not be met, he may fairly be taken to have made a deliberate or reckless representation of his present belief.

---

[1] *D.P.P.* v. *Ray*, [1974] A.C. 370 at 379, 382 385, 388, 391; SHC 527.
[2] *Ibid.*, at 379, 382.
[3] *Harris* (1975), 62 Cr. App. Rep. 28.
[4] *Doukas*, [1978] 1 All E.R. 1061; [1978] Crim. L.R. 177. The decision is to be preferred to *Rashid*, [1977] 2 All E.R. 237.
[5] *King*, [1979] Crim. L.R. 122.
[6] Cf. *Buckmaster* (1887), 2 Q.B.D. 182.
[7] Cf. *Waterfall*, [1970] 1 Q.B. 148; [1969] 3 All E.R. 1048.
[8] [1976] 3 All E.R. 112 at 116; above para. [157].
[9] Below, para. [177].
[10] L.R. 2 C.C.R. 134 at the source of the proposition in Kenny, *Outlines*, 359, adopted in *Page*, [1971] 2 Q.B. 330 at 333.
[11] [1977] A.C. 177; [1976] 3 All E.R. 112.
[12] But see [1977] Crim. L.R. at 616.
[13] [1976] 3 All E.R. at 117.
[14] *Beckett* v. *Cohen*, [1973] 1 All E.R. 120, D.C.; *British Airways Board* v. *Taylor*, [1976] 1 All E.R. 65 H.L.
[15] [1976] 3 All E.R. at 113.
[16] *Ibid.* at 121, quoting Pollock, B. in *Hazelton*: " ... the real representation made is that the cheque will be paid. It may be said that that is a representation as to a future event. But that is not

really so. It means that the existing state of facts is such that in ordinary course the cheque will be met".

---

[167] In *Greenstein*[1] DD made a practice of applying for very large quantities of shares sending a cheque for an amount far in excess of the money in their bank accounts. They had no authority to overdraw but they expected to be allotted a relatively small number of shares and to receive a "return cheque" for the difference between the prices of the shares applied for and the shares allotted. By paying the return cheques into their accounts they enabled the cheques drawn by them to be honoured, on most occasions on first presentation, on other occasions after, apparently, a very short interval, on second presentation. It was alleged that DD had obtained shares by *"Hazelton"* representations (the case being decided before *Charles*) that they had authority to draw the cheques and that they were good and valid orders. In some cases, where DD had given an undertaking required by the issuing houses that "the cheque sent herewith will be paid on first presentation", there was an allegation of a further representation to that effect. Since all the cheques were met on first or subsequent presentation, no one lost a penny but some applicants who might have got shares if DD had made more modest applications[3] did not get them because, as DD anticipated, there were not enough to go round.

It was held that DD had no authority, either from banking practice or the particular facts proved, to draw the inflated cheques; and that they were not valid orders because they could be met only by paying in the return cheques. There was, therefore, a deception. The deception was effective because the issuing houses would not have entertained the application had they known that their own return cheques were going to be used to fund it. The jury's verdict implied that DD were reckless whether their cheques would be honoured on first presentation; and, on the facts, the jury "were entitled if not bound to infer that the deception was deliberately dishonest".

It would seem then that *Greenstein* was correctly decided in the light of *Charles*. DD did not have the belief which they impliedly represented they had. As in Viscount Dilhorne's speech in *Charles*, there is a disturbing and, it is submitted, unwarranted suggestion that a representation as to something other than present fact will do.

The court distinguished the dicta of Buckley, J. in *Re London and Globe Finance Corporation*[2] on the ground that Buckley, J. "did not have in mind a case where the thing in which a person is induced to believe is a future state of affairs which comes about by a lucky chance, or as here by the act of the very person who was induced by the deception to do it." With respect, the inducing of a belief "in a future state of things" is incapable of being a deception. The deception must be as to present facts, including D's present intention or belief; and, so long as it is understood that "believe" does not require complete conviction[3] and that P sufficiently believes if he relies on the truth of the representation though he is not completely convinced it is true,[4] there should be no qualification to Buckley, J.'s proposition that there can be no deception unless a person is induced to believe that a thing is true which is false in fact.

---

[1] [1976] 1 All E.R. 1.
[2] [1903] 1 Ch. 728 at 732; [1900–3] All E.R. Rep. 891 at 893.

[3] *Cf.* Griew in Glazebrook, *Essays* 69 et seq.
[4] See [1977] Crim. L.R. at 621.

[168] It is certainly not enough to establish an implied deception that there is an implied term for the purposes of the law of contract and that the party bound by the term knows that it is unfulfilled. Suppose, for example, that the seller of goods, in circumstances in which the law implies an undertaking on his part that the goods are of merchantable quality, knows that this is not the case, but says nothing. It will be necessary to prove that the seller knew that he was being taken by the buyer to be making a particular assertion and that he knew the assertion to be false or that he did not believe it to be true. An obvious example of a sufficient deception is where the seller induces a sale of an inferior article by producing a sample of superior quality.[1] Though he does not say so in terms, the seller inevitably knows[2] that the buyer understands him to assert that the bulk corresponds with the sample in quality.

An apparently innocent act may constitute deception when considered in the light of a previous course of conduct. D laid before P a number of bars of metal of little value, saying "Eight ounces at four shillings an ounce". The fact that he had previously pledged ingots of silver, which were similar in appearance to the bars now produced, established fraud.[3]

[1] *Goss* (1860), Bell C.C. 208.
[2] The question must still be left to the jury—"Did *this* seller know?" Criminal Justice Act 1967, s. 8.
[3] *Stevens* (1884), 1 Cox C.C. 83.

[169] A civil case which has been criticised as going too far in discerning an implied false pretence is *Berg* v. *Sadler and Moore*.[1] D, a tobacconist, was unable to obtain supplies because he had been put upon the stop-list by the Tobacco Trade Association. He procured E to buy cigarettes, ostensibly on E's own behalf, from P. E and P were members of the Association and P would not have sold the cigarettes had he known they were for D. The Court of Appeal decided that, because D was guilty of an attempt to obtain by false pretences, he could not recover the money he had paid to P, although P, having discovered the truth, never delivered the cigarettes. The false pretence found to have been practised by E would seem to be an implied representation that the tobacco was not intended for any person to whom P would have been unwilling to sell it. This seems to go farther than is justifiable in the implication of a false representation.

> "If X buys from Y cigarettes with the intention of selling or giving them to a small boy to whom Y would not be willing to sell them; or if he buys a bottle of whisky with the intention, unknown to the seller, of giving it or selling it to a drunken man to whom the publican would not be willing to sell it, or indeed, if he buys weed-killer with the concealed intention of killing not weeds but his wife; can it be said that he is guilty of obtaining the goods by false pretences? Whatever the morality of the matter may be, it is submitted that this would be a new and dangerous interpretation of the contract of sale of goods."[2]

Presumably it never crossed P's mind to inquire whether D was buying the cigarettes for another. Could he then be said to be deceived? It may never cross the mind of the waiter in the restaurant that the customer does not intend to pay but, if he does not so intend, the food is clearly obtained by deception. It may never cross the mind of the customer that the wine offered by the waiter belongs not to the restaurant but to the waiter himself; but if the customer would not have bought the waiter's own wine, the price is obtained from him by deception.[3] To be implied, however, a representation must be one which very clearly "goes without saying", and the representation in *Berg* v. *Sadler and Moore* hardly passes this test.

There is one further objection to the decision, which is that the facts do not seem to be distinguishable from civil cases in which the person in the position of D has been held able to enforce the contract of sale made by E on the ground that D was an undisclosed principal.[4] It would be intolerable that the civil division of the Court of Appeal should find itself holding a transaction to be enforceable by a plaintiff, while the criminal division was sending him to prison for entering into it.

---

[1] [1937] 2 K.B. 158. Perhaps justified, however, in the light of *Metropolitan Police Commissioner* v. *Charles*, above, para. **[151]**.
[2] C. K. Allen, "Fraud, Quasi-Contract and False Pretences", 54 L.Q.R. 200 at 210–211. See also [1972B] C.L.J. at pp. 218–224.
[3] *Doukas*, [1978] 1 All E.R. 1061.
[4] *Dyster* v. *Randall & Sons*, [1926] Ch. 932 (*per* Lawrence, J.); *Nash* v. *Dix* (1898), 78 L.T. 445 (*per* North, J.). See C. K. Allen, above, footnote 19. This objection does not apply to *Doukas*. The wine waiter could not recover the price of the wine because there was no intention to contract with him.

---

[170] (v) *Passive acquiescence in self-deception.*—There are other cases in which D may be thought to be to some extent dishonest, in which it is thought that the court will probably be unwilling—and, it is submitted, rightly so—to hold that D has deceived P. These are cases in which there is no implied representation in the civil law. For example.

> (a) D contracts to sell a specific parcel or part of a specific parcel of oats to P. P wants old oats. D knows this and he also knows that the oats are in fact new oats.[1]

Provided that D has done and said nothing to lead P to suppose that the oats are old, it is submitted that he is guilty of no offence. A contrary holding would be quite incongruous since, under the civil law, there is a valid contract, enforceable by D against P.[2] It would be absurd if D were to be held guilty of obtaining by the crime of deception money which he could recover by action in a civil court. Indeed to hold that an offence was committed in these circumstances might have the effect of altering the civil law; for the civil court could hardly be seen to lend its aid to enable D to recover the fruits of his crime. In the absence of any expression of Parliament's intention to alter the civil law, it would be wrong to attribute such an effect to the Theft Act.

Supposing that, after an undoubted obtaining by deception by D from P, P, having discovered the deception, chooses to affirm the contract. In such a case D *may* sue upon the transaction which amounts in law to a crime. For instance, D obtains the deposit on a sale of goods to P, by deception. P affirms the contract. D may recover the balance of the price. This might have occurred under the old law and may be distinguished on the ground that D's right arises from P's conduct after the crime has been committed. D remains guilty of obtaining by deception; P's action cannot absolve him from criminal responsibility.

---

[1] *Smith* v. *Hughes* (1871), L.R. 6 Q.B. 597.
[2] This assumes *Smith* v. *Hughes* still represents the law. *Cf.*, however, *Solle* v. *Butcher*, [1950] 1 K.B. 671; [1949] 2 All E.R. 1107; *Grist* v. *Bailey*, [1967] Ch. 532; [1966] 2 All E.R. 876.

---

[171] The situation might conceivably be otherwise in only slightly different circumstances:

> (*b*) P believes, not merely that the oats are old, but that D is *contracting to sell the oats as old oats.* D knows that P so believes but has done and said nothing to induce such a belief.

Here the position in the civil law is different. Though the matter is not entirely free from doubt, the better view is probably that there is a contract for the sale of oats, guaranteed by D to be old oats.[1] Here D probably has no right to recover the price for P may rescind the contract for breach of condition.[2] It would be no more incongrous to hold this to be an obtaining by deception than so to hold in many other cases where contracts for the sale of property have been induced by fraud. The two questions are: (i) is D dishonest? and (ii) has there been any deception? It is certainly arguable that the first question should be answered in the affirmative. Even in 1871 the court evidently thought that the seller's conduct was not that of a "man of scrupulous morality or nice honour" and that in such circumstances "a man of tender conscience or high honour would be unwilling to take advantage of the ignorance of the seller".[3] Today the view might be taken that these standards should be required of everyone and not merely exceptional people. The second question poses greater difficulties for the prosecution. The fact is that this is an instance of "passive acquiescence of the seller in the self-deception of the buyer".[4] However, it is just arguable that D's remaining silent is conduct which deceives P into continuing to think that D acquiesces in his view of the contract. In either of the "oats" examples there would be a sufficient deception if the seller had done anything at all to confirm the buyer's belief. Even silence, if intended to mislead and actually misleading, would have been enough.

> "If, indeed, the buyer, instead of acting on his own opinion, had asked the question whether the oats were old or new, or had said anything which intimated his understanding that the seller was selling the oats as old oats, the case would have been wholly different; or even if he had said anything which showed that he was not acting on his own inspection and judgment, but assumed as the foundation of the contract that the oats were old, the silence of the seller as a means of misleading him might have amounted to a fraudulent concealment such as would have entitled the buyer to avoid the contract."[5]

---

[1] *Cf. A. Roberts & Co.* v. *Leicestershire County Council*, [1961] Ch. 555; [1961] 2 All E.R. 545.
[2] Rescission is no longer barred by the fact that the contract has been performed; Misrepresentation Act 1967, s. 1; see Atiyah, *Sale of Goods* (4th ed.), 289.
[3] (1871), L.R. 6 Q.B. at 604, *per* Cockburn, C.J.

⁴ *Ibid.*
⁵ (1871), L.R. 6 Q.B. 597 at 605, *per* Cockburn, C.J.

[172] (vi) *Omission to undeceive as a deception.*—Where D's statement is true at the time it is made but later to his knowledge becomes false, he will be guilty of obtaining by deception if P acts on the false statement by tendering property or a pecuniary advantage which D dishonestly accepts. In *D.P.P.* v. *Ray*¹ the statement was D's implied representation that he intended to pay for his meal. This statement was true when made and continued true until the end of the meal, but when D changed his mind it became false. It was held that the waiter acted on the false statement by leaving the room, when he would not have done so had he known the truth, that D intended to leave without paying. If D had changed his mind during the meal, it is clear that any part of the meal served and any service performed by the waiter thereafter would have been obtained by deception. It is essential to prove that P acted on the false representation and that the result of P's so acting was that D obtained the property or the service as the case may be.

The same result must follow in the case where the statement is false when made but believed by D to be true, if D discovers that the statement is false and thereafter accepts property or a service from P who, as D knows, is acting on the false statement.

In these situations there is, in effect, a duty on D either to correct P's false belief or, at least, to decline any property or service deriving from that belief.

This is not to argue that criminal liability should be imposed in all cases where the civil law imposes a duty to speak. This is a highly technical matter and there are instances where it would not be obvious to the layman that to remain silent would be tantamount to deception. Such cases may be unsuitable for the imposition of criminal sanctions. The point is that criminal liability should not be imposed where the civil law imposes no duty to speak. Where it does impose such a duty then the act may reasonably be held criminal if the words of the Act may fairly be said to cover the case.

¹ [1974] A.C. 370; [1973] 3 All E.R. 131; SHC 527; *Nordeng* (1975), 62 Cr. App. Rep. 123, at 129.

[173] (vii) *As to fact or law.*—In the old law of false pretences the books unanimously stated that the misrepresentation must be as to a matter of fact.¹ They then went on to contrast representation of fact with representation of opinion or intention. No discussion is to be found of representations of law and no authority is cited to show that a misrepresentation of law would not have been a sufficient false pretence. Indeed there appears to be no authority to that effect. On the other hand there is no authority to show that a misrepresentation of law was enough. It is thus uncertain to what extent the express inclusion of deception as to a matter of law extends the law. Certainly it seems desirable that misrepresentations of law should be within the terms of the Act. Consider the following cases:

(i) D and P are reading a legal document and D deliberately misrepresents its legal effect. This would seem to be misrepresentation of law since the construction of documents is a question of law. If D does so with the object of leading P to believe that D has some right over P's land so as to induce P to pay money for the release of that right, this would seem to amount to obtaining by deception.

(ii) P and his wife, D, have entered into a separation agreement whereby P covenanted to pay D an annual sum "free of any deduction whatever". D, knowing that the true legal construction of the document is to the contrary,[2] represents to P that this prevents P from deducting income tax. This is a misrepresentation of law and it would seem that D is guilty of obtaining the money (or at least that portion of it which represents the tax which ought to have been deducted) by deception.

---

[1] Archbold (36th ed.) 1945; Russell, 1171; Smith and Hogan (1st ed.), 408; Kenny, 358.
[2] *Ord* v. *Ord*, [1923] 2 K.B. 432.

---

[174] There are other cases which might fall within the Act, however, which some might regard as legitimate stratagems.

(i) D has entered into an oral agreement to purchase P's land. P now wishes to escape from the bargain. D, knowing that the contract is unenforceable for lack of a memorandum in writing,[1] writes to P pointing out that they have entered into a legally binding agreement and offering to release P from his liability on payment of £200.

(ii) P owes D a debt which, as D knows but P does not, is statute-barred. D writes to P stating that the money is recoverable by action and that he will sue unless it is paid.

Difficult questions might arise here since the contract in (i) is valid and only unenforceable by action; and the debt in (ii) remains due—the effect of the Limitation Act is to extinguish only the remedy and not the right. It is only the representation that an action will lie which may be false; and there are difficulties even about this, for an action *will* lie in both cases unless the Law of Property Act 1925 in the one case and the Limitation Act 1939 in the other is expressly pleaded.

There is the further point that D may well have a claim of right to the money which will negative dishonesty. Indeed since he may have an actual right to keep the money in both cases if it is paid, it might be thought to be incongruous that the obtaining of it should amount to an offence.[2]

A slightly different case arises where the right to recover land or a chattel is barred by the Limitation Act for in these cases the owner's title is extinguished.[3] In these instances a claim that the chattel or land was due in law to the claimant would be a misrepresentation, a belief in the existence of a moral right would not necessarily negative dishonesty[4] and if the land or chattel were handed over to D he would not be entitled to retain it.

It would appear therefore that to recover land or a chattel by misrepresenting the effect of the Limitation Act could amount to an offence under s. 15 (1). To recover a debt by a similar misrepresentation would probably not do so.

---

[1] Law of Property Act 1925, s. 40.
[2] See above, para. **[79]**. But this is not necessarily a defence to blackmail, below, para. **[297]**.
[3] Sections 16 (land) and 3 (2) (chattels).
[4] Above, para. **[111]**.

[175] In the cases just considered, it has been assumed that the law is quite clear and definite and D knows what it is. Many legal disputes arise, of course, where the law is uncertain. In these instances it is most unlikely that an offence could be committed under the Act. It must often happen that counsel make submissions as to the law in court which do not accord with, or are in direct opposition to the propositions which the same counsel would formulate if he were writing a text-book on the matter. The nature of his submission where the law is uncertain is governed by the interests of his client. A solicitor making similar submissions so as to exact money by way of compromise could not be said to be committing an offence because it is impossible to prove that the statement is (or was at the time) false—the law, *ex hypothesi*, being uncertain.

[176] The following proposition formulated by Street[1] for the law of the tort of deceit is probably equally true of deception under s. 15:

> "If the representations refer to legal principles as distinct from the facts on which those principles operate and the parties are on an equal footing, those representations are only expressions of belief and of the same effect as expressions of opinion between parties on an equal footing. In other cases where the defendant professes legal information beyond that of the plaintiff the ordinary rules of liability for deceit apply".

---

[1] *Torts* (6th ed.), 378.

---

[177] (viii) *Deception as to intention.*—Deception includes a deception as to the present intentions of the person using the deception or any other person. A representation as to present intention may be expressed or implied. Several examples of implied representations have been considered above.[1]

It should be emphasised that it must be clearly proved in these cases that D had no intention of carrying out his promise at the time he made it. If he intended to carry out his promise at that time but later changed his mind he is guilty of a breach of contract but of no criminal offence. It has long been recognised that a misrepresentation as to present state of mind will found a civil action for deceit and this is no more difficult to prove in the criminal than in the civil case—though the standard of proof is, of course, higher. Evidence as to the circumstances in which the promise was made, or as to a systematic course of conduct by D or, of course, as to a confession are examples of ways in which a jury might be convinced beyond reasonable doubt that D was deceiving P as to his present intentions.

---

[1] Para [166].

---

[178] Deceptions as to the present intentions of another person are likely to be rare. The most likely case is that where an agent obtains property for his principal by representing that the principal intends to render services or supply goods, well knowing that the principal has no such intention. There are other possible cases as where an estate agent says that a particular building society is willing to advance half the purchase price of a house, knowing that this is not so, and thus induces a purchaser to pay a deposit.

[179] (ix) *Statements of opinion.*—A statement of opinion was not a sufficient false pretence under s. 32 of the Larceny Act 1916. The leading case, *Bryan*,[1] carried this doctrine to extreme lengths. There D obtained money from P by representing that certain spoons were of the best quality, equal to Elkington's A, and having as much silver on them as Elkington's A. These statements were false to D's knowledge.[2] Nevertheless ten out of twelve judges[3] held that his conviction must be quashed on the ground that this was mere exaggerated praise by a seller of his goods to which the statute was not intended to apply. Erle, J. said "Whether these spoons ... were equal to Elkington's A or not, cannot be, as far as I know, decidedly affirmed or denied in the same way as a past fact can be affirmed or denied, but it is in the nature of a matter of opinion". This can hardly be true, however, of the statement that the spoons had as much silver on them as Elkington's A. This seems to be no less a misrepresentation of fact than that a six-carat gold chain is of fifteen carat gold which has subsequently been held to be a sufficient false pretence.[4] Recently it has been held[5] that it is a misrepresentation of fact for the accused to state "that they [had] effected necessary repairs to a roof [which repairs were specified] that they had done the work in a proper and workmanlike manner and that [a specified sum] was a fair and reasonable sum to charge for the work involved". The evidence showed that nothing needed to be done to the roof, what had been done served no useful purpose and it could have been done for £5, whereas £35 was charged.

---

[1] (1857), Dears. & B. 265.
[2] D's counsel said: "I cannot contend that the prisoner did not tell a wilful lie ...".
[3] Willes, J. *dissentiente* and Bramwell, B. *dubitante.*
[4] *Ardley* (1871), L.R. 1 C.C.R. 301.
[5] *Jeff and Bassett* (1966), 51 Cr. App. Rep. 28. *Cf. Hawkins* v. *Smith*, [1978] Crim. L.R. 578 ("Showroom condition throughout" a false trade description of a car which has interior and mechanical defects).

---

[180] The Theft Act gives no guidance as to whether a misrepresentation of opinion is capable of being a deception. In principle there is no reason why it should not be, where the opinion is not honestly held. A vendor's description of his tenant as "a most desirable tenant" when the rent was in arrears and, in the past, had only been paid under pressure was held by the Court of Appeal to be a sufficient misrepresentation to found an action in deceit.[1]

> "In a case where the facts are equally well-known to both parties, what one of them says to the other is frequently nothing but an expression of opinion. ... But if the facts are not equally well-known to both sides, then a statement of opinion by one who knows the facts best involves very often a statement of a material fact, for he impliedly states that he knows facts which justify his opinion"[2]

The way seems open to the courts, if they so wish, to hold that "deception" extends to this kind of case. The use of that term frees them from the fetters of false pretences. A view of commercial morality very different from that of the majority of the judges in *Bryan* now prevails and deliberate mis-statements of opinion would today be generally condemned as dishonest, no less dishonest, indeed, than mis-statements of other facts—for whether an opinion is held or not is a fact—and the law should follow the changed attitude. It may, moreover, be a significant fact that at the time *Bryan* was decided, it was not possible for the prisoner to give evidence in his own defence.[3]

Against this view, it might be argued that, since the Act has expressly removed one limitation on false pretences (representations as to intention) and has said nothing about this limitation, Parliament's intention is to allow it to continue. It is submitted that this would be a quite unjustifiable assumption. Parliament, in fact, has left it to the judges and, by the use of new terminology, given them a more or less free hand. The question now ought to be not "Is it a matter of opinion?" but, "If it is a matter of opinion, was it D's real opinion?" If the opinion is not honestly held there is, in truth, a misrepresentation of fact for the accused's state of mind is a question of fact. The Act indeed recognises this by holding false promises to be deception. If "I intend ..." (not intending) is a deception, is not "I believe ..." (not believing) equally a deception?

---

[1] *Smith v. Land and House Property Corporation* (1884), 28 Ch.D. 7.
[2] *Ibid.*, at 15, *per* Bowen, L.J.
[3] In *Ragg* (1860), Bell 214 at 219, Erle, C.J., referring to *Bryan*, said "... if such statements are indictable a purchaser who wishes to get out of a bad bargain made by his own negligence, might have recourse to an indictment, on the trial of which the vendor's statement on oath would be excluded, instead of being obliged to bring an action where each party would be heard on equal terms."

(c) Dishonestly

[181] (i) *Where there is or may be a claim of right.*—The deception must also be done "dishonestly". Dishonesty is a subjective concept. The jury must assess D's actual beliefs, whether reasonable or not. The reasonableness or otherwise of the alleged belief is relevant only to the question whether it is actually held or not.[1] Section 32 of the Larceny Act 1916 required an "intent to defraud" and the Court of Criminal Appeal said repeatedly that this meant "dishonestly"[2] so the law would appear to be unchanged. The Court of Appeal has said,[3] however, that "dishonestly" has a wider ambit without indicating the respects in which it is wider. D may deceive deliberately or recklessly, yet not obtain dishonestly.[4] "Dishonestly" is a separate element in the *mens rea*. The jury should *always* be directed that they must be satisfied that the deception was done dishonestly; though the absence of direction on this point may not be fatal where dishonesty is, in the particular circumstances, an inevitable inference from a deliberate deception.[5] There is no definition of dishonesty for the purposes of this section and the partial definition in s. 2 (1) applies only for the purposes of section 1 of the Act. Obviously the provisions of s. 2 (1) (c) (finder who believes that owner cannot be discovered by taking reasonable steps) are inapplicable to the offences now under discussion. In other respects it is likely that the meaning is the same. It may be, however, that the judge will be reluctant to direct the jury in the matter as there is no statutory provision and *Feely*[6] declares that the question, dishonest or not? is one for the jury. It is thought that it is reasonable to assume that one who obtains property, a service, or a pecuniary advantage by deception but under a claim of right made in good faith is not guilty.

Against this view might be cited (i) the case of *Parker*[7] and (ii) the provisions regarding blackmail[8] in the Theft Act. In *Parker*, Ridley, J. held that D, a moneylender, was guilty of demanding money upon a forged document, *with intent to defraud*, where he sent to his debtor, P, a letter which purported to come from P's superior officer and demanded that P repay the debt to D.[9] Ridley, J. said:

> "... if a man insists upon payment of debt which is due to him, or recovery of a chattel to which he is entitled, and for this purpose resorts to a forged instrument, that would afford evidence of an intent to defraud".

[1] *Lewis,* [1976] Crim. L.R. 383, C.A. .
[2] *Wright,* [1960] Crim. L.R. 366.
[3] *Potger* (1971), 55 Cr. App. Rep. 42 at 46.
[4] See *Wright* (above) and *Griffiths,* [1966] 1 Q.B. 589; [1965] 2 All E.R. 448.
[5] *Potger* (above), footnote 3.
[6] [1973] 1 Q.B. 530; [1973] 1 All E.R. 341; SHC 509.
[7] (1910), 74 J.P. 208.
[8] Below, para. **[315]**.
[9] According to the *Justice of the Peace* report, counsel argued that intent to defraud might be inferred from the fact that the sum demanded was more than P agreed to pay. But P did not allege that he was overcharged and the judge directed that there was evidence of an intent to defraud even if the debt was due. See 152 C.C.C. Sess. Pap. 321.

[182] It is clear, furthermore, that D may be guilty of blackmail under the Theft Act though he has not only a claim of right, but also an actual right to the property demanded.[1] It appears then that, if D believes he is entitled to a sum of money (and even if he *is* entitled to it):

   (i) he is guilty of forgery if he demands it with a forged instrument;
   (ii) he is guilty of blackmail if he demands it with menaces; but
   (iii) he is *not* guilty of theft if he appropriates it.

Should the "obtaining" offences be grouped with forgery and blackmail or with theft?[2] It is submitted that they belong with theft. Obtaining and blackmail are grouped together in the Act but (i) the definition of blackmail does not contain the word "dishonestly", and (ii) the relationship between theft and obtaining property is in fact closer than that between blackmail and obtaining property. Even if the *Lawrence* (C.A.) principle[3] is wrong and theft does not embrace virtually the whole of obtaining property, it is certain that theft and obtaining property overlap and are intended to overlap. If D induces P to let him have a horse on hire, dishonestly intending to sell it, D is *prima facie* guilty of offences contrary to both s. 1 and s. 15. If D believes the horse to be his, it would be unfortunate that he should have a defence under s. 1 but not under s. 15. The two offences should be in harmony on this fundamental point.

[1] Below, paras. **[315]**–**[317]**.
[2] If, as submitted above there is no *actus reus* where D is entitled to have the property which he obtains by deception, the question of *mens rea* does not arise. It deserves consideration, however, in case that view is wrong.
[3] Above, para. **[37]**.

[183] If this be correct, D would have a defence in the following case:
D's car has been obtained from him by X who gave a cheque drawn on a bank where he had no account and who never paid the price. X has sold the car to a *bona fide* purchaser, P. P refuses to give up the car to D. D, believing that

he is entitled to have the car back, recovers possession by pretending to be a mechanic from P's garage collecting the car for servicing.

Here D has no actual right to recover possession of the car; he is certainly guilty of a deliberate deception; but if he genuinely believes he is entitled to possession of the car, it is submitted that the jury should be told that he is not "dishonest" for the purposes of the section.

Probably the same result must follow where D's belief relates not to any specific property but to the repayment of a debt:

D, a Hungarian woman, has been P's mistress. On the termination of the relationship, P promises to pay D £100. Later he declines to do so. D is advised by a Hungarian lawyer that she is entitled to the money. By a deliberate deception she causes P to pay her £100.[1]

In such a case there was, and no doubt is, a sufficient claim of right to negative an "intent to steal"; and, if so, there should equally be a defence to obtaining by deception.

A more difficult case is that where D obtains something other than the thing to which he has a claim of right.

D's employer, E, cannot pay D's wages because he cannot obtain payment of a debt owed by P to E. D, by deception, obtains some of P's property and delivers it to E, hoping thereby to enable E to procure the payment of the debt—and the means to pay D's wages.

In such a case[2] Coleridge, J. thought that the facts negatived an intent to defraud; and in a subsequent case[3] Pollock, C. B. put this on the ground that D must have thought he had some right to obtain the property which he did obtain. Of course, he had no right in law so to do, in which case the decision on these facts must depend on the state of D's mind in the particular case. Did he, or did he not, believe he had, or that E had, a legal right to act in this way? Looked at in this way, it would seem rather unlikely that a claim of right could often be made out. D had a claim of right to his wages; E had a claim of right to payment by P of the debt (both being actual rights) but the question is whether D had a claim of right to the particular property he obtained by the deception. Few people would suppose today that they have a right to take the property of a debtor to compel him to pay his creditor.

---

[1] *Cf. Bernhard*, [1938] 2 K.B. 264, above, para. [**110**]; below, para. [**329**].
[2] *Williams* (1836), 7 C. & P. 354. *Cf. Close*, [1977] Crim. L.R. 107.
[3] *Hamilton* (1845), 1 Cox C.C. 244.

[**184**] (ii) *Where there is no claim of right.*—Prior to *Feely*[1] the courts were inclined to decide as a matter of law that certain common types of conduct were dishonest. In *McCall*[2] the Court of Appeal decided that to obtain a loan by deception was dishonest even though D intended to repay. D's submission that such conduct "is not necessarily tainted with dishonesty" was rejected. There was "an unanswerable case" against him. In *Halstead* v. *Patel*[3] D knowingly overdrew on a Giro account, intending to repay at some future date when a strike was over. It was held, relying on decisions which were not followed in *Feely*, that the "pious hope" of repaying at some future date was no defence; the justices were bound to convict. In *Potger*,[4] where D induced P to subscribe for magazines by the false representation that he was a student

taking part in a points competition, it was no answer that magazines worth the money would have been delivered in due course. The Court of Appeal came close to giving a definition of dishonesty in obtaining cases:

> "... once the jury had come to the conclusion that these were deliberate lies intended to induce the various persons to do acts which would benefit[5] the appellant and that they were or would have been induced so to act by those lies, it was inevitable that the jury should reach the conclusion at which they did arrive."

[1] Above, para. **[116]**.
[2] (1970), 55 Cr. App. Rep. 175; *cf. Duru*, [1973] 3 All E.R. 715.
[3] [1972] 2 All E.R. 147. The judgment is clearly wrong in so far as it refers to a "belief based on reasonable grounds". See [1972] Crim. L.R. 236; *Lewis*, [1976] Crim. L.R. 383 C.A.
[4] (1971), 55 Cr. App. R. 42.
[5] But should not the emphasis have been on prejudice to P rather than benefit to D? *Cf. Welham v. D.P.P.*, [1961] A.C. 103; [1960] 1 All E.R. 805; SHC 621, 622.

[185] *Feely* was a case of theft under s. 1 but it seems clear that the principles of that case and of *Boggeln v. Williams*[1] apply to all other offences under the Theft Acts which use the word "dishonestly". In *Feely*, Lawton, L.J. contrasted the case of the man who takes money from a till intending to repay (presumably before it is missed); and the man who obtains cash by passing a cheque on an account with no funds, intending to pay funds in to meet the cheque when it is presented. According to *Cockburn* (overruled in *Feely*) the first man was dishonest in law whereas:

> "the man who passes the cheque is deemed in law not to act dishonestly if he genuinely believes on reasonable grounds that when it is presented to the paying bank there will be funds to meet it."

Lawton, L.J. commented:

> "Lawyers may be able to appreciate why one man should be adjudged to be a criminal and the other not; but we doubt whether anyone else would."

Admittedly, these two cases should stand or fall together. If so, following *Feely*, the man who passes the cheque can no longer be "*deemed in law* not to act dishonestly". It is now a question for the jury in the particular case. *Feely* was followed in an obtaining case, *Greenstein*,[2] the first prosecution brought in respect of a particular method of "stagging". The judge told the jury:

> "... this is the first prosecution. It has not yet been decided if what they did did amount to a dishonest criminal deception and it will be you who will decide the answer to that question."

But the answer given by the jury is of no authority in any future case, even on exactly similar material facts. Surely the law should supply the answer to the question whether this practice is lawful or not—just as the law should say whether it is or is not lawful to obtain a loan by deception with intent to repay in due course. It is not the function of the jury to make law.

¹ [1978] 2 All E.R. 1061, above, para. **[117]**.
² [1976] 1 All E.R. 1, above, para. **[167]**.

[186] *Greenstein* shows that it is not necessarily a defence to a charge of dishonesty that D did not intend anyone to suffer any financial loss. Where D who has no money in his bank account and no authority to overdraw, obtains goods by using a cheque card, he knows that the person from whom the goods are obtained will suffer no financial loss—the loss will fall on the bank. For this reason, it may be that a charge of obtaining a pecuniary advantage from the bank will be preferred to one of obtaining goods from the seller; but it is submitted that there is evidence of dishonesty towards the seller as well, *if* he was induced by the deception to part with his property.[1]

¹ See the discussion of cheque card frauds, above para. **[157]**.

[187] Suppose that D, by making false statements as to his assets, persuades his bank manager to allow him to borrow by way of overdraft. Section 16 (2) (*b*) of the 1968 Act says that he is to be regarded as having obtained a pecuniary advantage. It is now for the jury to decide whether it is a defence that D intended (and was able) to repay the loan with interest in the agreed time. In a sense he has not obtained a "pecuniary advantage" at all, since he is going to give a full economic return for what he gets but that is not necessarily an answer.[1] If D, aged 48, applies for an appointment for which the maximum age is 45, stating that he is 44, he commits the *actus reus* of the offence if he is appointed (and of an attempt if he is not). It is for the jury to decide whether he is dishonest if he can say truthfully "I was the best qualified candidate and would have earned every penny of my salary if appointed". It is true that s. 16 (2) (*c*) defines only "pecuniary advantage" and the advantage must be obtained "dishonestly"; but it is thought that it would defeat the intention behind s. 16 (2) if the meaning given to "dishonestly" excluded these cases.

¹ Below, para. **[212]**.

B. OBTAINING PROPERTY BY DECEPTION

[188] By s. 15 of the Act:

"(1) A person who by any deception dishonestly obtains property belonging to another, with the intention of permanently depriving the other of it, shall on conviction on indictment be liable to imprisonment for a term not exceeding ten years.

(2) For purposes of this section a person is to be treated as obtaining property if he obtains ownership, possession or control of it, and 'obtain' includes obtaining for another or enabling another to obtain or to retain."

These subsections replace the old crime of obtaining by false pretences contrary to s. 32 of the Larceny Act 1916. Their scope is, however, considerably wider than that of the old provision. The most important change is that the new offence embraces cases which were formerly larceny by a trick as well as false pretences[1] but it also extends the law to cover some cases which were previously not criminal at all. The various constituents of the offence are examined below.

[1] Above, para. **[33]**.

(a) *The obtaining*

[189] (i) *For one's self.—* There is a sufficient obtaining if D obtains ownership, possession or control.[1] Under the old law it was doubtful whether obtaining ownership without also getting possession amounted to an offence.[2] It seems now to be clear that it does. If D is lawfully in possession of P's goods, for example, as a bailee, and he dishonestly by deception induces P to sell him the goods, the offence is complete when the ownership passes to D. Conversely if D, by deception, induces P to enter into an unconditional contract to sell to D specific goods which are in a deliverable state, the offence is complete although the goods never leave P's possession. The ownership in the goods passes as soon as the contract is made and it is immaterial that the time of payment and of delivery is postponed.[3] Similarly if D, by deception, induces P to transfer to him a bill of lading in respect of goods which are at sea,[4] he will be guilty of obtaining not merely the bill of lading but also the goods which it represents, for title to them passes on indorsement and delivery of the bill. It may be that, in these cases, P will suffer no loss; but it is right that such conduct should be criminal since it puts P's property at risk. D has probably obtained a voidable title to it and, if he can re-sell to a *bona fide* purchaser before P succeeds in avoiding the contract, the *bona fide* purchaser will get an unimpeachable title to the property and P will be permanently deprived of it.

[1] It is unnecessary to prove that D obtained the whole of the property mentioned in the information or indictment, but the sentence should relate only to property proved to have been obtained: *Levene* v. *Pearcey*, [1976] Crim. L.R. 63, above, para. **[53]**, footnote 1.
[2] Kenny thought it did not: *Outlines* (5th ed.), 243.
[3] Sale of Goods Act 1893, s. 18, rule 1.
[4] *Cf.* Kenny, footnote 2, above.

[190] It follows that if D, being in a foreign country, say France, sends a letter to England deceiving P into selling him goods which are in England, D is guilty of obtaining by deception in England as soon as the property passes to him. It is immaterial that he never sets foot within the jurisdiction. If the letter arrives within the jurisdiction but does not deceive P, (or, it is submitted, is lost before it reaches him) D is liable in England for an attempt:[1]

"... he who despatches a missile or a missive, arranges for its transport and delivery (essential parts of the attempt), and is thus committing part of the crime within the jurisdiction by the means which he has arranged".

Even if the "missile or missive" never reaches the jurisdiction (for example, the ship containing the missive sinks outside territorial waters) it is thought that D should be convicted. Though nothing has actually happened in England, it is the consequences here that the accused has in view, and it is to the consequences *intended* that we have regard when dealing with attempts (and conspiracy or incitement).

[191] The position regarding the converse case is less certain. D, in England, sends a letter to France, deceiving P into transferring property in goods to D in France. According to *Harden*¹, a case decided under the Larceny Act 1916, the English courts have no jurisdiction, but Lord Diplock has said² that that case should be reconsidered. According to his Lordship's view of jurisdiction under the Theft Act,³ D would clearly be liable to conviction here. Not all the members of the House of Lords appear to take the same view; but even if Lord Diplock's approach is not upheld, it may well be held that obtaining by deception, like blackmail, is a continuing offence, committed both in the country from which, and in the country to which, a letter is despatched.

Even if *Harden* is right, so that no offence is committed in England when the property passes abroad, it may be that there will be an offence if the goods are subsequently delivered in England. Possession of the goods has now been obtained within the jurisdiction by the deception which is still operating (the seller would not have despatched the goods had he known the truth). It might be argued that this is not obtaining the property "of another", since D is now the owner. But it is clear that an offence would be committed if, *after* the contract of sale, D had by a fresh deception induced P to part with possession of the goods before payment of the price, P being deprived of his lien over the goods;⁴ and it is submitted that the position is the same where an earlier deception which induced the transference of the property is still operative.⁵ Where, however, both ownership and possession are transferred to D abroad, according to *Harden* no offence is committed within the jurisdiction.

It must, of course, be decided *whether* D obtained the property abroad. In *Harden* it was held that the ownership in a cheque passed in Jersey when it was posted there to D in England. D had made an offer to P which stated that it could be accepted by *sending* the cheque. In *Tirado*⁶ the court said:

> "... we are not minded to take the law an inch beyond that which *Harden* determined, namely, that if a recipient of a valuable security wishes to show that he obtained it when it was posted to him, he has to be able to show an agreement, express or implied, whereby he had undertaken and accepted that posting should be equivalent to personal delivery as far as he was concerned."

It was held, no such agreement having been shown, that money delivered to a bank in Morocco for transmission by a banker's draft to Oxford was not obtained by D until it reached Oxford. P clearly parted with his ownership to the bank in Morocco, but if the money at that stage was held by the bank at P's rather than D's disposal, it had not yet been obtained by D.

¹ [1963] 1 Q.B. 8; [1962] 1 All E.R. 286.
² *Treacy* v. *D.P.P.*, [1971] A.C. 537 at 563; [1971] 1 All E.R. 110 at 123. *Cf. Markus*, [1976] A.C. 35; [1974] 3 All E.R. 705, at 712–713 C.A. where the court did not act on Lord Diplock's suggestion.
³ Below, para. **[431]**.
⁴ Below, para. **[206]**.
⁵ It must be conceded that it appears to follow from this argument that *two* offences are committed when D, by a single deception, causes P (i) to sell and (ii) subsequently to deliver goods

to him. But if there are two deceptions, one causing the property to pass, another causing delivery, it is inescapable that this must be so. And it is thought the position is exactly the same, in the case where there is only one deception. Of course, it would be improper to indict for both offences except where it is doubtful whether one count will lie because, e.g., of the jurisdictional difficulties referred to above.

[6] (1974) 59 Cr. App. Rep. 80 at 85.

[192] If D merely obtains possession, ownership remaining in P, his offence under the old law would have been larceny by a trick. Such conduct continues to be theft[1] but it is now also obtaining by deception and should always be indicted as such and not as theft. It is an offence under s. 15 (1) where D, by deception, induces P to let him have goods on hire, or hire-purchase, or on loan, with the appropriate *mens rea*. All sorts of difficult questions about whether the property passed or not, which had to be decided by criminal courts under the old law, are now irrelevant—provided the charge is brought under this section and not under section 1.

[1] See above, para. [33].

[193] It is enough that D obtains control. So if D, a servant, by deception induces his master, P, to entrust goods to D for use in the course of D's employment, D may be guilty of the offence though he has obtained not possession of the goods but control or "custody" as this particular relation to goods is sometimes called.

[194] (ii) *For another*—"'Obtain' includes obtaining for another or enabling another to obtain or retain".[1] So if D, by deception, induces P to make a gift of goods to E, D is guilty. That would be a case where D obtained for another. An instance of D's enabling another to obtain would be where E is negotiating with P for the sale of goods by E to P and D deceives P as to the quality of the goods so as to induce him to enter into the contract with and pay the price to E. Of course E, in these examples, would also be guilty if he was a party to D's fraud.

[1] Section 15 (1). *D.P.P.* v. *Stonehouse,*[1977] 2 All E.R. 909; [1977] Crim. L.R. 544.

[195] The meaning of "enabling another ... to retain" presents more difficulties. If E is in possession of P's goods and D, by deception, induces P to agree to transfer the ownership in the goods to E, this would be "obtaining for another" and not "enabling another to retain". The latter provision must be intended to apply to the situation where D induces P to allow E to retain some interest which E already has, for, if P is induced to transfer any new interest, this is obtaining for another.

There seem to be three possible cases:

(i)   E is P's bailee at will and D, by deception and with the appropriate intent, induces P not to terminate E's possession.

(ii) E is P's servant and has custody of P's goods. D, by deception, induces P not to terminate that custody, again with the appropriate intent.

(iii) E has obtained the ownership of property from P under the terms of a contract voidable by P. P is proposing to rescind that contract. D, by deception, induces him to refrain from doing so. It is clear that D has enabled E to retain ownership and therefore he is to be "treated as" obtaining property.

It might be argued in the third case, however, that D is not guilty because he is not enabling E to retain property *"belonging to another"*. It has been seen that this expression must have a wide meaning but in this example P has neither ownership, possession nor control. The question is whether property can be said to "belong to" a person for the purpose of the section when he has nothing more than the right, by rescinding a contract, to resume ownership of it. *Prima facie*, one would have thought that the answer to this question would be in the negative; P has no proprietary right or interest in the property.[1] It is true that s. 15 (2) gives an extended meaning to the words "obtains property"—D is, in the specified circumstances, to be "treated as obtaining property", whether he does so or not—but it does not, in terms, extend the meaning of the equally important phrase, "belonging to another". Case (iii) can be brought within the section only by holding that the extended meaning of "obtains property" extends by implication the meaning of "belonging to another".[2] D is probably not guilty of obtaining by deception in that case.

[1] *Cf.* s. 5 (1), above, para. **[53]**.
[2] The meaning given to this phrase by s. 5 applies only for the purposes of s. 1 (theft); above, para. **[53]**.

[196] It will be noticed that the Act makes no provision for the case where D by deception retains goods for himself. In most cases this will clearly fall under theft contrary to s. 1 so there will be no problem. (Of course in examples (i) and (ii), above, E, if he has *mens rea*, will be guilty of theft by "keeping [the property] as owner",[1] and D of aiding and abetting him: whereas if E has no *mens rea*, D might well be thought to be guilty of theft through an innocent agent. But it is very doubtful if D or E would be guilty of theft in example (iii)).[2]

If D is in possession or custody of P's property and, by deception, he induces P to allow him to retain that possession or custody as the case may be, with the intention of permanently depriving P of the property, D will be guilty of theft. If, however, D has acquired ownership and possession of the property from P before deception, it is difficult to see how he can be said to have appropriated the property of another. Suppose that D has acquired ownership and possession of P's property under a contract voidable by P for an innocent misrepresentation committed by D. P is about to rescind the contract and thus regain his ownership in the goods. D, by deception induces him to refrain from doing so, intending to keep the goods permanently for himself. D can hardly be said to have appropriated the property of another since P has no interest, legal or equitable, in the property at this time;[3] nor is this obtaining under s. 15 (1). As has been seen, in the corresponding case where D enables E to retain his ownership and possession of property, it is just arguable that D is guilty of an offence. If so, this is a curious anomaly for the argument is applicable where D enables himself to retain; but such cases are likely to be extremely rare.

[1] Section 3 (1), above, para. **[24]**.
[2] Above, paras. **[80]**–**[81]**.
[3] It is submitted above, para. **[80]**, that s. 5 (4) is inapplicable to this situation.

[197] (iii) *Necessity for specific property.*—It should be emphasised that, for D to be guilty of enabling E to retain, there must be some specific property which is the subject of the retention. So if D, E's accountant, deceives the Inland Revenue Inspector whereby E's liability to tax is reduced by £50, no offence is committed under this section. In a sense, of course, D has, by deception, enabled E to retain property; but it is not the property *of another*. It is submitted that the provision cannot have been intended to apply to the mere non-payment of a debt which is all that this is. D would, however, be guilty of an offence under 1978, s. 2 (1) (*b*).[1]

---

[1] Below, para. [**238**].

(b) Property

[198] The limitations put upon the meaning of "property" for the purposes of theft by s. 4 are inapplicable to deception. It seems clear, then, that s. 15 extends far beyond the "chattel, money or valuable security" which could be the subject of obtaining by false pretences under the Larceny Act 1916, s. 32. Non-larcenable chattels, which were not the subject of false pretences[1] may be obtained by deception. Other cases require more detailed consideration.

---

[1] *Robinson* (1859), Bell C.C. 34.

[199] (i) *Land,* —Land presents peculiarly difficult problems because of the nature of interests in land and the fact that the terminology of the Theft Act is geared to the traditional subject-matter of obtaining by false pretences, namely goods.[1] Under English law, ownership subsists not in the land itself but in an abstract entity called "an estate". The freeholder owns not the land but the fee simple estate in the land, and the leaseholder has a leasehold estate. The land itself may however be possessed. The offence may be committed therefore by obtaining the ownership of an estate in the land or by obtaining possession or control of the land, provided that there is an intention to deprive the victim permanently of his interest, whatever it is.

---

[1] See Griew, 6–34.

[200] 1. Where P parts with his estate.—There is little difficulty where the owner is induced to convey his whole estate to the rogue. For example, P, the owner of the freehold, is induced to convey the fee simple to D; or a lessee is induced to assign his whole leasehold interest to D. An obvious case is where an imposter procures the transference to himself of trust property or a deceased person's estate. But there are other cases. Suppose D induces P to sell him land for use as a coach-station, by agreeing that he will purchase all the petrol he needs for his coach-business from P. D never has any intention of honouring his promise. If the legal estate in the land is conveyed to D, or if D is given possession before conveyance, it seems clear that the offence is complete. It may be thought, however, that the offence is complete at an earlier stage. The general rule is that when A *contracts* to sell land to B, an equitable interest in the land passes at once to B. This arises from the fact that a decree of specific performance will normally be granted for a contract for the sale of land and "equity looks on as done that which ought to be done". If the contract is not specifically enforceable, no interest passes.[1] When there has been deception, it seems inevitably to follow that the contract is voidable for fraud by the vendor and thus not specifically enforceable against him.[2] If the transaction has got no further than the contract, it seems, then, that D could not be convicted of the full offence, though he might be convicted of an attempt.

---

[1] Megarry and Wade, *Law of Real Property* (4th ed.) 582.
[2] *Ibid.*, 585.

---

[201] 2. Where P creates a smaller estate.—The main difficulty arises out of the necessity for an intention permanently to deprive the owner of the property. Such an intent may be difficult or impossible to discover where the owner is induced not to part with his whole estate, but to carve some smaller estate out of it. Suppose that D, by deception, induces P, the owner of the freehold, to grant him a lease of the land for two years. Clearly D does not intend to deprive P permanently, or indeed at all, of the property which belongs to him—i.e., his freehold interest. Nor, if he intends to vacate the property after two years, does he intend to deprive P permanently of possession of the land. The position would be the same if P were himself a lessee whose lease had three years to run and he granted D a sub-lease for two years. These cases look much the same as that of the owner of a ship who charters it for two years. If the charterer has induced the charter by deception but intends to comply with its terms, he does not commit an offence, because of his lack of intention permanently to deprive. There is a possible answer to this analogy. A lease of land differs from the letting of a chattel in that an estate in land is created by the granting of the lease. That estate is regarded in law as a separate piece of property; and D intends that P shall never have that particular piece of property. The snag about this is that it is impossible to say that the leasehold estate ever "belonged to", or could belong to P, the owner of the freehold. If it were surrendered to P it would cease to exist as a separate piece of property and merge in P's larger interest. The leasehold interest does not exist until the lease is granted—and then it belongs to D. This case may, however, now be dealt with as an obtaining of services contrary to 1978, s. 1.[1]

---

[1] Below, para. **[219]**.

---

[202] 3. Where P retains his estate but D obtains possession.—What is the effect of obtaining possession of land by deception? If P's only interest in the land is his possession of it, then, clearly the offence may be committed. For example, P is a squatter on the land with no title to it other than his actual possession. Even where P has a good title to the land which he does not lose through the deception, it is thought that the offence will be committed if he is to be deprived of possession for a period coincident with this interest. For example, D deceives P, who is a lessee of land for two years, to allow him into possession as a licensee for those two years. P's leasehold estate continues unimpaired. What then of the case where D obtains from P, the freeholder, a lease of the land for 99— or 999—years? P has not been deprived of his freehold interest but, fairly clearly, D has an intention to deprive him of possession of the land for the rest of his natural life. Is it an answer that the land will some day revert to some remote successor in title? It is submitted that when the Act speaks of permanently depriving "another", it means the living person whose property is taken or obtained; so that if he is never to have it back in his lifetime, this element of the offence is made out. (So it would be theft if D were to take P's property, intending to restore it to P's executor after his death.) Even if this argument is correct, it provides no answer to the case of the man who obtains a short lease by deception and there is an awkward question as to where the line is to be drawn; but this too may be treated as a case of obtaining services contrary to 1978, s. 1.[1]

---

[1] Below, para. [219].

[203] 4. Where P parts with a portion of his estate.—The position is thought to be different where P is induced to transfer to D parts of his fee simple or other interest. For example, to convey to D the fee simple in the shooting-rights, or the minerals or to grant D an easement or *profit à prendre.* Here there is evidence that D *does* intend to deprive P permanently of a portion of his freehold interest.

If D is granted only a lease of the mineral rights, then there is the same difficulty as with grants of other leasehold interests; but may he be convicted of obtaining the actual minerals which he removes from the land? He certainly intends to deprive P permanently of these. The difficulty here might be that he is entitled by virtue of the estate which he holds, albeit an estate voidable for fraud, to take the minerals. The problem is essentially one of remoteness, and the authorities[1] rather suggest that the obtaining of the minerals is too remote from the deception. It might well be otherwise, however, in a case where D by deception obtains not a lease but a mere contractual licence to take the minerals. This would not differ in principle from the common case of obtaining by deception, where D obtains the property in pursuance of a contract voidable for fraud.

---

[1] See above, para. [160].

[204] 5. Where the freeholder obtains from the lessee.—It has been seen that the offence is committed if a lessee is induced to assign his lease. What if he is induced to surrender it to his landlord? P is permanently deprived of his interest, so there is no difficulty on that score. But is it possible to say that D has *obtained* property, when P's estate has simply ceased to exist? It certainly looks very odd, however, that D, the landlord, should commit no offence when anyone else in the world who persuaded P to transfer his estate would be so guilty. Perhaps the answer is that D has obtained possession of the land with intent and P shall have it no more and that is enough.

[205] (ii) *Things in action*—Things in action and other intangible property (e.g., patents) are clearly property so that D will be guilty of an offence under s. 15 (1) if, by deception, he causes P to transfer his book debts, his copyright or patent to him.

An equitable assignment of a thing in action requires no formality.

"Where there is a contract between the owner of a chose in action and another person which shows a clear intention that such a person is to have the benefit of the chose, there is without more a sufficient assignment in the eye of equity". [1]

As in the case of a contract for the sale of land, this result is said to arise from the principle that equity looks on as done that which ought to be done.[2] It might therefore be argued by analogy that the assignment will not be complete where it has been induced by fraud. It is not clear that this result follows. The difference is that while the transference of the equitable interest in the land depends on the availability of specific performance, this does not seem to be true of the equitable assignment of an existing thing in action. Here it appears that the assignment may be regarded as completed, even though no consideration be given by the assignee.[3] In such a case, there is no question of a decree of specific performance being given. If the equitable ownership of the thing in action passes where there is no contract at all it would seem that, *a fortiori*, it must pass where there is a voidable contract. A purported assignment of a future thing in action can operate only as a contract to assign. One who, by deception, induces such an "assignment" will be guilty of an attempt to obtain by deception. If he gave consideration then, on the thing coming into existence, the full offence will be complete.

If D deceives P into negotiating to D a cheque drawn in P's favour, this will amount to obtaining the thing in action represented by the cheque. The right to sue on it has been transferred from P to D. If D deceives P into drawing a cheque in D's favour, he may be guilty of procuring the execution of a valuable security contrary to s. 20 (2)[4] but not of obtaining the thing in action represented by the cheque, contrary to s. 15 of the Act. The thing in action never belonged to P—he could not sue himself—it was a new item of property which, on its creation belonged to D.[5] D might, no doubt, be convicted of obtaining the piece of paper;[6] and a court could presumably take into account its real value in sentencing D.

---

[1] Cheshire and Fifoot, *Law of Contract* (10th ed.), 495. "Chose" is a synonym for "thing".
[2] *Ibid.*, 465.
[3] *Ibid.*, 472–475.
[4] Below para. **[245]**.
[5] It is not an assignment of part of the thing in action consisting in the debt owed by P's bank to P, because the holder of a cheque cannot sue the bank on the cheque: Bills of Exchange Act 1882, s. 53 and *Schroeder* v. *Central Bank of London, Ltd.* (1876), 34 L.T. 735.
[6] *Cf.*, above, para. **[129]**.

(c) *Belonging to another*

[206] Property "belongs to another" for the purposes of this section if the other has possession or control of it or any proprietary right or interest in it except an equitable interest arising only from an agreement to transfer or grant an interest.[1] Thus, the *owner* may be guilty of obtaining his own property by deception where, by deception, he dishonestly induces another to give up his lawful possession or control of that property. Suppose that D has pledged his clock with P as security for a loan and, by deception, he induces P to let him have the clock back again, intending neither to restore it nor to repay the loan.[2]

Or D, by deception, induces his servant, P, to surrender his custody of D's goods, intending, for example, to charge P with having stolen them.[3] Both these cases seem to fall within the section and both, incidentally, probably amount to theft contrary to section 1. In both cases, P is entitled to retain his interest until it is properly terminated.

If D is entitled under the civil law to have his property back again, but P declines to deliver it, it is submitted that D commits no offence by recovering possession by deception. Suppose D has made P a bailee at will. He terminates the bailment by demanding the return of the property. On P's refusal to restore it, D obtains it by deception. In most cases, of course, D will have a claim of right which will negative dishonesty; but, even if he does not, it is submitted that it ought to be held that there is no *actus reus* in such a case. It would generally be incongruous that a man should be guilty of an offence under the criminal law in obtaining property which, by the civil law, he is entitled to have. It is true that the manner of exercising such a right may be such that it justifies the intervention of the criminal law, as in the case where a right of entry on to premises is exercised by violence or threats,[4] blackmail[5] and demanding property on a forged instrument contrary to s. 7 of the Forgery Act 1913.[6] Though the attempt to recover property is an essential part of these offences, it is evidently the use of the force, of the menace and of the forged instrument which is the gist of the offence. It might be argued that deception should fall into the same category. Deception, however, is less socially dangerous than force and does not attract that revulsion which nowadays attaches to blackmail. Demanding on forged instruments is less easily distinguishable; but, like blackmail, it is an offence the gist of which is the demand. In the present case, the gist of the offence is the obtaining of property *belonging to another*: and, as against D, it ought not to be said that property belongs to P merely because P is in possession of it, if D is entitled to recover possession from him.

If, in the example given above, D had not terminated the bailment, the answer might be different. If he were then to recover possession by deception and with a dishonest intent—for example, intending to charge P with having lost the property—he should be guilty.[7]

---

[1] The definition of "belonging to another" in s. 5 (1) (above, para. [50]) applies to s. 15: see s. 34 (1), below, page 215.
[2] *Cf. Rose* v. *Matt*, [1951] 1 K.B. 810; [1951] 1 All E.R. 361.
[3] *Cf.* East 2 P.C. 558; *Smith* (1852), 2 Den. 449.
[4] Criminal Law Act 1977, Part II, Smith and Hogan, 771–779.
[5] Below, para. [315].
[6] *Parker*, above, para. [181].
[7] *Cf.* the corresponding case in theft, and *Turner* (No. 2), above, para. [58].

(d) The mens rea of obtaining property

[207] The constituents of the *mens rea* are:

(i) Deliberation or recklessness in making the deception;[1]
(ii) Dishonesty;[2]
(iii) Intention permanently to deprive;[3]
(iv) An intention, with or without a view to gain, to obtain property.

Constituents (i) and (ii) have been sufficiently examined above. Of (iii), it need be added only that the meaning of the term applies for the purposes of s. 15 with the necessary adaptation of the reference to appropriation.[4]

---

[1] Above, para. [162]–[163].
[2] Above, para. [181]–[187].
[3] Above, para. [118]–[133].
[4] Section 15 (3).

---

[208] There is no provision corresponding to that for theft that "it is immaterial whether the appropriation is made with a view to gain ..."[1] It can hardly be doubted, however, that no further element of this nature is required in addition to the elements of *mens rea* described above. The draftsman perhaps took the view that the intention to obtain property, which is implicit in the subsection, in itself constituted a view to gain so[2] that any further express requirement would be superfluous. The terms of the Act make it clear that if D appropriates P's diamond and throws it into a deep pond, intending to deprive both P and himself permanently of it, he is guilty of theft. It does not, in express terms, say that D is guilty of deception if he obtains the ownership in or possession of P's diamond by deception with the intention of throwing the diamond into the pond and depriving P and himself permanently of it. It is submitted, however, that the obtainer of the diamond would be guilty of obtaining by deception. It is desirable that the same principles should govern s. 15 as s. 1. If the property in the diamond did not pass, D might be charged under either section. It has been suggested above[3] that it will save a great deal of difficulty if, in such cases, the charge is always brought under s. 15. This advice would be vitiated if s. 15 were construed to require a view to gain.

---

[1] Section 1 (2), above, para. [108].
[2] See below, para. [209].
[3] See para. [33].

---

[209] It is submitted that an intention to obtain property for oneself or another is a constituent of the *mens rea*. The *actus reus* of the offence is not committed where D, dishonestly and by deception, causes P to be deprived of his property but neither D nor anyone else obtains it. An intention to deprive another of property is therefore not a sufficient *mens rea* for the offence.

If D dishonestly tells P that a work of art owned by P is obscene, that it is being looked for by the police and that the best thing he can do is to burn it, D is not guilty of an offence under the section, if P complies.[1] Suppose then, that D's object is to cause loss to one person, but that this will, incidentally, bring profit to another. For example, D induces P to exclude E from his will by telling P false stories of E's misconduct. D does not know or care who will profit as a result of E's exclusion from the will. Someone almost certainly will. Suppose that P, having substituted S's name for E's, dies and the executors pay the legacy to S. There is no doubt that D has dishonestly obtained property by deception for S. The *actus reus* is complete. Is it a defence for D to say that he did not *intend* to obtain property for anyone, that his only intention was to ensure that E did *not* benefit and that he would have been perfectly content with the outcome if P had decided to spend all his money in his lifetime?

It is arguable that the essence of the offence is the obtaining of property; that, in this example, the obtaining of the advantage is merely incidental to the fulfilment of D's plan and that, accordingly, D should not be guilty. If he were to be convicted, the iniquity of his conduct (when he came to be sentenced) would be found to lie in his malicious deprivation of E; but that is not an offence. This argument requires the adoption of the narrowest possible definition of "intention"—but there is precedent for it in other offences.[2]

---

[1] D might be guilty of criminal damage through an innocent agent.
[2] Smith and Hogan, 47–52.

C. OBTAINING A PECUNIARY ADVANTAGE BY DECEPTION

[210] The draft bill proposed by the Criminal Law Revision Committee would have created two offences of (i) obtaining credit by deception and (ii) inducing an act by deception with a view to gain. Part of the proposal did not commend itself to Parliament. Instead, a new clause, which became s. 16, was introduced to create the offence of obtaining a pecuniary advantage by deception. S. 16 (2) (a) proved to be so obscure that it amounted to "a judicial nightmare"[1] and it was repealed by the 1978 Act. Section 16, as amended, provides:

> "(1) A person who by any deception dishonestly obtains for himself or another any pecuniary advantage shall on conviction on indictment be liable to imprisonment for a term not exceeding five years.
> (2) The cases in which a pecuniary advantage within the meaning of this section is to be regarded as obtained for a person are cases where—
> (b) he is allowed to borrow by way of overdraft, or to take out any policy of insurance or annuity contract, or obtains an improvement of the terms on which he is allowed to do so; or
> (c) he is given the opportunity to earn remuneration or greater remuneration in an office or employment, or to win money by betting.
> (3) For purposes of this section 'deception' has the same meaning as in section 15 of this Act".

---

[1] *Royle* [1971] 3 All E.R. 1359 at *per* Edmund Davies, L.J.

---

[211] Section 16 creates only one offence.[1] Subsection (2) merely describes the various types of pecuniary advantage the obtaining of which will amount to an offence, just as s. 4 describes the property which may be stolen under s. 1. It is however important that the particulars of the offence should specify precisely what is the pecuniary advantage which the accused is alleged to have obtained. "If you indict a man for stealing your watch, you cannot convict him of attempting to steal your umbrella;"[2] and, equally a man who is charged with obtaining a pecuniary advantage of one sort should not be convicted of obtaining a pecuniary advantage of a completely different sort. So a conviction was quashed where D was charged with obtaining a pecuniary advantage within the meaning of s. 16 (2) (a) (now repealed) and the court held that he had obtained a pecuniary advantage, not within that provision, but within s. 16 (2) (c)[3].

[1] *Bale* v. *Rosier*, [1977] 2 All E.R. 160.
[2] *McPherson* (1857), Dears. & B. 197 at 200, *per* Cockburn, C.J.
[3] *Aston and Hadley*, [1970] 3 All E.R., 1045.

(a) Pecuniary advantage

[212] The meaning of this term is limited to the cases set out in the two remaining paragraphs of s. 16 (2). In these cases a pecuniary advantage is deemed to have been obtained. If the facts proved are within one of the paragraphs, it is no defence that D obtained no pecuniary advantage in fact.[1] Conversely, it is no offence to obtain a pecuniary advantage in fact, if the facts proved are not within one of the paragraphs. The pecuniary advantage may be obtained by the person practising the deception for himself, or it may be obtained for another. The words, "for a person" in subs. (2) refer not only to D but also to the other person referred to in subs. (1).[2] The following paragraphs[3] deal with the obtaining by D of a pecuniary advantage for himself; but it should be borne in mind that, in all cases, it is an offence to obtain a similar pecuniary advantage for another.

[1] *Turner*, [1974] A.C. 357 at 346–345 *per* Lord Reid; SHC 537; below, para. **[237]**. See criticism by Waters (1974), 37 M.L.R. 562.
[2] *Richardson* v. *Skells*, [1976] Crim. L.R. 448 (Recorder Self).
[3] **[213]**–**[218]**.

[213] (i) *Section 16 (2) (b)*.—It has been held that a person "is allowed to borrow by way of overdraft" when the overdraft facility is granted to him, though he never draws on it.[1] The judge pointed out that the subsection, says, "is allowed to borrow", not, "borrows"; that the alternative, "or obtains an improvement of the terms", plainly refers to the agreement: and (he thought) that actually borrowing might be an offence of obtaining property by deception, contrary to s. 15.[2] It appears that D is "allowed to borrow by way of overdraft" when, as a result of D's act, his bank becomes legally bound to grant, or extend, his overdraft, even though the act is a breach of contract with the bank.[3] This seems to strain the meaning of the words "allowed"—for the bank certainly did not consent to D's "borrowing" in this way— and "borrow by way of overdraft" for the bank might refuse, though it would be a breach of contract to do so, to honour the cheque.

It has been cogently argued[4] that the words "by way of overdraft" would not extend to a bank loan by crediting some other account in the same or another bank. If money were obtained there would probably be an offence under s. 15. If no money is obtained, there would be an offence of obtaining services by deception, contrary to 1978, s. 1, the payment for the service being the interest to be charged on the loan. That section would indeed seem to cover virtually all cases under s. 16 (2) (b).

[1] *Watkins*, [1976] 1 All E.R. 578 (Judge Paul Clarke).
[2] Possibly the obtaining of the money might be held to be too remote by analogy to the employment and betting cases (above, para. **[160]**), the obtaining of the overdraft facility corresponding to the obtaining of employment; but it is thought this would not be a good analogy.
[3] *Cf.* Williams, *TBCL*, 846 fn. 4.
[4] Griew, 7–23.

[214] It may be that insurance and annuity contracts were singled out because they are cases where the insurer is peculiarly dependent on the assured's good faith, since the special facts which affect the risk lie peculiarly within the latter's knowledge. It may, therefore, have been thought that the insurer needs special protection against the assured's fraud. Even if the increased sum were actually paid, the payment would probably be too remote[1] from the deception to constitute an offence under s. 15.

Contracts of insurance are contracts *uberrimae fidei*, so that, under the civil law, there is an obligation to make disclosure of any material circumstance. Failure to do so renders the contract voidable. No action will lie for damages, however—i.e., the non-disclosure is not "deceit"—and it is submitted that a mere non-disclosure will not amount to a deception ("by words or conduct") for the purposes of s. 16, unless the non-disclosure makes, and is known by the accused to make, the words or conduct which have been used positively misleading.[2]

---

[1] See above, para. [160].
[2] *Kylsant*, [1932] 1 K.B. 442; [1931] All E.R. Rep. 179. A case where "... a document has been put forward ... in such a form that though it stated every fact correctly, fact by fact, and everything was correctly stated by the card, yet the true effect of what was said was completely false and completely misleading."

---

[215] (ii) *Section 16 (2) (c)*.—Obtaining an office or employment by false pretences did not amount to an offence under the Larceny Act 1916, and will probably not be an offence under s. 15 of the Theft Act since the obtaining of the salary or wages is too remote from the false pretence or deception.[1] This case is now specifically dealt with. D commits an offence if he obtains an appointment by stating that he has a qualification which he does not possess; or if he obtains the appointment at a higher salary by stating that he has that qualification. The offence is also committed by one who obtains an appointment, or an appointment on better terms, for another in a similar way.

---

[1] *Lewis* (1922), Russell, 1186.

---

[216] It is not an offence under the section to obtain the opportunity to earn remuneration otherwise than in an office or in employment. The exact scope of the provision is doubtful. It has been argued[1] that a freelance author does not earn money "*in* employment" by his publishers, nor a solicitor "*in* employment" by his client; that "'employment' seems to be confined to a fairly narrow range of relationships and may in fact be limited to the relationship of master and servant." If this is so, it is unfortunate; but it may be that the provision is not so severely limited. The following cases which have actually occurred (without giving rise to any authoritative decision) might reasonably be regarded as instances of earning "in employment":

D calls at P's house and says, falsely, that the Forestry Commission has said that a tree in P's garden should be cut down and that he will do the job for £8. P employs him to cut down the tree.

D offers to clean P's windows. P says E is his regular window cleaner. D says, falsely, that E has retired. P employs D to clean the windows.

These are instances of the "employment" of independent contractors. Even the solicitor and the author may be said to be employed—in the "simple language ... used and understood by ordinary literate men and women"—[2] and, if they are employed, their remuneration is surely earned "in employment."

Before the 1968 Act, it was no offence where D induced P to take bets on credit by false pretences. If the horse backed by D happened to win, the money, it was held, was paid out because D had backed a winning horse, not because he had made a false pretence.[3] That case is also specifically dealt with; and D would apparently now be guilty whether he was allowed to bet on cash or credit terms.

---

[1] Griew, 7–25. *Cf. Levene* v. *Pearcey*, [1976] Crim. L.R. 63 and commentary thereon.
[2] *Treacy* v. *D.P.P.*, [1971] A.C. 537 at 565; [1971] 1 All E.R. 110 at 124, *per* Lord Diplock.
[3] *Clucas*, [1949] 2 K.B. 226; [1949] 2 All E.R. 40.

---

[217] (iii) *The mens rea of obtaining a pecuniary advantage.*—The constituents of the *mens rea* are:

(1) Intention or recklessness in making the deception.[1]
(2) Dishonesty.[2]
(3) An intention to obtain a pecuniary advantage.

Constituents (1) and (2) have been sufficiently examined above. Constituent (3) requires further discussion.

---

[1] Above, para. [162]–[163].
[2] Above, para. [181]–[187].

---

[218] Causing a pecuniary disadvantage to another is not necessarily the same thing as obtaining a pecuniary advantage for oneself or another. An exactly similar argument to that employed in relation to obtaining property by deception[1] may be relied on here. Suppose that D's object is to cause loss to one person, but that this will, incidentally, bring a pecuniary advantage to another. For example, E is a candidate for an appointment with P. D sends to P a reference containing false statements, so as to ensure that E will not be appointed. D does not know who the other candidates are, but, if his deception is the reason why E is not appointed, one of them will obtain a pecuniary advantage as the direct result of D's deception. Suppose that the deception is successful and, consequently, S is appointed and E is not. There is no doubt that D has dishonestly obtained a pecuniary advantage by deception for S. The *actus reus* is complete. Is it a defence for D to say that he did not *intend* to obtain a pecuniary advantage for anyone, that his only intention was to ensure that E did *not* obtain a pecuniary advantage and that he would have been perfectly content with the outcome if P had decided not to make an appointment at all?

It is arguable that the essence of the offence is the obtaining of the advantage; that, in this example, the obtaining of the advantage is merely incidental to the fulfilment of D's plan and that, accordingly, D should not be guilty.

---

[1] Above, para. [209].

D. OBTAINING SERVICES BY DECEPTION

[219] A person's labour is something of economic value. It is the principal means by which most people acquire property but it is not in itself property. To cause another by deception to do certain work is not an offence of obtaining property even though the deceived person has suffered an economic loss and the deceiver has made a corresponding gain as a result of the deception. The mischief is very much the same as where property is obtained but it is only since 1978 that this fact has been expressly recognised by the law. Where D induced P to render services in advance of payment, this might have been treated as an obtaining of credit by fraud contrary to the Debtor's Act 1869 (now repealed) or possibly the obtaining of a pecuniary advantage through the deferment of a debt by deception contrary to s. 16 (2) (a) of the Theft Act 1968 (also repealed). These offences did not however relate to the gist of the offence which was that P had been wrongly caused to expend his labour and thereby suffered an economic loss.

Section 1 of the Theft Act 1978[1] provides:

"(1) A person who by any deception dishonestly obtains services from another shall be guilty of an offence.

(2) It is an obtaining of services where the other is induced to confer a benefit by doing some act, or causing or permitting some act to be done, on the understanding that the benefit has been or will be paid for."

[1] See CLRC Working Paper, *Section 16 of the Theft Act*, (1974), *Thirteenth Report* (1977) Cmnd. 6733; Griew, Appendix 2; Spencer, [1979] Crim. L.R. 24; Leng (1979), 143 J.P. 16 & 33; Syrota, Annotations in *Current Law Statutes* and 42 M.L.R. 301; Williams, [1979] C.L.J. 4.

By Deception

[220] The service must be obtained by deception. D does not commit the offence where he succeeds in dishonestly enjoying the service without deception as where he secretly enters a cinema or cricket ground or where he induces a taxi-driver to carry him by threats. As in the case of other obtaining offences,[1] it must be proved that P was deceived and did, or caused or permitted the act conferring the benefit in consequence of the deception.

Section 5 (1) provides that "deception" has the same meaning as in s. 15 of the 1968 Act. This has been considered above[2] and only one matter calls for comment here. Because s. 1 requires that P must do the act, or cause or permit the act to be done, *on the understanding that it will be paid for,* it might be argued that the deception must relate to D's intention to pay. It is submitted that this is not so. The function of the words, "on the understanding that the benefit has been or will be paid for", is to exclude from the operation of the section services which are rendered gratuitously. If D induces his neighbour, P, to mow D's lawn as an act of friendship by falsely stating that he has sprained his ankle, no offence is committed. If D makes the same false statement and, at the same time, offers P £10 to do the job, an offence is committed if P mows the lawn on the understanding that he will be paid *and* because he believes the story of the sprained ankle, even though D always intends to pay and does pay. The lie is clearly a deception within s. 15 of the 1968 Act and it induces P to confer a benefit on the understanding that it will be paid for. Clause 1 of the Committee's draft bill and the bill first introduced into Parliament was restricted to "a deception going to the prospect of payment being duly made".[3] There is no such restriction in s. 1 of the Act and no warrant in the words used for implying it. The effect is that the section is rather wider than one might expect in a Theft Act. The offence may be committed where no economic loss is contemplated or caused. An example is the case where D induces P to let him have the hire of a car for the day by falsely stating that he has a driving licence. D may intend to pay or even have paid in advance but he is still guilty of an offence under the section. The result is consistent with s. 15 of the 1968 Act as applied in *Potger*.[4] A possible answer to this view is that the jury might not find D's conduct to be dishonest where he intends no economic loss. While the courts continue to leave a wide discretion to juries in deciding whether conduct is or is not dishonest, it is impossible to state the law with any degree of certainty; but if the conduct envisaged is not dishonest, then Potger was wrongly convicted.

---

[1] Above, paras. [154]–[187].
[2] Para. [161].
[3] Cmnd. 6733, p. 23.
[4] (1970), 55 Cr. App. R. 42; above, para. [184].

(a) Services

[221] The difficulty of defining "services" deterred the CLRC from proposing an offence of obtaining services by deception[1]. The CLRC thought that services would have to be defined to include *any* act which would not be materially different from the offence proposed in Clause 12 (3) of the draft bill attached to the Eighth Report and that had proved to be unacceptable to Parliament. The Committee therefore proposed a narrower offence of "Deception as to the prospect of payment".[2] This was included in the Bill introduced by the government but this time Parliament took a different view. A preference was expressed for an offence of obtaining services, widely defined, and, after reference back to the CLRC, the provision which became s. 1 emerged. Under s. 1 "services" may be:

(i) *any* act done by P provided that
(*a*) it confers a benefit on someone other than P and
(*b*) it is done on the understanding that the benefit has been or will be paid for; or
(ii) *any* act which P causes or permits to be done, whether by D or another, provided that
(*a*) it amounts to a benefit to, or confers a benefit on, someone other than P and
(*b*) it is caused or permitted on the understanding that the benefit has been or will be paid for.

---

[1] Cmnd. 6733, para. 7.
[2] Cmnd. 6733, p. 23.

(b) Some act

[222] It is submitted that any act which satisfies the conditions stated is enough. If this is right there is a substantial overlap with ss. 15 and 16 (2) (*b*) and (*c*) of the 1968 Act. To give property is undoubtedly to confer a benefit and in most cases under s. 15 the property is to be paid for. To allow D to borrow by way of overdraft or to take out a policy of insurance is to confer a benefit and the benefits are to be paid for by the interest on the overdraft and the payment of the premiums. The fact that the transfer of property is not ordinarily described as "services"[1] is not sufficient, it is submitted, to take the case out of s. 1 since subsection (2) states positively, "It is an obtaining of services where ..." It is true that 1978, s. 3 distinguishes between the supply of goods and the doing of a "service"; but it is clear that "services" in s. 1 is intended to include some types of supply of goods, for example, hire; and it is thought that there is no sufficient ground for distinguishing between one type of supply and another.

P must be induced to do or to cause or permit some act. A mere omission will not do. This is not likely to be a serious limitation on the operation of the section. Even where D seeks to induce P to refrain from doing something, it is probable that this will require some act, or the causing or permitting of some act. P, a bank manager has stated that he proposes to withdraw D's overdraft facility. D, by deception, persuades him not to do so. It is probable that P will do such acts as giving instructions to his staff and writing to D to confirm that the facility is still available; and P will, of course, permit D to draw further cheques on the bank though his account is overdrawn. What, however, if D, while recumbent in a deck chair at the seaside, falsely tells the attendant that he has paid the hire? The attendant permits D to continue to lie motionless in the chair. That is a benefit, but can it be described as an act? If a case of this kind, serious enough to deserve prosecution, should arise, it would be better dealt with under s. 2 (1) (*b*).[2]

---

[1] *Cf.* Spencer, [1979] Crim. L.R. at p. 28.
[2] Below, para. [237].

---

[223] The offence is not complete until the act which confers the benefit and which is to be paid for, is done. If, by deception, D obtains a high place on the local authority waiting list for council houses, he may well be said to have obtained a benefit but that benefit is not to be paid for. If, in due course, he is granted the tenancy the continuing deception has induced an act for which it is understood that he will pay through the rent and the offence is now complete. Obtaining a high place on the list should, however, be regarded as sufficiently proximate to amount to an attempt to commit an offence under the section. D has probably done the last act which it is necessary for him to do. Where, on the other hand, D obtains a contract under which *he* is to render services for payment, for example, to paint P's house, it seems that there is no offence under s. 1. The contract is not to be paid for. It might be argued that P has been induced by deception to cause or permit an act to be done, namely the performance of the contract by D and that act is to be paid for—it is to be paid for by P himself. This argument is fallacious because it is the *causing or*

permitting the act which is the benefit and which must be done on the understanding that it will be paid for. P's causing or permitting D to paint his house is not to be paid for. The case may be contrasted with that where a car-hire firm is induced by deception to cause a car to be delivered to D or to permit D to take the car. Here it is the causing or permitting which is to be paid for, not the taking of the car by D, and the case is covered by s. 1. When P does the act or causes the act to be done it is clear that the offence is complete only when the act has been done. It is less obvious when the allegation is that P permitted the act to be done. It might be argued that the offence is complete when P gives permission.[1] It is submitted that the better view is that the act conferring the benefit must be done in all cases. Only then are services obtained. If P has given permission for the act to be done, D will be guilty of an attempt.

---

[1] *Cf. Watkins*, [1976] 1 All E.R. 578, above para. **[213]** where "allowed" in 1968, s. 16 (2) (*b*) was held to mean the act of allowing; but that depended on the context.

(c) A benefit

[224] The act must be done, or caused or permitted, by P but it is sufficient that it is a benefit to anyone, not necessarily to D. The offence might be committed where, for example, D obtains education at a school or university for his son, beauty treatment for his wife, lodging for his mistress, the transfer of a centre-forward to his favourite football club or the cleaning of his employer's offices. There is unlikely to be much difficulty in determining that the act confers a benefit where it is done on the understanding that it has been or will be paid for. Men do not generally pay for the acts of others unless they will be beneficial. There may, however, be occasional cases which give rise to difficulty.

(d) "A benefit"—in whose eyes?

[225] In the great majority of cases the "benefit" will be something of economic value. D need not be financially enriched, as he is in the case where he obtains property. The service might be, for example a massage, which makes him feel better or a haircut which makes him look smarter. It is submitted that the effect of the service does not fail to be a benefit because the person acting or the jury, or persons generally, would not regard it as beneficial. Suppose D instructs the barber to shave his magnificent head of hair; the woodcutter to fell a splendid tree; the painter to respray his new Rolls Royce in shocking pink.[1] In each case P protests at what he regards as an act of barbarity but is finally persuaded by the offer of money to do the act. It would be quite inappropriate that D's liability should depend on the subjective judgment of others as to whether the act was beneficial. It is submitted that it is sufficient that it was a benefit in D's eyes.

In these examples, the act done—haircutting, tree-felling, painting—is a service in the ordinary commercial sense.

---

[1] But what if the tree or Rolls Royce belongs to D's estranged wife, E, who is horrified at what is done? Is the satisfaction of D's malice against E a benefit to him? D should be charged with criminal damage.

---

[226] Where the act done, or caused or permitted, has no apparent commercial value, it may be argued that it is incapable of being a benefit within the Act. It is submitted that, again, it is a sufficient answer that D was willing to pay, or expressed a willingness to pay, for the act in question. D promises P £100 if P will walk to York. It is well recognised in the law of contract that P's walking to York is such a "benefit" to D as to amount to a sufficient consideration to make D's promise enforceable. To borrow (and modify) the facts of a well-known case in the law of contract:[1] D says to P, the owner of certain boilers: "Let me weigh your boilers and I will pay you £100." D has no intention of paying but, on the understanding that he will be paid, P allows him to weigh the boilers. In the actual case, the Court appears to have had no idea why D had this strange wish to weigh someone else's boilers (and generations of law students have puzzled in vain over the matter) but they had no doubt that P had given consideration to D by allowing him to do so. It is submitted that in such a case P has conferred a benefit on D. This does not mean that the words "to confer a benefit" are deprived of all meaning, as the following cases show.

---

[1] *Bainbridge* v. *Firmstone* (1838), 1 Per. Dev. 2.

[227] Can the act be a benefit where the doing of it amounts to a criminal offence? The answer, it is submitted, depends on the purpose for which the offence was created. If the object of the law is to protect D (or the third party on whom the alleged benefit is conferred) against the act in question, the doing of it cannot be regarded as a benefit. The law would be inconsistent if it were otherwise. If D, aged 17, induces P to tattoo him by falsely representing that he intends to pay, P is *prima facie* guilty of an offence under the Tattooing of Minors Act 1969. P could not, of course, recover the price of the tattooing from D but, as is shown below[1] that is not in itself enough to rule out an offence under s. 1. However, the object of the law is to protect minors from being tattooed. The law regards this as an evil to be prevented. It cannot consistently regard it at the same time as a benefit. If P can show that he believed and had reasonable cause to believe that D was over 18, then he is not guilty of the offence. It is submitted, however, that this makes no difference—the act which the law aims to prevent has been done and it is incapable of amounting to a benefit.

Also falling into this category is the case where the act is done to D and is an act to which he cannot effectively consent. He promises to pay P if she will whip him so as to inflict actual bodily harm upn him. P (it seems) is guilty of an offence against D, notwithstanding his consent.[2] If the law regards the act as an offence against D, it cannot also regard it as a benefit to him. A rather more likely example, perhaps is that where D, a pregnant woman, promises to pay P to perform an illegal abortion on her. This is unlikely to be regarded as a benefit to D in law, whatever view she may take of it.

---

[1] Para. **[230]**.
[2] *Donovan*, [1934] 2 K.B. 498; SHC 423.

[228] Where the object of the law is something other than the protection of

D, the forbidden act may well amount to a benefit to D although it is an offence. Where D obtains the hire of the car by falsely representing that he has a licence he commits an offence by driving it but there seems to be no reason why the use of the car should not be regarded as a benefit to him. The law requiring a licence is not for the protection of the driver (or at least not primarily for his protection). If D obtains a television set on hire-purchase terms without paying the deposit required by the law, the whole transaction is illegal but the use of the set appears to be plainly a benefit to D. There are cases where the act done is a grave crime yet an undoubted benefit to D, as where he hires P to kill X who is blackmailing D or who stands between D and a vast inheritance. To be free of the blackmailer, to inherit the great estate, is undoubtedly a benefit to D.

[229] Some acts which are not criminal offences but are regarded by the law as immoral may also be incapable of amounting to benefits. D, by deception, induces P, a prostitute, to allow him to have intercourse with her. This is not an act forbidden by the criminal law. However, extra-marital sexual intercourse has always been regarded with disfavour by the law and, indeed, it is described as "unlawful" not only in the law of contract but also in the law of sexual offences. It may be that the courts will regard the prostitute's favours as incapable of amounting to a benefit in which case D will be guilty of no offence if he obtains them by deception.

(e) The understanding

[230] Where D is induced by deception to render for nothing a service for which he would normally charge, it is impossible to contend that the act has been done on the understanding that it has been or will be paid for and thus there is no offence against s. 1. For example, D, by a false hard-luck story, induces P, a taxi-driver, to give him a free ride. This is a gratuitous service and so not within the terms of s. 1. D is, however, probably guilty of the offence of obtaining exemption from liability to make a payment, contrary to 1978, s. 2 (1) (c).[1]

The understanding is that someone, not necessarily P, has been or will be paid. It will, for example, commonly be the case that P, an employee, will confer a benefit on the understanding that his employer has been or will be paid. The understanding may be that the payment will be made not by D but by a third party. For example, D represents that his firm will pay his hotel bill.

The understanding is that of P. D must know that P understands that payment has been or will be made. It should be irrelevant that P's understanding is unreasonable if D knows that it exists.[2] The understanding will usually amount to a contract but it is not necessary that it should do so.

Sections 2 and 3 of the 1978 Act are both confined to cases in which there is an enforceable liability. No such limitation is expressed in s. 1 and there is no ground for implying it. Suppose that D, a minor, by falsely representing that he intends to pay the fee of £100, induces P to give him flying lessons. P will probably be unable to sue successfully for the fee because it is most unlikely that flying lessons will be held to be a necessary for a minor. P has, however, undoubtedly conferred a benefit on D and D is guilty of an offence of obtaining services by deception. The case is much the same in principle as that where D, a minor, obtains non-necessary goods from P by deception. P is unable to sue D for the price of the goods but he can prosecute him to conviction for an offence under s. 15 of the 1968 Act.

---

[1] Below, para. **[240]**.
[2] *Contra*, Syrota, *CLS*.

(f) Paid for

[231] In the great majority of cases, the benefit will be paid for in money—whether in cash or by cheque. The CLRC intended the offence in clause 1 of their draft bill to be—

"... essentially an offence of dishonestly obtaining by deception services on which a monetary value is placed ..."[1]

The Committee relied on the word "payment" to confine the offence to services on which a monetary value is placed. Section 1 is different from the draft clause in important respects but in this respect it appears to be the same, "paid for" having the same effect as "payment." The question is whether "paid for" might include "payment" by goods or services instead of money. For example,

D agrees with P that, if P will paint D's house with D's paint, D will put a new engine in P's car when it has done 60,000 miles. P paints the house. D, as he intended all along, refuses to supply the engine. Or,

D promises P that, if P will dig D's garden, D will give him a night's lodging. P digs the garden and D, as he intended all along, refuses to give him the lodging.[2]

In these cases, it could scarcely be said that a monetary value had been placed on the services in question and, if "paid for" does indeed require the fixing of a monetary value, no offence is committed. Clearly, however, D's acts are within the mischief at which the section is aimed, as it is by no means impossible for "paid for" to be construed to include "payment" by goods or services,[3] and it is submitted that it should be so construed.

"Paid for" does not imply a payment appropriated to this particular service. D commits the offence if he induces P to repair his television by falsely representing that he has an annual maintenance contract with P's employer or if he borrows books from a University library by falsely representing that he is a student, thus implying that he has paid or will pay the fees which entitle him to this service; or if he induces an AA scout to repair his car by pretending that he is a member who has omitted to bring his membership card with him.

---

[1] 13th Report, para. 9.
[2] See the 2nd edition of this work, paras **[268]**–**[269]**, where these examples were considered in relation to 1968, s. 16 (1) (a). They amounted to offences only if the word "charge" were to be construed broadly so as to include "obligation". The point was never decided. See 3rd edition, para. **[208]**.
[3] *Cf. White* v. *Elmdene Estates*, [1959] 2 All E.R. 605 at 610–611 *per* Lord Evershed, M.R., below, para. **[248]**.

E. EVASION OF LIABILITY BY DECEPTION

[232] Section 2 of the Act might be held to create three offences. There are material differences in both *mens rea* and *actus reus* between the three paragraphs, (*a*), (*b*) and (*c*), and the section does not contain the common unifying element which enabled the court to hold that s. 16 of the 1968 Act creates only one offence.[1]

---

[1] *Bale* v. *Rosier*, [1977] 2 All E.R. 160, above, para. [211].

(a) Securing the remission of a liability

[233] S. 2 (1) (*a*) provides that a person is guilty of an offence where, by any deception, he:

> "dishonestly secures the remission of the whole or part of any existing liability to make a payment whether his own liability or another's."

This provision is limited to cases where there is an existing debt. It does not apply to the case where D by deception induces P to agree to render a service without charge or at a lower price than he would have charged in the absence of the deception. That case is covered by paragraph (*c*).[J] It applies only to legally enforceable liability. It has no application to a "debt" which is unenforceable because it arises out of a transaction which is illegal because it contravenes a statute,[2] or which, as in the case of a wagering debt, is declared void by statute or which, as in the case of money promised to a prostitute[3] for her services, is treated as illegal in the law of contract.[4]

Section 2 (2) provides: "subsection (1) shall not apply in relation to a liability that has not been accepted or established to pay compensation for a wrongful act or omission." The CLRC explained that this subsection would prevent the offence being committed where, for example, "a person lies about the circumstances of an accident in order to avoid the bringing of civil proceedings for negligence against him".[5] The reason is that the Committee could see no justification "for extending the criminal law to cases where the existence of any liability is disputed:" "the claimant can launch civil proceedings if he thinks he has been deceived when he absolved the other party from liability." They thought, however that "the dividing line is reached where liability is not disputed even though the amount of that liability is. On this basis it would be an offence ... for an antique dealer to lie about the age and value of jewellery sent to him for valuation which had been lost as a result of his admitted negligence." It may seem strange that D should be liable if he dishonestly induces P to reduce his claim from £500 to £100 but not liable if he induces him to drop the claim altogether. The latter seems a greater offence. The difference, perhaps, is that the former may result in a compromise and, while the compromise would be voidable for fraud, the onus would be on P to establish the fraud. Liability may sometimes be accepted or established before the quantum is agreed[6] but more often negotiations will lead to a single agreement covering both. If, in the course of such negotiations D tells lies which cause P to settle for £500 when otherwise he would have pursued his claim for £1000 no offence is committed for no liability has been accepted or established until the agreement is concluded. Nor is it by any means completely clear that the section fulfils the intention of the CLRC. Suppose that liability but not quantum has been accepted; that the true measure of

119

damages is £1000 and that D deceives P into accepting £500. It is difficult to see that any *liability to pay £1000* has been accepted or established so as to be capable of being remitted in part.

[1] Below, para. [**240**].
[2] *Cf. Garlick* (1958), 42 Cr. App. Rep. 141.
[3] *Cf. Caslin*, [1961] 1 All E.R. 246.
[4] Cheshire & Fifoot, *Law of Contract* (10th ed.) Part IV, Chapter 4.
[5] *Thirteenth Report*, para. 16.
[6] *Tomlin v. Standard Telephones and Cables Ltd.*, [1969] 3 All E.R. 201.

(b) Remission

[234] There is some doubt as to the meaning of "secures the remission of ... any existing liability". The words must be read in the light of the fact that it is an offence under paragraph (*b*) to induce a creditor to forgo payment with intent to make permanent default. Paragraph (*a*) does not require any intention to make permanent default. Plainly a difference is intended between remitting liability and forgoing payment. The obvious difference seems to be that forgoing payment does not affect the existing liability whereas remitting liability does. Similarly paragraph (*c*)[1] seems to be concerned with a deception which affects the legal relationship between two persons, whereas, quite clearly, (*b*) does not require any modification of the legal relationship but only a forbearance to enforce unchanged rights. A remission of a liability, like an exemption from or abatement of a liability, suggests some change in legal rights and duties.

It is thus arguable that remission is some act of the creditor which has the effect in law of wiping out the legal liability; that the defendant must intend to secure remission and therefore intend the legal liability to be wiped out. This would explain the absence of the words, "with intent to make permanent default", in (*a*) and in (*c*). If a person intends that something shall cease to exist he intends to deprive the owner of it for ever. If there were an offence consisting in intentionally destroying physical property belonging to another[2] it would be absurd to add, "with intent permanently to deprive the other of it". Destruction of a physical thing necessarily entails permanent deprivation of it. A thing in action, on the other hand, is a legal concept and capable of re-constitution. Since the remission has been obtained by fraud, P can rescind the remission whereupon the thing in action revives. It may be said therefore that the analogy is specious;[3] but we are concerned with intention and, even if D does intend one day to pay the debt which has been remitted (or from which he has obtained an exemption or abatement), he does not intend to restore the *legal right* of which he has deprived P. He intends permanently to deprive him of that. A mere agreement by a creditor that he will not enforce a legal liability does not destroy the debt in law.[4]

> "... it is a daily occurrence that a merchant or tradesman, who is owed a sum of money, is asked to take less. The debtor says he is in difficulties. He offers a lesser sum in settlement, cash down. He says he cannot pay more. The creditor is considerate. He accepts the proferred sum and forgives him the rest of the debt. The question arises: is the settlement binding on the creditor? The answer is that, in point of law, the creditor is

120

not bound by the settlement. He can the next day sue the debtor for the balance, and get judgment."[5]

---

[1] Below, para. [239].
[2] The Criminal Damage Act 1971, of course, makes it an offence to destroy *or damage* property belonging to another.
[3] *Cf. Spencer*, [1979] Crim. L.R. at p. 34.
[4] *Jorden* v. *Money* (1854), 5 H.L.C. 185, H.L.; *D. and C. Builders, Ltd.* v. *Rees*, [1966] 2 Q.B. 617; [1965] 3 All E.R. 837, C.A.
[5] [1966] 2 Q.B. 617 at 623, [1965] 3 All E.R. 837 at p. 839, 40 *per* Lord Denning M.R. There is no question of the debt being remitted in equity. Equity will not assist D because of his fraud.

---

[235] If the debtor's statement of his difficulties is a lie, he has dishonestly and by deception induced his creditor to forgo payment but he has not induced him to remit the debt. Suppose, however, that the debtor, D, meets all his creditors who agree together and with D to accept a dividend of 50%—that is, to forgive D one half of each of the debts he owes. Because each creditor is supplying consideration to the others by agreeing to surrender one-half of his debt, this agreement is enforceable in law and D's debt has been remitted in part. If he has practised a dishonest deception, he is guilty of an offence under (*a*). It is immaterial that D does not intend to make permanent default because he intends to deprive P permanently of his legal thing in action, his property. If D does not intend to make permanent default—he intends one day to pay up—this is a defence only if the jury find that it negatives dishonesty. The case is very much the same as of the person who, without authority, takes money from a till, intending to spend it but hoping that one day he will be able to repay the owner. In both types of case D intends to deprive the owner of his property permanently and, if he is dishonest, that is sufficient to entail liability.

[236] Others[1] think that the paragraph has a wider operation and this was, indeed, the opinion of the CLRC:

> "An example would be where a man borrows £100 from a neighbour and, when repayment is due, tells a false story of some family tragedy which makes it impossible for him to find the money; this deception persuades the neighbour to tell him that he need never repay."[2]

Has the man secured the remission of the liability to pay £100 when the liability continues unimpaired throughout? The neighbour may, of course, have intended to remit the liability but in law he did not do so. The draftsman used a strong word, "secured", and it is difficult to see that it has been satisfied. On the other hand, there is no doubt that the neighbour has been induced to forgo payment (of the existing, unremitted, debt) and, if the debtor intends to make permanent default, this is an offence under paragraph (*b*).

Another case which has been thought to come within paragraph (*a*) is that of a seller, P, who believes the buyer's, D's, false story that certain goods were never delivered and are not now needed and cancels the invoice which was sent. If the goods were delivered in fact, the debt exists throughout. There has been no rescission nor, indeed, any intention to rescind. P had no intention of remitting any debt because he had been led to believe that no debt existed. This again seems to be better regarded as a case of forgoing payment.

The effect would be that paragraph (*b*) would have a much wider sphere of operation than paragraph (*a*). This would be contrary to the expectations of the Committee. However criminal sanctions are imposed on defaulting debtors sparingly and it is not inappropriate that they should be applicable only where D causes P actually to give up his legal right or where he has an intent to make permanent default.[3] The limitation on the combined effect of paragraphs (*a*) and (*b*) would not be a serious one. If, however, a construction similar to that suggested for paragraph (*a*) were applied to paragraph (*c*), the latter paragraph would also be rendered largely though not entirely inoperative. This might be thought more serious because (*c*) is the only provision which extends to prospective as well as existing liability.[4] Unless a lot of weight is put on the use of the word "secures" in (*a*) as contrasted with "obtains" in (*c*), it would be difficult to construe (*a*) so as to require an effect on liability in law and (*c*) so as not to do so; and, in order to salvage (*c*), it may be argued that the right interpretation is to construe "secure the remission" in (*a*) to mean "secure an agreement to remit"[5] and to accept that the words "or to forgo payment" in (*b*) are inoperative. Even so, it is submitted that the offence would be committed only where P knows that there is a liability and intends to remit it.[6] If he is deceived into believing that there is no liability he is induced to forgo payment but not to agree to remit anything. It is argued below that the consequences of a strict and (it is submitted) true construction of (*c*) are by no means disastrous; and it is submitted that the right course is to construe "secure the remission of liability" to mean what it says.

---

[1] *Cf.* Syrota, Current Law Statutes; Griew, 15–32.
[2] 13th Report, para. 13.
[3] Even if it is held then that D has not secured the remission of the debt, may he be held guilty of an attempt to do so? It seems not. In cases such as these, both D and P may believe that the debt has been remitted. If they are not lawyers, they may well believe that the promise not to sue for the debt is binding. But D has achieved the precise factual result which he intended and that result is not a crime. The steps taken towards the result and the accomplishment of it cannot therefore be regarded as an attempt. *Percy Dalton, (London) Ltd.* (1949), 33 Cr. App. Rep. 102, C.C.A., at 110, per Birkett J.; *Haughton* v. *Smith*, [1973] 3 All E.R. 1109 at 1118.
[4] Though even here s. 1 would fill much of the function intended by the CLRC for para. (*c*)—where a person obtains services at a reduced rate: see *Thirteenth Report*, Cmnd. 6733, para. 14.
[5] Professor Williams in his Note of Reservation accepted that this was the meaning of para. (*a*): *Thirteenth Report* Cmnd. 6733, p. 19.
[6] Griew, 15–33.

(c) Inducing creditor to wait for or forgo payment

[237] Section 2 (1) (*b*) provides that a person commits an offence where, by any deception, he—

> "with intent to make permanent default in whole or in part on any existing liability to make a payment, or with intent to let another do so, dishonestly induces the creditor or any person claiming payment on behalf of the creditor to wait for payment (whether or not the due date for payment is deferred) or to forgo payment;"

This clearly applies where the liability is neither remitted nor postponed. D remains liable to pay throughout but the creditor is induced to refrain from taking steps to enforce that liability for the time being or at all. The paragraph is concerned with the "stalling debtor." It was held in *D.P.P.* v. *Turner*[1] that it was an offence under s. 16 (2) (*a*) of the 1968 Act where D, by deception, secured relief from the claims of his creditor for only a short period. D, being pressed one Saturday for the payment of £38, gave his creditor a cheque for that sum knowing that it would not be honoured. It was dishonoured on Monday. It was held that the debt had been "evaded." All that D got, or could have hoped to get, from his deception was relief from the demands of his creditor for a day or two. This should certainly not be a serious offence and it is now not criminal at all, in the absence of an intent to make permanent default. If, as soon as P goes off with the worthless cheque, D moves to another town, leaving no forwarding address, he may now be guilty of an offence if the court or jury is satisfied that he intended never to pay.

It is presumably not necessary that the creditor should agree to wait for or forgo payment. He may be induced to wait or forgo because he is led to believe that he has no choice in the matter. For example, D, seeing the rent-collector at the door sends his small son to say, "Daddy's out." If the disgruntled rent-collector goes away, he has been induced to wait for payment even though his present claim to the money is not waived for an instant. Similarly where a tradesman is induced to write off the liability as a bad debt because he is persuaded, falsely, that D will never have the means to pay.

---

[1] [1974] A.C. 357; [1973] 3 All E.R. 124, above, para. [212]; cf. *Smith* v. *Koumourou*, [1979] Crim. L.R. 116 and commentary.

---

[238] Section 2 (3) provides:

"For purposes of subsection (1) (*b*) a person induced to take in payment a cheque or other security for money by way of conditional satisfaction of a pre-existing liability is to be treated not as being paid but as being induced to wait for payment."

Apart from this provision, acceptance of a cheque amounts to a conditional payment of a pre-existing debt which suspends the creditor's remedies until the cheque has either been met or dishonoured. In the absence of the provision, then, a creditor who had accepted as valid a worthless cheque might well have been held neither to have waited for nor to have forgone payment. The effect of s. 2 (3) is that D commits an offence under paragraph (*b*) if, having honestly bought and received goods at a shop, or honestly enjoyed the services of a hotel, he pays by a cheque which he knows to be worthless and goes off leaving a false address, intending never to pay.[1]

---

[1] He is probably also guilty of an offence under s. 3; below, para. [241].

(d) Obtaining exemption from or abatement of liability

[239] Section 2 (1) (*c*) provides that a person commits an offence where, by any deception, he—

"dishonestly obtains any exemption from or abatement of liability to make a payment."

Whereas paragraphs (*a*) and (*b*) are confined to existing liabilities, (*c*) applies simply to "liability to make a payment" which, in the context, must include, though it is not confined to, a prospective liability. Like paragraph (a) and unlike (b) it is expressed to be concerned with an effect on liability. If the Act is strictly construed, the offence is not committed where P makes a wholly inoperative agreement to grant D an exemption from or abatement of liability to make a payment. It was intended to apply to the case where D dishonestly obtains a rate rebate or a reduction in his rent for the future.[1] Probably D's legal liability is unaffected in either case. In the case of the rates his liability will be for the full rateable value of the property as it is, not as he has misrepresented it to be; and the reduction of the rent is likely to be inoperative either because of the lack of consideration rather than the fraud which would render a contract for the reduced rent voidable but not void. Paragraph (b) cannot be invoked because there is not yet an existing liability. However, a day will come when there will be an existing liability. The rates or rent fall due. P demands the lesser sum. He does so because the deception is continuing. If D intends to make permanent default has he not now induced P to forgo payment of an existing liability? It is submitted that he has. Thus, the effect of giving paragraph (c) its strict and, it is submitted, true, construction, is that (i) para. (c), like para. (a), is confined to a small number of cases; and (ii) in other cases guilt is limited to those where there is an intent to make permanent default and (iii) is postponed until the time when an actual liability exists and is forgone. The consequences are not serious and may indeed be held to be a very proper limitation on criminal liability. Another type of case to which (c) was intended to apply is that where D induces P to provide him with goods or services at a cheap rate by falsely stating that he belongs to a particular organisation or that he is an old age pensioner. Probably the offence is committed in these cases. There is a voidable contract to supply the goods or service at the reduced rate so that, arguably, liability, *pro tem*, has abated. If P actually supplies the goods or service he could no doubt recover the full value in an action in quasi-contract[2] but, until he does so, his only rights are to have the price agreed or to rescind the contract for fraud. Even if there is no offence under (c) at the time of the agreement, however, an offence would be committed under (b) so soon as the goods or service was supplied and P forbore from demanding the balance of the price because of the continuing deception. These acts will also amount to offences against 1968, s. 15 and 1978, s. 1, depending on whether it is goods or services which are obtained, but a charge under s. 2 (1) (c) more accurately describes the gist of the offence. What D has really done wrong is not to get the thing at all but to get it more cheaply. Where D obtains goods for nothing he is again guilty under both 1968, s. 15 and paragraph (c); but where he obtains services for nothing, the only charge is under paragraph (c). He is not guilty under 1978, s. 1, because there is no understanding that the services will be paid for.

---

[1] *Thirteenth Report*, Cmnd. 6733, para. 15.
[2] See [1971] Crim. L.R. 448 at 453 *et seq.*

(e) Evasion of the liability of another

[240] All the offences under s. 2 may be committed in respect of the liability of another. Under s. 2 (1) (a) the liability remitted may be "his own liability or another's." Under s. 2 (1) (*b*) the intent may be to let another make default on an existing liability. Section 2 (4) provides—

> For purposes of subsection 1 (*c*) "obtains" includes obtaining for another or enabling another to obtain.

So an offence may be committed by an accountant who secures the remission of a client's existing liability, a wife who persuades her husband's creditor to forgo payment of the husband's debt or a company secretary who obtains exemption of the company from liability to make a payment.

CHAPTER V

MAKING OFF WITHOUT PAYMENT

[241] The Theft Act 1978,[1] s. 3 (1) provides:

"Subject to subsection (3) below, a person who, knowing that payment on the spot for any goods supplied or service done is required or expected from him, dishonestly makes off without having paid as required or expected and with intent to avoid payment of the amount due shall be guilty of an offence."

This section is intended to deal with troublesome cases such as that of the customer in the restaurant or at the petrol station who departs without paying in such circumstances that it is not possible to prove that he had a dishonest intention before he received the food or the petrol as the case may be. In *D.P.P.* v. *Ray*[2] such a case was brought within the law of evading a debt by deception but the deception found by the court was of a highly artificial character and in many other similar cases it would be impossible to discern any deception at all.

---

[1] For discussion of the 1978 Act, see para. **[219]**, footnote 1, above.
[2] [1974] A.C. 370; [1973] 3 All E.R. 131 above, para. **[156]**.

(a) Makes off

[242] It is the dishonest departure from "the spot" which is the offence. If D leaves a café, absent-mindedly forgetting to pay and, on getting home, remembers and resolves not to do so, he commits no offence. Most offences (though not all) under this section will occur on business premises and if D forms the dishonest intention at any time while he is on the premises he may be guilty. If he is 100 yards down the road before he remembers that he has not paid his bill, the position is more doubtful. Since it is escaping his creditor's demand for the price which is the gist of the offence, he should perhaps be regarded as immune from liability once he has moved innocently "out of range of the creditor." If so, it might be different if, 100 yards down the road, he realises he has not paid because he hears the waiter in hot pursuit and, at that moment, decides to make a run for it.

"Makes off" has a pejorative connotation and is aimed primarily at the person who walks out secretly or runs or drives off at top speed. It is not necessarily confined to such cases, however. Suppose that D, a heavyweight boxer, tells the small and timorous café owner, that he has decided not to pay and walks out at a leisurely pace. If he has no good reason for doing so and is acting dishonestly, he is surely guilty of the offence. Similarly where D succeeds in getting away by means of a trick or deception (as there was held to be in *Ray*). In all these cases the departure is made without the consent of the creditor. Arguably it is different where the creditor is tricked into agreeing that D may go without paying.[1] It may be said that "makes off" is used instead of the neutral "departs" with some purpose and that the most likely purpose is to exclude the case of departure with consent. This puts a lot of weight on the pejorative nature of "makes off". Moreover, "departure by deception" is also bad and may fairly be considered a variety of making off. If, at the end of a taxi-ride, D tells the driver that he must go into a house to get some money and disappears, never to return to the spot, it is submitted that he is guilty notwithstanding the driver's concurrence in his departure.

---

[1] *Cf.* Spencer, [1979] Crim. L.R. at p. 37.

(b) Goods supplied or service done

[243] The debt must arise from the supply of goods or the doing of a service. A shoplifter in a shop which is not a self-service store is not guilty of the offence when he makes off, because no goods have been *supplied* to him. It is submitted, however, that goods are supplied by P to D where P has made them available to be taken and they are taken by D. If it were not so, the section would fail to cover one of the primary cases at which it is aimed—the self-service petrol station. The customer who honestly fills up his car and then dishonestly makes off has been supplied with petrol. What if he took the petrol dishonestly? Since this is an appropriation and theft of the petrol[1] it is arguable that it cannot be regarded as a "supply" of it. If that were right, the offences under 1968, s. 1 and 1978, s. 3 would be mutually exclusive, which might be inconvenient. Probably D is "supplied" whether he is honest or dishonest when he takes the petrol and the dishonest customer in the self-service shop is also "supplied" with goods.

There is no definition of goods or of service. "Service" is not the same as the "services" of section 1 but in practice "goods supplied or service done" in s. 3 may turn out to be more or less coincident with "services" in s. 1.[2] The service must however be "done", presumably by P or his agents. Is a service "done" where D takes advantage of a proferred facility? For example, he parks his car in an unmanned car park and leaves by lifting up the barrier and driving off without paying. Probably the custody of the car by the proprietor of the park while it was left there would be regarded as a "service done." It might be otherwise, however, if D were to leave his car in a street parking bay and drive off without putting money in the meter. The highway authority could not be said to have custody of the car, but it is arguable that the provision of a parking space on the highway is a service. That case is, in any event better dealt with under the appropriate regulations.

---

[1] Above, para. **[32]**.
[2] See above, para. **[221]**.

---

[244] Section 3 (2) provides:

"For the purposes of this section "payment on the spot" includes payment at the time of collecting goods on which work has been done or in respect of which service has been provided."

It is not clear that this provision is really necessary. The cases to which it applies are probably adequately covered by the words of subsection (1). It is made clear beyond all doubt that D may commit the offence where he makes off with his clothes which have been cleaned, his shoes which have been repaired or his car which has been serviced. The existence of subsection (2) may, however, cast a little doubt on another type of case. D makes off without paying the shoeshine boy who has cleaned his shoes. Work has been done on the goods but D was not "collecting" them. "Collecting" seems to imply that D is acquiring possession of the goods. He has never parted with possession of his shoes. Similarly where D calls a mechanic to repair his car which is broken down by the roadside. In no sense does the motorist "collect" his car when he drives off. It is submitted that these cases, though not within s. 3 (2) are adequately covered by s. 3 (1). If so, subsection (2) is indeed superfluous.

(c) Unenforceable Debts

[245] Section 3 (3) provides:

> "Subsection (1) above shall not apply where the supply of the goods or the doing of the service is contrary to law, or where the service done is such that payment is not legally enforceable."

The CLRC explained this provision on the ground that "the new offence is essentially a protection for the legitimate business".[1] The offence is thus not committed where D makes off from a prostitute's flat, a brothel, a disorderly house, an obscene performance in a night-club, a drug-pedlar's premises or a betting shop, without paying for the principal service or goods provided therein. If some goods or service has been legitimately provided—for example, drinks in the night-club—the answer will depend on whether the vice of the principal service infects collateral transactions, which it may do where it amounts to illegality but should not do where the principal transaction is merely void, as in the case of the wager in the betting shop.

Where the transaction is "contrary to law", there is no distinction between goods and a service but where it is merely "not legally enforceable", services only are affected. Thus the subsection applies where there is a merely void contract for services—for example, the wager—but it seems that it does not apply where there is a merely void contract for the supply of goods. If an impecunious minor has her hair done at the most expensive salon in London and walks off without paying it seems she commits no offence because the service done was not "necessary" and payment for it is unenforceable. If, however, the same impecunious minor dines on caviar and champagne she may be guilty of making off without payment even though—as is most probable—these expensive items cannot be proved to be necessaries for her. There is nothing contrary to law in supplying non-necessary goods to a minor. A seller may properly do so if he chooses but he will not be able to recover the price. Since goods and not services are involved, it is immaterial that payment is not legally enforceable.

---

[1] 13th Report, para. 19.

(d) Without having paid

[246] The only problem which seems to arise here concerns the person who gives a worthless cheque in "payment" of the debt. Since s. 2 (3) applies only to the offence under s. 2 (1) (*b*) it is arguable that, for the purposes of other offences under the Act, a person who takes a cheque by way of conditional satisfaction of a pre-existing liability is to be treated as being paid.[1] As D will be guilty of the more serious offence under s. 2 (1) (*b*), the question may not be of great importance. If it arises, the answer may well be that D has not paid "as required or expected". P requires and expects payment in legal tender or by a good cheque. Payment by a worthless cheque no more satisfies his requirement or expectation than payment in counterfeit money. If the cheque is backed by a cheque card, D has probably paid as required or expected even though D has no authority to use the card.

[1] Syrota, Current Law Statutes.

(e) Mens Rea

[247] (i) *Dishonestly.*[1] D must be dishonest when he makes off. He may have been dishonest from the start (in which case he will also be guilty of obtaining property or services by deception) or have formed the dishonest intention only after the goods were supplied or the service done. Whether D was dishonest or not will be a question for the jury but it seems clear that he could not be held to be dishonest if he believed that payment was not due (even though required and expected by P) because the goods supplied or service done was deficient in some fundamental respect. If D were prepared to leave his name and address, that would be cogent evidence of honesty whereas secret departure or flight would be strong evidence of dishonesty.

[1] Above, paras. [109]–[117].

[248] (ii) *Knowing that payment on the spot ... is required or expected from him.* Clearly D is not guilty if he wrongly supposes that the goods have been supplied or the service done on credit and that he is going to receive a bill through the post; or if, for example, he is under the impression that his firm has arranged to pay his hotel bill. D's belief that he has been given credit, whether reasonable or not, is inconsistent with the *mens rea* required. A problem of some practical importance arises from the common use of credit cards in shops, restaurants and garages. For example D, who is carrying a valid credit card, sees a notice at a garage, "Credit Cards Accepted," and drives in, intending to "pay" by use of his credit card. Having filled his tank, or had it filled by an attendant, he notices that he is unobserved, decides that there is a chance to have the petrol for nothing and drives off. His conduct is clearly within the mischief at which the section is aimed but is it within the words of the section? When D drives off does he know "that payment on the spot ... is required or expected from him"? The notice may fairly be considered to have become a term in the contract of sale when D entered the garage and bought petrol in reliance on it. The retailer of the petrol, P, is no longer entitled to require payment in cash as he would have been in the absence of the notice and he can hardly "expect" payment in cash from a customer with a valid credit card in his pocket. D could not be held to know that payment in cash is required or expected. He must know that he is required or expected *either* to pay in cash *or* to produce his credit card and sign the sales voucher. Only if the production of the card can be said to be "payment" within the meaning of s. 3 is the offence committed.

P is bound by his contract with the Credit Card Company to honour D's valid credit card and, if he does so, the Company is bound to credit his bank account with the value of the sales voucher. D is getting credit, but the credit is being given to him by the Company, not by P. P is giving credit, but he is giving it to the Company for, henceforth, he will look to the Company for payment. He expects to have nothing more to do with D. By producing his credit card, D, *in practice*, discharges his obligation to pay P for the petrol. In strict legal theory the obligation is not discharged for, if the Credit Card Company failed to fulfil its obligations, P could no doubt recover the price of the petrol from D—but this is a highly improbable contingency, unlikely to be present to the mind of either. Both will regard D's obligation as discharged. It is submitted then that the production of the credit card and signing of the sales voucher is fairly regarded as "payment" by D.[1] It follows that D knows that "payment" is required and expected from him and commits an offence when he makes off.

Similar considerations apply where P has indicated that he will take a cheque, whether backed by a cheque card or not. In modern usage, a cheque is treated as the equivalent of cash[2] and the debtor's obligation is discharged conditionally on the cheque being honoured. It is common to speak of payment by cheque and this should be regarded as a payment within s. 3. Because the debt is discharged, though only conditionally, the case is stronger than that of the credit card. On the other hand, the seller who honours a credit card has much better security for payment than one who takes a cheque not backed by a cheque card so it would be strange to regard the latter as paid and the former as not paid.

---

[1] "... the word 'payment' in itself is one which, in an appropriate context, may cover many ways of discharging obligations ..." *White* v. *Elmdene Estates, Ltd.*, [1959] 2 All E.R. 605 at 610–611 *per* Lord Evershed, M.R.
[2] *D. and C. Builders, Ltd.* v. *Rees*, [1965] 3 All E.R. 837 at 843 *per* Winn, L.J.

[249] (iii) *With intent to avoid payment.* The question which arises here is whether there must be an intention *permanently* to avoid payment. It was evidently at one time the intention of the Committee so to require[1] but it is not clear if the Act carries out this intention. Comparison may be made with s. 2 (1) (*b*) which expressly requires *permanent* default. In *Corbyn* v. *Saunders*[2] the Divisional Court declined to import "permanently" into the same phrase in the Regulation of Railways Act 1889, s. 5 (3). Probably, then, an intention to avoid payment temporarily will be enough, provided, of course, that it is a dishonest intention. If the defendant, having eaten an exceptionally expensive meal, discovers that he has lost his wallet and, realising that it will be weeks before he can raise the price of the meal, makes off, it will be for the jury to say whether his intention to pay when he is able negatives dishonesty.[3]

[1] Working Paper, para. 38.
[2] [1978] 2 All E.R. 697; [1978] Crim. L.R. 169.
[3] *Cf. Feely*, above, para. [**116**].

CHAPTER VI

OTHER OFFENCES INVOLVING FRAUD

1 FALSE ACCOUNTING

[250] Section 17 of the Theft Act replaces ss. 82 and 83 of the Larceny Act 1861 and the Falsification of Accounts Act 1875. It provides:

> "(1) Where a person dishonestly, with a view to gain for himself or another or with intent to cause loss to another,—
> (a) destroys, defaces, conceals or falsifies any account or any record or document made or required for any accounting purpose; or
> (b) in furnishing information for any purpose produces or makes use of any account, or any such record or document as aforesaid, which to his knowledge is or may be misleading, false or deceptive in a material particular;
> he shall, on conviction on indictment, be liable to imprisonment for a term not exceeding seven years.
> (2) For purposes of this section a person who makes or concurs in making in an account or other document an entry which is or may be misleading, false or deceptive in a material particular, or who omits or concurs in omitting a material particular from an account or other document, is to be treated as falsifying the account or document".

A. THE ACTUS REUS

[251] The two new offences created by this section may be committed by anyone whereas the 1861 offences applied only to officers of companies and the 1875 Act was confined to "any clerk, officer or servant". The new provisions, unlike the old, would apply, for example, to the honorary treasurer of a members' club who is not a servant.

[252] The section is confined to records or documents "made or required for any accounting purpose". In the context, this plainly means accounting in the financial sense. The wording is clearly wide enough to cover an account produced by mechanical means, as in the case of a taximeter.[1] Falsifying the gas-meter or electricity-meter would seem to be an offence within the section. On the other hand, dishonestly to falsify the odometer of a car with a view to gain would not normally be an offence under this section since the odometer of a car is not usually a record made or required for any accounting purpose. It would be otherwise, however, if the odometer reading were used to calculate a mileage allowance due to the driver. It would then be indistinguishable from the taximeter case. The information in the document may be furnished for other purposes in addition to accounting. It is sufficient that accounting is one of the purposes for which it is required. So a hire-purchase agreement was held to be a document within the section[2]. The "material particular" need not be one which is directly connected with the accounting purpose. If it is required for an accounting purpose, it is sufficient that it is "false in some respect that matters".[3]

---

[1] *Cf. Solomons*, [1909] 2 K.B. 980.
[2] *Mallett* (1978), 66 Cr. App. Rep. 239 C.A.
[3] Ibid.

B. THE MENS REA

[253] The act must be done:
  (i) dishonestly,
  (ii) with a view to gain for himself or another or with intent to cause loss to another and, in the case of s. 17 (1) (*b*),
  (iii) with knowledge that the document is or *may be* misleading, false or deceptive in a material particular. Recklessness is sufficient.

[254] As to dishonesty, reference may be made to the discussion of this element in other crimes.[1] Similar problems arise here. For example, the bookmaker's clerk may "borrow" his employer's money to place bets (with a view to gain) and falsify the accounts to cover up his action but with every intention and expectation of replacing the money before it is missed. Is he dishonest?

---

[1] Above, paras. [109]–[114] and [181–[186].

---

[255] As to the view to gain or intent to cause loss, see the discussion of these elements in connection with other crimes.[1] Suppose D falsifies the accounts so as to deceive his employer into thinking that D's department is more profitable than it really is, in order to ensure that D's employment will not be terminated.[2] It may be argued that D has no view to gain in such a case, since he intends to give full economic value for the wages he receives;[3] but, whether or not this is a sound argument (and it is probably not) he perhaps has an intent to cause loss in that he knows that the effect of his deception will be that his employer will keep open an uneconomic department. This, however, is only an "oblique" intention[4] and it is arguable that a direct intention must be proved.

---

[1] Below, paras. [312]–[322].
[2] *Cf. Wines*, [1953] 2 All E.R. 1497.
[3] See below, paras. [315]–[318].
[4] Smith and Hogan, 47–52.

---

[256] Has D a view to gain or an intent to cause loss where he falsifies an account in order to conceal losses or defalcations which have already occurred? Since, by s. 34 (2) (*a*)[1]:
  "(i) 'gain' includes a gain by keeping what one has, as well as a gain by getting what one has not; and
  (ii) 'loss' includes a loss by not getting what one might get, as well as a loss by parting with what one has;"
the answers will be generally in the affirmative. At least one of the objects

which D will have in view will be that of avoiding or postponing making restitution—"keeping what one has" and preventing P from getting what he might. The Court of Appeal has said[2] that putting off the evil day of having to pay is a sufficient gain. If D's *sole* object is to avoid prosecution, it is arguable that he is not guilty of the offence.[3] This result has been criticised[4] but it is perhaps not unreasonable. Telling lies to avoid prosecution, whether in an account or elsewhere, if it is to be an offence, would more naturally find a place in the offence of perverting the course of justice[5] than in the Theft Act. If D is penniless, there may be a difficulty in proving that he intended to do more than avoid prosecution; but, if he is employed, he may find it difficult credibly to deny that one of his objects was the continuance of his wages; and, as has been seen, this is almost certainly enough. Gain need not be D's sole object.

---

[1] Below, para. [**312**].
[2] *Eden* (1971), 55 Cr. App. Rep. 193 at 197.
[3] If D has an intent to make permanent default he is guilty of evading liability by deception, contrary to 1978, s. 2 (1) (*b*), above, para. [**237**].
[4] Griew, 8–05.
[5] Smith and Hogan, 722–726.

---

2 LIABILITY OF COMPANY OFFICERS FOR OFFENCES UNDER SECTIONS 18 AND 19

[**257**] Section 18 of the Act provides:

> "(1) Where an offence committed by a body corporate under section 15, 16 or 17 of this Act is proved to have been committed with the consent or connivance of any director, manager, secretary or other similar officer of the body corporate, or any other person who was purporting to act in any such capacity, he as well as the body corporate shall be guilty of that offence, and shall be liable to be proceeded against and punished accordingly.
>
> (2) Where the affairs of a body corporate are managed by its members, this section shall apply in relation to the acts and defaults of a member in connection with his functions of management as if he were a director of the body corporate."

An offence can be committed by a body corporate only through one of its responsible officers.[1] In every case where a corporation is guilty of an offence, then, there must be at least one of the officers referred to in the section who consented or connived. If he is unidentifiable, then only the corporation may be convicted; if he can be identified, he will, in the great majority of cases be guilty of an offence under ss. 15, 16 and 17 independently of s. 18, either as a principal offender or as a secondary party. Connivance or an express consent to an offence would seem sufficient to found liability under the general law,[2] apart from s. 18. The section is intended to go farther than this:

> "The clause follows a form of provision commonly included in statutes where an offence is of a kind to be committed by bodies corporate and where it is desired to put the management under a positive obligation to prevent irregularities, if aware of them. Passive acquiescence does not,

under the general law, make a person liable as a party to the offence, but there are clearly cases (of which we think this is one) where the director's responsibilities for his company require him to intervene to prevent fraud and where consent or connivance amounts to guilt."[3]

---

[1] Smith and Hogan, 148–154; *Tesco Supermarkets* v. *Nattrass*, [1972] A.C. 153: [1971] 2 All E.R. 127, H.L.
[2] Smith & Hogan, 153–154.
[3] *Eighth Report*, Cmnd. 2977, para. 104.

[258] The "positive obligation" clearly does not go so far as to impose liability for negligence; you cannot consent to that of which you are unaware,[1] and "connivance" involves turning a blind eye, which has always been regarded as equivalent to knowledge.[2] Even "passive acquiescence" has sometimes been held sufficient to found liability as a secondary party, under the general law, but probably only on the ground that inactivity was a positive encouragement to others to commit the unlawful act in question.[3] Section 14 may go a little beyond this, though that is not entirely clear and the provision does not seem yet to have been interpreted by the courts.[4] At least it eases the Crown's task to the extent that they have proved their case if they prove consent and they do not have to go on to establish that the consent amounted to an aiding and abetting, etc.

---

[1] *Re Caughey, Ex parte Ford* (1876), 1 Ch.D. 521 at 528, C.A., *per* Jessel, M.R. and *Lamb* v. *Wright & Co.,* [1924] 1 K.B. 857 at 864.
[2] Edwards, *Mens Rea in Statutory Offences*, 202–205; *Williams*, C.L.G.P. 159; Smith and Hogan, 102–103.
[3] Smith and Hogan, 118–120.
[4] *Cf.* the draconian provision in the Borrowing (Control and Guarantees) Act 1946, s. 4 (2), criticised by Upjohn, J. in *London and Country Commercial Property Investments, Ltd.* v. *A.-G.,* [1953] 1 All E.R. 436 at 441.

---

3 FALSE STATEMENTS BY COMPANY DIRECTORS, ETC.

[259] Section 19 (see page 243, below) replaces s. 84 of the Larceny Act 1861. It is wider than the earlier provision in that it applies to officers of unincorporated as well as incorporated bodies—for example, the chairman of a club. It is narrower in that:

    (i) there must be an intent to deceive *members or creditors*, whereas the earlier provision extended to an intent to induce *any person* to become a shareholder or partner, or to advance money, etc.;
    (ii) the written statement or account must be about the body's affairs.

[260] Examples of the kind of case to which the section is intended to apply are:

"A prospectus might include a false statement, made in order to inspire confidence, that some well-known person had agreed to become a director. It might also include a false statement, made in order to appeal to persons interested in a particular area, that a company had arranged to build a factory in that area."[1]

---

[1] *Eighth Report*, Cmnd. 2977, para. 105. False statements in prospectuses are also punishable by two years, imprisonment under the Companies Act 1948, s. 44. Offences under that section may, however, be committed negligently and the onus of disproving negligence is on the accused; whereas under s. 19 of the Theft Act the Crown must prove at least recklessness.

---

[261] The *mens rea* consists in:
  (i) an intent to deceive;
  (ii) knowledge that the statement is or may be misleading, false or deceptive in a material particular.

Though no intent to *defraud* is required, the effect seems to be much the same, since the statement must be false in a *material* particular. A particular is hardly likely to be held to be material unless the person to whom it is addressed is likely to take action of some kind on it and, thus, almost invariably, to be defrauded in the wide meaning now given to "fraud".[1]

As the Criminal Law Revision Committee thought, statements made recklessly will be within the section.[2] It is enough that D knows that the statement is or *may be* false, etc.

---

[1] *Welham* v. *D.P.P.*, [1961] A.C. 103; [1960] 1 All E.R. 805.
[2] *Eighth Report*, Cmnd. 2977, para. 104.

---

4 SUPPRESSION, ETC., OF DOCUMENTS

[262] Section 20 (1) replaces an elaborate group of offences in ss. 27–30 of the Larceny Act 1861. These offences have been little used in recent times and the Criminal Law Revision Committee had doubts as to whether any part of them should be retained, but s. 20 (1) was included because:

> "It seemed to us that it might provide the only way of dealing with a person who, for example, suppressed a public document as a first step towards committing a fraud but did not get so far as attempting to commit the fraud."[1]

It should be noted that the subsection does not apply to local government documents, the Committee being of the opinion that these were adequately protected by existing statutory provisions.

The main constituents of the offence are considered in connection with other offences.[2]

Section 20 (2) reproduces the substance of the offence under the Larceny Act 1916, s. 32 (2), modified so as to conform to the scheme of the Theft Act.[3]

It should be noted that where D deceives P into drawing a cheque in D's favour the appropriate charge is under s. 20 (2) and not under s. 15[4].

---

[1] *Eighth Report*, Cmnd. 2977, para. 106.
[2] As to "dishonestly", see above, paras. **[109]**–**[114]** and **[181]**–**[186]**; "with a view to gain" and "with intent to cause loss", see below, paras. **[294]**–**[304]**.

[3] As to "deception" see above, paras. **[154]**–**[180]**; and as to the other constituents of the offence see footnote 2 above. For s. 20, see p. 243, below.
[4] Above, para. **[205]**.

CHAPTER VII

REMOVAL OF ARTICLES FROM PLACES OPEN TO THE PUBLIC

[263] By s. 11 of the Theft Act:

"(1) Subject to subsections (2) and (3) below, where the public have access to a building in order to view the building or part of it, or a collection or part of a collection housed in it, any person who without lawful authority removes from the building or its grounds the whole or part of any article displayed or kept for display to the public in the building or that part of it or in its grounds shall be guilty of an offence.

For this purpose 'collection' includes a collection got together for a temporary purpose, but references in this section to a collection do not apply to a collection made or exhibited for the purpose of effecting sales or other commercial dealings.

(2) It is immaterial for purposes of subsection (1) above, that the public's access to a building is limited to a particular period or particular occasion; but where anything removed from a building or its grounds is there otherwise than as forming part of, or being on loan for exhibition with, a collection intended for permanent exhibition to the public, the person removing it does not thereby commit an offence under this section unless he removes it on a day when the public have access to the building as mentioned in subsection (1) above.

(3) A person does not commit an offence under this section if he believes that he has lawful authority for the removal of the thing in question or that he would have it if the person entitled to give it knew of the removal and the circumstances of it.

(4) A person guilty of an offence under this section shall, on conviction on indictment, be liable to imprisonment for a term not exceeding five years."

[264] It has been seen that an intention permanently to deprive is an essential constituent of theft, as it was of larceny. The CLRC considered the matter and came down against either (i) extending theft to include temporary deprivation, or (ii) creating a general offence of temporary deprivation of property.

"The former course seems to the Committee wrong because in their view an intention to return the property, even after a long time, makes the conduct essentially different from stealing. Apart from this either course would be a considerable extension of the criminal law, which does not

138

seem to be called for by an existing serious evil. It might moreover have undesirable social consequences. Quarrelling neighbours and families would be able to threaten one another with prosecution. Students and young people sharing accommodation who might be tempted to borrow one another's property in disregard of a prohibition by the owner would be in danger of acquiring a criminal record. Further, it would be difficult for the police to avoid being involved in wasteful and undesirable investigations into alleged offences which had no social importance."[1]

[1] *Eighth Report*, Cmnd. 2977, para. 56.

[265] The question whether temporary deprivation should be criminal attracted more attention than any other issue, both in and out of Parliament, during the passage of the Theft Bill;[1] but the government stuck firmly to the view expressed by the Committee. In two instances, the Committee found that there was a case for making temporary deprivation an offence, though not theft. These two cases are the subjects of this and the following chapter.

[1] See Samuels, 118 N.L.J. 281; Hadden, 118 N.L.J. 305; Smith, 118 N.L.J. 401. Parl. Debates, Official Report (H.L.), Vol. 289, cols. 1305–1325, 1480–1485, Vol. 290, cols. 51–71, 1390–1421, Vol. 291, cols. 59–71; (H.C.) Standing Committee H, cols. 3–18.

[266] Section 11 undoubtedly owes its existence to one particular and very unusual case—the removal from the National Gallery of Goya's portrait of the Duke of Wellington. The portrait was returned after a period of four years. There was evidence that the taker tried to make it a condition of his returning it that a large sum should be paid to charity. It has been argued above[1] that this should constitute a sufficient intent to deprive, but the accused was acquitted of larceny of the portrait, though convicted of larceny of the frame which was never recovered. The CLRC referred to two other cases, both of a very unusual nature.

> "... an art student took a statuette by Rodin from an exhibition, intending, as he said, to live with it for a while, and returned it over four months later. (Meanwhile the exhibitors, who had insured the statuette, had paid the insurance money to the owners, with result that the statuette, when returned, became the property of the exhibitors.[2]) Yet another case was the removal of the coronation stone from Westminster Abbey."

It may well be doubted whether these instances amounted to a case for the creation of a special offence but the government acted on the Committee's suggestion and produced a clause which, after much debate and amendment, became s. 11. The object of the section is to protect things which are put at hazard by being displayed to the public. Where, however, the purpose of the display is "effecting sales or other commercial dealings", it was thought reasonable to expect the person mounting the exhibition to bear the resulting hazards and to take adequate precautions against them.

[1] See para. **[127]**.

[2] If this had been foreseen by the taker then he might have been held to have an intention permanently to deprive; but this kind of foresight could probably only be attributed to a lawyer!

A. THE ACTUS REUS

[267] The ingredients of the offence are as follows:

(i) The *public* must have access. So the contents of a building will not be protected where only a particular small class of persons is permitted to have access; as where the owner opens the building to the members of a club, school or similar body.

[268] (ii) The public must have access *to a building in order to view.* The purpose is that of the invitor, not the invitee.[1] If the public have access to the building for this purpose, then articles in the grounds are protected. If the public do not have access to the building or have access only for some purpose other than viewing, articles in the grounds to which they do have access in order to view are not protected. If an exhibition of sculpture is put on in the grounds of a house, it will be not be an offence to "borrow" an item unless the public are also invited into the house for the purpose of viewing. If one piece of sculpture is displayed in the hall, then the fifty pieces in the grounds will also be protected. If, however, the public are invited into the house only for some purpose other than viewing—for example, to have tea—none of the articles will be protected. If follows, of course, that exhibitions in streets and squares are not protected.

[1] *Barr,* [1978] Crim. L.R. 244 (Judge Lowery).

[269] (iii) The article must be *displayed or kept for display.* "Displayed" means exhibited in the sense in which an art gallery exhibits a painting. A cross placed in a church solely for devotional purposes is not "displayed".[1] If D, while touring the art gallery, removes the fire extinguisher, he commits no offence against this section. If the article is in a store, it may be "kept for display" though not presently displayed.

[1] *Barr, supra.*

[270] (iv) If the article is displayed in a building, it must be removed *from the building.* If it is displayed in the grounds of the building, it must be removed *from the grounds.* Presumably it would be enough to take the article from the grounds into the building. If D is apprehended in the course of removing the article either from the grounds or the building then, no doubt he is guilty of an attempt.

[271] (v) The thing taken must be an *article.* The meaning of the word depends on its context. The expression, "any article whatsoever," in the Public Health Act 1936 was held not to include a goldfish, the court evidently taking the view that the word did not cover animate things.[1] On the other hand, a horse has been held to be an article for the purposes of a local Act dealing with exposure for sale at a market.[2] Bearing in mind the mischief at which the section is aimed, it is submitted that, if the other conditions are satisfied, any thing is protected, from an elephant in the London Zoo to a flower growing in the grounds of the stately home to which the public have access.

¹ *Daly* v. *Cannon*, [1954] 1 All E.R. 315.
² *Llandaff and Canton District Market Co.* v. *Lyndon* (1860), 8 C.B.N.S. 515.

[272] (vi) Where the article is in the building or its grounds as forming part of, or being on loan for exhibition with, a collection intended for permanent exhibition to the public, the offence may be committed at any time.¹ A collection is "intended for permanent exhibition to the public" if it is intended to be permanently *available* for exhibition to the public. It may be so intended though the pictures are exhibited in rotation and kept in store when not exhibited.² So it may be committed during the night when the building is closed, or on Sunday, even though the public are not admitted on Sunday, or in the middle of a month when the building is closed for renovation. Where this condition is not satisfied, then the article is protected only on a day when the public have access to the building. If P opens his stately home to the public on Easter Monday, then for the duration of that day only, articles displayed to the public in the building or its grounds are protected by the section. If D hides in the building until after midnight and removes an article on Tuesday he commits no offence under this section.

¹ Section 11(2).
² *Durkin*, [1973] 1 Q.B. 786; [1973] 2 All E.R. 872; SHC 552.

[273] (vii) If the public are admitted to view *the building* or part of it, then anything displayed is protected. If they are not admitted to view the building or part of it, then articles are protected only if a collection or part of a collection is displayed. Where a cathedral is open to the public to view and D removes an article which is displayed there, it is immaterial whether a collection is displayed or not. The term "collection" was used because it helps to indicate the intended purpose of the section—to protect articles assembled as objects of artistic or other merit or of public interest. It seems clear that it is not necessary that the contents should have been brought together for the purposes of exhibition in order to amount to a collection. If that were so, the contents of the stately home would be excluded from protection, for they were brought together for the edification of the collector, not for exhibition. It is no doubt sufficient that articles are preserved together. A single article could hardly constitute "a collection"; but, if it were on loan from a collection, might it not be "part of" a collection? A single article, not forming part of a collection, which was displayed to the public, would not be protected unless the public were admitted to view the building in which it was housed, as well as the article. Thus, if it were exhibited in a Nissen hut, it would not be protected, but it might be otherwise if the surroundings were more elegant.

[274] (viii) If the public are admitted to view a collection made or exhibited for the purpose of effecting sales or other commercial dealings, the articles will not be protected.¹ If the public are admitted to view the *building*, it would seem that articles will be protected even though they do form part of an exhibition for the purpose of effecting sales or commercial dealings. This will be so even

where the public are admitted for the dual purpose of viewing ᴛᴧᴇ building and the collection; when the public are admitted to view a building, any article which is displayed is protected.

---

¹ Section 11 (1).

---

[275] The definition of "collection" excludes not only commercial art galleries but also shops, salerooms and exhibitions for advertising purposes. Had it not been for this limitation, it is obvious that the scope of the section would have been immensely wider than is necessary to deal with the narrow class of cases at which the provision is aimed. Of course, a particular collection may be protected if the conditions of the section are satisfied, even though it is housed in a sale room, as where Christie's gave an exhibition in their sale room of articles which had been purchased from them and were lent by public galleries all over the world.

[276] (ix) It should be emphasised that the protection of the section is not lost because the articles displayed are for sale. It is a question of the purpose of the exhibitor in inviting the public to attend. Thus, it is clear that the pictures displayed at the Royal Academy exhibitions are protected, even though they are for sale. Neither sale, nor any other commercial dealing is the purpose of the Royal Academy in mounting the exhibition—though it may be the purpose of individual artists. There may be a difficult question where the exhibition has a dual purpose. Perhaps this is a case where it would be proper to have regard to the dominant purpose.

It is also clear that articles do not lose the protection of the section because a charge is made for admission with the object of making money in excess of the cost of upkeep. The sale or commercial dealing which is contemplated is one which is consequent upon the viewing of the exhibition.

B. THE MENS REA

[277] The *mens rea* of the offence is an intention to remove the article, knowing that there is no lawful authority for doing so and that the owner would not have authorised removal had he known of the circumstances. This closely follows the *mens rea* required for taking conveyances under s. 12. If the building were on fire and D removed a picture from it, he might well suppose that P would have authorised him to remove the picture had he known of the circumstances. The onus is, of course, on the Crown, once D has laid a foundation for such a defence, to prove beyond reasonable doubt that D did not so believe.

[278] As with s. 12, "dishonesty" is not a constituent of the offence. Where students borrow some article for the purpose of a "rag", it might be debatable whether they are dishonest or not; but the question need not be considered on a charge under s. 11; it is enough that they know that the removal is not and would not have been authorised by the owner had he known of it.

CHAPTER VIII

TAKING A MOTOR VEHICLE OR OTHER CONVEYANCE WITHOUT AUTHORITY

[279] Section 12 of the Act replaced the offence under s. 217 of the Road Traffic Act 1960. Section 12 (1) provides:

> "Subject to subsections (5) and (6) below, a person shall be guilty of an offence if, without having the consent of the owner or other lawful authority, he takes any conveyance for his own or another's use or, knowing that any conveyance has been taken without such authority, drives it or allows himself to be carried in or on it."

There seem to be two offences here and it is convenient to treat them separately.

1 TAKING A CONVEYANCE

A. TAKES

[280] A person "takes" if he assumes possession or control of the conveyance and moves it or causes it to be moved.[1] It does not matter how small the movement is. One who fails to move a car which he intends to take is guilty of an attempt.

The Theft Act omits the words "and drives away" which were in the Road Traffic Acts.[2] The object of this omission was not to bring the mere acquisition of possession within the ambit of the offence but to include the case where the conveyance is removed without being "driven" or, in the case of an aircraft "flown", a boat "sailed" and so on. So the offence was committed where a man took an inflatable rubber dinghy from outside a lifeboat depot, put it on a trailer and drove it away.[3] The essence of the offence is not stealing a ride but depriving the owner, though only temporarily, of his conveyance.[4]

In the Larceny Acts the word "takes" connoted merely the acquisition of possession and the requirement of "asportation" rested upon the further words, "and carries away". In *Bogacki*[5] it was held that, because "takes" is not a synonym for "uses", it imports a requirement of some degree of movement. A courting couple, occupying the back seat of a parked car as trespassers do not "take" it. If D takes possession of P's motorised caravan and lives in it for a month without moving it he does not commit this offence. This is not unreasonable. It is not different in substance from making use of P's bungalow.

The section is, after all, concerned with conveyances and the essence of a conveyance is that it moves.

---

[1] *Bogacki*, [1973] Q.B. 832; [1973] 2 All E.R. 864; SHC 556. *Webley* v. *Buxton*, [1977] Q.B. 481; [1977] 2 All E.R. 595. It is not enough that movement is caused accidentally: *Blayney* v. *Knight* (1975), 60 Cr. App. Rep. 269, D.C.

[2] The words were included in the Bill presented to Parliament but deleted so as to cover, e.g., the case of a boat which is towed away: H.L. Deb. Vol. 291, col. 106.

[3] *Bogacki*, [1973] Q.B. 832; [1973] 2 All E.R. 864.

[4] According to the Criminal Law Revision Committee, under the old law, "... the essence of the offence is stealing a ride" (*Eighth Report*, Cmnd. 2977, at para. 84); but there was more to it than that, as appears if the offence is compared with that of unlawful riding on public transport, where the authority is not deprived of the vehicle.

[5] Footnote 1, above.

---

[281] Where an employee has control, in the course of his employment, of a vehicle belonging to his employer, possession of the vehicle in law remains in the employer and the employee's control is known as custody. If the employee, without authority, so alters the character of his control of the vehicle that he no longer holds as employee but for his own purposes, he "takes" by assuming possession in the legal sense.[1] If, in the middle of the working day, he were to decide to drive his employer's van away for a fortnight's holiday, he would "take" it as soon as he departed from his authorised route with intent to control the vehicle for his own purpose. On the other hand, a lorry driver who diverted briefly from his authorised route merely to visit a favourite café would probably continue to hold as employee. The journey, though by an unnecessarily roundabout route, might still be in substance the journey he was employed to make. It is a question of degree. In *McKnight* v. *Davies*[2] a lorry driver was held guilty when, instead of returning the lorry to his employer's depot, as was his duty, he drove it to a public house, drove three men to their homes, back to another pub and then to his house, returning the vehicle to the depot the following morning.

While a deviation in the course of the working day raises a question of degree, it seems clear that when the working day is over and the driver resumes control over the vehicle for a purpose of his own, he commits the offence.[3]

---

[1] *McKnight* v. *Davies*, [1974] R.T.R. 4; SHC 561.

[2] *Mowe* v. *Perraton*, [1952] 1 All E.R. 423 appears to be wrongly decided.

[3] *Wibberley*, [1966] 2 Q.B. 214; [1965] 3 All E.R. 718.

---

[282] It is clear that a hirer under a hire-purchase agreement cannot commit the offence because he is the "owner" for this purpose.[1] Other bailees, however, may commit the offence. A bailee, unlike a servant, has possession of the thing entrusted to him; yet if he operates the conveyance after the purpose of the bailment has been fulfilled, that subsequent use may be held to amount to a taking, though he has never given up possession. In *McGill*,[2] D borrowed a car to take his wife to the station on the express condition that he brought it straight back. He did not return it that day, and the following day drove it to Hastings. It was held that his use of the car after the purpose of the borrowing was fulfilled constituted a taking. Once the conveyance has been *taken* by D, however, subsequent movement of it does not constitute a fresh taking,[3] unless

he has abandoned and then resumed possession; though it may be an offence under the second limb of the section.[4]

---

[1] Section 12 (7) (*b*), below, page 240.
[2] [1970] R.T.R. 209, C.A. See commentaries at [1970] Crim. L.R. 291 and 480.
[3] *Pearce*, [1961] Crim. L.R. 122.
[4] Below, para. **[290]**.

---

[283] The requirement of the Road Traffic Act that the vehicle be "driven away" led to some very subtle distinctions. It was held that, for example, a vehicle was not being driven where D released the handbrake so that it ran down a hill or where it was being towed or pushed by another vehicle. It would seem that there is a taking in each of these cases and convictions would now be possible, if the other constituents of the offence were present.[1]

---

[1] In *Roberts*, [1965] 1 Q.B. 85; [1964] 2 All E.R. 541, the court thought it "possible" that D's releasing the handbrake and allowing the vehicle to run down the hill amounted to a taking. It would clearly be sufficient taking for the purposes of larceny—suppose D had had an intent permanently to deprive, as by allowing the vehicle to run over a cliff into the sea; and it is thought that the requirements of this section should not be more stringent.

B. FOR HIS OWN OR ANOTHER'S USE

[284] The CLRC considered the essence of the offence they proposed in their draft bill to be "stealing a ride" but material amendments were made to the draft bill in Parliament which make the gist of the offence more doubtful. The words "and drives away" were omitted from the draft Bill and the words "for his own or another's use" were inserted. These words were intended to exclude from the offence one who let the conveyance run away, or float away, out of malice. In *Bow*[1] the Court of Appeal thought "use" meant "use as a conveyance;" but it seems that the actual taking need not involve the use of the conveyance at all—as in *Pearce*[2] where the conveyance, a rubber dinghy, was carried away on a trailer. An intention to use in the future may be enough and the court may have fairly assumed that D intended to use the dinghy for its normal purposes. If, however, he had intended to use it as a paddling pool for his children he would not (according to *Bow*) have been guilty of the offence, though the injury to the owner would have been the same. In *Bow*[3] D parked a vehicle in a private lane, allegedly for the purpose of poaching. P, a gamekeeper, blocked his exit with a Land-Rover and sent for the police. When P declined to move the Land-Rover, D got into it, released the handbrake and coasted 200 yards to allow his vehicle to be driven away. D's appeal, on the ground that he did not take the Land-Rover "for his own use", was dismissed: the taking necessarily involved the use of the Land-Rover "as a conveyance" and D's motive—to remove an obstruction—was immaterial. If D had pushed the vehicle without getting into it, the answer would presumably have been different. Even on the facts, it seems somewhat dubious whether D's taking of the vehicle is properly regarded as "use as a conveyance" for his *purpose* was not to convey himself or any other person or thing.[4]

---

[1] (1976), 64 Cr. App. Rep. 54; [1977] Crim. L.R. 176 and commentary.
[2] [1973] Crim. L.R. 321, C.A.
[3] (1976), 64 Cr. App. Rep. 54.

⁴ The decision is also open to criticism on the ground that P had no right to detain D: Williams, *TBCL*, 470–471. Presumably he had no right to detain D's vehicle either.

C. A CONVEYANCE

[285] By s. 12 (7) (*a*) of the Act:

"'conveyance' means any conveyance constructed or adapted for the carriage of a person or persons whether by land, water or air, except that it does not include a conveyance constructed or adapted for use only under the control of a person not carried in or on it, and 'drive' shall be construed accordingly."

Thus conveyances for the carriage of goods are excluded, but only where the conveyance has no place for a driver. A lorry is clearly within the protection of the Act, since it is constructed for the carriage of at least one person. A goods trailer, however, would not be so protected, nor a barge with no provision for a passenger. A vehicle, such as some milk floats, which is operated by a man walking beside it, is expressly excluded. A horse-drawn carriage is clearly a conveyance, but a horse is not.¹ A conveyance evidently means something that is manufactured. Moreover, it has been held that attaching a halter or bridle to the horse is not "adapting" it but only making it easier to ride.²

The elimination of the requirement of "driving" may bring within the section (or, at least, the first part of it) certain conveyances which otherwise would be outside it—that is any conveyance with accommodation for a passenger or passengers which has no means of self-propulsion and so cannot be driven but must be towed.

¹ *Neal v. Gribble*, [1978] R.T.R. 409; [1978] Crim. L.R. 500.
² *Ibid.* See commentary [1978] Crim. L.R. 500–501.

[286] Bicycles are expressly excluded by s. 12 (5):

"Subsection (1) above¹ shall not apply in relation to pedal cycles; but subject to subsection (6) below,² a person who, without having the consent of the owner or other lawful authority,³ takes a pedal cycle for his own or another's use, or rides a pedal cycle knowing it to have been taken without such authority, shall on summary conviction be liable to a fine not exceeding fifty pounds."

¹ Above, para. **[279]**.
² Below, para. **[289]**.
³ Below, para. **[287]**.

D. "WITHOUT HAVING THE CONSENT OF THE OWNER OR OTHER LAWFUL AUTHORITY"

[287] If the owner had not given his consent at the time of the taking, his later declaration that he would have done so if asked is not a defence.¹ It would seem clear that a consent extracted by intimidation would not amount to a defence.² In principle a consent induced by fraud would be no consent if the mistake induced in the owner was as to the identity of the taker or the nature of the transaction. Fraud going to less fundamental matters would not be sufficient. Thus if, for example, D borrowed P's car on a pretence that he wished to drive to Derby to visit his sick grandmother, when really he wanted to go there to see his girlfriend, he would not commit the offence; but it is thought that he would do so if his real intention was not to go to Derby at all, but to drive the car on the Monte Carlo rally. Against this view is the decision in *Peart*.[3] D induced P to lend his van, for a payment of £2, by representing that he wanted to drive to Alnwick and would return the van by 7.30 p.m. Instead, as presumably he intended all along, he drove to Burnley where he was found at 9 p.m. It was held that there was no taking; the misrepresentation did not vitiate P's consent. The court reserved the question whether a misrepresentation can ever be so fundamental as to vitiate consent for the purposes of this crime. The case is difficult to reconcile with the earlier case of *McGill*.[4] If, when a conveyance has been borrowed for a particular purpose, it is "taking" to use it for a quite different purpose *after* the declared purpose has been fulfilled, it is difficult to see why it is not "taking" to use it *immediately* for a purpose quite different from that declared. It is submitted that *McGill* is to be preferred to *Peart*. Similar principles should apply to a consent obtained without fraud, but under a mistake by P known to D.

[1] *Ambler*, (1979) 28 March, *Guardian Gazette*, CA.
[2] *Hogdon*, [1962] Crim. L.R. 563.
[3] [1970] 2 Q.B. 672; [1970] 2 All E.R. 823 C.A.; SHC 559.
[4] Above, para. [**282**].

[**288**] "Other lawful authority" would apply to the removal of a vehicle, in accordance with a statutory power such as the regulations made under s. 20 of the Road Traffic Regulation Act 1967, where the vehicle had been parked in contravention of a statutory prohibition, or in a dangerous situation, or in such circumstances as to appear to have been abandoned.

It would also cover any removal of a vehicle in pursuance of a common law right such as that of abating a nuisance,[1] or of a contractual right such as that of a letter under a hire-purchase agreement to resume possession in certain circumstances.

[1] *Cf. Webb v. Stansfield*, [1966] Crim. L.R. 449.

E.   THE MENS REA

[**289**] Section 12 (6) provides:

> "A person does not commit an offence under this section by anything done in the belief that he has lawful authority to do it or that he would have the owner's consent if the owner knew of his doing it and the circumstances of it."

It is clear then that the prosecution must prove that D knew that he was taking the vehicle without the owner's consent and did not believe that the owner would have consented if asked. This is an important change in the law for, under s. 217 of the Road Traffic Act 1960, the onus was on D to satisfy the court, on a balance of probabilities, that he acted in the *reasonable* belief that he had lawful authority, etc. This was a highly unsatisfactory situation.

Suppose D had been charged with (i) taking and driving away and (ii) stealing petrol, both charges arising out of his taking P's car, and had raised the defence in both cases that he believed he had P's authority to drive the vehicle. It would have been necessary to direct as to (i), that the onus was on D to prove his belief on a balance of probabilities and that the defence was made out if only the belief was reasonable; and as to (ii) that the onus was on the Crown to disprove his belief beyond reasonable doubt and that if they failed to do this, he was entitled to be acquitted even if his belief was an unreasonable one. This was preposterous. The Act brings the law of taking conveyances into line with that of stealing.[1] On the facts envisaged, the direction in relation to both charges would now be the same.

---

[1] *Cf.* the discussion of s. 2 (1) (*a*), above, para. [110].

---

2   DRIVING OR ALLOWING ONESELF TO BE CARRIED BY A "TAKEN" CONVEYANCE

A.   THE ACTUS REUS

[290] Where a conveyance has been unlawfully taken, D does not commit an offence of "taking" by driving or allowing himself to be carried in or on the taken conveyance.[1] Special provision was made to meet this case in the Road Traffic Act 1962, s. 44 and that provision is reproduced in s. 12 of the Theft Act. It seems clear that at least one offence, separate and distinct from taking a conveyance is created; and there are two such offences if *driving*[2] and *allowing oneself to be carried* cannot be regarded as alternative modes of commission of a single offence. It does not seem to matter greatly whether the provision is construed as creating two offences or one. It is true that if the courts should adopt the latter construction it would dispense with the necessity for proving which of several accused was driving a taken vehicle—a matter which might sometimes be difficult—since all would be principal offenders in the same offence. Even if "driving" is a separate offence, so long as it is clear that one of several passengers was driving, all may be convicted of driving, provided the necessary knowledge can be proved, although the actual driver cannot be identified, since each of them, if he was not the principal, was an aider and abettor.[3] One case in which it might matter would be where there was no evidence of *mens rea* against one of two or more possible drivers of the vehicle. If that person were the driver, there was no principal offender and there are difficulties about convicting of aiding and abetting where there is no principal offender.[4] The chance that he was the driver might thus create a reasonable doubt whether any of the parties was guilty of driving, even though there was conclusive evidence of *mens rea* against some of them.

---

[1] *Stally,* [1959] 3 All E.R. 814; *D. (Infant)* v. *Parsons,* [1960] 2 All E.R. 493.
[2] "Driving" now includes the activity of a person who sets in motion and controls an aircraft, hovercraft, boat or any other conveyance: s. 12 (7) (*a*). It is conceivable that the old technicalities of what is "driving" might arise again here. It is submitted that D is driving when he is in or on the vehicle and is in control of its forward or backward motion. *Cf. Wallace* v. *Major,* [1946] K.B. 473; [1946] 2 All E.R. 87; *Saycell* v. *Bool,* [1948] 2 All E.R. 83; *Shimmell* v. *Fisher,* [1951] 2 All E.R. 672; *Spindley,* [1961] Crim. L.R. 486; *Roberts,* [1965] 1 Q.B. 85; [1964] 2 All E.R. 541; *Arnold,* [1964] Crim. L.R. 664.

³ *Du Cros v. Lambourne*, [1907] 1 K.B. 40; *Swindall and Osborne* (1846), 2 Car. & Kir. 230.
⁴ Smith and Hogan, 132–136, *Cogan and Leak*, [1976] Q.B. 217; [1975] 2 All E.R. 1059.

[291] It has been held that a person is not "carried" in a conveyance merely because he is present in it. Carriage imports some movement. A person is not carried in a stationary launch though he is borne by its buoyancy.¹ It would presumably be no different where the boat rises or falls with the waves or the tide. This is not distinguishable from the movement of a stationary car on its springs as people get in or out. The slightest vertical motion of a hovercraft, however, should suffice.

"Drives" similarly seems to import movement. One who starts up a vehicle and engages the gear has reached the stage of an attempt but has not yet committed the offence.

¹ *Miller*, [1976] Crim. L.R. 147. Similarly, presumably, where D climbs up a rope into a tethered airborne balloon.

[292] The vehicle must actually have been taken; one cannot know a thing to be so, unless it is so.¹

The provision is intended to deal with persons other than the original taker, but it is not limited to such persons. The taker would appear to commit another offence on each subsequent occasion when he drives the vehicle or allows himself to be carried in or on it. Where the original taking is not an offence because of lack of *mens rea*, a subsequent driving of it may make the taker liable. For example, D takes P's car, wrongly supposing that P consents to his doing so. The car has been taken without P's consent but no offence has been committed. Having learnt that P does not consent to his having the car, D continues to drive it. He appears to commit the offence though it is arguable that a "taken" conveyance is one taken with *mens rea*.

¹ D would not be guilty of an attempt where he wrongly thought he knew that the vehicle had been taken: *Haughton v. Smith*, [1973] A.C. at 485; [1973] 3 All E.R. 1109; SHC 311.

B. THE MENS REA

[293] It must be proved that D knew that the conveyance had been taken without authority when he drove it or allowed himself to be carried in or on it as the case may be. Probably "wilful blindness" would be enough as in the case of other statutes.¹ Such a state of mind is, however, barely distinguishable from that of *belief* that the conveyance had been so taken. The Criminal Law Revision Committee thought that belief was not knowledge for the purpose of the old law of receiving² and made special provision for that state of mind in the new offence of handling.³ It is inevitable that comparison will be made between s. 12 (1) and s. 22, with the implication that belief will not do in the case of s. 12; but it is submitted that such an argument should not be accepted.⁴

¹ Smith and Hogan, 102–103; Edwards, *Mens Rea in Statutory Offences*, 202–205; Williams, *C.L.G.P. 159.*
² *Eighth Report*, Cmnd. 2977, para. 134; below, para. **[423]**.
³ See s. 22 (1), para. **[379]**.
⁴ Below, para. **[423]**.

3 SENTENCE

[294] The maximum punishment for the offences is raised from one to three years' imprisonment. In this case, the increase *does* represent an invitation to the court to impose stiffer penalties: the Criminal Law Revision Committee thought that the penalties under the old law were

"... far too low having regard to the prevalence of the offence, to the danger, loss and inconvenience which often result from it and to the fact that courts are commonly called on to deal with offenders who have committed the offence many times."[1]

---

[1] *Eighth Report,* Cmnd. 2977, para. 82.

CHAPTER IX

ABSTRACTING OF ELECTRICITY

[295] The Larceny Act of 1916 made special provision for the stealing of electricity because, no doubt, it was not capable of being taken and carried away. The notion of appropriation in the Theft Act might perhaps have been applied without incongruity to the abstraction of electricity but the unique nature of this kind of property was thought to call for a special provision. It has now been held that electricity is not "property" within section 4 of the Act and that it is not appropriated by switching on the current.[1] Section 13 of the Act provides:

> "A person who dishonestly uses without due authority, or dishonestly causes to be wasted or diverted, any electricity shall on conviction on indictment be liable to imprisonment for a term not exceeding five years."

Thus the offence would be committed by an employee who dishonestly used his employer's electrically-operated machinery without authority; by a householder who, having had his electricity supply cut off, dishonestly[2] reconnected it or who by-passed the meter; and by a tramp who, having trespassed into a house to obtain a night's shelter, turned on the electric fire to keep himself warm. If the tramp found the electric fire already burning, would he "use" the electricity by warming himself in front of it? Probably not. "Use" implies some consumption of electricity which would not occur but for the accused's act. If squatters switch on the electricity, not intending to pay for it, they appear to use it dishonestly. Suppose that D subsequently joins them and enjoys the heat and light provided. He appears to be a party to the dishonest use which is taking place.

---

[1] *Low* v. *Blease* (1975), 119 Sol. Jo. 695; [1975] Crim. L.R. 513.
[2] See *Boggeln* v. *Williams*, [1978] 2 All E.R. 1061, above, para. **[117]**.

---

[296] The tramp would not be guilty of burglary, since abstracting electricity is not one of the ulterior offences specified in s. 9 (1) (*b*).[1] Yet, oddly, it would seem that the person who did the acts described in the previous paragraph would be guilty of theft if it were gas he consumed, instead of electricity; so the tramp would be a burglar, if it were a gas fire. Not a very happy result.

---

[1] Below, para. **[358]**.

[297] There is nothing in the section to suggest that the electricity must come from the mains. Therefore it is probable that D commits the offence if he borrows my flashlight or portable radio and uses the dry battery.[1] Is the offence committed then by the dishonest "borrower" of a conveyance, such as a motor car, which consumes electricity from the battery when it is operated? If so, we have the incongruous result that the—merely incidental—use of the electricity is a more serious offence than the use of the vehicle as a whole.[2] It might be argued that if, as will usually be the case, the battery is charging properly, there will be as much electricity stored in it at the end of the journey as at the beginning; and that, therefore, the use is not dishonest. An analogy might be drawn with the case where D takes P's coins, intending permanently to deprive him of them but to replace an equivalent sum from D's own money, not causing any injury to P.[3] It is not a fair analogy, however. In the case of the coins, the replacements are D's property; in the case of the electricity, the replacement is generated by the use of P's petrol and P's machinery and belongs to P as much as the electricity consumed. It seems likely, therefore, that the dishonest borrower of a motor vehicle (or motor boat, aircraft, etc.) does commit an offence against s. 13.[4]

---

[1] Or if he operates an electrically-powered milk-float or similar vehicle. Taking such a vehicle is not an offence under s. 12 if the operator is not carried in or on it.
[2] This incongruity has always been present with regard to the petrol which is consumed.
[3] Above, para. **[116]**–**[117]**.
[4] This incongruity would not have arisen under the draft bill proposed by the Criminal Law Revision Committee, since the draft clause contained the words, "with intent to cause loss to another". These words were cut out by the House of Lords.

---

[298] What if D obtains the benefit of the use of the electricity by fraud? Lord Airedale put the case[1] of a woodworking company allowing sea scouts to use their electrically-operated machinery and D's obtaining the use of the machinery by falsely stating that he is a sea scout. Lord Airedale thought D might escape because he had obtained authority, albeit by false pretences, and was therefore not acting "without due authority". One answer to this might be that some meaning should be given to the word "due"; and that, while D was acting with actual authority, he was not acting with "due" authority, since the authority was voidable on the ground of fraud. D is not guilty of obtaining services contrary to 1978, s. 1,[2] unless the use of the machinery had been, or was to be, paid for.

---

[1] Parl. Debates (H. of L.), Vol. 190, col. 154.
[2] Above, para. **[219]**.

---

[299] The corresponding provision in the Larceny Act was sometimes used to deal with persons who dishonestly used a telephone and this would seem to be perfectly possible under the Theft Act. For example, the employee who dishonestly uses his employer's telephone for his own private purposes would seem to be in no different situation from the employee who uses any other electrically operated machine. Specific provision for the dishonest use of a *public* telephone or telex is now made by the insertion of a new section, s. 65A, in the Post Office Act 1953.[1] This creates a merely summary offence. It is submitted that such cases should now be prosecuted as summary offences and not under s. 13; but where the telephone is a private one, there is no reason why s. 13 should not be invoked.

---

[1] See Schedule 2, para. 8, below.

CHAPTER X

BLACKMAIL[1]

[300] "Blackmail" is the name which was commonly given to the group of offences contained in ss. 29–31 of the Larceny Act 1916. That term is officially adopted for the first time as the name of the offence which replaces these sections of the Larceny Act. Section 21 (1) of the 1968 Act provides:

> "A person is guilty of blackmail if, with a view to gain for himself or another or with intent to cause loss to another, he makes any unwarranted demand with menaces; and for this purpose a demand with menaces is unwarranted unless the person making it does so in the belief—
> (*a*) that he has reasonable grounds for making the demand; and
> (*b*) that the use of the menaces is a proper means of reinforcing the demand."

---

[1] *Eighth Report*, Cmnd. 2977, paras. 108–125.

---

1 THE ACTUS REUS

[301] The *actus reus* consists in a demand with menaces; and the two problems here are to determine the meaning of the expressions, "demand" and "menaces".

A. DEMAND

[302] Under the Larceny Act, the demand had to be for "any property or valuable thing"[1] or something capable of being stolen[2] or for an appointment or office of profit or trust.[3] The Theft Act is not so limited. Section 21 (2) provides:

> "The nature of the act or omission demanded is immaterial, and it is also immaterial whether the menaces relate to action to be taken by the person making the demand."

In effect, this is limited by the requirement that the demand be made with a view to gain or intent to cause loss[4] so that the change in the law is probably slight. In the vast majority of cases, the blackmailer will be demanding money or other property, intending both a gain to himself and a loss to another. It is clearly intended that the demand for a remunerated appointment or office[5] be covered, though whether such a case satisfies the requirement of view to gain or loss requires further consideration.[6] It would seem, however, that a demand for an unremunerated office, which would formerly have been an offence, would now, *prima facie*, not be. To threaten one believed to have influence in these matters, if he did not procure D's appointment as a justice of the peace,

154

or Lord Lieutenant of the County, or Chairman of the Trustees of the British Museum would appear no longer to be an offence of blackmail. The limitation would seem to be in pursuance of a general policy of limiting the provisions of the Act to the protection of economic interests. Had there been no such limitation, the section would have extended to such cases as that where D demands with menaces that P shall have sexual intercourse with him—a case which is obviously outside the scope of an enactment dealing with "theft and similar or associated offences" and which is provided for by other legislation.[7]

---

[1] Sections 29 and 31 (*a*).
[2] Section 30.
[3] Section 31 (*b*).
[4] See below, para. [312].
[5] *Eighth Report*, Cmnd. 2977, para. 117.
[6] Below, para. [318].
[7] Sexual Offences Act 1956, s. 2.

---

[303] In other respects, the Act extends the scope of the law. To demand with menaces that a person abandon a claim to property or release D from some legal liability of an economic nature may now be an offence. To demand with menaces that P discontinue divorce proceedings would not, however, be within the section. Whereas under s. 29 of the Larceny Act the demand had to be in writing, it is quite immaterial whether the demand under the Theft Act be oral or written.

[304] Whether an utterance amounts to a "demand" seems to depend on whether an ordinary literate person would so describe it.[1] A demand is made when and where a letter containing it is posted; and it probably continues to be made until it arrives and is read by the recipient.[2] To post such a letter in England addressed to P in Germany amounts to an offence in England. To post the letter in Germany addressed to P in England would be an offence here, at least if it arrived within the jurisdiction and, according to Lord Diplock,[3] even if it did not.

An oral demand would appear to be made when uttered, though unheard by the person addressed. If an emissary, other than the Post Office, be despatched bearing a demand, whether written or oral, it would seem that it could scarcely be held to be "made" until delivered.[4] The test would seem to be whether D has done, personally or through an agent, the final act necessary in the normal course to result in a communication. The Post Office, though sometimes treated as such, is not an agent in any real sense. The posted letter is as irrevocable as the bullet expelled from a gun. Any emissary other than the Post Office, whether he carries a demand or a loaded gun, may be recalled; so the principal of the one has, as yet, no more demanded than the principal of the other has shot. As was the case under the old law, it is likely that there may be a demand although it is not expressed in words, "a demand may be implicit or explicit".[5] It is probably enough that "the demeanour of the accused and the circumstances of the case were such that an ordinary reasonable man would understand that a demand ... was being made upon him ...".[6] There may also be a demand although it is couched in terms of request and obsequious in tone;[7]

the addition of the menace is sufficient to show that it is truly a demand that is made.

[1] *Treacy* v. *D.P.P.*, [1971] A.C. 537 at 565; [1971] 1 All E.R. 110 at 124, *per* Lord Diplock.
[2] *Ibid. Cf. Baxter*, above, para. [**190**].
[3] *Ibid.*
[4] See Griew, 9–12, and the discussion by Lord Reid (dissenting) in *Treacy*: [1971] A.C. at 550, and [1971] 1 All E.R. at 111.
[5] *Clear*, [1968] 1 Q.B. 670; [1968] 1 All E.R. 74 at 77.
[6] *Collister and Warhurst* (1955), 39 Cr. App. Rep. 100 at 102.
[7] *Robinson* (1796), 2 East P.C. 1110; *Studer* (1915), 11 Cr. App. Rep. 307.

B. MENACES

[305] The Criminal Law Revision Committee states:[1]

"We have chosen the word 'menaces' instead of 'threats' because, notwithstanding the wide meaning given to 'menaces' in *Thorne's* case ... we regard that word as stronger than 'threats', and the consequent slight restriction of the scope of the offence seems to us right."

It is reasonably clear then, that it was the intention that the old law should be preserved here. In the case referred to, *Thorne* v. *Motor Trade Association*,[2] Lord Wright said:

"I think the word 'menace' is to be liberally construed and not as limited to threats of violence but as including threats of any action detrimental to or unpleasant to the person addressed. It may also include a warning that in certain events such action is intended."

[1] *Eighth Report*, Cmnd. 2977, para. 123.
[2] [1937] A.C. 797 at 817, H.L.

[306] In view of the breadth of this definition, it is apparent that any restriction imposed by the use of the word "menaces" rather than "threats" must be slight. In most cases, there is no need to spell out the meaning of the word to a jury, since it is "an ordinary English word which a jury could be expected to understand".[1]

The one limitation is that the threat does not amount to a menace unless "it is of such a nature and extent that the mind of an ordinary person of normal stability and courage might be influenced or made apprehensive so as to accede unwillingly to the demand".[2] If the threat is "of such a character that it is not calculated to deprive any person of reasonably sound and ordinarily firm mind of the free and voluntary action of his mind",[3] then it does not amount to a menace; but it has been said this doctrine should receive "a liberal construction in practice"[4]—that is, the court should be slow to hold that the threat would not influence an ordinary man.

[1] *Lawrence* (1971), 57 Cr. App. Rep. 64; [1971] Crim. L.R. 645.
[2] *Clear*, [1968] 1 Q.B. 670; [1968] 1 All E.R. 74, C.A.
[3] *Boyle and Merchant*, [1914] 3 K.B. 339 at 345, C.C.A.
[4] *Tomlinson*, [1895] 1 Q.B. 706 at 710, *per* Wills, J.; *Clear* (*supra*) at 80.

[307] If the threat is one of so trivial a nature that it would not influence anybody[1] to respond to the demand, it is certainly reasonable to say that it is not a menace. A letter from a student rag committee to shopkeepers offering to sell "indemnity posters" reading "these premises are immune from all rag '73 activities whatever they may be" has been held not to amount to a menace.[2] It would no doubt have been different if the '72 rag activities had been of such a nature as to cause apprehension in ordinary shopkeepers. The doctrine is satisfactory enough, then, where the person to whom the demand is addressed is a person of normal stability and courage, but it has been said that "persons who are thus practised upon are not as a rule of average firmness".[3] Suppose that P is a weak-minded person, likely to be swayed by a fanciful or trivial threat which an ordinary person would ignore; and that this is known to the threatener. It is submitted that the threat should be regarded as a menace; and that to hold the contrary would be hardly more reasonable than to say that robbery was not committed because the victim allowed himself to be overcome by a degree of force which a courageous man would have successfully resisted; or that there was no obtaining by deception because the victim was excessively gullible and was taken in by a pretence which anyone with his wits about him would have seen through.

---

[1] *Cf. Tomlinson* (*supra*), *per* Wills, J.; *Boyle and Merchant,* [1914] 3 K.B. at 344.
[2] *Harry,* [1974] Crim. L.R. 32: SHC 564 (Judge Petre).
[3] *Tomlinson,* [1895] 1 Q.B. at 710, *per* Wills, J.

---

[308] Whether a threat amounts to a menace within this principle appears, at first sight, to be an objective question to be answered by looking at the actual facts of the case. It appears from *Clear*,[1] however, that the question is to be answered by reference to the facts known to the accused, if these are different from the actual facts—that, in effect, the question is one of intention. In that case, D had received a sub-poena to appear as a witness in an action in which P was the defendant. D demanded money from P with a threat that, if the money were not paid, he would alter the statement he had made to the police and so cause P to lose the action. P was quite unmoved by this threat since the action was being defended by his insurers and, if the action succeeded, it was they and not he who would pay. D's conviction was upheld. It might be said that, in the actual circumstances of the case, the words used could not influence a person of normal stability and courage; but the court appears to have held that regard must be had, not to the actual circumstances, but to the circumstances as they appeared to the person making the demand:

> "There may be special circumstances unknown to an accused which would make the threats innocuous and unavailing for the accused's demand, but such circumstances would have no bearing on the accused's state of mind and of his intention. If an accused knew that what he threatened would have no effect on the victim it might be different."[2]

---

[1] Above, para. [306], [1968] 1 All E.R. at 80.
[2] *Ibid.*

---

[309] It is submitted, therefore, that there is a sufficient menace if, in the circumstances known to the accused, the threat might:

(i) influence the mind of an ordinary person of normal stability and courage, whether or not it in fact influences the person addressed; or

(ii) influence the mind of the person addressed, though it would not influence an ordinary person.

It is assumed, of course, that in both cases there is an intention to influence the person addressed to accede to the demand by means of the threat.

2   THE MENS REA

[310] The *mens rea* of blackmail comprises a number of elements:
(1) An intent to make a demand with menaces.[1]
(2) A view to gain for himself or another, *or* intent to cause loss to another.
(3) Either
    (*a*) no belief that he has reasonable grounds for making the demand, *or*
    (*b*) no belief that the use of the menaces is a proper means of reinforcing the demand.

---

[1] Above, paras. [301]–[309].

---

[311] It is clear that the onus of proof of each of these elements is on the Crown; but it is enough to establish (1) and (2) and *either* (3) (*a*) or (3) (*b*). It may well be that, once the Crown has introduced evidence of elements (1) and (2), an evidential burden is put upon the accused as regards (3); that is he must introduce some evidence of his belief of *both* (*a*) and (*b*), whereupon it will be for the Crown to prove that he did not believe one, or the other, or both. Where, on the face of it, the means used to reinforce the demand are improper, and D does not set up the case that he believed in its propriety, the jury need not be directed on the point.[1] It will be noted that whether or not a demand is "unwarranted" is exclusively a question of the accused's belief, as to which no one is better informed than he; and the phraseology of the section—"a demand with menaces is unwarranted unless ..."—suggests that it is for the accused to assert that his demand was warranted.

Where, however, D does not set up such a defence, but the evidence is such that a jury might reasonably think he had the beliefs in question, it is the duty of the judge to direct the jury not to convict unless satisfied that he did not have the beliefs or one of them.[2] The first element requires no further consideration.

---

[1] *Lawrence* (1971), 57 Cr. App. Rep. 64; [1971] Crim. L.R. 645; SHC 570.
[2] "It is always the duty of the judge to leave to the jury any issue (whether raised by the defence or not) which, on the evidence in the case, is an issue fit to be left to them": *Palmer* v. *R.*, [1971] 1 All E.R. 1077 at 1080, P.C., *per* Lord Morris.

A.   A VIEW TO GAIN OR INTENT TO CAUSE LOSS

[312] "Gain" and "loss" are defined by s. 34 (2) (*a*) of the Theft Act:

" 'gain' and 'loss' are to be construed as extending only to gain or loss in money or other property, but as extending to any such gain or loss whether temporary or permanent; and

> (i) 'gain' includes a gain by keeping what one has, as well as a gain by getting what one has not; and
>
> (ii) 'loss' includes a loss by not getting what one might get, as well as a loss by parting with what one has."

[313] As has already been noted,[1] this definition limits the offence to the protection of economic interests. Without it, the scope of s. 21—demanding with menaces the performance of *any act or omission*—would have been very wide indeed and would certainly have extended far beyond "theft and similar or associated offences" which it is the object of the 1968 Act to revise. In most cases, the blackmailer is trying to obtain money to which he knows he has no right and there will be no doubt about his view to gain. It is clearly not necessary, however, that there should be evidence of a direct demand for money or other property. It is enough that D's purpose in demanding the act or omission, whatever it may be, is gain or loss in terms of money or other property. Suppose that D demands with menaces that P should marry him. If P is an heiress and D's object is to enrich himself, he is guilty of blackmail. But if D's object is the satisfaction of his carnal desires, or the social advancement which the marriage will bring, then he is not guilty. No doubt it is enough that the acquisition of money or other property is one of several objects which D has in mind in making the demand. The gain or loss must be in money or other property so it is probable that, though obtaining services by deception is now an offence,[2] obtaining them by threats is not, though D is enriched thereby.

---

[1] Above, para. [**302**].
[2] Theft Act 1978, s. 1, above, para. [**219**].

---

[314] Is it enough that D foresees that the fulfilment of his demand will result in a gain to him, even though gain is not one of the objects of the demand? D is so consumed with desire for the heiress that he would have made exactly the same demand with menaces even if she had been a pauper: but he knows that the marriage will be profitable. It is thought that this will probably not be enough. Where it is a case of causing loss rather than making a gain, "intent" is specifically required and this is likely to be construed to require a desire that loss should ensue. D demands with menaces that P should jump into a muddy pool. D's object is that P, who has offended him, should suffer discomfort and humiliation. As D foresaw, P's clothes are ruined by immersion in the pool and so he suffers a loss. It is probable that D is not guilty. If that be correct with regard to "intent to cause loss", it would seem appropriate that a similar principle should govern "view to gain".

(a) Belief in a right to the gain

[315] It is not necessarily a good defence that D believes he has a right to the gain. If he has such a belief, then he certainly believes that he has reasonable grounds for making the demand, but it will be recalled that this does not cause the demand to be warranted unless it is coupled with a belief that the use of the menaces is a proper means of reinforcing the demand. Section 21 does not use the word "dishonestly" which, in ss. 1, 15, 16, 17 and 20, ensures that a claim of right to the property is a defence. It is clear that the

Criminal Law Revision Committee intended that the offence might be committed where D had both a claim of right and an actual right to the property which he intended to acquire.[1]

> "A may be owed £100 by B and be unable to get payment. Perhaps A needs the money badly and B is in a position to pay; or perhaps A can easily afford to wait and B is in difficulty. Should it be blackmail for A to threaten B that, if he does not pay, A will assault him—or slash the tyres of his car—or tell people that B is a homosexual, which he is (or which he is not)—or tell people about the debt and anything discreditable about the way in which it was incurred? On one view none of these threats should be enough to make the demand amount to blackmail. For it is no offence merely to utter the threats without making the demand (unless for some particular reason such as breach of the peace or defamation); nor would the threat become criminal merely because it was uttered to reinforce a demand of a kind quite different from those associated with blackmail. Why then should it be blackmail merely because it is uttered to reinforce a demand for money which is owed? On this view no demand with menaces would amount to blackmail, however harsh the action threatened, unless there was dishonesty. This is a tenable view, though an extreme one. In our opinion it goes too far and there are some threats which should make the demand amount to blackmail even if there is a valid claim to the thing demanded. For example, we believe that most people would say that it should be blackmail to threaten to denounce a person, however truly, as a homosexual unless he paid a debt. It does not seem to follow from the existence of a debt that the creditor should be entitled to resort to any method, otherwise non-criminal, to obtain payment. There are limits to the methods permissible for the purpose of enforcing payment of a debt without recourse to the courts. For example, a creditor cannot seize the debtor's goods; and in *Parker*[2] it was held (as mentioned in para. [181]) that a creditor who forged a letter from the Admiralty to a sailor warning him to pay a debt was guilty of forgery notwithstanding the existence of the debt."

---

[1] *Eighth Report*, Cmnd. 2977, para. 119.
[2] (1910), 74 J.P. 208.

---

[316] Acts of Parliament, however, do not always carry out the intention of those who frame them, and it has been argued that the use of the words "with a view to gain" will defeat the object of the Committee in this case:[1] "There is surely no gain or loss where a person merely secures the payment of that which he is owed."

The argument might be elaborated as follows:

> "... If I liquidate a just debt, I suffer no economic loss. In my personal balance sheet, the amount of cash in hand on the credit side is reduced, but this is offset by a corresponding reduction on the debit side in the item 'sundry creditors'."[2]

If the debtor has suffered no economic loss it follows that the creditor has acquired no economic gain for, while his cash in hand will increase, his credit balance under "sundry debtors" will diminish. If "gain in money or other property" means economic enrichment, then it is arguable that D has no view to gain when he demands that to which he is entitled.

¹ Hogan, [1966] Crim. L.R. at 476.
² R. N. Gooderson, [1960] C.L.J. 199 at 205, discussing the meaning of "fraud" in relation of *Welham v. D.P.P.*, [1961] A.C. 103; [1960] 1 All E.R. 805.

[317] The answer turns on the meaning of the word "gain". That word has frequently been the subject of interpretation in other statutes.¹ The meaning given to a word in one statute is by no means conclusive as to that which it should bear in another; but it may give some guidance. "Gain" certainly might mean "profit"² and if that is its meaning in the Theft Act, then the argument in the preceding paragraph seems a sound one. On the other hand, Jessel, M.R. has said " 'Gain' means exactly acquisition ... Gain is something obtained or acquired."³ Though he found that there was a profit, and therefore a gain, in that case, it would seem that he did not think that gain was necessarily to be equated with profit. If then, "gain" includes acquisition, whether at a profit or not, the difficulty disappears. A man may properly be said to have *acquired* that which he is entitled to have, if he secures ownership or possession of it. Apart from the intentions of the Committee which have been quoted above, the Act itself suggests that this is the right view, (a) through the omission of the word "dishonestly", which would have imported a defence of claim of right, (b) because s. 21 requires not merely a belief that D is entitled to the thing demanded but also a belief that the use of the menaces is proper, and (c) because "gain" is defined to include "getting what one has not." It is submitted therefore that "gain" includes the acquisition of money or other property whether it is due in law or not.⁴ This view appears to be accepted by the courts. It has been held that "getting hard cash as opposed to a mere right of action is getting more than one already has".⁵ It should be noted that it may also be a summary offence to harass a debtor where the debt is due.⁶

¹ Particularly the Companies Acts and Factories Acts. See Companies Act 1948, s. 434 (1) and Factories Act 1961, s. 175 (1). See also Obscene Publications Act 1964, and *Chief Constable of Blackpool v. Woodhall*, [1965] Crim. L.R. 660.
² "Any gain consequent on death" in the New Zealand Law Reform Act 1939, means "any increase in financial resources", *per* Ostler, J. in *Alley v. Alfred Bucklands & Sons, Ltd.*, [1941] N.Z.L.R. 575.
³ *Re Arthur Average Association* (1875), 10 Ch. App. 542, at 546.
⁴ *Cf. Lawrence*, [1971] Crim. L.R. 645, where it appears that D believed the debt to be due.
⁵ *Parkes*, [1973] Crim. L.R. 358; SHC 571 (Judge Dean); *cf. Parkes*, [1974] Crim. L.R. 320.
⁶ Administration of Justice Act 1970, s. 40. Smith & Hogan, 581.

(b) Intention to return an economic equivalent

[318] If the view expressed in the preceding paragraph is wrong, similar problems arise where D intends to restore to P an economic equivalent of the alleged gain which he has in mind. As a starting point, suppose that D wishes to acquire a particular florin belonging to P which has a sentimental value for both P and D. D demands of P with menaces that he exchange the desired florin for another. Obviously D intends to acquire the florin but he does not

intend to make any profit in terms of money.[1] If there were no view to gain in this situation, many cases would be excluded from the section which it is reasonably clear that it is intended to cover. If D demands with menaces that he be given an appointment, he may have every intention of doing a good day's work and earning his wages.[2] The runner who, by menaces, gains admission to a race may have every intention of supplying a first-class performance which will be worth as much· or more in terms of money to the organisers of the meeting as any prize he may win. The gambler who, by menaces, causes the bookmaker's clerk to let him bet on credit may have every intention of paying up if the horse backed loses—he is prepared to pay the full economic value of the chance he has bought. In each of these examples, D has a view to the acquisition of money or other property—his wages, the prize, the winnings—and in each case it is submitted that he is guilty of blackmail.

If this be correct, the same principle must govern "loss". D intends P to suffer a loss if he intends him to be deprived of particular money or property, though he may also intend that P be fully compensated in economic terms.

---

[1] Of course, the problem under consideration would not arise if the coin had a higher market value than its nominal value. Cf. *Moss* v. *Hancock*, [1899] 2 Q.B. 110.

[2] Lord Denning has expressed the view that, in such a case, there is no intention to cause economic loss to the employer: *Welham* v. *D.P.P.*, [1961] A.C. at 131. It follows that the employee has no intention to make an economic gain.

(c) Temporary gain and loss

[319] The intent permanently to deprive which is an essential ingredient of theft, robbery and obtaining property by deception is not a requisite of blackmail. Suppose that D, by menaces, causes P to let him have a car on hire for a week. If D intends to return the car at the end of the week, he cannot be guilty of theft or of robbery.[1] He has, however, a view to a temporary gain which is sufficient under s. 21 and he is guilty of blackmail.

This may seem strange, but it is consistent with the theory that it is the method of obtaining the property—the demand with menaces—which is the gist of the offence and not the unlawful profit made or contemplated by D or the corresponding loss to P. As we have seen D may be demanding property which he is entitled to have.

---

[1] Above, para. [118].

(d) Intent to cause loss

[320] In most cases "a view to gain" and an "intent to cause loss" will go hand in hand; P's loss will be D's gain. The phrase, "intent to cause loss" is not, however, superfluous. There may be circumstances in which D intends to cause a loss to P without any corresponding gain to D. If P has written his memoirs and D demands with menaces that P destroy them, D has an intent to cause loss but no view to gain.

Another instance would be the case where D demands with menaces that P dismiss Q from a remunerated office or employment or that P should not promote Q. D intends to cause Q a loss (by not getting what he might get[1]) and it is immaterial whether D has in view any gain to himself or another. Likewise

162

where D demands with menaces that P resign his own appointment, or not apply for, or refuse promotion.

[1] Above, para. [312].

(e) Gain by keeping and loss by not getting

[321] A view to gain includes an intent to keep what one has; and intent to cause a loss includes causing another not to get what he might get.[1] Thus if D owes P £10 and, by menaces, he induces him to accept £5 in full satisfaction he has caused a gain and a loss within the meaning of s. 21.

If D, knowing that P is in financial difficulties and in urgent need of money, takes advantage of this situation in order to induce P to accept a less sum in satisfaction, he may be in danger of conviction of blackmail. D can hardly say, to any effect, that he had reasonable grounds for making the demand if he knew the larger sum was due; and in that case it is immaterial whether the use of the menaces is a proper means of reinforcing the demand. The Court of Appeal has taken the view that it is "intimidation" and holding a creditor "to ransom" to say "We cannot pay you the £480. But we will pay you £300 if you will accept it in settlement. If you do not accept it on those terms you will get nothing. £300 is better than nothing."[2] This suggests that that court, at least, would regard such pressure on a creditor as a "menace".

[1] Section 34 (2) (i) and (ii), above, para. [312].
[2] *D. and C. Builders v. Rees*, [1966] 2 Q.B. 617 at 625, *per* Lord Denning, M.R.

(f) Remoteness

[322] Where a number of intermediate steps are required between the act caused by D's menace and the acquisition by him of any gain, problems of remoteness may arise.

If D gains admission to an Inn of Court by menacing the Under-Treasurer,[1] is he guilty of an offence under the section? If he intends ultimately to practise and thereby to earn fees it would seem that his action is taken with a view to gain—though this is rather far to seek. But if he has no intention to practise and merely wants the prestige of the barrister's qualification, it is difficult to see that he can have committed the offence. It must appear that D at least contemplated the *possibility* of using his qualification to earn money, probably that this was his actual intention.

What, then, if D menaces the headmaster of the public school with a view to gaining admission for his newly-born son? If D believes that the only advantage of education at that school is that it will produce a more cultured person with a greater capacity for the enjoyment of life than education in a state school, he has no view to gain. If, however, he believes and is motivated by his belief that his son will (in about twenty years' time) have a greater earning power, is it to be said that he has a view to gain? Literally he does. Yet the gain is so distant in time and subject to so many contingencies that its connection with the demand with menaces may be thought too remote. A stronger case is that of a candidate for a university examination who menaces the examiner with a view to passing or getting a better class degree than he would otherwise obtain. Most candidates have an eye on their earning capacity and this might be *prima facie* evidence of a view to gain.

---

¹ *Cf. Bassey* (1931), 22 Cr. App. Rep. 160.

B.   UNWARRANTED DEMANDS¹

[323] Whether a demand is "warranted" or not appears to be exclusively a question of the accused's belief. Theoretically a demand with menaces may be unwarranted although D is entitled to recover the property demanded and the menace is a perfectly proper means of enforcing the demand. Suppose P has stolen and disposed of D's picture. D threatens to report him to the police unless he pays D £1,000. D believes the picture is only worth £100; so he does not believe that he has reasonable grounds for making the demand. The picture is in fact worth £1,000, so he does actually have reasonable grounds. D who has looked up an out-of-date law book believes that it is the offence of compounding a felony to accept any consideration for not disclosing a theft; so he does not believe that the use of the menace is a proper means of enforcing the demand. But by the Criminal Law Act 1967, s. 5 (1) it is lawful to accept reasonable compensation for making good the injury or loss caused by an arrestable offence, in consideration for not disclosing it. The use of the menaces then—or so it seems—is a proper means of reinforcing the demand. Looking at the facts objectively, D has done nothing wrong; but he is guilty of blackmail.

It does not seem likely that this will be a serious issue in practice. Where D's conduct is objectively innocent, it is unlikely that a prosecution will ever be instituted. If it is, the onus of proof on the Crown will be very difficult to satisfy. The usual way of satisfying the jury that D did not have the beliefs referred to in s. 21 (1) (*a*) and (*b*) will be by showing that no reasonable person could have held such a belief. For example, if D says that he believed that he had reasonable grounds for demanding £1,000 from his neighbour in return for not disclosing to the neighbour's wife that her husband had committed adultery, it is safe to assume, in the absence of some extraordinary circumstances, that the jury will disbelieve him and be satisfied beyond reasonable doubt of his guilt. They will be so satisfied because they will feel that no man in his right mind could entertain such a belief for a moment.² If then, D's beliefs are entirely reasonable, the normal mode of proof fails; and, in the absence of some confession by D as to his belief in the unreasonableness of his demand, or the impropriety of his threat, conviction will be impossible.

---

¹ See Williams, *TBCL*, 799–803.
² The ultimate question is as to the state of mind of the accused person and this should always be stresséd to a jury.

---

[324] The problem that does arise is the converse. That is, the grounds for making the demand were not reasonable but D asserts that he believed they were; the use of the menaces is not a proper means of reinforcing the demand but D asserts that he believed it was. The question for the jury then is simply whether D is speaking the truth. Juries have to determine this question often

enough; but the difference about this case is that it is not a question of the accused's belief in *fact*, but the accused's belief in *standards.*

This provision of the Act has been criticised by a judicial writer:[1]

> "If a defendant has acted disgracefully by making a certain demand reinforced by threats of a particular kind, I see no injustice in holding him responsible in a criminal court, even though he may have acted according to his own standard in these matters. On the other hand I see some danger to our general standards of right and wrong, if each man can claim to act according to his own, however low that standard may be. That is one objection. Another is the difficulty of the jury's ascertaining the defendant's standard, so that it may be decided whether in the case before them he acted in accordance with it. A man whose standard is below the general may fail in a particular case to observe even his own standard in which event he would, I suppose, be punishable under clause 17 [now section 21]. But are questions of this kind triable?"

[1] Sir Bernard MacKenna, "Blackmail: A Criticism", [1966] Crim. L.R. 467 at 472.

[325] The matter has not yet been considered by an appeal court and the only reported case adopts this wholly subjective view. In *Lambert*,[1] D, suspecting his wife to be having an affair with P, offered to sell P his "rights" to the wife for £250, stating that he would inform P's employer of his conduct if P did not accept. On a direction that they must be satisfied that D, in his own opinion, was acting wrongly in the circumstances, the jury acquitted.

If no regard whatever were paid to external standards, the crime of blackmail would virtually disappear. It is almost invariably a pre-meditated offence. By the accused's own standards, it is something which he might do, whatever others might think. It is his belief at the time of making the demand which is relevant. If he should later admit that his conduct was unreasonable or improper, this is probably because he knows full well that people generally regard it as unreasonable or improper. It would be unreasonable to attribute to Parliament an intention to enact an offence which would be a dead letter. It was certainly not the intention of the Committee. If we look first at the question of the propriety of the threat, some clear guidance as to their intentions can be found in the Report.[2] Some care was devoted to the choice of the word "proper":

> "... we chose the word 'proper' after considering 'legitimate' or 'fair' instead. Any of the three words would, we think, be suitable. 'Fair' would provide a good test for a jury to apply. It might also be a little more favourable to the accused, because the jury might think that, even if the accused behaved improperly the prosecutor behaved so badly that it was fair that he should be treated as he was. There seems little difference between 'legitimate' and 'proper'. On the whole, 'proper' seems the best word. 'Proper' directs the mind to consideration of what is morally and socially acceptable, which seems right on a matter of this kind; 'legitimate' might suggest that it is a purely legal question whether the accused had a right to utter the menaces."

This passage clearly shows that it was intended that the jury should apply a standard and that the standard should be "what is morally and socially acceptable".

[1] [1972] Crim. L.R. 422; SHC 569 (Deputy circuit Judge Arnold). In *Harry*, [1974] Crim. L.R. 32; SHC 564, it appears that the prosecution conceded that *Lambert* was correct.
[2] Para. 123.

[326] We are of course concerned with D's beliefs in the matter, not the jury's. Once D's belief has been ascertained, it has to be decided whether it fits the words of the section. The word "proper" has to be given a meaning. According to this interpretation then, the test is: "Did the accused person believe that what he threatened to do was morally and socially acceptable?" The effect might be illustrated by considering the effect on the case, decided under the Larceny Act, of *Dymond*.[1] D wrote to P alleging that he had indecently assaulted her and adding, "I leave this to you to think what you are going to do, paid or gett summons ... If you dont send to and apologise I shall let everybody knowed in the town it." Her conviction was upheld by the Court of Criminal Appeal holding that an honest belief in "reasonable cause" for making the demand, as opposed to reasonable cause in fact, was not a defence. Probably a jury would take the view that Miss Dymond's conduct was, by their standards, morally and socially unacceptable; but the question would be whether *she* knew that it was morally and socially unacceptable. In the circles in which Emily Dymond moved it may well be that the advice of the neighbours was "If he won't pay up, you ought to summons him and tell everyone." If these were the only standards known to Emily, she ought to be acquitted.

[1] [1920] 2 K.B. 260.

[327] This is not to say that the standards of the small group to which D belongs will necessarily govern in every case. D may belong to a terrorist organisation, the members of which think it right to demand money as the price of releasing a hostage in order to further their political ends. The conduct may be morally and socially acceptable within the small group; but it is safe to assume that these are not the only standards known to D. He is well aware that, in English society generally, such conduct is morally and socially unacceptable; and it must be the known standards of English society generally which apply.

[328] Where D admits that he knew that the act he threatened to do was a crime, it is submitted that the judge would be within his rights if he withdrew the defence from the jury. What is criminal cannot be "proper" within the meaning of a statute and if D knows the act to be a crime he cannot believe it to be "proper".

Where the act amounts to a crime but D does not know that, the test should again be whether he believed the threat to be socially and morally acceptable by persons generally. Even if D does not know that it is unlawful to threaten another with a dagger in order to compel the payment of a debt,[1] a jury might well find that he knew that it was a socially and morally unacceptable way of compelling the wages clerk to pay his wages. If so, D, though not guilty of robbery or attempted robbery, would be guilty of blackmail.

In many cases of blackmail the threat is to do something not amounting to a crime. Here the exclusive test must be whether D knew that the threat in the circumstances would be condemned as improper by the community generally.

[1] Cf. *Skivington*, [1968] 1 Q.B. 166; [1967] 1 All E.R. 483; above, para. [138].

[329] D's plea might very well be accepted in the following cases. D, a bookmaker, being unable to obtain payment of a wagering debt due from P, another bookmaker, threatens to report P to Tattersalls if he does not pay up. D threatens P that she will tell P's wife of their immoral relationship if P does not pay her the money he promised for her immoral services. D threatens that he will warn his friends against doing business with P if P does not pay up a statute-barred debt.

A similar test might be applied to determine whether D believed he had reasonable grounds for making the demand. If he had a claim of legal right then, clearly, he believed he had reasonable grounds for making the demand. A lady who believed, wrongly but on the advice of a Hungarian lawyer, that she was entitled to money promised to her as the price of her past immoral services, would have a good defence.[1] If she knew that she had no legal right, she might nevertheless believe that the man was under a moral obligation to compensate her, and a jury could find that she believed that she had reasonable grounds for her demand. Similarly where D demands money won on a wager with P, though he knows that wagers are unenforceable in law, or demands payment of a statute-barred debt, being aware of the statute of limitations.

[1] *Bernhard*, [1938] 2 K.B. 264; [1938] 2 All E.R. 140.

[330] If this view is accepted, the law is certainly lacking in precision; but this is a branch of the law in which precision is not easily obtainable. From the point of view of justice, however, the law seems unexceptionable. The defendant is not to be held liable unless it is proved that he knew he was doing something which he ought not to do, in the broad sense described, *either* in making the demand, *or* in making the threat.

CHAPTER XI

BURGLARY AND AGGRAVATED BURGLARY

1 BURGLARY

[331] The law relating to burglary and other breaking offences contained in the Larceny Act 1916, ss. 24–27, was very complicated.[1] The Theft Act effected a considerable simplification of the law. The Act eliminated entirely the concept of "breaking" which was a requisite of burglary and most forms of house-breaking under the Larceny Act. "Breaking" was a highly technical term on which there was a great deal of case law and it no longer served a useful purpose in the definition of the offences. The Act also got rid of the distinction between breaking "in the night" and breaking "in the day" which was the most conspicuous difference between the old offences of burglary and housebreaking. So far as the definition of the new offence is concerned, the concept of "dwelling house" is also eliminated; but, unfortunately, it is still necessary to distinguish between "dwellings" and other buildings for the purposes of ascertaining the jurisdiction of magistrates' courts.[2] The new offence of burglary comprehends all[3] that was formerly burglary and house-breaking—and a good deal more besides.

---

[1] Smith and Hogan (1st ed.), 397–401.
[2] Section 29 (2), below, para. [434].
[3] With some unimportant exceptions.

---

[332] Section 9 of the Act provides:

"(1) A person is guilty of burglary if—
(a) he enters any building or part of a building as a trespasser and with intent to commit any such offence as is mentioned in subsection (2) below; or
(b) having entered any building or part of a building as a trespasser he steals or attempts to steal anything in the building or that part of it or inflicts or attempts to inflict on any person therein any grievous bodily harm.

(2) The offences referred to in subsection (1) (a) above are offences of stealing anything in the building or part of a building in question, of inflicting on any person therein any grievous bodily harm or raping any woman therein, and of doing unlawful damage to the building or anything therein.

(3) References in subsections (1) and (2) above to a building shall apply also to an inhabited vehicle or vessel, and shall apply to any such

168

vehicle or vessel at times when the person having a habitation in it is not
there as well as at times when he is.

(4) A person guilty of burglary shall on conviction on indictment be
liable to imprisonment for a term not exceeding fourteen years."

Paragraphs (*a*) and (*b*) of s. 9 (1) create separate offences. A person indicted
under one paragraph may not be convicted of an offence under the other.[1]
When there is a doubt as to which offence was committed, it is desirable to
have two counts.

[1] *Hollis*, [1971] Crim. L.R. 525.

A. THE ACTUS REUS

(a) Enters

[333] The common law rule was that the insertion of any part of the body,
however small, was a sufficient entry. So where D pushed in a window pane
and the forepart of his finger was observed to be inside the building, that was
enough.[1] The Act gives no express guidance and it seems to have been assumed
in Parliament that the common law rules would apply.[2] In *Collins*,[3] D, naked
but for his socks, had climbed up a ladder on to a bedroom window sill, as a
trespasser and with intent to rape, when the lady in the bedroom invited him
in. It was not clear whether he was on the sill outside the window or on the
inner sill at the moment when he ceased to be a trespasser and became an
invitee. Edmund Davies, L.J. said that there must be "an effective and
substantial entry" as a trespasser to constitute burglary. This suggests that it is
no longer enough that any part of the body however small is intruded; but it is
not clear what "effective and substantial" means. The insertion of an arm may
be "effective" if it is long enough to reach property and remove it. Yet it
cannot have been intended that D must have got so far into the building as to
be able to accomplish his unlawful purpose. Probably the safest and best course
is to assume the continued existence of the common law rule.

The common law went further. If an instrument was inserted into the
building *for the purpose of committing the ulterior offence*, there was an entry
even though no part of the body was introduced into the building. So it was
enough that hooks were inserted into the premises to drag out the carpets[4] or
that the muzzle of a gun was introduced with a view to shooting someone
inside.[5] It would amount to an entry if holes were bored in the side of a granary
so that wheat would run out and be stolen by D,[6] provided that the boring
implement emerged on the inside. On the other hand, the insertion of an
instrument *for the purpose of gaining entry* and not for the purpose of
committing the ulterior offence, was not an entry if no part of the body
entered.[7] If D bored a hole in a door with a centre bit for the purpose of
gaining entry, the emergence of the point of the bit on the inside of the door
was not an entry.

[1] *Davis* (1823), Russ & Ry. 499.
[2] Parl. Debates, Official Report (H.L.), Vol. 290, cols. 85–86.
[3] [1973] 1 Q.B. 100 at 106; [1972] 2 All E.R. 1105 at 1111; SHC 574.
[4] (1583), 1 Anderson 114.

⁵ O. East P.C. 492.
⁶ *State* v. *Crawford* (1899), 46 L.R.A. 312 (Alabama).
⁷ *Hughes* (1785), 1 Leach 406; but *cf. Tucker* (1844), 1 Cox C.C. 73.

[334] Even if the courts are willing to follow the common law in holding that the intrusion of any part of the body is an entry, they may be reluctant to preserve these technical rules regarding instruments, for they seem to lead to outlandish results. Thus it seems to follow from the common law rules that there may be an entry if a stick of dynamite is thrown into the building or if a bullet is fired from outside the building into it.[1] What then if a time bomb is sent by parcel post? Has D "entered", even though he is not on the scene at all?—perhaps even abroad and outside the jurisdiction? Whether D enters or not can hardly depend on how far away he is and the case seems indistinguishable from the others put. Yet this is hardly an "entry" in the "simple language as used and understood by ordinary literate men and women" in which the Act is said to be written.[2]

---

[1] 1 Hawk. P.C., c. 17, s. 11; 2 East P.C. 490; *contra*, Hale, 1 P.C. 554.
[2] Above, para. **[8]**, footnote 3, and see Griew 4–08.

---

[335] There is, however, a cogent argument in favour of the common law rules which may be put as follows. If D sends a child, under the age of ten, into the building to steal, this is obviously an entry by D,[1] through an "innocent agent", under ordinary principles. Suppose that, instead of a child, D sends in a monkey. It is hard to see that this should not equally be an entry by D. But if that point be conceded, it is admitted that the insertion of an *animate* instrument is an entry; and are we to distinguish between animate and inanimate instruments? Unless we are, the insertion of the hooks, etc., must also be an entry.[2]

If D puts a child under ten through the window, so that child may open a door and admit D who will himself steal, it is by no means so clear that the innocent agency argument is open; and the common law rule regarding instruments would suggest it is not an entry; since the child is being used to gain entry and not to commit the ulterior offence.

---

[1] Hale, 1 P.C. 555; Smith and Hogan, 112–113.
[2] Transvestites who hooked dresses worth £600 through letter boxes of shops pleaded guilty to burglary in a metropolitan magistrate's court: *Daily Telegraph*, 4-3-79.

(b) As a trespasser

[336] Trespass is a legal concept and we must resort to the law of tort in order to ascertain its meaning.[1] It would appear that any intentional, reckless or negligent entry into a building is a trespass if the building is in fact in the possession of another who does not consent to the entry. Entry with the consent of the occupier cannot be a trespass. In *Collins*[2] it was held that, whatever the position in the law of tort, an invitation by the occupier's daughter to enter her bedroom and have intercourse with her, without the knowledge or consent of the occupier, precluded trespass for this purpose. Suppose, however, that the occupier's daughter or servant invites her lover into the house to steal the occupier's property. This ought to be burglary if the lover realises, as he surely must, that the daughter or servant has no right to invite him in for this purpose. Where the invitation is issued by a member of the household, it is submitted that the question is whether the accused knew that the invitation was issued without authority. In *Jones and Smith*[3] where the occupier's son had a general permission to enter the house, entry with an accomplice, and with an intent to steal, constituted burglary. The accused had knowingly exceeded the permission. Williams[4] argues that *Jones and Smith* is wrongly decided, being inconsistent with *Collins*,[5] because Collins also exceeded the permission since he entered intending to use force if necessary. But as the girl saw him to be "a naked male with an erect penis" it seems clear that she invited him in for the purpose of sexual intercourse, that he knew he was so invited and that any intention to rape must have lapsed.

In *Collins* the invitation to enter was issued under a mistake as to the man's identity. It is submitted that, if he had known of the mistake, he would have intentionally entered as a trespasser. Mistake as to identity, where identity is material, generally vitiates consent. Mistake by the person entering is no defence to an action in tort; so that, if D on a very dark night were to enter the house next door in mistake for his own, this would be regarded as an intentional entry and a trespass. This would apparently be so even if D's mistake was a reasonable one, *a fortiori* if it were negligent as, for example, if he made the mistake because he was befuddled with drink. It is established, however, that it is not sufficient (though it is necessary) that D is a trespasser in the civil law. In the criminal law he must be shown to have *mens rea*. If he is charged under s. 9 (1) (*a*), it must appear that, when he entered, he knew the facts which caused him to be a trespasser or at least that he was reckless whether those facts existed.[6] A merely negligent entry, as where D enters another's house, honestly but unreasonably believing it to be his own, should not be enough. So too a belief in a *right* to enter the house of another should be a defence, for then there is no intention to enter *as a trespasser.* Suppose that D, being separated from his wife, wrongly supposes that he has a right to enter the matrimonial home of which she is the owner-occupier and does enter with intent to inflict grievous bodily harm upon her. Even if he is in law a trespasser it is submitted that he is not a burglar.

---

[1] Salmond on *Torts* (16th ed.), 38; Winfield on *Tort* (9th ed.), 323; Street, *Law of Torts* (6th ed.), 13, 63.
[2] [1973] 1 Q.B. 100 at 107; [1972] 2 All E.R. 1105 at 1111; SHC 574; above, para. [**315**]. *Cf. Robson* v. *Hallett*, [1967] 2 Q.B. 939; [1967] 2 All E.R. 407, (invitation by occupier's son effective until withdrawn by occupier).
[3] [1976], 3 All E.R. 54, C.A.
[4] *TBCL*, 812–814.
[5] Above, para. [**333**].
[6] *Collins*, [1973] 1 Q.B. 100, at 100, at pp. 104–105; [1972] 2 All E.R. 1105 at 1109–1110.

[**337**] If D's entry is involuntary, he is not a trespasser and cannot be guilty of burglary. So if he is dragged against his will into P's house and left there by his drunken companions and he steals P's vase and leaves, this is not burglary. If, however, D had intentionally entered the building, believing it to be his own house and committed theft on discovering the truth, it appears from the previous paragraph that he would have committed theft after entering as a trespasser and thus committed the *actus reus* of burglary. In this case it seems

that D has *mens rea* as well, for burglary under s. 9 (1) (*b*) is committed, not at the time of entry, but when the ulterior crime is committed; and at that time, he knows that he has entered as a trespasser.[1]

---

[1] The common law doctrine of trespass *ab initio* has no application to burglary under the Theft Act: *Collins*, [1973] 1 Q.B. 100 at 107; [1972] 2 All E.R. 1105 at 1111; SHC 574. See the second edition of this work at paras. 377–378.

---

[338] (i) *Entry under false pretences.*—Since trespass is an entry without consent, difficulties may arise where consent is obtained by fraud. If the fraud is such as to render the transaction void, then it is safe to say that any apparent consent is not real consent and a trespass will be committed.

For example (to borrow the names from a well-known civil case), if Blenkarn by pretending to be the well-known firm of picture cleaners, Blenkiron & Co., [1] causes P to enter into "a contract" with him for the cleaning of P's pictures and thereby gains admission to P's premises, he does so as a trespasser and will be guilty of burglary if he steals while on the premises.

Similarly if D, by impersonating X who has a reader's ticket, gains admission to the P University library with intent to steal the books.

---

[1] *Cf. Cundy v. Lindsay* (1878), 3 App. Cas. 459.

---

[339] Mistake as to identity in these examples rendered the contract, in the first case, and licence, in the second case, void. The problem is more difficult where the fraud is such as to render the transaction not void but merely voidable.

For example, D, by producing forged references, causes P to enter into a contract with him, D, for the cleaning of P's pictures. D obtains a reader's ticket to the P University library by falsely pretending that he, D, is reading for a degree at another university. In these situations, the contract and the licence are not void but voidable. It may therefore be argued that since D enters the premises under an existing contract or licence, he does not do so as a trespasser. P may rescind the transaction but, until he does so, it is a perfectly good contract or licence. If this argument is sound, the consequences could be serious, for some acts which were (and rightly) burglary or house-breaking under the old law would be outside the terms of s. 9. For example, D gains admission to P's house by falsely pretending that he has been sent by the B.B.C. to examine the radio set in order to trace disturbances in transmission. It was held[1] under the old law, that there was a constructive breaking since the householder had been deceived by a trick and he would not have admitted the man had he known the true facts. "Breaking" is no longer an issue and the sole question is whether there was a trespassory entry.

There are English and Commonwealth authorities which suggest that there is a trespass in all the examples considered in this paragraph. In *Taylor* v. *Jackson*[2] D had permission to go on P's land and hunt for rabbits. He went there to hunt for hares and the Divisional Court held that this was evidence of trespass in pursuit of game, contrary to the Game Act 1831, s. 30. In *Hillen and Pettigrew* v. *I.C.I. (Alkali), Ltd.*[3] members of a stevedore's gang employed to unload a barge were held to be trespassers when they placed kegs on the hatch covers, knowing that this was a wrong and dangerous thing to do. They were, therefore, not entitled to damages when the hatch covers collapsed and they were injured. Lord Atkin said:

> "As Scrutton, L.J. has pointedly said: 'When you invite a person into your house to use the staircase you do not invite him to slide down the bannisters.'[4] So far as he sets foot on so much of the premises as lie outside the invitation or *uses them for purposes which are alien to the invitation* he is not an invitee but a trespasser, and his rights must be determined accordingly. In the present case the stevedores knew that they ought not to use the covered hatch in order to load cargo from it; for them *for such a purpose it was out of bounds*: they were trespassers."

In *Farrington* v. *Thomson and Bridgland*[5] an Australian court held that a police officer who entered a hotel for the purpose of committing a tort was a trespasser. The tacit invitation to the public to enter the hotel did not extend to persons entering for the purpose of committing a tort or a criminal offence.

---

[1] *Boyle*, [1954] 2 Q.B. 292; [1954] 2 All E.R. 721.
[2] (1898), 78 L.T. 555.
[3] [1936] A.C. 65.
[4] *The Carlgarth*, [1927] P. 93 at 110.
[5] [1959] V.R. 286 (Smith, J.). See also *Gross* v. *Wright*, [1923] 2 D.L.R. 171.

[340] (ii) *Entry for a purpose alien to a licence to enter.*—Such cases are not only authority for saying that all the hypothetical examples considered above are cases of trespass and therefore of burglary, but they go much further. In the examples, a false pretence is made with a view to gaining entry. These authorities suggest that it is enough to negative a licence to enter, that entry is made with a secret unlawful intent, even though no false pretence is made. If this is right, D, who enters a shop for the purpose of shoplifting, is a burglar.[1] This is perhaps fair enough. Few would object to the conviction of burglary of intending bank robbers who enter the bank flourishing pistols; yet banks are no more and no less open to the public than shops—that is, an invitation is extended by both to those members of the public who wish to enter for the transaction of the business for which the premises exist—the sale of goods, the cashing of cheques, the opening of an account and so on. One decision goes against this view. In *Byrne* v. *Kinematograph Renters Society, Ltd.*[2] Harman, J. held that it was not trespass to gain entry to a cinema by buying tickets with the purpose, not of seeing the film, but of counting the patrons. It is submitted that this decision is against the weight of authority and should not be followed.

---

[1] *Contra*, Williams, *TBCL*, 814.
[2] [1958] 2 All E.R. 579 at 593; distinguished in *Jones*, above, para. [336], footnote 3.

[341] This is not to say that all shoplifters are burglars. In order to convict of burglary, it is necessary to prove that D entered with intent to steal and this will often be difficult or impossible. If D entered the shop in order to make a purchase or to look at the stock in order to decide whether to make a purchase, he is not a trespasser. If he then yields to temptation and steals, he probably becomes a trespasser but it remains a fact that he did not *enter* as a trespasser. Where there is evidence that the shoplifting was pre-meditated, as a previous conspiracy, or system, or preparatory acts, as the wearing of a jacket with special pockets, then a conviction for burglary may be possible.

[342] (iii) *Who is the victim of the burglary?*—Trespass is an interference with possession. Burglary is therefore committed against the person in possession of the building entered. Where the premises are let, the burglary is committed against the tenant and not against the landlord. The landlord could commit burglary of the premises, the tenant could not. Even if the tenant is only a tenant at will, he may maintain trespass. So may a deserted wife, though she has no proprietary interest in the matrimonial home.[1] On the other hand, "The guest at a hotel will not ordinarily have sufficient possession of his room to enable him to sue in trespass."[2] It has been held that, where a servant occupies premises belonging to his master for the more convenient performance of his duties as servant, he cannot maintain an action for trespass against the master.[3] In such a case it is, of course, necessary to look at the precise terms of the arrangement between the parties; if the servant has been given exclusive possession, he and not the master is the victim of a trespass. And it does not necessarily follow that, because the servant in a particular case may not maintain trespass against the master, he cannot do so against third parties.[4]

---

[1] *National Provincial Bank, Ltd.* v. *Ainsworth*, [1965] A.C. 1175; [1965] 2 All E.R. 472.
[2] Street, *Law of Torts* (3rd ed.), 67.
[3] *Mayhew* v. *Suttle* (1854), 4 E. & B. 347; *White* v. *Bayley* (1861), 10 C.B.N.S. 227.
[4] Though in *White* v. *Bayley* (above, footnote 3) Byles, J. thought, *obiter*, that an action could not have been maintained by the servant against a stranger (10 C.B.N.S. at 235).

---

[343] The position of a lodger depends on the precise terms of his contract. If he has exclusive possession so that he can refuse entry to the landlord then, no doubt, he may maintain trespass. Many lodgers, however, do not have such possession and in such cases an unauthorised entry by a third party is a trespass against the landlord.

It seems to follow that burglary is not committed where an innkeeper enters the room of a guest, even though the entry is without the guest's consent and with intent to steal; and that, depending on the terms of the contract, the same may be true in the case of a master entering premises occupied by his servant for the purposes of his employment and a landlord entering the rooms of his lodger.

[344] It seems that an indictment will lie although it does not allege that the building was the property of anyone. Whereas the Larceny Act 1916 required that the breaking and entering be of the dwelling house *of another*, there is no such expression in the Theft Act. The requirement of trespass means that evidence must be offered that someone other than the accused was in possession. If that is all that is necessary, evidence that A or B was in possession should suffice—it is equally a trespass in either event. But if a statement of ownership is required in the indictment, "A or B" will hardly do. It is submitted, therefore, that it should be sufficient that the indictment alleges that D trespassed in a building without alleging who is the owner of the building.

(c) Any building or part of a building

[345] The meaning of "building" in various statutes has frequently been considered by the courts. Clearly the meaning of the term varies according to the context and many things which have been held to be buildings for other purposes will not be buildings for the purpose of the Theft Act—for example, a garden wall, a railway embankment or a tunnel under the road. According to Lord Esher, M.R., its "ordinary and usual meaning is, a block of brick or stone work, covered in by a roof".[1] It seems clear, however, that it is not necessary that the structure be of brick or stone to be a building within this Act. Clearly all dwelling houses are intended to be protected and these may be built of wood; while "the inhabited vehicle or vessel" which is expressly included is likely to be built of steel or of wood. More helpful is the view of Byles, J., that a building in its ordinary sense is "a structure of considerable size and intended to be permanent or at least to endure for a considerable time."[2]

To be a building, the structure must have some degree of permanence. A substantial portable structure may be a building[3] but probably not a tent even though it is someone's home. It is again a question of the meaning of the word in the language of ordinary literate men; and this perhaps suggests that a telephone kiosk is not a building. If it is, the wreckers of these places are probably burglars.

---

[1] *Moir* v. *Williams*, [1892] 1 Q.B. 264.
[2] *Stevens* v. *Gourley* (1859), 7 C.B.N.S. 99 at 112; SHC 579. For other descriptions, see *Stroud's Judicial Dictionary* (4th ed.), 1, 334.
[3] *B. & S.* v. *Leathley*, [1979] Crim. L.R. 314 (Carlisle Crown Court).

---

[346] The outbuildings of a house seem to be buildings for the purpose of the Act so that burglary may now be committed in a detached garage, a wooden toolshed or a greenhouse. Similarly, farm buildings such as a stable, cow-byre, pig-stye, barn or silo and industrial buildings such as factories, warehouses and stores. Other cases are more difficult. It is not uncommon for trespassers to enter unfinished buildings and do damage. If they enter with intent to cause damage by fire or explosion are they now guilty of burglary? An unfinished building was a building within s. 6 of the Malicious Damage Act 1861.[1] Why not for the purposes of burglary? Clearly there is a difficult question as to the point in its erection at which a structure becomes a building. In *Manning*,[2] Lush, J. said:

> "... it is sufficient that it should be a connected and entire structure. I do not think four walls erected a foot high would be a building."

In that case all the walls were built and finished and the roof was on. It may be that a roof will be thought necessary for a structure to be a building under the present Act, for it clearly is not intended to extend to a walled garden, yard or paddock. What if there is a roof but no walls, as in the case of a bandstand?[3] There is no obvious answer to borderline cases such as this but they are likely to be rare.

---

[1] *Manning* (1871), L.R. 1 C.C.R. 338.
[2] *Ibid.*, at 341.

[3] Held to be a building for the purposes of a private act regulating the provision of public entertainments in buildings: *A.G.* v. *Eastbourne Corporation* (1934), 78 Sol. Jo. 633.

---

[347] (i) *Part of a building.*—It is sufficient if the trespass takes place in part of a building so that one lodger may commit burglary by entering the room of another lodger within the same house, or by entering the part of the house occupied by the landlord. A guest in a hotel may commit burglary by entering the room of another guest. A customer in a shop who goes behind the counter and takes money from the till during a short absence of the shopkeeper would be guilty of burglary even though he entered the shop with the shopkeeper's permission. The permission did not extend to his going behind the counter. It is enough that there is a defined area within the building into which D was not permitted to go and that he knew this when he entered the area or when he stole or attempted to steal, etc., within the area. It is not necessary that the building be permanently divided into parts. A temporary physical division is enough if it clearly marks out a part of the building into which D is not allowed to go. In *Walkington*[1] there was a moveable, three-sided, rectangular counter in a shop. It was held that the rectangle bounded by the three sides of the counter was capable of being "part" of the building. A customer who entered the area with intent to steal from the till on the counter was held to have knowingly entered that part of the building as a trespasser and to be guilty of burglary.

---

[1] No. 1293/C/78, 22/2/79, C.A. Below, para. **[359]**.

---

[348] Take a case put by the Criminal Law Revision Committee.[1] D enters a shop lawfully,[2] but conceals himself on the premises until closing time and then emerges with intent to steal. When concealing himself he may or may not have entered a part of the building to which customers are not permitted to go; but even if he did commit a trespass at this stage, he may not have done so with intent to commit an offence in that part of the building into which he has trespassed. For example, he hides in the broom cupboard of a supermarket, intending to emerge and steal tins of food. Entering the broom cupboard, though a trespass committed with intent to steal, is not burglary, for he has no intent to steal in the part of the building which he has entered as a trespasser. When he emerges from the broom cupboard after the shop has closed, he is a trespasser and it is submitted that he has entered a part of the building with intent to steal. He is just as much a trespasser as if he had been told in express terms to go, for he knows perfectly well that his licence to remain on the premises terminated when the shop closed.[3] Suppose, however, having entered lawfully, he merely remained concealed behind a pile of tins of soup in the main hall of the supermarket. This was not a trespass because he had a right to be there. When he emerged and proceeded to steal, still in the main hall of the supermarket, was he entering another part of the building? It is submitted that every step he took was " as a trespasser", but it is difficult to see that he entered any part of the building as a trespasser; the whole transaction took place in a single part of the building which he had entered lawfully.

---

[1] *Eighth Report*, Cmnd. 2977, para. 75.
[2] *I.e.*, without intent to steal; above, para. **[341]**.

[3] The Criminal Law Revision Committee thought "The case is not important, because the offender is likely to go into a part of the building where he has no right to be, and this will be a trespassory entry into that part". But he has no right to be in any part of the building after closing time and the only question, it is submitted, is whether he went into *another* part.

---

[349] It would seem that the whole reason for the words "or part of a building," is that D may enter or be in part of a building without trespass and it is desirable that he should be liable as a burglar if he trespasses in the remainder of the building with the necessary intent. It is submitted that the building need not be physically divided into "parts". It ought to be sufficient if a notice in the middle of a hall stated, "No customers beyond this point". These considerations suggest that, for present purposes, a building falls into two parts only: first, that part in which D was lawfully present and, second, the remainder of the building. This interpretation avoids anomalies which arise if physical divisions within a building are held to create "parts".[1]

---

[1] See para. [352]; Griew, 4–15, n. 30, finds this interpretation "desirable but strained" and rejects it.

---

[350] (ii) *The extent of a "building" and its "parts".*—Under the old law, the entry had to be into a particular dwelling house, office, shop, garage, etc. A single structure might contain many dwelling houses—for example a block of flats—many offices, shops or garages. If D broke into Flat 1 with intent to pass through it, go upstairs and steal in Flat 45, the breaking and entering of Flat 1 was neither burglary nor housebreaking for D did not intend to commit a felony therein.[1] It was probably not even an attempt, not being sufficiently proximate to the intended crime. If D broke into a flat above a jeweller's shop with intent to break through the ceiling and steal in the shop, he could be convicted of burglary in the flat only if it could be said that he broke and entered the flat with intent to commit a felony therein, namely to break and enter the shop.[2] The difficulty about this argument is that while the breaking may reasonably be said to have occurred in the flat, the entering, strictly speaking, took place in the shop. On that view, there was no intent to commit a felony in the flat and it was not, therefore, burglary or housebreaking to break and enter it.

---

[1] *Cf. Wrigley*, [1957] Crim. L.R. 57.
[2] *Cf.* comment on *Wrigley*, [1957] Crim. L.R. 58.

---

[351] The effect on this situation of the Theft Act depends on what is the extent of a "building". In its ordinary natural meaning, this term could certainly include a block of flats. If that meaning be adopted, D's entering Flat 1 as a trespasser with intent to pass through it, go upstairs and steal in Flat 45 is an entry of a building as a trespasser with intent to steal therein—that is, it is burglary. Similarly the intending jewel thief would be guilty of burglary when he entered the flat above the jeweller's shop as a trespasser. The effect would be to make the full offence of what was previously, at the most, an attempt, and probably was only an act of preparation. There seems no good reason, however, why the law should not be extended in this way. On the contrary, there is everything to be said for enabling the police to intervene at

the earliest possible moment to prevent such offences; and for forestalling defences such as "I had no intention to steal in the flat—I was only using it as a passage to another flat which I never reached". It is submitted therefore that the word "building" should be given its natural meaning.

[352] Suppose, however, that D is lawfully in Flat 1, and that he can get to Flat 45 where he intends to steal only by trespassing into Flat 2. Suppose he is apprehended in Flat 2. He is guilty of burglary only if he can be shown to have intended to steal in "the part of the building in question". If Flat 2 is a separate part, he had no such intention and his act is probably too remote to constitute an attempt to enter Flat 45. But it is very odd that entering Flat 1 (from outside where D lawfully was) as a trespasser with intent to steal in Flat 45 should be burglary, and entering Flat 2 as a trespasser (from Flat 1 where D lawfully was) with intent to steal in Flat 45 should be nothing. It is therefore submitted that, as physical divisions are *unnecessary* to create "parts", so the existence of such divisions is insufficient to create them. If the building is divided into the part into which D may lawfully go and the part into which he may not, then Flats 2 and 45 are in the same "part" of the building and D is guilty of burglary as soon as he enters Flat 2.

[353] Is a row of terrace houses a single building?[1] Suppose D breaks into no. 1, climbs into the rafters and makes his way above no. 2, intending to continue to no. 36, descend into the house and steal therein. Has he already committed burglary? It is difficult to discern any satisfactory principle by which this case can be distinguished from those of the block of flats and the flat above the shop considered above. In both the block of flats and the terrace a series of dwelling houses are contained within a single structure and it cannot matter that the arrangement is horizontal rather than vertical. It is true that there is internal communication between the flats; but it can hardly be said that the block of flats would cease to be "a building" because access to them was confined to an external staircase. In policy and in principle there seems to be no reason why "building" should not include the whole terrace.

---

[1] In *Hedley* v. *Webb*, [1901] 2 Ch. 126, Cozens-Hardy, J. held that two semi-detached houses were a single building for the purpose of determining whether there was a sewer within the meaning of the Public Health Act 1875, s. 4. In *Birch* v. *Wigan Corporation*, [1953] 1 Q.B. 136; [1952] 2 All E.R. 893, the Court of Appeal (Denning, L.J. dissenting) held that one house in a terrace of six was a "house" within the meaning of s. 11 (1) and (4) of the Housing Act 1936 and not "part of a building" within s. 12 of that Act. But, since the sections were mutually exclusive, the house could not be both a "house" and "part of a building" for the purpose of the Act. Otherwise, Denning, L.J. would have been disposed to say that the house was both and Romer, L.J. also thought that "for some purposes and in other contexts two 'houses' may constitute one building."

---

[354] (iii) *Inhabited vehicle or vessel.*—The obvious cases which are brought within the protection of burglary by this provision are a caravan or a houseboat which is someone's home. There seems to be no reason whatever why a home should lack the ordinary protection of the law because it is mobile and this extension is welcome. Its limits should be noted. "Inhabited" implies, not merely that there is someone inside the vehicle, but that someone is *living* there. My saloon car is not an inhabited vehicle because I happen to be sitting in it when D enters against my will. The caravan or houseboat which is a man's

home is, however, expressly protected, whether or not he is there at the time of the burglary. He may, for example, be away on his holidays.

[355] The provision is not free from difficulty. Many people now own "dormobiles" or motorised caravans which they use for the ordinary purposes of a motor car during most of the year but on occasions they live in them, generally while on holiday. While the vehicle is being lived in, it is undoubtedly an inhabited vehicle. When it is being used for the ordinary purposes of a motor car, it is submitted that it is not an inhabited vehicle. The exact moment at which the dormobile becomes an inhabited vehicle may be difficult to ascertain. Is it when the family have loaded it with their belongings before departing on their holiday? When they take to the road on their journey to the sea-side? When they park the vehicle at the place where they intend to sleep? Or when they actually go to sleep in the vehicle? It can hardly be later than that. Since the vehicle is not really distinguishable from any other family car going on holiday until it reaches its destination, it probably becomes "inhabited" when it reaches the place at which it is to be used as a home. But does it then cease, for the time being, to be inhabited, if the family go for a spin in it next day? Is it burglary if a thief enters it in the car park of the swimming pool where they have gone for a swim? Similar problems arise when the holiday is concluding. If the answer tentatively suggested above regarding the beginning of the holiday is correct, then it ought to follow that when the vehicle embarks on its homeward journey, after the last night on which it is intended to sleep in it, it then ceases to be inhabited.

Very similar problems will arise in connection with boats with living accommodation. Ships where the passengers or crew sleep aboard, are clearly covered. The person who trespasses into a passenger's cabin on the Queen Elizabeth in order to steal is clearly guilty of burglary.[1]

---

[1] Presumably, in such a case, the trespass is committed against the owners since, under modern conditions, they, and not the master, are in possession of the ship: *The Jupiter* (No. 3), [1927] P. 122 at 131; affirmed, [1927] P. 250. The passengers would seem to be in the same situation as the guests in a hotel. See above, para. [343].

---

[356] Difficult problems of *mens rea* may arise. According to ordinary principles, D should not be convicted unless he knew of the facts which make the thing entered "a building" in law. Suppose D enters a dormobile parked by the side of the road. If he knew that P was living in the vehicle, there is no problem. But what if he did not know? In principle it would seem that he ought to be acquitted of burglary, unless it can be shown that he was at least reckless whether anyone was living there or not; and this seems to involve showing that the possibility was present to his mind.

B.   THE MENS REA

(a) Intention to enter as a trespasser; or knowledge of having trespassed

[357] As pointed out above,[1] it must be proved on a charge under s. 9 (1) (a) that D intended to enter, knowing of the facts which, in law, made his entry trespassory; or, at least, being reckless whether such facts existed; and, on a charge under s. 9 (1) (b), that, at the time of committing the ulterior offence, D knew of or was reckless as to the facts which had made his entry a trespass.

If, in a case under either paragraph, D sets up an honest belief in a right to enter, it should be for the Crown to prove the belief was not held.

¹ See para. [337].

(b) The ulterior offence

[358] It must be proved that D, *either—*
  (i) entered with intent to commit one of the following offences:
    (*a*) stealing,
    (*b*) inflicting grievous bodily harm,
    (*c*) rape,
    (*d*) unlawful damage to the building or anything therein;
  or
  (ii) entered and committed or attempted to commit one of the following offences:
    (*a*) stealing,
    (*b*) inflicting grievous bodily harm.

[359] Is a conditional intention to commit one of these offences enough? In *Collins*¹ the Court of Appeal appeared to accept that an intention to rape a woman if she did not consent to intercourse was sufficient; but, in *Husseyn,*² on a charge of attempted theft, it was held that one who intends to steal only if what he finds is worth stealing does not have a present intention to steal. Following this, it was held that a trespasser with such a state of mind had no case to answer on a burglary charge.³ In *Walkington,*⁴ where D entered intending to steal any money which there might be in a till, the court had no doubt that he intended to steal within s. 9 (1) (*b*). The fact that the till was empty was irrelevant on the burglary charge. The decision does not necessarily apply where D does not intend to steal money or any specific thing but is looking for anything worth stealing. Though the court thought it plain that different considerations apply to a charge of attempt to steal a specific thing, it would be odd if a person with such a state of mind were held to have an intention to steal when he entered a building but no such intention when, later, he was examining the contents to see whether they were worth stealing. The better view is that he had an intention to steal throughout.

¹ Above, para. [333], footnote 3.
² (1978) 67 Cr. App. Rep. 131, above, para. [124].
³ *Bozickovic*, [1978] Crim. L.R. 686 (Recorder McAulay).
⁴ Court of Appeal, No. 1293/C/78, 22/2/79; [1979] Crim. L.R. (August) and commentary; above, para. [347]. *Greenhoff*,[1979] Crim. L.R. 108 (Judge Randolph) must now be regarded as wrongly decided.

[360] (i) *Stealing.*—This clearly means theft, contrary to s. 1.¹ So an entry with the intention of dishonestly using electricity contrary to s. 13 is not burglary.² Nor is it enough to prove that D has entered with intent to commit an offence contrary to s. 15 or s. 16 of the Act. If the *Lawrence* (C.A.) principle³ is valid, virtually all s. 15 offences are theft, contrary to s. 1; but, if it is not, the old distinction between larceny by a trick and obtaining by false pretences becomes important here. Thus D gains admission to P's house or place of business by pretending to be the agent of E, a person well-known to P. This is an entry as a trespasser.[4] D then induces P to sell goods to E, and departs, taking the goods and leaving a forged cheque. There is, of course, no contract with E, the ownership in the goods remains in P, and D has dishonestly appropriated property belonging to another with the intention of permanently depriving the other of it. He is guilty of theft (as well, of course, as obtaining by deception) and, therefore, he is guilty of burglary. But the position is different where D gains admission to P's building by pretending that her (D's) husband is ill and then, by the same pretence, induces P to lend her £20 intending to deprive P permanently of it. Here too D enters as a trespasser but (subject to the *Lawrence* (C.A.) principle) the offence committed inside is only obtaining by deception and not theft (because the ownership in the money passes to D) and therefore burglary is not committed. The difference lies in whether the property passes or not. If D goes into P's shop and induces P to let him have a television set on credit by giving a false address and false references, the nature of D's crime depends on the nature of the transaction in the civil law. If it is hire or hire-purchase, the ownership does not pass and D is guilty of theft as well as obtaining by deception; if it is a credit sale, the ownership passes and D is guilty only of obtaining by deception. Thus, it is burglary in the former case[5] but not in the latter.

---

[1] See s. 1 (1).
[2] *Low* v. *Blease,* [1975] Crim. L.R. 513; above, para. [295].
[3] Above, para. [37].
[4] Above, para. [338].
[5] Assuming that entry with intent to commit a fraud of this nature is a trespass: see above, para. [338].

---

[361] (ii) *Grievous bodily harm.*—The infliction of grievous bodily harm must be an "offence". There are three offences under the Offences against the Person Act 1861 in which the infliction of grievous bodily harm may be a constituent. They are causing grievous bodily harm with intent (s. 18),[1] unlawfully and maliciously inflicting grievous bodily harm (s. 20)[2] and unlawfully and maliciously administering poison so as to inflict grievous bodily harm (s. 23).[3]

Where the charge is one of entering with intent under s. 9 (i) (*a*) it would seem that the evidence must establish an intent to commit the first and most serious of these three offences.[4] To satisfy the terms of s. 9 (1) (*a*), an actual intention to inflict grievous bodily harm must be proved. Under s. 9 (1) (*b*), however, the position seems to be different. Here it is only necessary to prove that D entered and committed an offence of inflicting grievous bodily harm. Suppose D enters P's house as a trespasser[5] and throws a stone intending to smash a vase, knowing that there is a risk that by so doing he might cause serious bodily harm and either not caring whether he does or not, or hoping that he does not. He is not, so far, guilty of burglary. But, if he throws the stone and actually causes grievous bodily harm to P he is guilty of an offence under s. 20 of the Offences against the Person Act and therefore of burglary. If no more can be established than that the grievous bodily harm was caused negligently, then the offence of burglary is not made out.

What if D enters with intent to murder? It would be very strange if an entry

with intent to inflict grievous bodily harm amounted to burglary, and an entry
with intent to murder did not. It is submitted that the greater includes the less
and that an intention to kill, whether by inflicting physical injuries or by
poisoning is enough.

---

[1] Smith and Hogan, 369. "Cause" is wider than "inflict." An intention to cause grievous bodily
harm otherwise than by poison or assault seems to be insufficient *mens rea* for burglary.
[2] *Ibid.*
[3] Smith and Hogan, 377.
[4] The principal difference between s. 18 and s. 20 is that in the former an actual intention must be
proved, whereas in the latter it is enough that the accused was reckless whether or not he caused
grievous bodily harm.
[5] But without intent to commit any of the offences referred to in s. 9 (1) (a).

---

[362] (iii) *Rape.*—By s. 1 (1) and Schedule 2 of the Sexual Offences Act
1956 and s. 1 (1) of the Sexual Offences (Amendment) Act 1976 rape is an
offence punishable with life imprisonment and consisting in having sexual
intercourse with a woman who does not consent to it, knowing that she does not
consent or being reckless whether she consents.[1] The recklessness referred to
here can only exist at the moment of the intercourse. The fact that such
recklessness will suffice does not settle the question[2] whether a conditional
intention on entry is enough.

---

[1] Smith & Hogan, 400.
[2] Above, para. [359].

---

[363] (iv) *Unlawful damage to the building or anything therein.*—The
damage intended must be such that to cause it would amount to an offence. It
is an offence under s. 1 of the Criminal Damage Act 1971, intentionally or
recklessly to destroy or damage any property belonging to another.

Is it necessary that the object of the ulterior crime be in the building before
the trespassory entry? In other words, is it burglary if D drags P into a barn
with intent to rob, or inflict grievous bodily harm on, or rape her? The words of
the section do not supply a clear answer, but the purpose of the offence—the
protection of persons and things in a building—suggests that the crime does
not extend to these cases.

2   AGGRAVATED BURGLARY

[364] By s. 10 of the Theft Act:

"(1) A person is guilty of aggravated burglary if he commits any
burglary and at the time has with him any firearm or imitation firearm,
any weapon of offence, or any explosive; and for this purpose—
(a) 'firearm' includes an airgun or air pistol and 'imitation firearm' means
anything which has the appearance of being a firearm, whether
capable of being discharged or not; and
(b) 'weapon of offence' means any article made or adapted for use for
causing injury to or incapacitating a person, or intended by the person
having it with him for such use; and
(c) 'explosive' means any article manufactured for the purpose of

182

producing a practical effect by explosion, or intended by the person having it with him for that purpose.

(2) A person guilty of aggravated burglary shall on conviction on indictment be liable to imprisonment for life."

The reason given by the Criminal Law Revision Committee for the creation of this offence is that "burglary when in possession of the articles mentioned ... is so serious that is should in our opinion be punishable with imprisonment for life. The offence is comparable with robbery (which will be so punishable). It must be extremely frightening to those in the building, and it might well lead to loss of life."[1]

---

[1] *Eighth Report*, Cmnd. 2977, para. 80.

A. THE ARTICLES OF AGGRAVATION

[365] "Firearm" is not defined in the Act, except to the extent that it includes an airgun or air pistol. It would seem likely that the courts will seek guidance as to the meaning of this term from the definition in the Firearms Act 1968, s. 57 (1). The expression is given a wide meaning in that Act, however, and it does not necessarily follow that it should bear a similarly wide meaning in the Theft Act. Thus the definition includes any component part of a firearm, but the natural meaning of the term does not include parts. If I have the body locking pin of a Bren gun in my pocket, no one would say I was carrying a firearm. As the statutory definition has not been incorporated in the Theft Act, as could easily have been done, it is submitted that the word should not be given a meaning any wider than that which it naturally bears; and that, therefore, the term "imitation firearm" be similarly limited.

[366] The definition of "weapon of offence" is somewhat wider than that of "offensive weapon" in s. 1 (4) of the Prevention of Crime Act 1953. It would seem that (i) articles made for causing injury to a person, (ii) articles adapted for causing injury to a person, and (iii) articles which D has with him for that purpose are precisely the same as under the 1953 Act.[1] Thus, (i) would include a service rifle or bayonet, a revolver, a cosh, knuckleduster or dagger; (ii) would include razor blades inserted in a potato, a bottle broken for the purpose, a chair leg studded with nails; and (iii) would include anything that could cause injury to the person if so desired by the person using it—a sheath-knife, a razor, a shotgun, a sandbag, a pick-axe handle, a bicycle chain or a stone.[2] To these categories, however, s. 10 (1) (*b*) adds (iv) any article made for *incapacitating* a person, (v) any article adapted for *incapacitating* a person, and (vi) any article which D has with him for that purpose. Articles *made* for incapacitating a person might include a pair of handcuffs and a gag; articles *adapted* for incapacitating a person might include a pair of socks made into a gag, and articles *intended* for incapacitating a person might include sleeping pills to put in the night-watchman's tea, a rope to tie him up, a sack to put over his head, pepper to throw in his face, and so on.

In the cases of (i), (ii), (iv) and (v) the prosecution need prove no more than that the article was made or adapted for use for causing injury or incapacitating as the case may be. In the cases of (iii) and (vi) clearly they must go further and prove that D was carrying the thing with him with the intention of using it to injure or incapacitate, not necessarily in any event, but at least if the need arose.

¹ Smith and Hogan, 393.
² *Harrison* v. *Thornton,* [1966] Crim. L.R. 388.

[367] The definition of "explosive" closely follows that in s. 3 (1) of the Explosives Act 1875 which, after enumerating various explosives, adds:

"... and every other substance, whether similar to those above mentioned or not, used or manufactured with a view to produce a practical effect by explosion or by a pyrotechnic effect ..."

It will be observed that the definition in the Theft Act is narrower. The Explosives Act, if read literally, is wide enough to include a box of matches—these produce a "pyrotechnic effect"; but it seems clear that a box of matches would not be an "explosive" under the Theft Act.

The main difficulty about the definition—and this is unlikely to be important in practice—lies in determining the meaning of "practical effect". Perhaps it serves to exclude fireworks which, so it has been said in connection with another Act, are "things that are made for amusement";¹ but if the thing is *intended* to produce "a practical effect", it is immaterial that it was not manufactured for that purpose and that it is incapable of doing so.

¹ *Bliss* v. *Lilley* (1832), 32 L.J.M.C. 3, *per* Cockburn, C.J. and Blackburn, J.; but Wightman, J. thought that a fog-signal was a "firework".

B.   "AT THE TIME" OF COMMISSION OF BURGLARY

[368] It must be proved that D had the article of aggravation with him *at the time* of committing the burglary. Where the charge is one of entry with intent this is clearly at the time of entry. Where the charge is one of committing a specified offence, having entered, it is at the time of commission of the specified offence.

C.   "HAS WITH HIM"

[369] This again closely follows the wording of the Prevention of Crime Act 1953. It has been held that the words in that Act mean "*knowingly* has with him",¹ in the sense that D must be proved to have known that he had the thing which is an offensive weapon. Whether it must also be proved that he knew that it possessed those characteristics which make it an offensive weapon within the meaning of the Act has not been decided. It does not follow that it will be so decided. It has been held under the law relating to possession of dangerous drugs, that a mental element must be proven to establish possession, but that element falls short of knowledge that the thing is a dangerous drug.² It would be enough that D knew that it was a drug; or that he had had a reasonable opportunity to ascertain its nature; or that he suspected that there was "anything wrong" with the thing and took or retained control regardless. Similarly, under the Firearms Act 1968 it is unnecessary to prove that D knew the thing he used was a firearm within the meaning of the Act[3]—though it is no doubt necessary to prove that he knew he had that thing.

It may be predicted with some confidence, therefore, that proof will be required that D knew that he had the article of aggravation with him at the appropriate time. It is submitted that, in principle, proof should also be necessary that he knew the thing had the characteristics of an article of aggravation.

---

[1] *Cugullere*, [1961] 2 All E.R. 343 at 344.
[2] *Warner* v. *Metropolitan Police Commissioner*, [1969] 2 A.C. 256; [1968] 2 All E.R. 356.
[3] *Pierre*, [1963] Crim. L.R. 513; Smith and Hogan, 389.

---

[370] It has now been held that, under the Prevention of Crime Act, in effect overruling earlier decisions, a person carrying an inoffensive article for an innocent purpose does not become guilty of having an offensive weapon with him merely because he uses that article for an offensive purpose.[1] The 1953 Act is directed against the carrying abroad of articles intended to be used as weapons, not against the use of an article as a weapon. It seems clearly right that the same construction should be put upon s. 10 of the Theft Act. If then D carries a jemmy for the sole purpose of forcing a window, the jemmy does not become a weapon of offence merely because he uses it to strike P who has interrupted him. It has also been held under the 1953 Act that no offence is committed where a person arms himself with a weapon for *instant* attack on his victim.[2] So if D is interrupted in the course of stealing after a trespassory entry and picks up an inkstand (or any object) and throws it with intent to cause injury, he does not thereby become guilty of aggravated burglary. He can be adequately dealt with by a charge of whatever offence against the person he has committed. On the other hand, if D picked up a stone outside the house to use as a weapon if he should be disturbed after entry, the subsequent burglary would probably be aggravated. Here D has armed himself before an occasion to use violence has arisen; and the stone is a weapon of offence.

---

[1] *Dayle*, [1973] 3 All E.R. 1151.
[2] *Ohlson* v. *Hylton*, [1975] 2 All E.R. 490; *Giles*, [1976] Crim. L.R. 253; *Bates* v. *Bulman* (1979), 68 Cr. App. Rep. 21.

CHAPTER XII

POSSESSION OF HOUSEBREAKING IMPLEMENTS, ETC.[1]

[371] By s. 25 (1) and (2) of the Theft Act:

"(1) A person shall be guilty of an offence if, when not at his place of abode, he has with him any article for use in the course of or in connection with any burglary, theft or cheat.

(2) A person guilty of an offence under this section shall on conviction on indictment be liable to imprisonment for a term not exceeding three years."

This offence replaced the more complicated provisions contained in the Larceny Act 1916, s. 28. The 1916 Act was directed chiefly against,[2] though it was not limited to, preparatory acts in contemplation of offences of breaking and entering. The new provision is expressed to be directed against acts preparatory to:

    (i) burglary contrary to s. 9,

    (ii) theft contrary to s. 1,

    (iii) criminal deception contrary to s. 15,[3]

    (iv) taking and driving away a conveyance, contrary to s. 12.[4]

---

[1] See J. B. Bentil (1979) 143 J.P. 47.
[2] *Eighth Report*, Cmnd. 2977, p. 69.
[3] By s. 25 (5), "cheat" means an offence under s. 15.
[4] By s. 25 (5), "theft" in this section includes an offence of taking under s. 12 (1).

---

1 THE ACTUS REUS

A. ANY ARTICLE

[372] The *actus reus* consists in the accused's having with him any article. Clearly the article need not be made or adapted for use in committing one of the specified offences. It is sufficient that the *mens rea* is proved in respect of the article, that is, that the accused intended to use it in the course of, or in connection with, one of the specified offences. Thus, it might be a tin of treacle, intended for use in removing a pane of glass; a pair of gloves to be worn so as to avoid leaving fingerprints; a collecting box marked "Oxfam" when the possessor did not represent that organisation; and so on. There may occasionally be difficulty in deciding what is an "article". Does it include blacking on the face to prevent recognition, or "Bostik" on the fingers to prevent fingerprints? Having regard to the mischief at which the section is

186

aimed, it is submitted that a substance so applied to the body, remains an "article".

[373] The offence is thus very wide in its scope. But there must be some limits. Thus D can hardly be committing an offence because he is wearing his trousers when on his way to do a burglary. Yet he intends to wear them while he is committing the burglary and would not dream of undertaking such an enterprise without them. Similarly, he can hardly be committing an offence by wearing his shoes or any other item of everyday apparel. Yet it was suggested above that gloves for the avoidance of fingerprints would entail liability. This suggests that the article must be one which D would not be carrying with him but for the contemplated offence. If it is something which he would carry with him on a normal, innocent expedition, it should not fall within this section.[1] So there might be a difference between a pair of rubber gloves and a pair of fur-lined gloves which D was wearing to keep his hands warm on a freezing night, even though he did intend to keep them on so as to avoid leaving fingerprints. The latter pair of gloves is hardly distinguishable, for this purpose, from D's overcoat which seems to fall into the same category as his trousers. If D is carrying a pair of plimsolls in his car to facilitate his cat-burgling, this seems a plain enough case; but what if he has simply selected his ordinary crepe-sole shoes for wear because they are less noisy than his hob-nails?

It has been held that being in possession of a driving licence and other documents belonging to another, with intent to obtain a job that would give an opportunity to steal, is too remote from the intended theft to constitute the offence.[2]

---

[1] See Williams, *TBCL*, 819–820.
[2] *Mansfield*, [1975] Crim. L.R. 101, C.A. *Cf.*, above, para. [160]. D was guilty of an attempt to obtain a pecuniary advantage by deception contrary to s. 16 (2) (*c*), above, para. [229].

B.   "HAS WITH HIM"

[374] The expression "has with him"[1] is the same as in s. 10 (1) of the Act. Questions as to D's knowledge of the nature of the thing can hardly arise here, since it must be proved that he intended to use it in the course of or in connection with a specified offence. No doubt D has an article with him if it is in his immediate possession or control; so that he will be guilty if the article is only a short distance away and he can take it up as he needs it; as where a ladder has been left in a garden by an accomplice and D enters the garden intending to use the ladder to make an entry. If the article is found in D's car some distance from the scene of the crime this will be evidence that D was in possession of the article when driving the car.

It is probable that mere momentary possession will not suffice,[2] as where D is apprehended on picking up a stone which he intends to use to break a window in order to commit burglary.

---

[1] See above, para. [369].
[2] Above, para. [370].

C.   WHEN NOT AT HIS PLACE OF ABODE

[375] No offence is committed by being in possession of house-breaking implements in one's own home. The offence is committed as soon as D steps from his house into the street carrying the article with intent. Though the offence is primarily aimed at persons who have started out to commit crime, it extends well beyond that. It may be committed by possession of an article at a place of employment or, indeed, at any place other than D's place of abode. The burglar who keeps his housebreaking equipment in his car commits the offence every time he drives the car even though he is not starting out to commit crime but, for example, going to church. While the car is in his garage at home he is probably not committing an offence, both because the articles are at his place of abode and because he does not have them with him. Where a man had no home but his car, it was held that the car was his "place of abode" only when it was on a site where he intended to abide. While it was in transit he was committing the offence.[1]

---

[1] *Bundy*, [1977] 2 All E.R. 382, C.A. *Cf. Kelt*, [1977] 3 All E.R. 1099; [1977] Crim. L.R. 556 and commentary.

D.   USE IN THE COURSE OF OR IN CONNECTION WITH

[376] It is not necessarily a defence that D did not intend to use the article while actually committing the contemplated crime. If, for example he intended to use it only in the course of making his escape after the commission of the offence, this would be enough, being use "in connection with" the offence. Similarly if he intended to use the article while doing preparatory acts. The string used by D to tie himself up in *Robinson*[1] would seem to come within the provision, though it was to be used only in the course of a preparatory act and not in the course of the commission of the proposed criminal deception. Any insurance claim form he might have had, on the other hand, would have been for use in the course of commission of the offence.

The offence is directed at acts preparatory to the offences specified. It is not an offence under the section merely to be in possession of articles which *have been* used in the course of or in connection with one of the offences.[2] A person concealing or disposing of articles which have been so used may be guilty of an offence under s. 4 of the Criminal Law Act 1967.[3]

---

[1] (1915), 11 Cr. App. Rep. 124.
[2] *Ellames*, [1974] 3 All E.R. 130; SHC 582. *Cf. Eighth Report*, para. 150. *Cf. Allamby*, [1974] 3 All E.R. 126.
[3] Smith and Hogan, 728.

---

2   THE MENS REA

[377] The *mens rea* for the offence would appear to consist in:
   (i) knowledge that one possesses the article; and
   (ii) an intention that the article be used in the course of or in connection with any of the specified crimes.

D must have it in mind that, when he uses the article, he will do so with the intention required by any one of the specified crimes. In *Rashid*[1] a British Rail steward was charged with going equipped with his own sandwiches which he dishonestly intended to sell for personal gain to travellers instead of British Rail sandwiches. His conviction was quashed for misdirection but the court was inclined to think that D could not be guilty of the offence because it would be "a matter of complete indifference" to a passenger whether the sandwich was British Rail's or D's. In *Doukas*[2] however a wine waiter was held rightly convicted when he was equipped, contrary to his employer's instructions, with his own wine for sale to his employer's customers. It seemed to the court incredible that "any customer, to whom the true situation was made clear, would willingly make himself a party to what was obviously a fraud by the waiter upon his employers". *Doukas* is to be preferred to the dicta in *Rashid*. Of course D *might* meet dishonest customers who would not care whether the food supplied belonged to D or to his employer, but the point is that he was obviously prepared to deceive any honest customer he met.

In *Ellames*,[3] the court expressed the opinion that it is not necessary to prove that D intended to use the article in the course of or in connection with any specific burglary, theft or cheat; it is enough that he intended to use it for some burglary, theft or cheat. Although the Committee[4] stated that they regarded the offence as a preparatory one "in contemplation of a particular crime", the dictum in *Ellames* seems to be right. It is supported by the use of the word "any". If a man sets out with a jemmy looking for a suitable house to break into, he has the article with him for use in the course of a burglary and it should not be a defence that he has not yet decided which house to break into. His conditional intention is enough. If D is equipped with car keys, having it in mind to steal anything from the cars which he thinks is worth stealing, he ought to be guilty, notwithstanding *Husseyn*.[5] Similarly where a confidence trickster sets out with his equipment, looking for a gullible passer-by. The court in *Ellames*[6] also thought it enough that D intended the article to be used by another. There is nothing in the section to require that the contemplated use shall be by the accused.

---

[1] [1977] 2 All E.R. 237; [1977] Crim. L.R. 237 and commentary.
[2] [1978] 1 All E.R. 1061, C.A.; [1978] Crim. L.R. 177; above, para. **[169]**.
[3] [1974] 3 All E.R. 130 at 136.
[4] Report, para. 150.
[5] (1978) 67 Cr. App. Rep. 131, above, para. **[124]**. But *Lyons* v. *Owen*, [1963] Crim. L.R. 123 suggests the contrary.
[6] [1974] 3 All E.R. at 136.

---

[378] Section 25 (3) provides:

> "Where a person is charged with an offence under this section, proof that he had with him any article made or adapted for use in committing burglary, theft or cheat shall be evidence that he had it with him for such use."

This is probably no more than enactment of the general rules regarding proof of intent.[1] The jury may take this fact into account but it is entirely for them to say what weight, if any, is to be attached to it. If D offers no explanation then the jury may be told that there is evidence upon which they may find that he had the necessary intent; but it is submitted that they should be told so to find only if satisfied beyond reasonable doubt that he in fact had that intent.[2] If D does offer an explanation then the jury should be told to acquit if they think it may reasonably be true and to convict only if satisfied beyond reasonable doubt that the explanation is untrue.[3]

Where the article in question is not made or adapted for use in any specified offence,[4] mere proof of possession without more will not amount to *prima facie* evidence—*i.e.*, the case will have to be withdrawn from the jury. But, in certain circumstances, possession of articles not made or adapted for committing offences may amount to very cogent evidence of intent.[5] It is a question of law for the judge, at what point proof of other incriminating circumstances amounts to a case fit for submission to the jury.

---

[1] *Cf.* Criminal Justice Act 1967, s. 8.

[2] *Cf.* the case where the alleged receiver is proved to have been in possession of recently stolen property and offers no explanation: *Abramovitch* (1914), 11 Cr. App. Rep. 45.

[3] The decision in *Patterson*, [1962] 2 Q.B. 429 that the onus of proof under Larceny Act 1916, s. 28 was on the accused, was based on the express wording of that section and is entirely inapplicable to the new provision.

[4] *Cf. Harrison*, [1970] Crim. L.R. 415.

[5] Griew, 11–09.

CHAPTER XIII

HANDLING STOLEN GOODS

[379] The offence created by s. 22 replaced both the indictable offences under the Larceny Act 1916, s. 33 and the summary offences under the Larceny Act 1861, s. 97. Section 22 provides:

"(1) A person handles stolen goods if (otherwise than in the course of the stealing) knowing or believing them to be stolen goods he dishonestly receives the goods, or dishonestly undertakes or assists in their retention, removal, disposal or realisation by or for the benefit of another person, or if he arranges to do so.

(2) A person guilty of handling stolen goods shall on conviction on indictment be liable to imprisonment for a term not exceeding fourteen years."

1   THE ACTUS REUS

A.   STOLEN GOODS

[380] By s. 34 (2) (*b*):

" 'goods', except in so far as the context otherwise requires, includes money and every other description of property except land, and includes things severed from the land by stealing."

It will be noted that this definition differs from and is narrower than the definition of "property" for the purposes of theft in s. 4 (1).[1] Since, however, land generally is excluded from theft by s. 4 (2), the effect seems to be that, with small exceptions to be discussed below, the property which can be the subject of handling is co-extensive with that which can be the subject of theft.

---

[1] Above, para. **[83]**.

(a)   Things in action

[381] Things in action are expressly mentioned in s. 4 (1) and not in s. 34 (2) (*b*). They must however be included in the words "every other description of property except land". The remaining question is whether the context of s. 22 *requires* the exclusion of things in action. If s. 22 were confined, like the old law, to *receiving*, no doubt the context would so require. Receiving connoted taking possession or control of a physical thing and was wholly inapplicable to a thing in action. It may well be that this continues to be so under the Theft Act and that a charge of handling by receiving a thing in action, contrary to s. 22, would be bad. The new offence, however, is not

191

confined to receiving but can be committed in a variety of ways.[1] "Removal" may be thought appropriate only to a physical thing and possibly the same is true of "retention"; but "disposal" and "realisation" are both words which are perfectly apt to include dealings with a thing in action and therefore it would seem that the context does not require the exclusion of things in action from the definition of goods as the object of disposal or realisation. It is, of course, arguable that "goods" must mean the same for the whole of s. 22 and that its meaning should not vary according to the particular verb selected by the prosecution as appropriate to describe the accused's conduct. But, if it had been the intention to exclude things in action from handling, this would surely have been done expressly, as in the case of land. The definition of goods clearly leaves it open to the court to hold that it includes things in action where the context permits and, as handling is the only crime to which the definition is relevant, it seems to follow that provision is made for a variable meaning of "goods" within s. 22.

---

[1] Below, para. [408].

---

[382] Cases of handling a stolen thing in action are likely to be rare but they are certainly quite possible. Perhaps the most likely case is that where a thief pays stolen money into a bank account. The legal position is that he no longer owns any money but is owed a debt by the bank.[1] The debt is a thing in action—and it is stolen. If D assists the thief to retain the "money in the bank" he will be guilty of handling the thing in action. Another example would be where E, an executor, dishonestly sells to F a copyright which belongs to a beneficiary under the will, P. Even if an indictment for receiving a thing in action will lie, this may not be handling by F, though he knows all the facts, because his participation may be "in the course of the stealing"—since the stealing consists in the sale.[2] The copyright is, however, stolen goods in F's hands. D then assists F to dispose of, or realise the copyright for F's benefit. D is guilty of handling and F is presumably guilty of aiding and abetting him in handling.

---

[1] This point seems to have been overlooked in *Pitchley* (1973), 57 Cr. App. Rep. 30; SHC 592; below, para. [416].
[2] But cf. *Pitham and Hehl*, above, paras. [23] and [48]. If the receiving is in the course of the stealing F is, of course, guilty of aiding and abetting the theft.

(b) Land

[383] "Land" which is stolen contrary to s. 4 (2) (b) can always be the subject of handling since the stealing necessarily involves severance of the thing in question. A fixture or structure which is stolen contrary to s. 4 (2) (c), on the other hand, may or may not be severed from the land. Only if it is severed can it be the subject of handling. If E, an outgoing tenant, dishonestly sells to D, the incoming tenant, a fixture belonging to P, D cannot be guilty of handling (whether or not his act is in the course of stealing) if the fixture is not severed; nor, of course, is F guilty of handling if he, knowing all the facts, takes over the premises, including the fixture, from D; yet he has knowingly taken possession of a stolen fixture.

Land which is stolen contrary to s. 4 (2) (*a*) will rarely be capable of being handled since the kind of conduct contemplated by 4 (2) (*a*) will not normally involve severance.

Land may be the subject of both obtaining by deception and blackmail. Again, severance may or may not take place and handling is possible only if it does so.

(c) Meaning of "stolen"

[384] By s. 24 (4):

"For purposes of the provisions of this Act relating to goods which have been stolen (including subsections (1) to (3) above) goods obtained in England or Wales or elsewhere either by blackmail or in circumstances described in section 15 (1) of this Act shall be regarded as stolen; and 'steal', 'theft' and 'thief' shall be construed accordingly."

By s. 24 (1):

"The provisions of this Act relating to goods which have been stolen shall apply whether the stealing occurred in England or Wales or elsewhere, and whether it occurred before or after the commencement of this Act, provided that the stealing (if not an offence under this Act) amounted to an offence where and at the time when the goods were stolen; and references to stolen goods shall be construed accordingly."

[385] Thus goods are "stolen" for the purposes of the Act if:
  (i) they have been stolen contrary to s. 1;
 (ii) they have been obtained by blackmail contrary to s. 21;
(iii) they have been obtained by deception contrary to s. 15 (1);
(iv) they have been the subject of an act done in a foreign country which was (a) a crime by the law of that country and which (b), had it been done in England, would have been theft, blackmail or obtaining by deception contrary to s. 1 or s. 21 or s. 15 (1) respectively.

These provisions narrow the previous law in two ways:

[386] (i) Section 33 (1) of the 1916 Act extended to goods obtained by any felony or misdemeanour until the Criminal Law Act 1967, and thereafter to goods obtained by any offence. Thus it was sufficient to prove that the goods had been obtained through a conspiracy to defraud. This is no longer so. Goods which have been obtained through such a conspiracy will, generally, have been obtained by deception but this is not invariably so. Suppose D receives from E money which E and F have obtained from P by backing a winning horse after inducing P to bet with them by deception.[1] E and F are guilty of a conspiracy to defraud and of obtaining a pecuniary advantage by deception[2] but they have not obtained the money by deception. Thus, while D may have been guilty of receiving[3] under the old law, he is guilty of no offence under the new.

The opinion also has been expressed[4] that s. 33 (1) of the 1916 Act might have extended to receiving goods obtained by a mere summary offence, as, for example, beer bought from a publican who has not renewed his licence.

However that may be, it is quite clear that such conduct is no longer an offence.

---

[1] *Clucas*, [1949] 2 K.B. 226; above, paras. [160] and [216].
[2] Contrary to s. 16 above, para. [210]. Where, on a sale of goods, credit is obtained by deception, the goods are "stolen" because there is an offence under s. 15 as well as under s. 16: *Dabek*,[1973] Crim. L.R. 527.
[3] It is submitted that this is not absolutely clear. P was defrauded by being induced to bet, not by being induced to pay out the money. See above, para. [216]. If so, it is arguable that, though a misdemeanour was committed, the money was not *obtained by* a misdemeanour.
[4] *Eighth Report*, Cmnd. 2977, at p. 67.

---

[387] (ii) The second respect in which the law is narrowed concerns property stolen abroad. Under the 1916 Act, s. 33 (4), it was an offence merely to have possession of property stolen abroad and that irrespective of whether the act was an offence by the law of the place where it was committed. Now, mere possession is not enough[1]—there must, as in the case of property stolen in England, be proof of handling by the accused—and the "stealing" must be an offence by the law of the place where it was committed—though not necessarily the crime equivalent to stealing. These seem highly desirable reforms. It was most anomalous that the owner of property stolen abroad should have been afforded greater protection by the English criminal law than the owner of property stolen in England;[2] and it seems wrong in principle that English Law should, in effect, attribute criminality to an act innocent by the law of the place where it is done.

---

[1] But it may be theft by "keeping ... as owner": s. 3 (1), above, para. [51].
[2] For example, suppose D was in possession of two pictures, one stolen in Glasgow and the other stolen in London. He received both innocently but kept them after discovering that they were stolen. This was an offence in respect of the Glasgow picture, but no offence in respect of the London picture. Under the Theft Act it would not be handling in respect of either picture—but it might be theft in respect of both, if D was not a purchaser for value in good faith. See s. 3, above, paras. [24] and [46].

---

[388] While the offence is narrowed in these two respects, it is widened in another and important respect. It was no offence under s. 33 (1) of the 1916 Act to receive goods, knowing them to have been fraudulently converted, contrary to s. 20 of that Act, since the goods were neither stolen nor *obtained* in circumstances which amounted to felony or misdemeanour,[1] as s. 33 (1) required. Now, of course, acts which amounted only to fraudulent conversion contrary to s. 20 of the Larceny Act are ordinary theft and present no problem.

---

[1] *Misell* (1926), Cr. App. Rep. 109; *Bianchi*, [1958] Crim. L.R. 813.

(d) The "thief " must be guilty

[389] Section 22 does not expressly state that the goods must actually be stolen. While a person cannot *know* goods to be stolen unless this is so, he may *believe* them to be stolen although they are not. It is now established that, to constitute the offence, the goods in question must not only be believed to be stolen, but actually be stolen at the time of the alleged offence.[1] A person who dishonestly handles goods, mistakenly believing them to be stolen, is guilty neither of handling nor of attempting to handle. The Crown must prove that

the goods were stolen. D's admission that the goods in his possession are stolen goods goes to prove *mens rea* but it is of no value as evidence that the goods are actually stolen if he did not have personal knowledge of that fact but was merely saying what he had been told or what he inferred from the circumstances. Of course, the circumstances which satisfied D that the goods were stolen may also satisfy the jury of that fact.[2]

If, then, the alleged thief is not guilty, the handler cannot be convicted for there are no *stolen* goods for him to handle. So if the alleged thief turns out to have been under the age of ten at the time of the alleged theft, then the goods appropriated cannot be stolen goods and there can be no conviction for handling them.[3] In such circumstances, however, the receiver is now guilty of theft.[4] The wider ambit of theft than larceny means that problems of this type are likely to occur less often under the 1968 Act. Where a wife took her husband's goods and vice versa there could be no larceny unless they were not living together or the goods were taken with a view to their ceasing to live together. The abolition of this rule[5] gets rid of some difficult problems[6] which would otherwise have arisen on a handling charge. As it is, where the goods of one spouse are appropriated by another, this is an ordinary theft and the goods are "stolen" as in any other theft.

---

[1] *Haughton* v. *Smith*, [1973] 3 All E.R. 1109 at 1112, 1119 and 1124; SHC 311 at 312 and 318.
[2] *Porter*, [1976] Crim. L.R. 58; *Marshall*, [1977] Crim. L.R. 106; *Lang* v. *Evans (Inspector of Police)*, [1977] Crim. L.R. 286; *Hack*, [1978] Crim. L.R. 359; *Overington*, [1978] Crim. L.R. 692, C.A.
[3] *Walters* v. *Lunt*, [1951] 2 All E.R. 645, thus remains good law.
[4] Above, para. [51].
[5] Section 30 (1), below, para. [458].
[6] Cf. *Creamer*, [1919] 1 K.B. 564.

---

[390] If the appropriator of the goods is guilty of theft, it is submitted that the goods appropriated may be the subject of handling although the appropriator is immune from prosecution by reason, for example, of diplomatic immunity.[1] The thief could be prosecuted for the theft if diplomatic immunity were waived. The handler may be convicted whether that immunity is waived or not—unless, of course, he too is entitled to diplomatic immunity.

---

[1] Cf. *Dickinson* v. *Del Solar*, [1930] 1 K.B. 376; *A.B.*, [1941] 1 K.B. 454; *Madan* (1961), 45 Cr. App. Rep. 80.

---

[391] It is submitted that the question whether the thief was guilty must be decided on the evidence of that fact produced at the trial of the receiver. Thus the fact that the "thief" has been acquitted is no bar to the prosecution of an alleged receiver of the goods which he has been acquitted of stealing and should not even be admitted as evidence that the goods were not stolen.[1] Similarly, the fact that the "thief" has been convicted, far from being conclusive against the alleged receiver, is not even admissible evidence that the goods were stolen.[2]

---

[1] The rule in *Hollington* v. *Hewthorn*, [1943] K.B. 587; [1943] 2 All E.R. 35, though abolished for civil proceedings by s. 11 of the Civil Evidence Act 1968, continues to apply in criminal cases.
[2] *Hollington* v. *Hewthorn*, [1943] K.B. 587; [1943] 2 All E.R. 35. Cf. *Humphreys and Turner*, [1965] 3 All E.R. 689; *Remillard* v. *R.* (1921), 62 S.C.R. 21.

B. WHEN GOODS CEASE TO BE STOLEN

[392] By s. 24 (3) of the Act:

"But no goods shall be regarded as having continued to be stolen goods after they have been restored to the person from whom they were stolen or to other lawful possession or custody, or after that person and any other person claiming through him have otherwise ceased as regards those goods to have any right to restitution in respect of the theft."

It is obvious that goods which have once been stolen cannot continue to be regarded as "stolen" so long as they continue to exist thereafter. A line must be drawn somewhere; and the Act draws it in the same place as did the common law. Though the word "restored" seems inappropriate to the case where the goods are taken into possession by the police, the Court of Appeal has held that the subsection applies to that case.[1] So if the stolen goods are taken from the thief by the owner or someone acting on his behalf, or by the police, and subsequently returned to the thief so that he may hand them over to a receiver, the receiver will not be guilty of handling because the goods are no longer stolen goods.[2] Difficult questions may continue to arise whether goods have in fact been "restored to the person from whom they were stolen or to other lawful possession or custody". Thus in *King*[3] a parcel containing the stolen goods (a fur coat) was handed by E, the thief, to a policeman who was in the act of examining the contents when the telephone rang. The caller was D, the proposed receiver. The policeman discontinued his examination, D was told to come along as arranged, he did so and received the coat. It was held that D was guilty of receiving stolen goods on the ground that the coat had not been reduced into the possession of the police—though it was admitted that there was no doubt that, in a very few minutes, it would have been so reduced, if the telephone had not rung. Presumably the same result would follow under the Theft Act. The case has, however, been subjected to criticism. It is easy to see that if the police are examining a parcel to see whether it contains stolen goods they do not take possession or even custody of the contents until they decide that this is what they are looking for.[4] In *King*, however, E had admitted the theft of the coat and produced the parcel. One might have expected, therefore, that the policeman had in fact made up his mind to take charge of it before the telephone rang. The decision presumably proceeds on the assumption that he had not done so. The Court of Appeal has recently affirmed[5] that the question is one of the intention of the police officer. An officer correctly suspected that goods on the back seat of a car were stolen. He removed the rotor arm from the car, kept observation until D appeared and got into the car, and then questioned him. It was held that the jury ought to have been asked to consider whether the officer had decided before D's appearance to take possession of the goods or whether he was of an entirely open mind, intending to decide when he had questioned D. To immobilise a car is not the same thing as to take possession of it or its contents.

---

[1] *Re A.-G.'s Reference (No. 1 of 1974)*, [1974] Q.B. 744; [1974] 2 All E.R. 899; SHC 585. Was it the inappropriateness of the word "restored" which led some members of the House of Lords in *Haughton* v. *Smith* to doubt whether it had properly been conceded that the goods in that case had ceased to be stolen?

² *Cf. Dolan* (1855), Dears. C.C. 436; *Schmidt* (1866), L.R. 1 C.C.R. 15; *Villensky*, [1892] 2 Q.B. 597.
³ [1938] 2 All E.R. 662, C.C.A.
⁴ *Cf. Warner* v. *Metropolitan Police Commissioner*, [1969] 2 A.C. 256; [1968] 2 All E.R. 356; SHC 61, H.L.
⁵ *Re A.-G.'s Reference (No. 1 of 1974)*, above, footnote 1.

[393] It is now quite clear that the goods may cease to be stolen in the case where the police are acting without the authority of the owner for they are clearly in "other lawful possession or custody" of the goods.[1]

---

[1] *Cf.* the dictum of Cresswell, J. in *Dolan* (above, footnote 2) that goods retained their stolen character in this situation. Presumably the police in *King* were acting with the owner's authority. The point is not discussed, but it would seem likely that the theft had been reported to the police by the owner.

---

[394] Section 24 (3) also provides that the goods lose their character of stolen goods if the person from whom they were stolen has ceased to have any *right to restitution* in respect of the theft.

Whether a "right to restitution" exists is a question of civil law. A person whose goods have been wrongfully converted does not have a *right* to have those goods restored to him. He has a right to damages but it is in the discretion of the court whether to order the goods to be delivered to him.[1] It is quite clear that s. 24 (3) is not intended to be confined to those cases in which a court would exercise its discretion to order the goods to be returned to P. In the criminal proceedings, it would be impossible to identify such cases and it is submitted that the subsection is applicable to all cases in which P could succeed in a civil action based on his proprietary interest in the thing, whether in conversion or for the protection of an equitable interest.

---

[1] Torts (Interference with Goods) Act 1977, s. 3.

---

[395] The provision seems to have been intended to bear a still wider meaning. The Criminal Law Revision Committee explained it as follows:[1]

> "This is because, if the person who owned the goods when they were stolen no longer has any title to them, there will be no reason why the goods should continue to have the taint of being stolen goods. For example, the offence of handling stolen goods will ... apply also to goods obtained by criminal deception under [section 15]. If the owner of the goods who has been deceived chooses on discovering the deception to ratify his disposal of the goods he will cease to have any title to them."

---

[1] *Eighth Report*, Cmnd. 2977, para. 139.

---

[396] It is clear that "title" is here used in a broad sense to include a right to rescind. The Committee clearly has in mind a case where property passes from P to D at the moment when the goods are obtained by deception. In such a case, P, strictly, has no "title" and his right to recover the goods (or, much more likely, their value) will only arise on his rescinding the contract.[1] Such a potential right, it is submitted, is clearly a "right to restitution" within the Act.

---

[1] *Cf.* above, para. [75] where it is argued in relation to s. 5 (4) that a person holding property under a voidable title is not "under an obligation to make restoration".

[397] Goods will cease to be stolen in the following cases:—

E obtains goods by deception from P. There is a voidable contract of sale. On discovering the deception, P ratifies the contract. D, not knowing of the ratification, receives the goods believing them to be stolen. D is not guilty of handling.

E obtains goods by deception from P. There is a voidable contract of sale. E sells the goods to F, a *bona fide* purchaser for value without notice of the deception. F gets a good title.[1] He delivers the goods to D who knows they have been obtained by but was not a party to the deception.[2] D is not guilty of handling.[3]

E steals goods from P. He sells them in market overt to F, a *bona fide* purchaser for value without notice of the theft. F gets a good title.[4] D receives the goods knowing that they were stolen by E from P. He is not guilty of handling.

P entrusts his goods to E, a mercantile agent. E, dishonestly and in breach of his agreement with P, sells the goods to F who is a *bona fide* purchaser for value without notice of E's dishonesty. This is theft by E but F gets a good title to the goods.[5] D receives the goods knowing that they have been dishonestly appropriated by E. D is not guilty of handling.

P delivers a motor vehicle to E under a hire-purchase or conditional sale agreement. Before the property in the vehicle has passed to E, he dishonestly sells it to F, a *bona fide* purchaser for value without notice of the agreement and who is not a "trade or finance purchaser" as defined in s. 29 (2) of the Hire-Purchase Act 1964. This is theft by E but F gets a good title to[6] the vehicle. D receives the vehicle knowing that it has been dishonestly appropriated by E. He is not guilty of handling.[7]

---

[1] Sale of Goods Act 1893, s. 23.
[2] *Cf. Peirce v. London Horse and Carriage Depository,* [1922] W.N. 170, C.A.
[3] F is not guilty of theft even if he realises the goods have been obtained by deception before he sells them to D: s. 3 (2) above. Nor, of course, is D.
[4] Sale of Goods Act 1893, s. 22.
[5] Factors' Act 1889, s. 2.
[6] Hire-Purchase Act 1964, s. 27; Consumer Credit Act 1974, Sch. 4, para. 22.
[7] In none of these examples is D guilty of theft from P, for P has no proprietary right or interest in the goods.

C. GOODS REPRESENTING THOSE ORIGINALLY STOLEN MAY BE STOLEN
GOODS

[398] By s. 24 (2) of the Act:

> "For purposes of those provisions reference to stolen goods shall include, in addition to the goods originally stolen and parts of them (whether in their original state or not)—
> (*a*) any other goods which directly or indirectly represent or have at any time represented the stolen goods in the hands of the thief as being the proceeds of any disposal or realisation of the whole or part of the goods stolen or of goods so representing the stolen goods; and

(*b*) any other goods which directly or indirectly represent or have at any time represented the stolen goods in the hands of a handler of the stolen goods or any part of them as being the proceeds of any disposal or realisation of the whole or part of the stolen goods handled by him or of goods so representing them."

The effect of the interpretation put upon the corresponding provision in the Larceny Act 1916 (s. 46 (1)) was that anything into or for which the stolen goods were converted or exchanged, whether immediately or otherwise, acquired the character of stolen goods. Thus if A stole an Austin motor car from P and exchanged it with B for a Bentley; B exchanged the Austin with C for a Citroen; and A exchanged the Bentley with D for a Daimler, all four cars would now be stolen goods even though B, C and D might be innocent. And if A, B, C and D each sold the car he had in his possession, the proceeds of each sale (as well as the cars) would be stolen, as would any property purchased with the proceeds. Thus the stolen goods might be multiplied to an alarming extent. The provision did not seem to give rise to any difficulty in practice and it seems that it was very rarely invoked; but it was clearly undesirable to re-enact a provision with such far-reaching theoretical possibilities. Section 24 (2) imposes a limitation upon the possible multiplication of stolen goods.

[399] The Criminal Law Revision Committee stated[1] of this provision:

"It may seem technical; but the effect will be that the goods which the accused is charged with handling must, at the time of the handling or at some previous time, (i) have been in the hands of the thief or of a handler, and (ii) have represented the original stolen goods in the sense of being the proceeds, direct or indirect, of a sale or other realization of the original goods."

[400] Thus, in the example above, if B, C and D were innocent (i) the Austin would continue to be stolen throughout unless P ceased to have any right to restitution of it in respect of the theft;[1] (ii) the Bentley would be stolen goods since it directly represented the goods originally stolen in the hands of the thief as the proceeds of a disposition of them; (iii) the Citroen would not be stolen since B was neither a thief nor a handler; (iv) the Daimler would be stolen since it indirectly represented the stolen goods in the hands of the thief; and the proceeds of sale of the Daimler would also be stolen goods; but the proceeds of sale of the Austin, the Bentley and the Citroen would not, since they came into the hands of C, D and B respectively, none of whom was a thief or a handler.

The difference between the old law and the new is, of course, that a disposition or realisation of the stolen goods by a person who is neither a thief nor a handler (i.e., by one who is in fact appropriating or handling the goods but who has no *mens rea*) no longer causes the proceeds to be stolen. So if D innocently receives stolen goods and converts them into another form—for example, he buys a car with stolen money, or pays stolen money into a bank—the property in the changed form is not stolen; and the dishonest retention of it by D is not handling;[2] nor is it theft if value was given for the goods.[3]

[1] Section 24 (3), above, para. **[392]**.
[2] The point seems to have been overlooked in *Pitchley* (1972), 57 Cr. App. Rep. 30; SHC 592. *Cf.* Griew 10–12, footnote 33.
[3] Above, para. **[46]**.

(a) Handling the proceeds of goods got by theft

[401] In the vast majority of cases, stolen goods will have been got by theft,[1] contrary to s. 1 (1). Where this is the case, s. 24 (2) effects only a very slight extension of the law. That is, in almost every case where goods are notionally stolen by virtue of s. 24 (2), they are probably "stolen" by virtue of some other provision in the Act, if the original "stealing" was theft.

There are two reasons for this:

(i) In most cases where a thief or a handler disposes of stolen goods to an innocent person he will commit an offence against that person which will result in the proceeds being stolen within the meaning of s. 24 (4). In most such cases the thief will, inevitably, represent that he has a greater interest in the goods than is in fact the case and so will be guilty of obtaining by deception. Thus, in the example of the cars, A appears to be guilty of obtaining both the Bentley and the Daimler by deception—they were "stolen" independently of s. 24 (2). The Citroen, on the other hand, which was not the subject of any offence under the Act, did not become stolen by virtue of s. 24 (2). Thus s. 24 (2) in fact adds precisely nothing in this situation.

(ii) Section 24 (2) only operates in the case of proceeds of stolen goods which are or have been in the hands of a thief or handler. It is almost inevitable that the thief or handler will have done some act in relation to the proceeds which amounts to an appropriation of them. If, then, the proceeds are the property of another, there will be a theft of them; and it would seem that the proceeds *will* generally be the property of another. A thief does not usually obtain the proprietary interest[2] of the "owner" in the goods stolen. When a person's property is wrongfully converted into another form, he continues to own the property in its changed form: *Taylor* v. *Plumer.*[3] It is generally said that the legal owner of the property is the legal owner of the proceeds, but this has been disputed.[4] It is irrelevant, however, whether P's rights are legal or equitable, provided only that they are proprietary rights within s. 5.[5] So, even if the thief or handler does not commit an offence against the person to whom he disposes of the stolen goods, he probably does commit theft against the owner of the original goods when he appropriates the proceeds of those goods.

[1] *Cf. D.P.P.* v. *Neiser*, [1959] 1 Q.B. 254; [1958] 3 All E.R. 662.
[2] See s. 5 (1), above, para. **[53]**.
[3] (1815), 3 M. & S. 562.
[4] By Turner, [1956] Crim. L.R. at 664, Goode (1976), 92 L.Q.R. 360 at 367–371 and Khurshid and Matthews (1979),95 L.Q.R. 79; *Cf.* Williams, *TBCL*, 713 footnote 2 and 715, footnote 6.
[5] Above, para. **[53]**.

[402] Suppose that A steals £1,000 in cash from P and with it buys a necklace from B who is *bona fide* and without notice of the theft. A then delivers the necklace to D who knows all the facts. There was certainly no theft of the necklace from B, and it may be that it was not obtained by deception.

The necklace, however, belongs to P[1] and A's receipt of it is an appropriation of property belonging to P and is theft.

In that example, P's interest in the original property, the money, was a legal interest. The position is similar where P's interest is an equitable one. Suppose D is a trustee who holds a valuable painting on trust for P. Intending to appropriate the proceeds, he dishonestly sells the picture (theft) to E, who is *bona fide*. E gets good title to the picture, but P can trace his equitable interest into the proceeds and D's appropriation of them is theft from him.

In these examples, then, the proceeds are stolen goods independently of s. 24 (2). The cases are thus likely to be few where the original offence is theft and the proceeds are "stolen" solely by virtue of s. 24 (2) and are not the subject of an independent offence.

---

[1] He cannot, of course, recover both the money and the necklace but, in this example, there can be no question of his having his money back since B now has a good title to it. P's only surviving proprietary interest is in the necklace.

[403] Though it will rarely be *necessary* to rely on s. 24 (2), it may, however, be simpler to do so rather than on the doctrine of *Taylor* v. *Plumer* (which is not entirely free from obscurity) or of tracing in equity, which requires an understanding of a difficult branch of the civil law. In general, it seems to be unimportant whether goods are regarded as stolen because they are the product of other stolen goods or because they are the subject of an independent theft. Occasionally it may be thought important because the gravity of the first theft outweighs that which consists in the appropriation of the proceeds; and, when it comes to sentencing, the gravity of the handling depends to some extent on the gravity of the theft which is in issue. An obvious example is that of the man who received a large sum which came indirectly from the Great Train Robbery.[1] The large sum was no doubt the property of the owner of the original stolen money. The appropriation of the proceeds of the original stolen money would now be theft from the owner, but a much less serious theft than the original robbery. It is the original robbery which the prosecution wish to rely on.

---

[1] Cf. *Eighth Report*, Cmnd. 2977, at p. 66.

(b) Handling the proceeds of goods got by deception or blackmail

[404] Where the goods are "stolen" within s. 24 (4), having been obtained by deception, the position is rather different. Here s. 24 (2) may have an important part to play. Where the ownership did not pass to D (i.e., it is a case of theft as well as obtaining by deception), the position is the same as where the goods are stolen contrary to s. 1. Where the ownership did pass to D so that D did not commit theft, s. 24 (2) may come into its own.

For example A induces P to sell him an Alvis by deception. A is guilty of obtaining by deception but the property passes to him, so, subject to the *Lawrence* (C.A.) principle,[1] he is not guilty of theft. He exchanges the Alvis with B, a *bona fide* purchaser, for a Buick. This is probably not obtaining of the Buick by deception, even though B does not know that the Alvis is "stolen", since A is able to give a good title to it. A now delivers the Buick[2] to D who

201

knows all the facts. D is guilty of handling stolen goods and the Buick is stolen solely by virtue of s. 24 (2).

Similar considerations apply where the goods have been obtained by blackmail. If the transaction is void, then subsequent dealing with the goods obtained or the proceeds is likely to amount to an independent theft. If the transaction is voidable merely so the ownership passes, subsequent dealings with the property or proceeds will not amount to theft so that the proceeds will be stolen solely by virtue of s. 24 (2).

---

[1] Above, para. [37].

[2] P has lost his right to restitution in respect of the Alvis if B is in good faith and it has, therefore, ceased to be stolen. But P still has a right to rescind as against A and D and so has a right to restitution in respect of the Buick which, therefore, continues to be stolen. See below, para. [407].

(c) When proceeds of stolen goods cease to be stolen

[405] It has already been seen that stolen goods cease to be stolen when the conditions laid down by s. 24 (3) are fulfilled. What then, is the position of goods which have been stolen notionally under s. 24 (2)? Do they cease to be notionally stolen when the goods which they represent cease to be stolen? They must do so when the original goods are *restored to the possession* of the owner, for then the right to restitution of the proceeds lapses. Do the proceeds also cease to be stolen when the owner loses his *right to restitution* of the original goods? It seems clear that the answer must be in the negative. If it were otherwise, s. 24 (2) would be almost completely ineffective. In the case of the Alvis and the Buick (above, para. [404]) the right to recover the stolen Alvis was lost at the same instant that the Buick became the proceeds of the stolen Alvis, so that s. 24 (3) would cancel out s. 24 (2). Suppose again, that A obtains a car by deception from P. The contract of sale is voidable, so that A gets ownership of the car. He sells it to B who knows all the facts and who re-sells it to C who is *bona fide* and without notice of A's dishonesty. C gets an unimpeachable title to the car and it ceases to be stolen goods. A then gives the proceeds of the sale to D who knows all the facts. This is just the situation in which it might be desirable to rely on s. 24 (2) but it would not be possible to do so if the money (notionally stolen, as the proceeds of the car) ceased to be stolen on the car's so ceasing. It is submitted, therefore, that the money does not cease to be stolen. It continues to be stolen until the conditions specified in s. 24 (3) are satisfied in respect of it.

[406] Section 24 (3) may be applicable to "stolen" proceeds since the person from whom the original goods were stolen may assert a right to restitution as against the proceeds. Suppose that some of the money stolen in the Great Train Robbery had been used to purchase a necklace from a *bona fide* seller so that the right to restitution of the money had been lost and it had ceased to be stolen. Suppose further that the necklace had been given to D who knew all the facts. The necklace would be stolen by virtue of s. 24 (2).[1] P would have a right to restitution in respect of it and there would be room for the application of s. 24 (3) in that this right might be lost in the various ways[2] in which the right to restitution of the original goods might be lost. Additionally, it would be lost

if the original property were restored to the possession of the owner, since he could not recover the value of his property twice.

---

[1] It would also be stolen independently of s. 24 (2); above, para. [401].
[2] Above, paras. [396]–[417].

---

[407] To sum up, it is submitted that:

1. Goods notionally stolen as being the proceeds of other stolen goods do not necessarily cease to be notionally stolen when the original stolen goods cease, by virtue of s. 24 (3), to be stolen.

2. Goods notionally stolen cease to be notionally stolen when the conditions of s. 24 (3) are satisfied in respect of those goods.

3. Goods notionally stolen are usually also actually stolen. They cease to be actually stolen when the conditions of s. 24 (3) are satisfied in respect of them—i.e., at the same moment as they cease to be notionally stolen.

D.   FORMS OF HANDLING

[408] The term "handling" has been adopted because "receiving"—the only way of committing the offence under s. 33 (1) of the 1916 Act—is now one of several ways in which the new offence can be committed. These are:

(i) *Receiving* the goods.
(ii) *Undertaking* the retention, removal, disposal or realisation of the goods by or for the benefit of another person.
(iii) *Assisting* in the retention, removal, disposal or realisation of the goods by or for the benefit of another person.
(iv) *Arranging* to do (i), (ii) or (iii).

It has been decided that s. 22 creates only one offence.[1] Since that offence may be committed in four or six or even eighteen ways, a contrary decision would have had a disastrously complicating effect on the section, giving wide scope to possible objections on the ground of duplicity.

Particulars should be given so as to enable the accused to understand the ingredients of the charge he has to meet.[2] In the case of an indictment where more than one variety of handling is alleged, the better practice is to have one count for receiving (or, perhaps, arranging to receive, where appropriate) and a second count for the other forms of handling.[3] If D is charged only with receiving he may not be convicted on that indictment of some other form of handling.[4] The maximum number of counts for a single instance of handling in the ordinary case is two.[5]

---

[1] *Griffiths* v. *Freeman*, [1970] 1 All E.R. 1117.
[2] *Sloggett*, [1972] 1 Q.B. 430; [1971] 3 All E.R. 264.
[3] *Willis and Syme*, [1972] 3 All E.R. 797, C.A.; *Deakin*, [1972] 3 All E.R. 803; SHC 590, C.A.
[4] *Nicklin*, [1977] 2 All E.R. 444; [1977] Crim. L.R. 221.
[5] *Ikpong*, [1972] Crim. L.R. 432, C.A.

(a) Receiving

[409] All forms of handling other than receiving or arranging to receive are subject to the qualification that it must be proved that D was assisting another person or acting "for the benefit of another person".[1] If there is no evidence of this—as will frequently be the case—then it must be proved that D *received* or

arranged to receive the goods and evidence of no other form of handling will suffice. The Act does not define receiving in any way and it must be assumed that all the old authorities remain valid.

It must be proved, then, that D took possession or control of the stolen property or joined with others to share possession or control of it. "Receiving" the thief who has the goods in his possession does not necessarily amount to receiving the goods. If the thief retains exclusive control, there is no receiving.[2] There may, however, be a joint possession in thief and receiver, so it is unnecessary to prove that the thief ever parted with possession—it is sufficient that he shared it with the alleged receiver. In *Smith*[3] it was held that a recorder had correctly directed a jury when he told them that if they believed "that the watch was then in the custody of a person with the cognizance of the prisoner, that person being one over whom the prisoner had absolute control, so that the watch would be forthcoming if the prisoner ordered it, there was ample evidence to justify them in convicting ...". Lord Campbell, C.J. said that if the thief had been employed by D to commit larceny, so that the watch was in D's control, D was guilty of receiving. In such a case D was an accessory before the fact to larceny and today he would be guilty of theft. If the facts were as put by Lord Campbell, when did D become a receiver? As soon as the theft was committed? If so, we have the extraordinary result that D became guilty of both theft and receiving at the same moment. But, if this moment is not selected, it is difficult to see what other is appropriate. This may, however, appear less anomalous under the new law than under the old. Virtually all handling is now theft, so it is the general rule that the two offences are committed simultaneously. In the ordinary case, however, the offence is handling because there has been a previous theft. The peculiarity of the present problem is that there has been no *previous* theft; and it may be, therefore, that the requirement that the handling be "otherwise than in the course of the stealing", would prevent D from being guilty of handling until he did some act amounting to that offence, *after* the theft was complete.

---

[1] Below, para. **[420]**.
[2] *Wiley* (1850), 2 Den. 37.
[3] (1855), Dears. C.C. 494.

[410] As is clear from *Smith*, actual manual possession by D need not be proved. It is enough if the goods are received by his servant or agent with his authority.[1] The receipt may be for a merely temporary purpose such as concealment from the police.[2] It is unnecessary that the receiver should receive any profit or advantage from the possession of the goods. If D took possession of the goods from the thief without his consent, this was formerly only larceny (from the thief) and not receiving.[3] There seems to be no reason why it should not be both theft and handling under the Act, since it is clear that the two offences can be committed by one and the same act.

---

[1] *Miller* (1854), 6 Cox C.C. 353.
[2] *Richardson* (1834), 6 C. & P. 335.
[3] *Wade* (1844), 1 Car. & Kir. 739.

[411] It continues to be essential for the judge to give a careful direction as to possession or control.[1] If the only evidence against D is that he ran away on being found by the police in a house where stolen property had been left, there would appear to be no case to leave to a jury. Likewise where the evidence is consistent with the view that D went to premises where stolen goods were stored with the intention of assuming possession, but had not actually done so;[2] or where the only evidence of receiving a stolen car is that D's finger-print was found on the driving mirror.[3] The mere fact that the stolen goods were found on D's premises is not sufficient evidence. It must be shown that the goods had come either by invitation or arrangement with him or that he had exercised some control over them.[4] D is not necessarily in possession of a stolen safe simply because he assists others in trying to open it.[5]

[1] *Frost and Hale* (1964), 48 Cr. App. Rep. 284.
[2] *Freedman* (1930), 22 Cr. App. Rep. 133.
[3] *Court* (1960), 44 Cr. App. Rep. 242.
[4] *Cavendish*, [1961] 2 All E.R. 856.
[5] *Tomblin*, [1964] Crim. L.R. 780.

(b) Arranging to receive

[412] D's preparations to receive, not yet amounting to an attempt to do so, may constitute a sufficient "arrangement". The goods must be stolen at the time the arrangement is made. An agreement to handle goods to be stolen in the future may be a conspiracy to handle but it is not handling until the goods are actually stolen. As soon as they are stolen the continuing agreement might become an "arrangement." Where the goods are already stolen the crime is complete as soon as the arrangement is made. It is not undone if D repents or does nothing to carry out the arrangement, or it becomes impossible of performance. So in a case like *King*[1] it might now be possible to get a conviction for handling by showing that the arrangement was made while the goods were still stolen. It is odd that the offence is committed both by arranging to receive and by actually doing so. Is it two offences or one continuing offence? The latter view is preferable, for *Griffiths* v. *Freeman*[2] by no means solves all the problems of duplicity. The arrangement must be made after the theft, since D must know or believe the goods to be stolen. Most arrangements will involve agreement with another. An arrangement with an innocent person will be enough. If the other knows the goods are stolen, there will usually be a conspiracy.

[1] Above, para. **[392]**.
[2] Above, para. **[408]**, footnote 12.

(c) Undertaking and assisting

[413] The provisions of the Act relating to handling by *undertaking and assisting* extend the law to cover cases which were formerly not criminal at all. They are far-reaching and overlapping. "Undertaking" presumably covers the case where D sets out to retain, etc., the stolen goods, on his own initiative, and "assisting", the case where he joins the thief or another handler in doing so. Some examples drawn from the old law will illustrate the kind of case to which the law extends.

D negotiates the sale to F of goods which he knows to have been stolen by E. D is never in possession or control of the goods.[1] He would appear to have arranged and undertaken or assisted in the disposal of stolen goods.

D assists E to lift from a van a barrel of gin which he knows to have been stolen by E or another. Even if he never has possession or control[2] he has arranged, assisted or undertaken the removal of the stolen goods.

D's fifteen-year-old son, E, brings home a bicycle which he has stolen. D assists in its retention if (i) he agrees that E may keep the bicycle in the house or (ii) he tells the police there is no bicycle in the house, or (iii) he gives E a tin of paint so that he may disguise it.

D lights the way for E to carry stolen goods from a house to a barn so that E may negotiate the sale of the goods. D has assisted in the removal of the goods.[3]

It has been held that where a seller employs a sub-contractor to make goods which are delivered to the buyer, the seller may be guilty of handling by assisting in the realisation of stolen goods if, knowing or believing the materials to have been stolen, he pays the sub-contractor for the goods.[4] It has also been decided that a buyer of stolen goods may be held to have undertaken the realisation of the stolen goods.[5] But it would seem more appropriate to the facts to charge *assisting* in the realisation or (if it be the fact) receiving the goods.

---

[1] *Cf. Watson*, [1916] 2 K.B. 385.
[2] *Gleed* (1916), 12 Cr. App. Rep. 32; *Hobson* v. *Impett* (1957), 41 Cr. App. Rep. 138.
[3] *Wiley* (1850), 2 Den. 37.
[4] *Tamm*, [1973] Crim. L.R. 115 (Judge R. David).
[5] *Deakin*, [1972] 3 All E.R. 803; SHC 590, C.A.

(d) Arranging or undertaking to assist

[414] Far-reaching though the extension of the law to undertaking and assisting is, the Act goes further. A mere arrangement to do any of the acts amounting to undertaking or assisting is enough. D simply agrees or prepares to negotiate the sale of stolen goods, to lift down the barrel of stolen gin or to do any act for the purpose of enabling E to retain, remove or dispose of the goods. Nothing more is required.

E. HANDLING BY OMISSION

[415] "Receiving", "undertaking" and "arranging" all suggest that an act of some kind is required. It is difficult to envisage any of these forms of handling being committed by omission. It is however possible to *assist* another by inactivity; but this will not constitute an offence except in the rather rare case where the law imposes a duty to act.

In *Brown*,[1] it was held that D's mere failure to reveal to the police the presence of stolen goods on his premises did not amount to assisting in their retention. (Nor did his advice to the police to "Get lost.") Clearly the thief was in fact assisted by D's silence in the sense that D's omission to disclose the truth delayed the finding of the stolen goods. There is, however, no duty to give information to the police.[2] No doubt the answer would have been different if D had not merely refused information but had told lies.[3]

The court thought that D's conduct was *evidence* that D was permitting the

goods to remain and thereby assisting in their retention. It would obviously l
an act of assistance for D, expressly or tacitly, to give a thief permission
keep stolen goods on D's premises. The court's remarks (and, indeed, decisio
for they applied the proviso) seem to go farther and suggest that it would t
enough if D did not communicate with the thief at all but simply allowed stole
goods which had been placed on his premises to remain there. This comes ver
close to making the mere omission to remove goods or report their presence a
offence. But the result is perhaps reasonable. If a lorry driver were to obserx
that his mate had secretly inserted some stolen goods in the lorry and wei
then to drive the lorry to its destination without comment, there would be n
difficulty in saying that he had assisted in the removal of the goods. Where th
goods are planted on static premises, the assistance consists in the maintenanc
of the premises where the goods lie and the exclusion of strangers, just as in th
lorry case it consists in driving the lorry.

---

[1] [1970] 1 Q.B. 105; [1969] 3 All E.R. 198, C.A.
[2] The "duty" referred to in Appendix A to the Judges' Rules appears to be no more than a mora
duty. Refusal to answer a constable is not an obstruction in the course of his duty: *Rice* v. *Connolly*
[1966] 2 Q.B. 414; [1966] 2 All E.R. 649; Smith & Hogan, 365–368.
[3] This probably is obstruction of the police: *Rice* v. *Connolly* (footnote 2, above); *Matthews* v
Dwan, [1949] N.Z.L.R. 1037.

---

[416] The *dicta* in *Brown* were followed in *Pitchley*.[1] D's son stole £150 anc
on November 5 gave it to D to look after for him. D may not have known the
money was stolen when he received it and, on November 6, he paid it into a
savings bank account. On November 7 D learnt that the money was stolen. He
did nothing about it. He was indicted for handling the sum of £150 betweer
November 5 and 11. The prosecution case was that he either received the
money dishonestly or assisted dishonestly in its retention. The court though
that the word "retain" in the section bears its dictionary meaning—"keep
possession of, not lose, continue to have".[2] D, by permitting the "money"[3] to
remain under his control, was retaining it,[4] and was guilty. He was, it appears.
under a duty to withdraw "the money" and return it to its owner.

---

[1] (1973), 57 Cr. App. Rep. 30; [1972] Crim. L.R. 705, C.A. and commentary thereon; SHC 592.
[2] "The meaning of the word 'retention' in the section is a matter of law in so far as the
construction of the word is necessary", *per* Cairns, L.J. at 57 Cr. App. Rep. 37. *Cf. Feely*, above,
para. [116].
[3] The stolen money in fact had ceased to exist and it appears that the thing in action which
replaced it was not "stolen": above, para. [400].It is thus very doubtful whether Pitchley was rightly
convicted. A better charge would have been theft. The thing in action being the proceeds of the
stolen money, probably continued to belong to P; and D, by keeping it as owner, appropriated it:
s. 3 (2).
[4] But is "retaining" an offence? If D alone retains, it is odd to describe him as *assisting* in
retention. D's conduct might have been better described as *undertaking* the retention, but he was
not dishonest when he "undertook".

F.   OTHERWISE THAN IN THE COURSE OF THE STEALING

[417] Whatever the form of handling alleged, it must be proved it was done
"otherwise than in the course of the stealing". This provision was obviously
necessary if a great many instances of perfectly ordinary theft were not
automatically to become handling as well. Thus, without the provision,
virtually every instance of theft by two or more persons would have been

handling by one or other or, more likely, both of them, since they would inevitably render mutual assistance to one another in the removal of the goods. Given the decision to keep handling as a separate crime, the provision was, then, necessary—but it adds further unfortunate complications to an already complicated offence.

[418] The position was in fact much the same under the old law of receiving, because of the rule that a principal in the felony of larceny could not be guilty of receiving as a principal in the first degree.[1] If D received the goods in the course of the stealing, it followed that he was a principal in the larceny and this necessarily meant that he could not be convicted of receiving. If a servant stole money from his master's till and handed it to an accomplice in his master's shop, the accomplice was guilty of larceny and not guilty of receiving.[2] Similarly, if a man committed larceny in the room in which he lodged and threw a bundle of stolen goods to an accomplice in the street, the accomplice was guilty of larceny and not guilty of receiving.[3] But where E broke into a warehouse, stole butter and deposited it in the street some thirty yards from the warehouse door, D who then came to assist in carrying it off was not guilty of larceny as a principal offender.[4] Similarly where D waited half a mile from the scene of a proposed larceny and there received a horse stolen by E.[5] Doubtless, in these cases, D was guilty of receiving. A similar problem arose under the repealed s. 5 (1) (a) of the Homicide Act 1957. Under this provision "any murder done in the course or furtherance of theft" was capital. In *Jones*[6] D committed murder when he was interrupted as he was about to leave a store in which he had committed larceny. The Court of Criminal Appeal had no doubts that this was a killing "in the course ... of theft".

---

[1] Below, para. **[422]**.
[2] *Coggins* (1873), 12 Cox C.C. 517.
[3] *Perkins* (1852), 5 Cox C.C. 554.
[4] *King* (1817), Russ. & Ry. 332; *cf. Gruncell and Hopkinson* (1839), 9 C. & P. 365.
[5] *Kelly* (1820), Russ. & Ry. 421.
[6] [1959] 1 Q.B. 291; [1959] 1 All E.R. 41; see also *H.M. Advocate v. Graham*, 1958 S.L.T. 167.

---

[419] Under the 1968 Act everything depends on the extent to which appropriation is a continuing act.[1] As has been observed, one case involving handling, *Pitham and Hehl*[2], suggests that appropriation is an instantaneous act. If this is right, the words "in the course of the stealing" are rendered nugatory and it is submitted that, in the light of *Hale*,[3] a robbery case, *Pitham* should be narrowly construed and the "transaction" test adopted. If so, it seems that, as in the larceny cases, the theft continues at least while the thief is on the premises in which he perpetrates it and while "the job" is incomplete. But is E still in the course of theft as he walks down the garden path with the swag? as he drives home? and as he shows it to his wife in the kitchen? On the other hand, is the theft necessarily in the course of commission because the stolen property has not yet been removed from the premises on which it was stolen, if E has completed "the job" and all that remains is for others to take possession of the goods? It is thought that, in such a case, E is no longer in the course of stealing. If so, some of the old cases on larceny are no longer in point. Thus in *Atwell and O'Donnell*[4] goods were left in the warehouse in which they had been stolen for *some time thereafter* and the court held that it was a continuing transaction as to those who joined in the plot *before the goods were finally carried away from the premises.* Presumably until this occurred, the asportation was incomplete. It does not necessarily follow that the course of stealing under the Theft Act continues so long. If E appropriates goods in his employer's warehouse and conceals them so that they may be taken by D who comes to the warehouse a week later, is it to be said that D's taking is in the course of the stealing? Surely not. It is thought that E must still be "on the job"—vague though that phase may be—if the receipt is to be "in the course of the stealing".

¹ Above, para. [**48**].
² (1977), 65 Cr. App. Rep. 45, above, para. [**23**], [**48**].
³ C.A., No. 5908/A/77, 28 Nov. 78., above, para. [**146**].
⁴ (1801), 2 East P.C. 768.

G.   BY OR FOR THE BENEFIT OF ANOTHER PERSON

[**420**] Each of the nouns, "retention", "removal", "disposal" and "realisation" is governed by the words "by or for the benefit of another person."¹ It must therefore be proved that:—

  (a) D undertook, assisted or arranged the retention, removal, disposal or realisation *for the benefit of another person*; or
  (b) D assisted or arranged the retention, removal, disposal or realisation *by another person.*²

There can hardly ever have been a thief who did not retain, remove, dispose of or realise the stolen goods, and the qualification created by the italicised words prevents all thieves from being handlers as well. The italicised words are an essential part of the offence and the indictment must allege that the handling was "by or for the benefit of another person".³ The thief may himself be guilty of handling (by undertaking) if he himself retains, removes, etc., the goods for the benefit of another person. It would seem to be immaterial that the other person is guilty of no offence and even unaware of what is going on.

D steals goods, sells them to E, a *bona fide* purchaser, and keeps the purchase price for himself. D is not guilty of handling unless merely performing the contract with E amounts to acting "for the benefit of" E. D sells the goods to E, a *bona fide* purchaser, and instructs E to pay the purchase price to F. D is guilty of handling the stolen goods. He has undertaken the disposal of the goods for the benefit of another person. Presumably D is guilty if he sells the goods and receives the purchase price from E with the intention of paying it over to F. Thus an inquiry into D's motives may be necessary.

¹ *Sloggett*, [1971] 3 All E.R. 264 at 267.
² *Cf.* Blake "The Innocent Purchaser and Section 22 of the Theft Act", [1972] Crim L.R. 494.
³ *Sloggett*, [1972] 1 Q.B. 430; [1971] 3 All E.R. 264.

H.   INNOCENT RECEIPT ·AND SUBSEQUENT RETENTION WITH MENS REA

[**421**] If D receives the stolen goods innocently, either, that is, believing them not to be stolen or knowing them to be stolen but intending to return them to the true owner, of course, he commits no offence. Suppose he subsequently discovers the goods to be stolen or decides not to return them to

the true owner or disposes of them. He has, presumably dishonestly, undertaken the retention of or has disposed of stolen goods knowing them to be stolen. Whether he is guilty of an offence depends on a number of factors.

1. Where D does not get ownership of the goods. (The normal situation where goods are stolen.):

    (i) D gives value for the goods.

        (*a*) D retains or disposes of the goods for his own benefit. This is not theft because of s. 3 (1);[1] nor is it handling by undertaking, assisting or arranging since it is not for the benefit of another. D might be guilty of handling by aiding and abetting the receiving by the person to whom he disposes of the goods, if that person has *mens rea.*

        (*b*) D retains or disposes of the goods for the benefit of another. This is not theft (s. 3 (2)) but is handling.

    (ii) D does not give value.

        (*a*) D retains or disposes of the goods for his own benefit. This is theft but not handling unless it amounts to aiding and abetting receipt by another.

        (*b*) D retains or disposes of the goods for the benefit of another. This is theft and handling.

2. Where D gets ownership of the goods. (Because the rogue obtained them by deception and acquired a voidable title or because of some exception to the *nemo dat* rule.)

(*a*) D gives value for the goods.

Retention or disposal of the goods cannot be theft, since P has no property in the goods, nor handling since P has lost his right to restitution,[2] his right to rescind being destroyed on the goods coming into the hands of D who was a *bona fide* purchaser for value.

(*b*) D does not give value.

Again this cannot be theft, since P has no property in the goods, but it may be handling since P's right to rescind and secure restitution of his property is not extinguished by the goods coming into the hands of one who does not give value. It will be handling if this is so *and* D either aids and abets a guilty receipt by another or disposes of the goods for the benefit of another.

---

[1] Above, para. [**46**].
[2] Above, para. [**392**].

I.   HANDLING BY THE THIEF

[422] The common law rules regulating the liability of a thief to a charge of receiving goods feloniously stolen by him were complicated by the distinction between principals and accessories.

That distinction[1] has now been abolished and all participants in a crime are classed as principals.[2] The effect is that any thief may be convicted of handling the goods stolen by him by receiving them—if the evidence warrants this conclusion.[3] In the majority of cases the thief can only be guilty of handling by receiving where he aids and abets the receipt by another. Since he is already in possession or control, he cannot receive as the principal offender. In some circumstances, however, a thief might be convicted of handling the stolen goods by receiving them as the principal offender. For example, D steals goods and, in the course of the theft, delivers them to E. Two days later E returns the goods to D.

---

[1] See the 3rd edition of this book, para. [404].
[2] Criminal Law Act 1967, s. 1.
[3] *Dolan* (1976), 62 Cr. App. Rep. 36 at 39, C.A. Cf. *Stapylton* v. *O'Callaghan*, [1973] 2 All E.R. 782; SHC 594; above, para. [45].

---

2 THE MENS REA

A. KNOWLEDGE OR BELIEF

[423] It must be proved that D handled the goods, "knowing or believing them to be stolen goods". The test is subjective. The fact that any reasonable man would have known that the goods were stolen is evidence, but no more, that D knew or believed that this was so.[1] There is some difficulty about the function of the words, "or believing." The law of receiving stolen goods under the Larceny Acts used the word "knowing" alone. To say that a person "knows" a thing to be so implies that it is so. To say that he "believes" it to be so means that he thinks it is (or, perhaps, probably is) so, whether it is in fact so or not. It might have been supposed that "believing" was introduced to extend the law to cover one who received the goods believing them to be stolen when they were not. It has already been noticed that this interpretation was considered and rejected by the House of Lords in *Haughton* v. *Smith*.[2] It seems that the CLRC intended the word to cover what is often called wilful blindness and equated by the courts with knowledge.[3] They said:[4]

> "It is a serious defect of the present law that actual knowledge that the property was stolen must be proved. Often the prosecution cannot prove this. In many cases indeed guilty knowledge does not exist, although the circumstances of the transaction are such that the receiver ought to be guilty of an offence. The man who buys goods at a ridiculously low price from an unknown seller whom he meets in a public house may not *know* that the goods were stolen, and he may take the precaution of asking no questions. Yet it may be clear on the evidence that he believes that the goods were stolen. In such cases the prosecution may fail (rightly, as the law now stands) for want of proof of guilty knowledge."

The case intended to be covered seems to be that of a person who has a very strong suspicion and who turns a blind eye. Yet the courts have constantly said that the belief is not to be equated with suspicion. It is a misdirection to tell the jury that the section is satisfied by "knowledge or belief or suspicion that the property was stolen;"[5] or by the fact that D, "suspecting that the goods were stolen deliberately shut his eyes to the consequences."[6] Where a dealer in second-hand goods bought a £29 watch from a youth for £5 and admitted that he knew he had taken a chance it was held to be a misdirection to tell the jury that D was guilty if he was suspicious and closed his eyes.[7] In *Reader*[8] a direction that the law was that D "believed" the goods to be stolen if he thought it more likely than not that they were stolen was not saved by the

211

qualification, "If you feel ['belief'] ought to have a definition or a test more favourable to [D], then take that more favourable definition as your test." The Court said "To believe that the goods are probably stolen is not to believe that the goods are stolen ..."[9] Thus the word "believing" does not appear to have achieved the result intended by the CLRC. "Wilful blindness" never amounts to more than a strong suspicion or belief that goods are probably stolen. If D must be virtually certain that the goods are stolen, he knows they are stolen and "believing" adds nothing to "knowing." At least, that seems to be the law stated by the judges; but, remarkably, they need not tell the jury to apply the law so stated. In *Reader* the Court said[10]

> "If the learned judge had left the word 'belief' entirely alone and left the jury to decide what is belief, that is something which everybody is concerned with almost every day of their lives and they would have been able to come to a proper conclusion without explanation being given."

Thus, the jury may find that wilful blindness amounts to belief if they want to.

It is sufficient that D knows or believes that goods, whatever they are, are stolen. His knowledge or belief need not extend to the identity of the thief, or the owner,[11] or the nature of the stolen goods.[12] If D knows he is in possession of a box containing stolen goods, it is no defence that he does not know what the contents are and is shocked to discover that the box contains guns; nor would it be a defence that he believed the box contained stolen watches.[13]

---

[1] *Stagg*, [1978] Crim. L.R. 227.

[2] [1975] A.C. at 485; above, para. **[389]**.

[3] Smith and Hogan, 102–103.

[4] *Eighth Report*, Cmnd. 2977, at p. 64.

[5] *Grainge*, [1974] 1 All E.R. 928; SHC 596, C.A. *Cf. Woods*, [1969] 1 Q.B. 447; [1968] 3 All E.R. 709, C.C.A.

[6] *Griffiths* (1974), 60 Cr. App. Rep. 14, C.A. *Atwal v. Massey*, [1971] 3 All E.R. 881 (D.C.) is definitely misleading on this point.

[7] *Ismail*, [1977] Crim. L.R. 557 and commentary. *Cf.* the discussion by Griew, 10–14 – 10–16; Williams, *TBCL*, 832–833.

[8] (1977), 66 Cr. App. Rep. 33, C.A.

[9] At p. 36.

[10] At p. 36.

[11] *Fuschillo*, [1940] 2 All E.R. 489; but it may be necessary to name the owner where the property is of a common and indistinctive type: *Gregory*, [1972] 2 All E.R. 861.

[12] *McCullum* (1973), 57 Cr. App. Rep. 645; SHC 599, C.A.

[13] *Ibid.* at 649–650. An argument that D was not in possession of the contents because he was mistaken as to their nature would probably fail because he knew there was "something wrong" with the goods: *Warner v. Metropolitan Police Commissioner*, [1969] 2 A.C. 256 at 308; [1968] 2 All E.R. 356 at 390: SHC 61 at 66.

B.   DISHONESTY

[424] Dishonesty was an essential ingredient of the old crime of receiving though it was not expressed in the statute. The inclusion of the word "dishonestly" thus makes no change in the law. D may receive goods knowing or believing them to be stolen and yet not be guilty if, for example, he intends to return them to the true owner or the police.[1] A claim of right will amount to a defence, but it will be difficult to establish such a claim where D knows or believes the goods to be stolen except in the case put above, where he intends to return the goods to the owner. Whether there is dishonesty is presumably now a question of fact for the jury in each case, as in theft.[2]

[1] *Cf. Matthews*, [1950] 1 All E.R. 137.
[2] *Feely*, [1973] 1 Q.B. 530; [1973] 1 All E.R. 341; SHC 509.

C. PROOF OF MENS REA

[425] The common law rules concerning proof of *mens rea* on a receiving charge hold good under the Act. In particular, where D is found in possession of recently stolen property the jury may be directed that they *may* infer guilty knowledge or belief if D offers no explanation of his possession or if they are satisfied beyond reasonable doubt that any explanation he has offered is untrue. The onus of proof remains on the Crown throughout, and, whether D offers an explanation or not, he should be convicted only if the jury are satisfied beyond reasonable doubt that he had the guilty knowledge or belief.[1]

[1] *Abramovitch* (1914), 11 Cr. App. Rep. 45; *Aves* (1950), 34 Cr. App. Rep. 159; *Hepworth*, [1955] 2 Q.B. 600. *Cf. Stapylton* v. *O'Callaghan*, [1973] 2 All E.R. 782; SHC 594; above, para. **[45]**.

[426] Because of the difficulty of proving guilty knowledge, the Larceny Act provided for the admission of certain evidence on a receiving charge which would not be admissible in criminal cases generally. The Theft Act has corresponding but somewhat different provisions. By s. 27 (3):

> "Where a person is being proceeded against for handling stolen goods (but not for any offence other than handling stolen goods), then at any stage of the proceedings, if evidence has been given of his having or arranging to have in his possession the goods the subject of the charge, or of his undertaking or assisting in, or arranging to undertake or assist in, their retention, removal, disposal or realisation, the following evidence shall be admissible for the purpose of proving that he knew or believed the goods to be stolen goods:—
>
> (*a*) evidence that he has had in his possession, or has undertaken or assisted in the retention, removal, disposal or realisation of, stolen goods from any theft taking place not earlier than twelve months before the offence charged; and
> (*b*) (provided that seven days' notice in writing has been given to him of the intention to prove the conviction) evidence that he has within the five years preceding the date of the offence charged been convicted of theft or of handling stolen goods."

Whereas under (*b*) the previous conviction must have occurred within five years preceding the offence charged, the possession, etc. under (*a*) must have occurred "not earlier" than twelve months before the offence charged. The possession, etc. which is admissible under (*a*) may have taken place *later* than the offence charged.[1]

[1] *Davis*, [1972] Crim. L.R. 431, C.A.

[427] It appears that these provisions supplement and do not replace the common law.[1] Thus a handling of goods stolen earlier than twelve months before the handling now charged might be admissible at common law if it fell within the "similar facts" rule of admissibility.[2] So too might a conviction of theft or handling after the date of the offence charged or more than five years before it—though this is rather unlikely. Section 27 (3) imposes limitations upon admissibility which do not exist at common law. The evidence in question may not be given until after some evidence of the *actus reus* has been given; and evidence admissible under (*b*) may not be given without seven days' notice in writing of intention to tender it. Commonly, evidence admissible under the Act will not be admissible at common law because there is an insufficient degree of similarity or other nexus. Where the evidence is admissible at common law as well as under the Act, it is submitted that the statutory restrictions must be observed. If the evidence is inadmissible under the Act—for example it is a handling of goods stolen more than twelve months before the offence charged—but is admissible at common law because of the striking similarity of the facts, the statutory restrictions cannot apply. It is submitted, however, that the rule requiring evidence of the *actus reus* of the offence charged to be given before the evidence of the other handling or theft ought to be observed as a rule of practice. If it is a desirable precaution in the case of evidence sanctioned by statute, it is equally desirable in the case of that admitted by the common law.

[1] *Davis*, above.
[2] Cross, *Evidence* (4th ed.) 310.

[428] Although evidence has been given of the *actus reus*—for example that D was in possession—D may dispute that fact. Evidence admitted under s. 27 (3) may not be considered on the question whether D was in possession. It is admissible for one purpose only—to prove the knowledge or belief that the goods were stolen. Since proof of possession also requires proof of a mental element, these questions may become virtually indistinguishable. In *Wilkins*[1] evidence was given that stolen goods were found in D's garden and behind a drawer in her bedroom. This was evidence that she was in possession, permitting the admission of evidence under s. 27 (3). Her defence was that the articles had been put there without her knowledge, that she did not know they were there, and, accordingly, that she was never in possession. Since the judge's direction failed to make clear that the evidence could be taken into account only on the issue of guilty knowledge or belief that the goods were stolen, the convictions were quashed. Where there is a danger that the jury may think the evidence relevant to some other issue, the judge might be wise to exercise his discretion to exclude the evidence.

[1] [1975] 2 All E.R. 734.

D. PROCEDURE

[429] By s. 27 (1):

"Any number of persons may be charged in one indictment with reference to the same theft, with having at different times or at the same time handled all or any of the stolen goods, and the persons so charged may be tried together."

If £500 is stolen from a bank and the thief, on separate occasions, hands £100 to each of five persons, all five may be tried together for handling the stolen money, though they have no connection with one another except through the thief.

By s. 27 (2):

"On the trial of two or more persons indicted for jointly handling any stolen goods the jury may find any of the accused guilty if the jury are satisfied that he handled all or any of the stolen goods, whether or not he did so jointly with the other accused or any of them."

Under the rule in *D.P.P.* v. *Merriman*[1] where two persons are jointly charged with committing the same act and it emerges that they were not acting in concert, each may be convicted of committing the act independently. The subsection goes further in that it allows conviction not only where there is separate participation in a single act but where there are different acts in relation to the same stolen goods. In *French*[2] D received stolen goods and took them to E's shop where E received them. It was held that they were properly jointly indicted, although the handlings were quite separate and the case against each must be considered separately.

---

[1] [1973] A.C. 584; [1972] 3 All E.R. 42.
[2] [1973] Crim. L.R. 632, C.A.

CHAPTER XIV

ENFORCEMENT AND PROCEDURE

1 SEARCH FOR STOLEN GOODS

[430] Power to issue a warrant or authority to search premises for stolen goods is given by s. 26 of the 1968 Act.[1]

Under the Larceny Act a search warrant might authorise search by any person specified in the warrant. Under the 1968 Act, only a policeman may be authorised to search, though the information may be sworn by any person. Other enactments authorising the issue of search warrants to persons other than police officers are, however, expressly preserved. In any such Act a reference to stolen goods shall be construed in accordance with s. 24 of the Theft Act.[2] The effect is to widen the power of search to include goods which have been obtained by blackmail and by deception.

The power given by s. 26 (2) to superintendents and above was formerly enjoyed only by Chief Constables. With the increasing size of police forces, this was thought by the Criminal Law Revision Committee to be too restrictive. A small restriction on the power given by s. 26 (2) (a) is that the occupier's offence of dishonesty must have been committed within the preceding five years whereas under the Larceny Act it might have been committed at any time.

It is submitted that the constable's authority to seize goods under s. 26 (3) extends to any goods on the premises in question which he believes to be stolen goods, whether they are named in the warrants or not.[3] Even if the section did not justify such a seizure, it would be lawful by the common law.[4]

---

[1] Below, page 246.
[2] See s. 32 (2) (b), below, page 251.
[3] Contrast the wording of s. 42 (1) of the Larceny Act 1916.
[4] *Chic Fashions (West Wales), Ltd.* v. *Jones*, [1968] 2 Q.B. 299; [1968] 1 All E.R. 229.

---

2 JURISDICTION

A. TERRITORIAL

[431] It is a general principle of the common law that criminal jurisdiction does not extend to acts committed abroad. Parliament may, of course, extend jurisdiction so far as it pleases but it is a general rule of construction that unless there is something which points to a contrary intention, a statute will be taken to apply only to the United Kingdom. The Acts expressly provide that, with small exceptions, they do not extend to Scotland or Northern Ireland.[1] The majority of the House of Lords in *Treacy* v. *D.P.P.*[2] assumed that the general principle of construction applied to offences under the 1968 Act, with the result that they are triable only if committed in England and Wales. Lord Diplock alone expressed the opinion that the only territorial limitations to be implied are those required by the rules of international comity which "do not call for more than that each sovereign state should refrain from punishing persons for their conduct within the territory of another sovereign state where that conduct has had no harmful consequences within the territory of the state which imposes the punishment."[3] It would look a little odd that the Act should provide that conduct should be an offence under English law if committed anywhere in the world *except* Scotland and Northern Ireland; but Lord Diplock explained the exception of these areas as depending on constitutional practice, not international comity. Probably the majority opinion will prevail; but it will be recalled that the interpretation of offences such as obtaining by deception and blackmail as continuing offences,[4] goes some way to achieving the effect desired by Lord Diplock.

An exception is created by 1968 ss. 14 and 33. Where a person is charged with theft, attempted theft, robbery, attempted robbery or assault with intent to rob, with respect to the theft of a mail bag or postal packet, or the contents of either when in course of transmission in the British postal area,[5] then he may be tried in England and Wales without proof that the offence was committed there.

---

[1] Section 36 (2).
[2] [1971] A.C. 537; [1971] 1 All E.R. 110.
[3] [1971] A.C. at 564.
[4] Above, paras. **[190]**–**[191]** and **[304]**.
[5] Section 14 (2).

---

[432] By Part I of Schedule 3, the provisions of the Post Office Act 1953 which relate to stealing and receiving were repealed for England and Wales (but not for Scotland). Anyone prosecuted in England and Wales for stealing or handling mail bags, etc. must therefore be prosecuted under the appropriate section of the Theft Act. If the charge is one of handling mail bags, etc., then it seems that it must be proved that the offence was committed in England and Wales. The other offences under the Post Office Act, including those akin to but not amounting to theft, such as unlawfully taking away or opening a mail bag, continue in force.

B. COURTS

(a) *The Crown Court*

[433] Under the Courts Act 1971, courts of assize and quarter sessions are abolished and all proceedings on indictment are to be brought in the Crown Court. Of the indictable offences under the Theft Acts, aggravated burglary, burglary in the circumstances described in s. 29 (2) (*b*) of the Act[1], blackmail and handling stolen goods from an offence not committed in the United Kingdom are "Class 3" offences and the remainder are "Class 4" offences[2]. The effect is that all the offences may be listed for trial by a High Court judge or by a circuit judge or recorder but the Class 4 offences will normally be listed for trial by a circuit judge or recorder.

---

[1] Below, para. **[397]**.
[2] Practice Note, [1971] 3 All E.R. 829.

(*b*) *Magistrates' Courts*

[434] All indictable offences under the Theft Acts 1968 and 1978 are triable either way except—

> (*a*) robbery, aggravated burglary, blackmail and assault with intent to rob;
> (*b*) burglary comprising the commission of, or an intention to commit, an offence which is triable only on indictment;
> (*c*) burglary in a dwelling if any person in the dwelling was subjected to violence or the threat of violence.[1]

The offences triable only on indictment which are likely to be relevant under (*b*) are causing grievous bodily harm with intent, contrary to s. 18 of the Offences against the Person Act 1961, rape and damaging property with intent to endanger life, contrary to the Criminal Damage Act 1971, s. 1 (2). "Dwelling" under (*c*) will include inhabited vehicles or vessels.

---

[1] Criminal Law Act 1977, Sch. 3, para. 28, replacing s. 29 (2) of the Theft Act 1968.

---

3 RESTITUTION[1]

[435] 1968, s. 28 provides a summary procedure whereby the court before which a person is convicted of certain offences may order that the property concerned be restored to the owner.[2] Under the old law, conviction might affect the title to goods. This is no longer so.[3] Who is the owner of property is a question for the civil law and the fact that there has been a conviction of any criminal offence with respect to the property is irrelevant, so far as title is concerned.

Section 28 (1) provides:

> "Where goods have been stolen, and either a person is convicted of any offence with reference to the theft (whether or not the stealing is the gist of his offence) or a person is convicted of any other offence but such an offence as aforesaid is taken into consideration in determining his sentence, the court by or before which the offender is convicted may on the conviction exercise any of the following powers:—
>
> (*a*) the court may order anyone having possession or control of the goods to restore them to any person entitled to recover them from him; or
> (*b*) on the application of a person entitled to recover from the person convicted any other goods directly or indirectly representing the first-mentioned goods (as being the proceeds of any disposal or realisation of the whole or part of them or of goods so representing them), the court may order those other goods to be delivered or transferred to the applicant; or
> (*c*) the court may order that a sum not exceeding the value of the first-mentioned goods shall be paid out of any money of the person convicted which was taken out of his possession on his apprehension to

any person who, if those goods were in the possession of the person convicted would be entitled to recover them from him.

---

[1] Macleod, "Restitution under the Theft Act", [1968] Crim. L.R. 577.
[2] Police have no power to retain property seized from accused solely in anticipation of a compensation, forfeiture or restitution order being made: *Malone* v. *Commissioner of Police*, [1979] 1 All E.R. 256.
[3] Section 31 (2), below, p. 251.

A. STOLEN GOODS

[436] "Goods" are defined in s. 34 (2) (*b*) which is considered above.[1] "Stolen" bears the same meaning as in s. 24 (4)[2] and thus extends to goods obtained by blackmail or by deception.[3]

---

[1] See para. [380].
[2] Above, para. [384].
[3] Sections 24 (4) and 28 (6).

B. THE CONVICTION

[437] The court's power arises on a conviction, or a taking into consideration, "of any offence with reference to the theft[1] (whether or not the stealing is the gist of his offence)". The convictions would include handling the stolen goods, robbery, burglary and aggravated burglary. The two latter offences do not necessarily involve theft and it would, of course, be necessary for the court to be satisfied on the evidence admissible under s. 28 (4)[2], that a theft of the goods which were the object of the burglary had in fact been committed. It is not necessary that the conviction should be an offence against the Act. It might be, for example, a conviction of assisting an arrestable offender under s. 4 (1) of the Criminal Law Act 1967 or of concealing an arrestable offence under s. 5 (1) of that Act; of conspiracy or an attempt to commit theft where there is proof that the theft was actually committed; or of a forgery done for the purpose of committing the theft in question.

---

[1] I.e., the theft, blackmail or deception.
[2] Below, para. [443].

C. AGAINST WHOM THE ORDER MAY BE MADE

[438] An order under s. 28 (1) (*a*) may be made against anyone having possession or control of the goods. A *bona fide* purchaser may thus be ordered to surrender the goods to someone with a better title. The order may be made against a person holding the goods on behalf of another as, for example, a servant who has custody of goods, possession being in the employer.

An order under s. 28 (1) (*b*)[1] may be made only against the person convicted.

---

[1] Cf. *Eighth Report*, Cmnd. 2977, para. 165.

D. IN WHOSE FAVOUR THE ORDER MAY BE MADE

[439] An order may be made in favour of any person who is entitled to recover the goods from the person in possession or control (para. (*a*)) or who would be entitled to recover the goods if they were in the possession of the person convicted (para. (*c*)); and any *applicant* entitled to recover the *proceeds* of the stolen goods from the person convicted (para. (*b*)).

As has been pointed out above,[1] it is only in exceptional cases that the owner of goods has a literal right to recover them, even from a thief, in civil law. Generally his remedy is an action in conversion in which he will be awarded damages. It is submitted that, as with "right to restitution", so also "entitled to recover" must be given a broad interpretation to extend to cases in which the claimant would be able to succeed in an action based upon his proprietary rights in the thing in question. This would therefore extend to a case in which the ownership has passed to the rogue under a voidable transaction[2] which the owner has rescinded.

The person entitled will generally be the victim of the theft or someone standing in his shoes, as his executor, administrator or trustee in bankruptcy. If the victim has received compensation for the loss of the stolen goods under an insurance policy, then the insurance company may be subrogated to his rights.[3] If the victim had not the best right to possession of the goods (as, for example, if he himself had stolen them from another) the person with that right is the person entitled.

[1] In discussing the meaning of "a right to restitution" in s. 24 (3); para. **[394]**.
[2] Above, para. **[394]**.
[3] *Church* (1970), 55 Cr. App. Rep. 65 at 71.

E. THE PROPERTY IN RESPECT OF WHICH THE ORDER MAY BE MADE

[440] The property in respect of which the order may be made is as follows:

Section 28 (1) (*a*): such of the goods[1] which have been stolen as are in the possession or control of the person against whom the order is made.

Section 28 (1) (*b*): such of the proceeds of the goods which have been stolen as are in the possession or control of the person against whom the order is made.

Section 28 (1) (*c*): any *money* of the person convicted which was taken out of his possession on his apprehension, not exceeding the value of the stolen goods.

Two questions arise here. The first relates to the meaning of "taken out of his possession on his apprehension". This is not confined, as might have been supposed, to money which is taken from D's person when he is arrested. In *Ferguson*[2], it was held to include money in a safe deposit box at Harrods, of which D had the key, which was properly appropriated by the police as the suspected proceeds of the theft, ten days after D's arrest. This decision seems to attribute to "possession" its legal rather than its popular meaning but the court said that it was "difficult to think of a clearer case of money being in the possession" of the accused and that, giving "'on his apprehension' a common-sense meaning", the money was so taken. If the money had been deposited in a bank account, the result would have been different since D would have been only a creditor of the bank and not in possession. It seems then that money at D's home or in his car is in his possession for this purpose.

Presumably the taking must be lawful. The police have no right to seize money which they do not reasonably believe to be the proceeds of a crime or evidence of its commission. It is submitted that money unlawfully seized, though literally taken from the accused on his apprehension, could not be used to compensate the victim. The provision may thus work somewhat capriciously. Money wrongly but reasonably suspected to be the proceeds of the theft may be taken and used to compensate, but other money in the possession of the accused may not. It is odd that a wrong, though reasonable, suspicion should make the difference.

Any provision containing the word "possession" is likely to present problems. In *Parker*,[3] D apparently threw away a wallet containing money shortly before his arrest, and this was found in a garden by the police the following day; the court refused to answer the question whether the money was taken from his possession on his apprehension. On one view, he had abandoned possession by throwing the wallet away; but so to hold would seem to depart from the broad "commonsense" view taken in *Ferguson*.[2]

Finally, the money must be "money of the person convicted" so that if, as in *Ferguson*, any doubt is raised as to D's ownership of the money, no order may be made.

[1] *Cf.* s. 34 (2) (*b*), above, paras. **[380]**–**[383]**.
[2] [1970] 2 All E.R. 820 C.A..
[3] [1970] 2 All E.R. 458 C.A..

[441] The second problem concerns the extent to which D may be required to make compensation. Section 28 (1) (*c*) says to the extent of "a sum not exceeding the value of the first mentioned goods"—i.e., the goods which have been stolen. This presents no difficulty where D is convicted of the theft. He may, however, be convicted of an offence "with reference to the theft" and his participation may relate only to a small part of the stolen property. For example, it may be proved that £1,000 was stolen from a bank and that D dishonestly received £10 of that money which was taken from him when he was arrested. On a literal reading, it would seem that D might be ordered to pay £990 out of other money taken from him on his arrest which was not the proceeds of the theft. However, in *Parker*[1] the court held that, whatever the proper construction of the section:

> "If a man is charged with handling stolen goods and the whole of the goods in respect of which he has been convicted are recovered, then it must, we hold, be an incorrect exercise of any discretion which exists under the section to make him pay compensation in addition in respect of other goods which are not the subject of a charge against him".

[1] [1970] 2 All E.R. at 462–463.

F. COMPENSATION TO A THIRD PARTY

[442] By s. 28 (3):

> "Where under subsection (1) above[1] the court on a person's conviction makes an order under paragraph (a) for the restoration of any goods, and

221

it appears to the court that the person convicted has sold the goods to a person acting in good faith, or has borrowed money on the security of them from a person so acting, the court may order that there shall be paid to the purchaser or lender, out of any money of the person convicted which was taken out of his possession on his apprehension, a sum not exceeding the amount paid for the purchase by the purchaser or, as the case may be, the amount owed to the lender in respect of the loan."

Thus if D has stolen a necklace from P and pawned it with Q for a loan of £100, on D's conviction, Q may be ordered to restore the necklace to P and be compensated out of the money taken from D on his apprehension. The provision is confined to money taken from D on his apprehension so Q will have no remedy under s. 28 if D, when apprehended, is wearing a gold watch but carrying no money, though he has large sums in his bank. Q, may, however, be compensated by an order made under s. 35 of the Powers of Criminal Courts Act 1973.[2]

---

[1] See above, para. [435].
[2] Below, para. [450].

G. WHEN AN ORDER SHOULD BE MADE

[443] It is provided by s. 28 (4)[1] that "The court shall not exercise the powers conferred by this section unless in the opinion of the court the relevant facts sufficiently appear from the evidence given at the trial or the available documents, together with admissions made by or on behalf of any person in connection with any proposed exercise of the powers ..."

The court must be satisfied on the evidence given *at the trial* that an order should be made; and the trial concludes when sentence is passed.[2] The court may not embark on a new inquiry at the end of the trial. The words, "on the conviction" in s. 28 (1) mean the same as "immediately after the conviction" in the Forfeiture Act 1870, s. 4 (repealed).

The court is never bound to make an order under s. 28; when the condition in s. 28 (4) is satisfied it is a matter for the discretion of the court. Clearly, however, when the relevant facts do sufficiently appear, an order should generally be made unless there is a real dispute as to the title to the goods. Even when the facts are absolutely clear the question of entitlement to the goods may involve difficult questions of law. Where they have been transferred to a third party, many of the subtleties of the old law of larceny by a trick and false pretences may arise. If there is any real dispute or any doubt as to title, then an order should not be made; the parties should be left to their civil remedies. Only in the plainest cases, where there is no doubt of fact or law, should an order be made.[3]

"In practice the power will be exercisable only where there is no real dispute as to ownership. It would seriously hamper the work of the criminal courts if at the end of a trial they had to investigate disputed titles."[4]

222

No right to be heard is given to a third party against whom an order might be made—and it has been said that he has no *locus standi*[5]—but it is submitted that it would be improper to make an order against a party without allowing him to be heard on the subject[6]—particularly since, where the order is made by the Crown Court, the third party has no right of appeal.[7] An order made against a person not afforded a hearing would seem to offend against the rules of natural justice and, where made by a magistrates' court, liable to be quashed by *certiorari*; but *certiorari* will not lie to the Crown Court, which is part of the Supreme Court.

---

[1] Below, p. 249.
[2] *Church* (1971), 55 Cr. App. Rep. 65.
[3] *Ferguson*, [1970] 2 All E.R. 820 C.A. .
[4] *Eighth Report*, Cmnd. 2977, para. 164: "it would probably be impracticable (as well as being undesirable) that an order should be made in any but straightforward cases".
[5] *Ferguson*, [1970] 2 All E.R. at 822.
[6] "... certainly it is intended that he should be heard, either in person or through counsel"—Parl. Debate Official Report (H.L.) 290, col. 865, *per* Lord Stonham. *Cf. Macklin* (1850), 5 Cox C.C. 216.
[7] Below, para. **[446]**.

H. EXERCISE OF MORE THAN ONE POWER

[444] The question may arise as to whether the court may exercise more than one of its powers in respect of the same theft.[1] Though paras. (*a*), (*b*) and (*c*) of s. 28 (1) are expressed in the alternative, s. 28 (2) contemplates that an order may be made against the thief under both (*b*) and (*c*). The situation contemplated is that where the thief has disposed of the goods for less than their true value. If power is exercised under (*b*) to award these proceeds to the applicant, the balance may be made up from money taken from D on his apprehension. Normally, where the power under (*a*) is exercised to restore the goods to the owner, no further compensation will be required. If, however, only a part of the goods can be restored by exercising power (*a*), there seems to be no reason why power (*b*) or (*c*) should not be exercised in relation to the remainder.

Where P gets the whole of his goods back under (*a*) but they are damaged, he might succeed in an application for compensation under (*c*). If a count for criminal damage were included in the indictment and the accused convicted, the court might, on application or otherwise, order the payment of up to £400 compensation under the Criminal Damage Act 1971, s. 8; and, if there were no such count, then the similar power under the Forfeiture Act might be exercised on application. There seems to be nothing to prevent the court exercising these various statutory powers on the same occasion and in combination if it thinks it just to do so.

Where D has succeeded in passing a good title to a *bona fide* purchaser (B), and the court, in the exercise of power (*a*), consequently orders possession to be given to B, may it then exercise power (*c*) in favour of the original owner, A? This is the converse of the more usual situation expressly provided for in s. 28 (3)[2] where the *bona fide* purchaser gets no title and consequently is ordered to surrender the goods to A. It is submitted that the above question should be answered in the affirmative. If the goods were in the possession of D, A "would be entitled to recover them from him". The superior right of B would not defeat an action by A against D. A therefore satisfies the condition in para. (*c*), and it seems entirely right that he should be compensated out of money taken from D where D has succeeded in depriving him of his title to the goods. The situation will probably rarely arise, since it will not often be absolutely clear that D has passed a good title to B; and where there is a doubt, the court must refrain from making orders.[3]

---

[1] *Cf.* Macleod, [1968] Crim. L.R. at 586–587.
[2] Above, para. [442].
[3] Above, para. [443].

I. ENFORCEMENT OF AN ORDER

[445] The Act makes no provision for the enforcement of orders made under s. 28.

> "Disobedience to an order made by a court of assize or quarter sessions for the handing over of goods could, we think, be dealt with as contempt. Disobedience to a similar order made by a magistrates' court could be dealt with under s. 54 (3) of the Magistrates' Courts Act 1952."[1]

---

[1] *Eighth Report*, Cmnd. 2977, para. 163.

J. THE EFFECT OF AN ORDER

[446] The Act contains no provision similar to that in the Police (Property) Act 1897, protecting the person in whose favour an order is made against claims to the property on the expiration of six months from the order.[1] It is submitted that an order should have no effect whatever on the rights under the civil law of any claimant to the property, except possibly where those rights consist in a merely possessory title.[2]

It may frequently happen that a magistrates' court is in a position to order the return of the property either under the Police (Property) Act or under the Theft Act and, when this is so, the court should make it clear under which provision it is acting since there is the difference in effect referred to.[3] In general it is thought that it would be better to utilise the power under the Theft Act, since the 1897 Act may interfere in a rather arbitrary fashion with the rights at civil law, even of persons who are unaware that the proceedings are taking place.[4]

---

[1] Below, para. [453].
[2] *Cf. Irving* v. *National Provincial Bank, Ltd.,* [1962] 2 Q.B. 73; [1962] 1 All E.R. 157 C.A., below, para. [453].
[3] Moreover the order under the Theft Act does not take effect if the conviction is quashed (below, para. [449]) whereas that under the Police (Property) Act is quite unaffected by the quashing of any conviction since the power does not depend upon the existence of a conviction, but only of a charge.
[4] Below, para. [453].

K. APPEAL

(a) From an order in the Crown Court

[447] It has now been decided[1] that where an order is made against a person convicted on indictment, he may appeal against it to the Court of Appeal.

Though the point has not been made clear by the courts, it seems that the appeal is an appeal against sentence under s. 9 of the Criminal Appeal Act 1968; for, by s. 50 (1) of that Act:

> "... 'sentence', in relation to an offence, includes any order made by a court when dealing with an offender ..."

It was held that this was wide enough to include an order made under s. 4 of the Forfeiture Act 1870 for payment of money by way of satisfaction or compensation,[2] and it would seem to follow that an order made under s. 24 is also part of the sentence.[3] Leave to appeal against sentence must be obtained from the Court of Appeal.

Where an order is made against a person other than the person convicted no appeal by him will lie;[4] though if the convicted person appeals, the court may then annul or vary[5] a restitution order made against a third party. This is anomalous—particularly since it is possible for an order to be made against a third party who has not been heard; but it will be of no practical importance if orders are made only in undisputed and straightforward cases.

---

[1] *Parker*, [1970] 2 All E.R. 458; *Ferguson*, [1970] 2 All E.R. 820.
[2] *Jones*, [1929] 1 K.B. 211; [1928] All E.R. Rep. 532.
[3] In *Thebith* (1969), 54 Cr. App. Rep. 35 at 37, it was stated that there was (unspecified) authority that a restitution order was not part of the sentence, and consequently there was no appeal. The author has been unable to trace the authority, and it would appear to be overruled by the cases cited above.
[4] *Cf. Elliott*, [1908] 2 K.B. 452; *JJ. of the Central Criminal Court* (1886), 18 Q.B.D. 314.
[5] Criminal Appeal Act 1968, s. 30 (4).

(b) From an order in the Magistrates' Court

[448] Section 83 of the Magistrates' Courts Act 1952 gives a right of appeal against sentence to the Crown Court and sentence includes (with inapplicable exceptions) "any order made on conviction". This clearly gives a right of appeal to the convicted person against an order made under s. 28. Both the convicted person and a third party against whom an order has been made might appeal by way of case stated to the High Court on a question of law or jurisdiction, under s. 87 (1) of the Magistrates' Courts Act which applies to any person aggrieved by an order.

L. SUSPENSION OF ORDERS MADE ON INDICTMENT

[449] The operation of an order for restitution is suspended for 28 days after the date of conviction on indictment unless, "in any case in which, in their opinion, the title to the property is not in dispute,"[1] the court directs otherwise. Where notice of appeal or leave to appeal is given within those 28 days, then the operation of the order is suspended until the conviction is quashed or, if it is not quashed, until time for applying for leave to the House of Lords has run out or so long as any appeal to that House is pending.[2] If the conviction is quashed by the Court of Appeal or the House of Lords then the order does not take effect. When a conviction is quashed by the Court of Appeal and restored by the House of Lords, the House may make any order for restitution which could have been made by the court which convicted the respondent.[3]

[1] *Ibid.*, s. 30; and Theft Act 1968, s. 28 (4).
[2] Criminal Appeal Act 1968, s. 42 (1).
[3] *Ibid.*, s. 42 (3).

M. OTHER POWERS TO AWARD COMPENSATION

(a) Under the Powers of Criminal Courts Act 1973

[450] Section 35 of the Powers of Criminal Courts Act 1973 provides that a court by or before which a person is convicted of any offence may, whether on application or otherwise, make an order requiring the offender to pay compensation for any personal injury, loss or damage resulting from that offence or any other offence which is taken into consideration in determining the sentence.[1] The court is required to have regard to the offender's means so far as they appear or are known to the court. In the Crown Court there is no other limit but in a magistrates' court the maximum for one offence is £1000.[2] In the case of an offence under the Theft Act, where the property in question is recovered, any damage to the property occurring while it was out of the owner's possession is to be treated as having resulted from the offence, however and by whomsoever the damage was caused.[3] If D takes P's car, contrary to 1968, s. 12, and crashes into Q's car, the damage to P's car is covered but not the damage to Q's car.[4]

Unlike s. 28 of the Theft Act, these provisions do not relate to any particular property. They may thus be relied on where neither the stolen property nor its proceeds has been recovered and nothing has been taken from D on his apprehension.

[1] For the principles to be applied, see *Kneeshaw*, [1975] Q.B. 57; [1974] 1 All E.R. 896 C.A.; *Oddy*, [1974] 2 All E.R. 666.
[2] Section 35 (4) and (5) as substituted by the Criminal Law Act 1977, s. 60 for offences committed after December 1, 1977. For offences committed earlier, £400.
[3] Section 35 (2).
[4] *Quigley* v. *Stokes*, [1977] 2 All E.R. 317, applying s. 35 (3).

(b) Under the Police (Property) Act 1897

[451] Where any property has come into the possession of the police in their investigation of a suspected offence, a magistrates' court may, under s. 1 (1) of the Police (Property) Act 1897, make an order for the delivery of the property to the person appearing to be the owner, or, if the owner cannot be ascertained, make "such order with respect to the property as to the magistrate or court may seem meet." The procedure should be used only in straightforward cases, where there is no difficulty of law.[1] The word "owner" is to be given its ordinary, popular meaning; so that a jeweller to whom a ring has been handed for valuation and who, suspecting it to be stolen, has given it to the police, is not "the owner". Though no one with a better title has appeared, somewhere (presumably) there is a person who "owns" the ring in the ordinary popular sense. No order may be made in favour of the jeweller.[2]

[1] *Raymond Lyons & Co., Ltd.* v. *Metropolitan Police Commissioner*, [1975] Q.B. 321; [1975] 1 All E.R. 335.
[2] *Ibid.*

[452] The property must not be restored to the person who is the owner in the popular sense, if it appears that there is some person with a better right to immediate possession, such as a person with a valid lien on the property. It was so held in *Marsh* v. *Commissioner of Police*,[1] though the court declined to decide whether the lienor was the "owner" for this purpose. According to *Raymond Lyons' case*,[2] he is not. The curious result is that where another person has a better right to possession than the owner, no order can be made in favour of either claimant. Moreover, the magistrates cannot exercise the discretion given to them by the section where "the owner cannot be ascertained", because the owner is ascertained. It is submitted that, notwithstanding *Raymond Lyons' case*, if it is wrong to deliver to the owner in the strict sense where there is another with a better right to possession, this can only be because the owner in the strict sense is not "the owner" for the purpose of the Act; and that it should follow that "the owner" is the person with the best right to possession.[3]

[1] [1945] K.B. 43 C.A.
[2] Above, para. **[451]**.
[3] Howard argues that the property must in all cases be awarded to the owner in the strict sense; [1958] Crim. L.R. 744. A forfeiture order made by the Crown Court under s. 43 of the Powers of Criminal Courts Act 1973 does not determine the issue of the ownership of the property: *Chester JJ. Ex parte Smith*, [1978] R.T.R. 373; [1978] Crim. L.R. 226, D.C.

[453] It is provided by s. 1 (2) of the Police (Property) Act 1897 that an order made under s. 1 (1) does not affect any person's right to bring legal proceedings within six months of the order to recover the property from the person to whom it has been delivered under the order of the court; but on the expiration of those six months, the right shall cease. An order may, however, affect the onus of proof: *Irving* v. *National Provincial Bank Ltd.*[1] where it was held that, in the absence of any evidence as to the ownership of the money, the defendant bank's title arising from an order made under the Act was superior to that of the plaintiff from whose possession the money had been taken by the police; the onus was on the plaintiff and not on the defendant to establish actual ownership in the money.

It is submitted that this provision should defeat the title only of one who might have asserted a better right to possess before the magistrates' court. If, for example, D steals a car from P and, on D's conviction, the magistrates order that it be returned to P, the rights of Q, from whom P had the car on hire or hire-purchase, should not be affected. If, after the expiration of six months, Q seeks to recover the car in accordance with the terms of the contract he should not be debarred from doing so by the order made under the Act.

Even thus limited, the provision could lead to arbitrary and unjust interference with civil rights. Suppose that the court makes an order in favour of P from whom goods have been stolen. The goods had been the subject of an earlier theft from Q. More than six months after the order, Q discovers that the goods are in the possession of P. His right to recover them would appear to be barred. It is not obvious why P should have this windfall arising out of the dishonest intervention of a third party.

[1] [1962] 2 Q.B. 73 C.A.

[454] It has been held by a metropolitan magistrate that "property" includes anything into or for which the property has been converted or exchanged, by analogy to s. 46 (1) of the Larceny Act 1916.[1] It is submitted that this was the correct decision, though it would be better to rely on the common law concerning ownership[2] than on the analogy of a criminal statute. Difficult questions might arise where the property has been converted into a more valuable thing by the expenditure of skill and labour.[3]

[1] (1959), 123 J.P.J. 640.
[2] *Taylor v. Plumer* (1815), 3 M. & S. 562. *Cf.* above, para. [**401**].
[3] See 104 L.J. 296 and Torts (Interference with Goods) Act 1977, s. 6.

[455] The Theft Act no longer provides that the 1897 Act shall apply to any property seized by the police under the authority of s. 26 of the Theft Act.[1] Such property appears to be covered by the amended words of s. (1) 1 of the 1897 Act.

[1] Section 26 (4) is repealed by the Criminal Justice Act 1972, s. 64 (2), Sch. 6, Part II.

4 HUSBAND AND WIFE[1]

[456] Under the Larceny Act 1916, a husband could steal from a wife and *vice versa* only if, at the time of the theft, *either*, they were not living together *or* the property was taken with a view to their ceasing to live together. So where a wife took her husband's property and gave it to her lover, the lover was not guilty of receiving stolen goods.[2] This rule is abolished by s. 30 (1) of the 1968 Act which also applies to the 1978 Act[3] and provides:

"This Act shall apply in relation to the parties to a marriage, and to property belonging to the wife or husband whether or not by reason of an interest derived from the marriage, as it would apply if they were not married and any such interest subsisted independently of the marriage."

The effect is that wives and husbands can steal, or commit any other offence under the Acts in relation to, the property of each other.

[1] *Eighth Report,* Cmnd. 2977, paras. 189–199.
[2] *Creamer,* [1919] 1 K.B. 564.
[3] 1978, s. 5 (2).

A. PROCEEDINGS INSTITUTED BY INJURED SPOUSE

[457] The proceedings may be instituted by the injured spouse. The 1968 Act, s. 30 (2) provides:

"Subject to subsection (4) below, a person shall have the same right to bring proceedings against that person's wife or husband for any offence (whether under this Act or otherwise) as if they were not married, and a person bringing any such proceedings shall be competent to give evidence for the prosecution at every stage of the proceedings."

This subsection is not confined to offences under the Acts but applies to "any offence". Thus, for example, a wife may prosecute her husband for stealing or damaging the property of a third party, for an offence against the person of a third party, or for perjury; and in any such prosecution the wife would now be a competent witness for the prosecution. The Act does not say whether the wife would be compellable and it might be argued that, since there is a proviso to s. 30 (3) (*b*) that the spouse shall not be compellable and no such proviso to s. 30 (2), the spouse *is* compellable under s. 30 (2).[1] Presumably it is very unlikely that the problem will arise, since the spouse who is bringing the proceedings is unlikely to be unwilling to give evidence. The problem could arise where the prosecuting spouse declines to give evidence and the court wishes to compel him to do so. It is unlikely that a spouse would be held to be compellable in the absence of express words.[2]

---

[1] *Cf. Tilley* v. *Tilley*, [1949] P. 240; [1948] 2 All E.R. 1113.
[2] See *Hoskyn* v. *Metropolitan Police Commissioner*, [1978] 2 All E. R. 136.

B. PROCEEDINGS INSTITUTED BY THIRD PARTY

[458] Section 30 (3) makes provision for the competence of a spouse in proceedings instituted by a third party for an offence committed by a person "with reference to" his spouse or his spouse's property:

> "Where a person is charged in proceedings not brought by that person's wife or husband with having committed any offence with reference to that person's wife or husband or to property belonging to the wife or husband, the wife or husband shall be competent to give evidence at every stage of the proceedings, whether for the defence or for the prosecution, and whether the accused is charged solely or jointly with any other person:

Provided that—

> (*a*) the wife or husband (unless compellable at common law) shall not be compellable either to give evidence or, in giving evidence, to disclose any communication made to her or him during the marriage by the accused; and
> (*b*) her or his failure to give evidence shall not be made the subject of any comment by the prosecution."

[459] This follows the form of earlier statutes which make one spouse competent for the prosecution or defence on the trial of the other. The effect is the same as that of s. 4 (1) of the Criminal Evidence Act 1898 in relation to the offences mentioned in the Schedule to that Act or of s. 39 of the Sexual Offences Act 1956 to offences under that Act, other than those expressly excluded from its provisions. The words in brackets in proviso (*a*) were intended to preserve what was believed to be a rule of common law that, where one spouse committed an offence of violence against the other, the aggrieved spouse was a compellable witness. The House of Lords has now decided[1] that this was never the law, the spouse in such cases being competent but not compellable. The bracketed words are now meaningless.

---

[1] *Hoskyn* v. *Metropolitan Police Commissioner*, [1978] 2 All E.R. 136.

---

[460] Where D is prosecuted by a third party for stealing his wife's property, obtaining it by deception or handling it when stolen, the wife is clearly a competent but not compellable witness for the prosecution. Likewise where the prosecution is for burglary of a building of which his wife is in possession[1] or of a building of which she is not in possession, if the burglary is committed with the intention of stealing or inflicting damage on her property, doing her grievous bodily harm or raping her.[2] Other cases are where one spouse is blackmailed by the other or where the one takes the other's motor vehicle or conveyance contrary to s. 12, or abstracts his electricity, contrary to s. 13, etc.

Offences committed "with reference to" a spouse would include such cases as that where the husband lives on the earnings of his wife's prostitution, or where he wilfully neglects to maintain her. There is corresponding provision for the former of these two cases in the Sexual Offences Act 1956 and for the latter under the Criminal Evidence Act 1898. The spouse's competence in such prosecutions could now be justified by reference to either the Theft Act or the earlier statute.

Evidence admissible under this provision is not limited to offences *against* the spouse or his property or to offences under the 1968 Act. So a husband was a competent witness where his wife forged his name on an application to a finance company for a loan.[3] The offence was committed against the finance company, not the husband, but it was committed with reference to him.

---

[1] If D burgled a building occupied by P as tenant of D's wife, would the wife be a competent witness for the prosecution? Strictly the offence is committed "with reference to" the wife's property, since she owns the freehold of the burgled premises; but the trespass is committed against P and unless there is an intention to damage the wife's property (e.g., the fabric of the building) her ownership of the freehold might be thought insufficient to bring the offence within the subsection.

[2] For the circumstances in which a husband may be guilty of rape upon his wife, see Smith and Hogan, 401–403.

[3] *Noble*, [1974] 2 All E.R. 811; [1974] Crim. L.R. 545 and commentary thereon.

C. RESTRICTIONS ON PROSECUTION

[461] The 1968 Act, s. 30 (4) provides:

"Proceedings shall not be instituted against a person for any offence of stealing or doing unlawful damage to property which at the time of the offence belongs to that person's wife or husband, or for any attempt, incitement or conspiracy to commit such an offence, unless the proceedings are instituted by or with the consent of the Director of Public Prosecutions:

Provided that—
  (*a*) this subsection shall not apply to proceedings against a person for an offence—
       (i) if that person is charged with committing the offence jointly with the wife or husband; or
       (ii) if by virtue of any judicial decree or order (wherever made) that person and the wife or husband are at the time of the offence under no obligation to cohabit; and
  (*b*) (Repealed)[1].

[462] Where it is a case of stealing or the doing of unlawful damage by one spouse to the property of the other, consent is required whether the proceedings are to be instituted by the aggrieved spouse or by a third party.¹ Outside these cases, however, no consent is required whether the proceedings be instituted by the aggrieved spouse or by a third party. If a wife alleges, or a third party alleges, that her husband has obtained her property by deception, blackmailed her, wounded her or committed sodomy with her, no consent is required. Presumably consent will be required on a robbery charge since this is within "any offence of stealing". It is not obvious why this clause (which was not in the draft bill produced by the Criminal Law Revision Committee) should be thus limited.

¹ *Withers*, [1975] Crim. L.R. 647.

[463] Proviso (*a*) (i) is not very clear. It is a proviso to a subsection dealing with a case of a person who steals or damages his spouse's property; and so one would expect a proviso to qualify the rule that *such a person* cannot be prosecuted except with the consent of the Director. That is, the natural meaning of "that person" in the proviso is the person who has stolen or damaged the property of his wife or husband.

If that be correct, proviso (*a*) (i) deals with the case where the husband and wife are jointly charged with theft of or criminal damage to property which belongs to one of them. This looks a little curious; but it will be recalled¹ that it is perfectly possible for a person to be convicted of stealing his own property where some third person has a proprietary interest in it. Suppose that a husband has pawned his watch. While his wife engages the pawnbroker's attention, he secretly takes the watch back again. Proceedings may be brought against the couple without the consent of the Director. It is very reasonable that consent should not be necessary in this case; and perhaps the proviso is required because the proceeding, literally, is for an offence of stealing property belonging to the husband.

¹ Above, para. [57].

[464] The position would seem to be much the same in the case of criminal damage. Generally a man may damage property which is his own with impunity, no matter how barbarous his action may be. But if another has a proprietary interest in the property, this would surely be an offence. For example, D has mortgaged a valuable painting to P by bill of sale. If he deliberately destroys the painting, he is surely guilty of an offence of criminal damage. If then, his wife destroys the painting with his connivance, they may both be prosecuted without consent.

If this interpretation is correct, it follows that if, in the above examples, the wife had taken the watch and destroyed the painting, without the husband's connivance, the Director's consent would have been required, for proceedings instituted by P. This looks strange because, though it is the husband's property which is destroyed, the *offence* is committed against a third party.

231

Moreover, property may "belong" to one of the spouses, at least for the purposes of theft,[1] although the ownership in the strict sense is in a third party. Suppose that H has a television set on hire or hire-purchase from P. If his wife, W, sells the television set without H's consent, it is clearly right that he should have to get consent to prosecute her for stealing from him. The same should apply if she smashes the set and he alleges that she has criminally damaged his property. On the other hand, it looks distinctly odd that P has to get the consent of the Director to prosecute W; but that appears to be the effect.

[1] See s. 5, above, para. [53].

[465] It may well be that the proviso was not actually intended to deal with this situation at all, but to apply to the case where D, a third party, assists H to steal or destroy W's property and D and H are prosecuted jointly. It may be intended to say that, in those circumstances, no consent shall be required so far as the proceedings against D are concerned. If that is the intention, the proviso is not strictly necessary because D is not within the main part of the subsection. It would mean, moreover, that consent would still be necessary for the proceedings against H; so that joint proceedings would still have to wait on consent. That would not be very sensible; so probably the better course (if not the only proper course) is to assume that the proviso means what it says. In that event, the situation envisaged in this paragraph is the same as if the proviso did apply to it. No consent is required so far as D is concerned (because he is not a person charged with an offence against his wife's property) but consent is required so far as H is concerned. There must either be separate trials or the Director's consent obtained.

Proviso (a) (ii) means that if H and W have been judicially separated or if a non-molestation order has been made[1] and one of them steals or damages the other's property, proceedings may be brought without the consent of the Director, whether they were in fact living together at the time of the offence or not. If the parties have merely separated in pursuance of an agreement, the Director's consent is required even if they are in fact living apart at the time of the alleged offence.

[1] *Woodley* v. *Woodley*, [1978] Crim. L.R. 629 D.C.

APPENDIX

THEFT ACT 1968

(1968 c. 60)

ARRANGEMENT OF SECTIONS

233

An Act to revise the law of England and Wales as to theft and similar or associated offences, and in connection therewith to make provision as to criminal proceedings by one party to a marriage against the other, and to make certain amendments extending beyond England and Wales in the Post Office Act 1953 and other enactments; and for other purposes connected therewith.

[26th July, 1968]

Definition of "theft"

1. Basic definition of theft

(1) A person is guilty of theft if he dishonestly appropriates property belonging to another with the intention of permanently depriving the other of it; and "thief" and "steal" shall be construed accordingly.

(2) It is immaterial whether the appropriation is made with a view to gain, or is made for the thief's own benefit.

(3) The five following sections of this Act shall have effect as regards the interpretation and operation of this section (and, except as otherwise provided by this Act, shall apply only for purposes of this section).

EFFECT OF SECTION
For the effect of this section see above, Chapter II, paras. **[17]**–**[134]**.

PREVIOUS CORRESPONDING OFFENCES
This offence replaces the offences of larceny, embezzlement and fraudulent conversion under ss. 1, 17 and 20 of the Larceny Act 1916 (5 Halsbury's Statutes (2nd ed.) 1012, 1021, 1022).

PUNISHMENT
For the maximum punishment for this offence, see s. 7, below.

"PERSON"
Under the Interpretation Acts 1889, s. 2 (32 Halsbury's Statutes (3rd ed.), 435) and 1978 s. 5 and Sched. 1, "person" includes a body corporate unless a contrary intention appears. It seems that a corporation may be guilty of any offence under the Act, other than under ss. 18, 19 and, probably, 25. (A corporation does not have a "place of abode".)

"THIEF" AND "STEAL"
For the meaning of "thief" and "steal" for the purpose of offences relating to stolen goods, see s. 24 (4), below.

"EXCEPT AS OTHERWISE PROVIDED BY THIS ACT"
See ss. 15 (3), 34 (1), below, in relation to offences under s. 15, below.

2. "Dishonestly"

(1) A person's appropriation of property belonging to another is not to be regarded as dishonest—

(a) if he appropriates the property in the belief that he has in law the right to deprive the other of it, on behalf of himself or of a third person; or

(b) if he appropriates the property in the belief that he would have the other's consent if the other knew of the appropriation and the circumstances of it; or

(c) (except where the property came to him as trustee or personal representative) if he appropriates the property in the belief that the person to whom the property belongs cannot be discovered by taking reasonable steps.

(2) A person's appropriation of property belonging to another may be dishonest notwithstanding that he is willing to pay for the property.

EFFECT OF SECTION
For the effect of this section see above, paras. [109]–[117].

3. "Appropriates"

(1) Any assumption by a person of the rights of an owner amounts to an appropriation, and this includes, where he has come by the property (innocently or not) without stealing it, any later assumption of a right to it by keeping or dealing with it as owner.

(2) Where property or a right or interest in property is or purports to be transferred for value to a person acting in good faith, no later assumption by him of rights which he believed himself to be acquiring shall, by reason of any defect in the transferor's title, amount to theft of the property.

EFFECT OF SECTION
For the effect of this section see above, paras. [18]–[52], [105]–[106].

4. "Property"

(1) "Property" includes money and all other property, real or personal, including things in action and other intangible property.

(2) A person cannot steal land, or things forming part of land and severed from it by him or by his direction, except in the following cases, that is to say—

(a) when he is a trustee or personal representative, or is authorised by power of attorney, or as liquidator of a company, or otherwise, to sell or dispose of land belonging to another, and he appropriates the land or anything forming part of it by dealing with it in breach of the confidence reposed in him; or

(b) when he is not in possession of the land and appropriates anything forming part of the land by severing it or causing it to be severed, or after it has been severed; or

(c) when, being in possession of the land under a tenancy, he appropriates the whole or part of any fixture or structure let to be used with the land.

For purposes of this subsection "land" does not include incorporeal hereditaments; "tenancy" means a tenancy for years or any less period and includes an agreement for such a tenancy, but a person who after the end of a tenancy remains in possession as statutory tenant or otherwise is to be treated as having possession under the tenancy, and "let" shall be construed accordingly.

(3) A person who picks mushrooms growing wild on any land, or who picks flowers, fruit or foliage from a plant growing wild on any land, does not (although not in possession of the land) steal what he picks, unless he does it for reward or for sale or other commercial purpose.

For purposes of this subsection "mushroom" includes any fungus, and "plant" includes any shrub or tree.

(4) Wild creatures, tamed or untamed, shall be regarded as property; but a person cannot steal a wild creature not tamed nor ordinarily kept in captivity, or the carcase of any such creature, unless either it has been reduced into possession by or on behalf of another person and possession of it has not since been lost or abandoned, or another person is in course of reducing it into possession.

EFFECT OF SECTION
For the effect of this section see above, paras. [83]–[104].

5. "Belonging to another"

(1) Property shall be regarded as belonging to any person having possession or control of it, or having in it any proprietary right or interest (not being an equitable interest arising only from an agreement to transfer or grant an interest).

(2) Where property is subject to a trust, the persons to whom it belongs shall be regarded as including any person having a right to enforce the trust, and an intention to defeat the trust shall be regarded accordingly as an intention to deprive of the property any person having that right.

(3) Where a person receives property from or on account of another, and is under an obligation to the other to retain and deal with that property or its proceeds in a particular way, the property or proceeds shall be regarded (as against him) as belonging to the other.

(4) Where a person gets property by an other's mistake, and is under an obligation to make restoration (in whole or in part) of the property or its proceeds or of the value thereof, then to the extent of that obligation the property or proceeds shall be regarded (as against him) as belonging to the person entitled to restoration, and an intention not to make restoration shall be regarded accordingly as an intention to deprive that person of the property or proceeds.

(5) Property of a corporation sole shall be regarded as belonging to the corporation notwithstanding a vacancy in the corporation.

EFFECT OF SECTION
For the effect of this section see above, paras. [53]–[82].

HUSBAND AND WIFE
As to property belonging to a husband or wife see s. 30 (1), below.

6. "With the intention of permanently depriving the other of it"

(1) A person appropriating property belonging to another without meaning the other permanently to lose the thing itself is nevertheless to be regarded as

having the intention of permanently depriving the other of it if his intention is to treat the thing as his own to dispose of regardless of the other's rights; and a borrowing or lending of it may amount to so treating it if, but only if, the borrowing or lending is for a period and in circumstances making it equivalent to an outright taking or disposal.

(2) Without prejudice to the generality of subsection (1) above, where a person, having possession or control (lawfully or not) of property belonging to another, parts with the property under a condition as to its return which he may not be able to perform, this (if done for purposes of his own and without the other's authority) amounts to treating the property as his own to dispose of regardless of the other's rights.

EFFECT OF SECTION
    For the effect of this section see above, paras. [118]–[134].

Theft, robbery, burglary, etc.

7. Theft

A person guilty of theft shall on conviction on indictment be liable to imprisonment for a term not exceeding ten years.

"THEFT"
    For the definition of "theft" see s. 1, above.

TRIAL
    This offence is triable either way: see para. [434].

8. Robbery

(1) A person is guilty of robbery if he steals, and immediately before or at the time of doing so, and in order to do so, he uses force on any person or puts or seeks to put any person in fear of being then and there subjected to force.

(2) A person guilty of robbery, or of an assault with intent to rob, shall on conviction on indictment be liable to imprisonment for life.

EFFECT OF SECTION
    For the effect of this section see above, Chapter III, paras. [137]–[152].

PREVIOUS CORRESPONDING OFFENCES
    This offence replaces the offences of robbery and aggravated robbery punishable under s. 23 of the Larceny Act 1916 (5 Halsbury's Statutes (2nd ed.) 1025).

"STEALS"
    For the meaning of "steals" see s. 1 (1) above.

TRIAL
    Offences under this section are triable only on indictment: see para. [434].

9. Burglary

(1) A person is guilty of burglary if—

    (a) he enters any building or part of a building as a trespasser and with intent to commit any such offence as is mentioned in subsection (2) below; or

    (b) having entered any building or part of a building as a trespasser he steals or attempts to steal anything in the building or that part of it or inflicts or attempts to inflict on any person therein any grievous bodily harm.

(2) The offences referred to in subsection (1) (*a*) above are offences of stealing anything in the building or part of a building in question, of inflicting on any person therein any grievous bodily harm or raping any woman therein, and of doing unlawful damage to the building or anything therein.

(3) References in subsections (1) and (2) above to a building shall apply also to an inhabited vehicle or vessel, and shall apply to any such vehicle or vessel at times when the person having a habitation in it is not there as well as at times when he is.

(4) A person guilty of burglary shall on conviction on indictment be liable to imprisonment for a term not exceeding fourteen years.

EFFECT OF SECTION
For the effect of this section see above, paras. [**331**]–[**363**].

PREVIOUS CORRESPONDING OFFENCES
This section and s. 10 below replace offences of burglary, housebreaking, etc. under ss. 24–27 of the Larceny Act 1916 (5 Halsbury's Statutes (2nd ed.) 1026, 1027).

"STEALS"
For the meaning of "steals" and "stealing" see s. 1 (1), above.

TRIAL
For offences under this section which may be tried either way, see s. 29 (2), below.

10. Aggravated burglary

(1) A person is guilty of aggravated burglary if he commits any burglary and at the time has with him any firearm or imitation firearm, any weapon of offence, or any explosive; and for this purpose—

(*a*) "firearm" includes an airgun or air pistol, and "imitation firearm" means anything which has the appearance of being a firearm, whether capable of being discharged or not; and

(*b*) "weapon of offence" means any article made or adapted for use for causing injury to or incapacitating a person, or intended by the person having it with him for such use; and

(*c*) "explosive" means any article manufactured for the purpose of producing a practical effect by explosion, or intended by the person having it with him for that purpose.

(2) A person guilty of aggravated burglary shall on conviction on indictment be liable to imprisonment for life.

EFFECT OF SECTION
For the effect of this section see above, paras. [**364**]–[**370**].

PREVIOUS CORRESPONDING OFFENCES
See notes to s. 9, above.

"STEALS"
For the meaning of "steals", "stealing" see s. 1 (1), above.

TRIAL
Offences under this section are triable only on indictment: see para. [**434**].

11. Removal of articles from places open to the public

(1) Subject to subsections (2) and (3) below, where the public have access to a building in order to view the building or part of it, or a collection or part of a collection housed in it, any person who without lawful authority removes from the building or its grounds the whole or part of any article displayed or kept for display to the public in the building or that part of it or in its grounds shall be guilty of an offence.

For this purpose "collection" includes a collection got together for a temporary purpose, but references in this section to a collection do not apply to a collection made or exhibited for the purpose of effecting sales or other commercial dealings.

(2) It is immaterial for purposes of subsection (1) above, that the public's access to a building is limited to a particular period or particular occasion; but where anything removed from a building or its grounds is there otherwise than as forming part of, or being on loan for exhibition with, a collection intended for permanent exhibition to the public, the person removing it does not thereby commit an offence under this section unless he removes it on a day when the public have access to the building as mentioned in subsection (1) above.

(3) A person does not commit an offence under this section if he believes that he has lawful authority for the removal of the thing in question or that he would have it if the person entitled to give it knew of the removal and the circumstances of it.

(4) A person guilty of an offence under this section shall, on conviction on indictment, be liable to imprisonment for a term not exceeding five years.

EFFECT OF SECTION
  For the effect of this section see above, Chapter VI, paras. [263]–[278].

TRIAL
  This offence is triable either way: see para. [434].

12. Taking motor vehicle or other conveyance without authority

(1) Subject to subsections (5) and (6) below, a person shall be guilty of an offence if, without having the consent of the owner or other lawful authority, he takes any conveyance for his own or another's use or, knowing that any conveyance has been taken without such authority, drives it or allows himself to be carried in or on it.

(2) A person guilty of an offence under subsection (1) above shall on conviction on indictment be liable to imprisonment for a term not exceeding three years.

(3) Offences under subsection (1) above and attempts to commit them shall be deemed for all purposes to be arrestable offences within the meaning of section 2 of the Criminal Law Act 1967.

(4) If on the trial of an indictment for theft the jury are not satisfied that the accused committed theft, but it is proved that the accused committed an offence under subsection (1) above, the jury may find him guilty of the offence under subsection (1).

(5) Subsection (1) above shall not apply in relation to pedal cycles; but, subject to subsection (6) below, a person who, without having the consent of the owner or other lawful authority, takes a pedal cycle for his own or

another's use, or rides a pedal cycle knowing it to have been taken without such authority, shall on summary conviction be liable to a fine not exceeding fifty pounds.

(6) A person does not commit an offence under this section by anything done in the belief that he has lawful authority to do it or that he would have the owner's consent if the owner knew of his doing it and the circumstances of it.

(7) For purposes of this section—

(a) "conveyance" means any conveyance constructed or adapted for the carriage of a person or persons whether by land, water or air, except that it does not include a conveyance constructed or adapted for use only under the control of a person not carried in or on it, and "drive" shall be construed accordingly; and

(b) "owner", in relation to a conveyance which is the subject of a hiring agreement or hire-purchase agreement, means the person in possession of the conveyance under that agreement.

EFFECT OF SECTION
For the effect of this section see above, Chapter VII, paras. [**280**]–[**294**].

PREVIOUS CORRESPONDING OFFENCES
This section replaces offences against s. 217 of the Road Traffic Act 1960, and the Vessels Protection Act 1967.

TRIAL
Offences under sub-s. (1) of this section are triable either way: see para. [**434**].

13. Abstracting of electricity

A person who dishonestly uses without due authority, or dishonestly causes to be wasted or diverted, any electricity shall on conviction on indictment be liable to imprisonment for a term not exceeding five years.

EFFECT OF SECTION
For the effect of this section see above, Chapter VIII, para. [**295**]–[**299**].

PREVIOUS CORRESPONDING OFFENCES
This section replaces offences against s. 10 of the Larceny Act 1916 (5 Halsbury's Statutes (2nd ed.) 1018).

TRIAL
This offence is triable summarily either way: see para. [**434**].

14. Extension to thefts from mails outside England and Wales, and robbery etc. on such a theft

(1) Where a person—

(a) steals or attempts to steal any mail bag or postal packet in the course of transmission as such between places in different jurisdictions in the British postal area, or any of the contents of such a mail bag or postal packet; or

(b) in stealing or with intent to steal any such mail bag or postal packet or any of its contents, commits any robbery, attempted robbery or assault with intent to rob;

then, notwithstanding that he does so outside England and Wales, he shall be guilty of committing or attempting to commit the offence against this Act as if he had done so in England or Wales, and he shall accordingly be liable to be prosecuted, tried and punished in England and Wales without proof that the offence was committed there.

(2) In subsection (1) above the reference to different jurisdictions in the British postal area is to be construed as referring to the several jurisdictions of England and Wales, of Scotland, of Northern Ireland, of the Isle of Man and of the Channel Islands.

(3) For purposes of this section "mail bag" includes any article serving the purpose of a mail bag.

EFFECT OF SECTION
    For the effect of this section see above, para. [**431**].

"STEALS"
    For the meaning of "steals" see s. 1 (1), above.

Fraud and blackmail

15. Obtaining property by deception

(1) A person who by any deception dishonestly obtains property belonging to another, with the intention of permanently depriving the other of it, shall on conviction on indictment be liable to imprisonment for a term not exceeding ten years.

(2) For purposes of this section a person is to be treated as obtaining property if he obtains ownership, possession or control of it, and "obtain" includes obtaining for another or enabling another to obtain or to retain.

(3) Section 6 above shall apply for purposes of this section, with the necessary adaptation of the reference to appropriating, as it applies for purposes of section 1.

(4) For purposes of this section "deception" means any deception (whether deliberate or reckless) by words or conduct as to fact or as to law, including a deception as to the present intentions of the person using the deception or any other person.

EFFECT OF SECTION
    For the effect of this section see above, paras. [**153**]–[**209**].

PREVIOUS CORRESPONDING OFFENCES
    The principal offence replaced by this section is obtaining by false pretences under s. 32 (1) of the Larceny Act 1916 (5 Halsbury's Statutes (2nd ed.) 1031).

PROPERTY BELONGING TO ANOTHER
    See the definitions in ss. 4 (1) and 5 (1), above, which apply for the purposes of this section by virtue of s. 34 (1), below.

TRIAL
    The offences under this section are triable either way: see para. [**434**].

16. Obtaining pecuniary advantage by deception

(1) A person who by any deception dishonestly obtains for himself or another any pecuniary advantage shall on conviction on indictment be liable to imprisonment for a term not exceeding five years.

(2) The cases in which a pecuniary advantage within the meaning of this section is to be regarded as obtained for a person are cases where—

(a) [Repealed]

(b) he is allowed to borrow by way of overdraft, or to take out any policy of insurance or annuity contract, or obtains an improvement of the terms on which he is allowed to do so; or

(c) he is given the opportunity to earn remuneration or greater remuneration in an office or employment, or to win money by betting.

(3) For purposes of this section "deception" has the same meaning as in section 15 of this Act.

REPEAL
> Paragraph (*a*) of subsection (2) is repealed by the Theft Act 1978.

EFFECT OF SECTION
> For the effect of this section see above, paras. **[153]**–**[187]** and **[210]**–**[218]**.

PREVIOUS CORRESPONDING OFFENCES
> This offence replaces the offence of obtaining credit by fraud under s. 13 (1) of the Debtors Act 1869 (3 Halsbury's Statutes (3rd ed.) 10).

TRIAL
> Offences under this section are triable either way: see para. **[434]**.

17. False accounting

(1) Where a person dishonestly, with a view to gain for himself or another or with intent to cause loss to another,—

(a) destroys, defaces, conceals or falsifies any account or any record or document made or required for any accounting purpose; or

(b) in furnishing information for any purpose produces or makes use of any account, or any such record or document as aforesaid, which to his knowledge is or may be misleading, false or deceptive in a material particular;

he shall, on conviction on indictment, be liable to imprisonment for a term not exceeding seven years.

(2) For purposes of this section a person who makes or concurs in making in an account or other document an entry which is or may be misleading, false or deceptive in a material particular, or who omits or concurs in omitting a material particular from an account or other document, is to be treated as falsifying the account or document.

EFFECT OF SECTION
> For the effect of this section see above, paras. **[250]**–**[256]**.

PREVIOUS CORRESPONDING OFFENCES
> This section replaces offences under ss. 82 and 83 of the Larceny Act 1861 (5 Halsbury's Statutes (2nd ed.) 741) and the Falsification of Accounts Act 1875 (5 Halsbury's Statutes (2nd ed.) 878).

"GAIN"; "LOSS"
> For the meaning of "gain" and "loss" see s. 34 (2) (*a*), below.

OFFENCES BY COMPANY OFFICERS
> For offences under this section by company officers see s. 18, below.

TRIAL
> Offences under this section are triable either way: see para. **[434]**.

18. Liability of company officers for certain offences by company

(1) Where an offence committed by a body corporate under section 15, 16 or 17 of this Act is proved to have been committed with the consent or connivance of any director, manager, secretary or other similar officer of the body corporate, or any person who was purporting to act in any such capacity, he as well as the body corporate shall be guilty of that offence, and shall be liable to be proceeded against and punished accordingly.

(2) Where the affairs of a body corporate are managed by its members, this section shall apply in relation to the acts and defaults of a member in connection with his functions of management as if he were a director of the body corporate.

EFFECT OF SECTION
    For the effect of this section see above, paras. [**257**]–[**258**].

19. False statements by company directors, etc.

(1) Where an officer of a body corporate or unincorporated association (or person purporting to act as such), with intent to deceive members or creditors of the body corporate or association about its affairs, publishes or concurs in publishing a written statement or account which to his knowledge is or may be misleading, false or deceptive in a material particular, he shall on conviction on indictment be liable to imprisonment for a term not exceeding seven years.

(2) For purposes of this section a person who has entered into a security for the benefit of a body corporate or association is to be treated as a creditor of it.

(3) Where the affairs of a body corporate or association are managed by its members, this section shall apply to any statement which a member publishes or concurs in publishing in connection with his functions of management as if he were an officer of the body corporate or association.

EFFECT OF SECTION
    For the effect of this section see above, paras. [**259**]–[**271**].

PREVIOUS CORRESPONDING OFFENCES
    This section replaces s. 84 of the Larceny Act 1861.

TRIAL
    Offences under this section are triable either way: see para. [**434**].

20. Suppression, etc. of documents

(1) A person who dishonestly, with a view to gain for himself or another or with intent to cause loss to another, destroys, defaces or conceals any valuable security, any will or other testamentary document or any original document of or belonging to, or filed or deposited in, any court of justice or any government department shall on conviction on indictment be liable to imprisonment for a term not exceeding seven years.

(2) A person who dishonestly, with a view to gain for himself or another or with intent to cause loss to another, by any deception procures the execution of a valuable security shall on conviction on indictment be liable to imprisonment for a term not exceeding seven years; and this subsection shall apply in relation to the making, acceptance, indorsement, alteration, cancellation or destruction in whole or in part of a valuable security, and in relation to the signing or sealing of any paper or other material in order that it may be made or

converted into, or used or dealt with as, a valuable security, as if that were the execution of a valuable security.

(3) For purposes of this section "deception" has the same meaning as in section 15 of this Act, and "valuable security" means any document creating, transferring, surrendering or releasing any right to, in or over property, or authorising the payment of money or delivery of any property, or evidencing the creation, transfer, surrender or release of any such right, or the payment of money or delivery of any property, or the satisfaction of any obligation.

EFFECT OF SECTION
For the effect of this section see above, para. [262].

PREVIOUS CORRESPONDING OFFENCES
This section replaces offences under ss. 27–30 of the Larceny Act 1861.

TRIAL
Offences under this section are triable either way: see para. [434].

21. Blackmail

(1) A person is guilty of blackmail if, with a view to gain for himself or another or with intent to cause loss to another, he makes any unwarranted demand with menaces; and for this purpose a demand with menaces is unwarranted unless the person making it does so in the belief—

  (a) that he has reasonable grounds for making the demand; and
  (b) that the use of the menaces is a proper means of reinforcing the demand.

(2) The nature of the act or omission demanded is immaterial, and it is also immaterial whether the menaces relate to action to be taken by the person making the demand.

(3) A person guilty of blackmail shall on conviction on indictment be liable to imprisonment for a term not exceeding fourteen years.

EFFECT OF SECTION
For the effect of this section see above, Chapter IX, paras. [300]–[330].

PREVIOUS CORRESPONDING OFFENCES
This section replaces offences against ss. 29–31 of the Larceny Act 1916 (5 Halsbury's Statutes (2nd ed.) 1028–1030).

"GAIN"; "LOSS"
For the meaning of "gain" and "loss", see s. 34 (2) (a), below.

TRIAL
Offences under this section are triable only on indictment: see para. [434].

Offences relating to goods stolen, etc.

22. Handling stolen goods

(1) A person handles stolen goods if (otherwise than in the course of the stealing) knowing or believing them to be stolen goods he dishonestly receives the goods, or dishonestly undertakes or assists in their retention, removal, disposal or realisation by or for the benefit of another person, or if he arranges to do so.

(2) A person guilty of handling stolen goods shall on conviction on indictment be liable to imprisonment for a term not exceeding fourteen years.

EFFECT OF SECTION
For the effect of this section see above, Chapter XII, paras. [**379**]–[**429**].

PREVIOUS CORRESPONDING OFFENCES
The section replaces offences under s. 97 of the Larceny Act 1861 (5 Halsbury's Statutes (2nd ed.) 743) and s. 33 of the Larceny Act 1916 (5 Halsbury's Statutes (2nd ed.) 1032).

"STOLEN GOODS"
For the meaning of stolen goods see s. 24, below.

TRIAL
Offences under this section are triable either way: see para. [**434**].

23. Advertising rewards for return of goods stolen or lost

Where any public advertisement of a reward for the return of any goods which have been stolen or lost uses any words to the effect that no questions will be asked, or that the person producing the goods will be safe from apprehension or inquiry, or that any money paid for the purchase of the goods or advanced by way of loan on them will be repaid, the person advertising the reward and any person who prints or publishes the advertisement shall on summary conviction be liable to a fine not exceeding one hundred pounds.

PREVIOUS CORRESPONDING OFFENCE
This section replaces offences under s. 102 of the Larceny Act 1861 (5 Halsbury's Statutes (2nd ed.) 744).

STOLEN GOODS
For the meaning of "stolen goods" see s. 24, below.

24. Scope of offences relating to stolen goods

(1) The provisions of this Act relating to goods which have been stolen shall apply whether the stealing occurred in England or Wales or elsewhere, and whether it occurred before or after the commencement of this Act, provided that the stealing (if not an offence under this Act) amounted to an offence where and at the time when the goods were stolen; and references to stolen goods shall be construed accordingly.

(2) For purposes of those provisions reference to stolen goods shall include, in addition to the goods originally stolen and parts of them (whether in their original state or not),—

(a) any other goods which directly or indirectly represent or have at any time represented the stolen goods in the hands of the thief as being the proceeds of any disposal or realisation of the whole or part of the goods stolen or of goods so representing the stolen goods; and

(b) any other goods which directly or indirectly represent or have at any time represented the stolen goods in the hands of a handler of the stolen goods or any part of them as being the proceeds of any disposal or realisation of the whole or part of the stolen goods handled by him or of goods so representing them.

(3) But no goods shall be regarded as having continued to be stolen goods after they have been restored to the person from whom they were stolen or to other lawful possession or custody, or after that person and any other person claiming through him have otherwise ceased as regards those goods to have any right to restitution in respect of the theft.

(4) For purposes of the provisions of this Act relating to goods which have

been stolen (including subsections (1) to (3) above) goods obtained in England or Wales or elsewhere either by blackmail or in the circumstances described in section 15 (1) of this Act shall be regarded as stolen; and "steal", "theft" and "thief" shall be construed accordingly.

EFFECT OF SECTION
For the effect of this section see above, paras. [384]–[388].

"GOODS"
For the meaning of "goods" see s. 34 (2) (*b*), below.

PROVISIONS OF THIS ACT RELATING TO GOODS WHICH HAVE BEEN STOLEN
I.e. ss. 22–23, 26–28 and 32.

Possession of housebreaking implements, etc.

25. Going equipped for stealing, etc.

(1) A person shall be guilty of an offence if, when not at his place of abode, he has with him any article for use in the course of or in connection with any burglary, theft or cheat.

(2) A person guilty of an offence under this section shall on conviction on indictment be liable to imprisonment for a term not exceeding three years.

(3) Where a person is charged with an offence under this section, proof that he had with him any article made or adapted for use in committing a burglary, theft or cheat shall be evidence that he had it with him for such use.

(4) Any person may arrest without warrant anyone who is, or whom he, with reasonable cause, suspects to be, committing an offence under this section.

(5) For purposes of this section an offence under section 12 (1) of this Act of taking a conveyance shall be treated as theft, and "cheat" means an offence under section 15 of this Act.

EFFECT OF SECTION
For the effect of this section see above, Chapter XI, paras. [371]–[378].

PREVIOUS CORRESPONDING OFFENCES
The section replaces offences against s. 28 of the Larceny Act 1916 (5 Halsbury's Statutes (2nd ed.) 1028).

"BURGLARY"
For the meaning of "burglary" see ss. 9, 10, above.

"THEFT"
For the meaning of theft see s. 1, above.

TRIAL
Offences under this section are triable either way: see para. [434].

Enforcement and procedure

26. Search for stolen goods

(1) If it is made to appear by information on oath before a justice of the peace that there is reasonable cause to believe that any person has in his custody or possession or on his premises any stolen goods, the justice may grant a warrant to search for and seize the same; but no warrant to search for stolen goods shall be addressed to a person other than a constable except under the authority of an enactment expressly so providing.

(2) An officer of police not below the rank of superintendent may give a constable written authority to search any premises for stolen goods—

   (a) if the person in occupation of the premises has been convicted within the preceding five years of handling stolen goods or of any offence involving dishonesty and punishable with imprisonment; or

   (b) if a person who has been convicted within the preceding five years of handling stolen goods has within the preceding twelve months been in occupation of the premises.

(3) Where under this section a person is authorised to search premises for stolen goods, he may enter and search the premises accordingly, and may seize any goods he believes to be stolen goods.

(4) [Repealed.]

(5) This section is to be construed in accordance with section 24 of this Act; and in subsection (2) above the references to handling stolen goods shall include any corresponding offence committed before the commencement of this Act.

REPEAL
   Subsection 4 is repealed by the Criminal Justice Act 1972, s. 64 (2), Sch. 6, Part II.

EFFECT OF SECTION
   For the effect of this section see above, para. [**430**].

27. Evidence and procedure on charge of theft or handling stolen goods

(1) Any number of persons may be charged in one indictment, with reference to the same theft, with having at different times or at the same time handled all or any of the stolen goods, and the persons so charged may be tried together.

(2) On the trial of two or more persons indicted for jointly handling any stolen goods the jury may find any of the accused guilty if the jury are satisfied that he handled all or any of the stolen goods, whether or not he did so jointly with the other accused or any of them.

(3) Where a person is being proceeded against for handling stolen goods (but not for any offence other than handling stolen goods), then at any stage of the proceedings, if evidence has been given of his having or arranging to have in his possession the goods the subject of the charge, or of his undertaking or assisting in, or arranging to undertake or assist in, their retention, removal, disposal or realisation, the following evidence shall be admissible for the purpose of proving that he knew or believed the goods to be stolen goods:—

   (a) evidence that he has had in his possession, or has undertaken or assisted in the retention, removal, disposal or realisation of, stolen goods from any theft taking place not earlier than twelve months before the offence charged; and

   (b) (provided that seven days' notice in writing has been given to him of the intention to prove the conviction) evidence that he has within the five years preceding the date of the offence charged been convicted of theft or of handling stolen goods.

(4) In any proceedings for the theft of anything in the course of transmis-

sion (whether by post or otherwise), or for handling stolen goods from such a theft, a statutory declaration made by any person that he despatched or received or failed to receive any goods or postal packet, or that any goods or postal packet when despatched or received by him were in a particular state or condition, shall be admissible as evidence of the facts stated in the declaration, subject to the following conditions:—

(a) a statutory declaration shall only be admissible where and to the extent to which oral evidence to the like effect would have been admissible in the proceedings; and

(b) a statutory declaration shall only be admissible if at least seven days before the hearing or trial a copy of it has been given to the person charged, and he has not, at least three days before the hearing or trial or within such further time as the court may in special circumstances allow, given the prosecutor written notice requiring the attendance at the hearing or trial of the person making the declaration.

(5) This section is to be construed in accordance with section 24 of this Act; and in subsection (3) (*b*) above the references to handling stolen goods shall include any corresponding offence committed before the commencement of this Act.

EFFECT OF SECTION
For the effect of this section see above, paras. [**425**]–[**429**].

TRANSITIONAL PROVISIONS
This section applies in relation to offences committed before the commencement of the Act: see s. 35 (2), below.

28. Orders for restitution

(1) Where goods have been stolen, and [either] a person is convicted of any offence with reference to the theft (whether or not the stealing is the gist of his offence) [or a person is convicted of any other offence but such an offence as aforesaid is taken into consideration in determining his sentence], the court by or before which the offender is convicted may on the conviction exercise any of the following powers:—

(a) the court may order anyone having possession or control of the goods to restore them to any person entitled to recover them from him; or

(b) on the application of a person entitled to recover from the person convicted any other goods directly or indirectly representing the first-mentioned goods (as being the proceeds of any disposal or realisation of the whole or part of them or of goods so representing them), the court may order those other goods to be delivered or transferred to the applicant; or

(c) ... the court may order that a sum not exceeding the value of [the first-mentioned] goods shall be paid ... out of any money of the person convicted which was taken out of his possession on his apprehension [to any person who, if those goods were in the possession of the person convicted, would be entitled to recover them from him].

(2) Where under subsection (1) above the court has power on a person's conviction to make an order against him both under paragraph (*b*) and under

paragraph (*c*) with reference to the stealing of the same goods, the court may make orders under both paragraphs provided that the [person in whose favour] the orders [are made] does not thereby recover more than the value of those goods.

(3) Where under subsection (1) above the court on a person's conviction makes an order under paragraph (*a*) for the restoration of any goods, and it appears to the court that the person convicted has sold the goods to a person acting in good faith, or has borrowed money on the security of them from a person so acting ... the court may order that there shall be paid to the [purchaser or lender] out of any money of the person convicted which was taken out of his possession on his apprehension, a sum not exceeding the amount paid for the purchase by the [purchaser] or, as the case may be, the amount owed to the [lender] in respect of the loan.

(4) The court shall not exercise the powers conferred by this section unless in the opinion of the court the relevant facts sufficiently appear from evidence given at the trial or the available documents, together with admissions made by or on behalf of any person in connection with any proposed exercise of the powers; and for this purpose "the available documents" means any written statements or admissions which were made for use, and would have been admissible, as evidence at the trial, the depositions taken at any committal proceedings and any written statements or admissions used as evidence in those proceedings.

(5) Any order under this section shall be treated as an order for the restitution of property within the meaning of sections 30 and 42 of the Criminal Appeal Act 1968 (which relate to the effect on such orders of appeals).

(6) References in this section to stealing are to be construed in accordance with section 24 (1) and (4) of this Act.

AMENDMENT
> The words in square brackets in sub-ss. (1)–(3) are substituted by the Criminal Justice Act 1972, s. 64 (1), Sch. 5.

EFFECT OF SECTION
> For the effect of this section see above, paras. [435]–[455].

TRANSITIONAL PROVISIONS
> This section applies in relation to offences committed before the commencement of the Act: see s. 35 (2), below.

29. [Repealed]

AMENDMENT
> Section 29 (1) related to the jurisdiction of Quarter Sessions and was repealed by the Courts Act 1971, s. 56 and Sched. 2, Part IV.
> Section 29 (2) related to the jurisdiction of Magistrates Courts and was replaced by the Criminal Law Act 1977, s. 16 and Sched. 3.
> See above, para. [434].

General and consequential provisions

30. Husband and wife

(1) This Act shall apply in relation to the parties to a marriage, and to property belonging to the wife or husband whether or not by reason of an

interest derived from the marriage, as it would apply if they were not married and any such interest subsisted independently of the marriage.

(2) Subject to subsection (4) below, a person shall have the same right to bring proceedings against that person's wife or husband for any offence (whether under this Act or otherwise) as if they were not married, and a person bringing any such proceedings shall be competent to give evidence for the prosecution at every stage of the proceedings.

(3) Where a person is charged in proceedings not brought by that person's wife or husband with having committed any offence with reference to that person's wife or husband or to property belonging to the wife or husband, the wife or husband shall be competent to give evidence at every stage of the proceedings, whether for the defence or for the prosecution, and whether the accused is charged solely or jointly with any other person:
Provided that—

(a) the wife or husband (unless compellable at common law) shall not be compellable either to give evidence or, in giving evidence, to disclose any communication made to her or him during the marriage by the accused; and

(b) her or his failure to give evidence shall not be made the subject of any comment by the prosecution.

(4) Proceedings shall not be instituted against a person for any offence of stealing or doing unlawful damage to property which at the time of the offence belongs to that person's wife or husband, or for any attempt, incitement or conspiracy to commit such an offence, unless the proceedings are instituted by or with the consent of the Director of Public Prosecutions:
Provided that—

(a) this subsection shall not apply to proceedings against a person for an offence—

(i) if that person is charged with committing the offence jointly with the wife or husband; or

(ii) if by virtue of any judicial decree or order (wherever made) that person and the wife or husband are at the time of the offence under no obligation to cohabit;

(b) [Repealed].

(5) Notwithstanding section 12 of the Criminal Jurisdiction Act 1975 subsection (4) of this section shall apply—

(a) to an arrest (if without warrant) made by the wife or husband and

(b) to a warrant of arrest issued on an information laid by the wife or husband.

AMENDMENT
Subsection (4) proviso (b) was repealed by the Criminal Jurisdiction Act 1975, section 14 (5), Sched. 6.
Subsection (5) was added by the Criminal Jurisdiction Act 1975, section 14 (4), Sched. 5.

EFFECT OF SECTION
For the effect of this section see above, paras. [456]–[465].

31. Effect on civil proceedings and rights

(1) A person shall not be excused, by reason that to do so may incriminate that person or the wife or husband of that person of an offence under this Act—

    (*a*) from answering any question put to that person in proceedings for the recovery or administration of any property, for the execution of any trust or for an account of any property or dealings with property; or

    (*b*) from complying with any order made in any such proceedings;

but no statement or admission made by a person in answering a question put or complying with an order made as aforesaid shall, in proceedings for an offence under this Act, be admissible in evidence against that person or (unless they married after the making of the statement or admission) against the wife or husband of that person.

(2) Notwithstanding any enactment to the contrary, where property has been stolen or obtained by fraud or other wrongful means, the title to that or any other property shall not be affected by reason only of the conviction of the offender.

32. Effect on existing law and construction of references to offences

(1) The following offences are hereby abolished for all purposes not relating to offences committed before the commencement of this Act, that is to say—

    (*a*) any offence at common law of larceny, robbery, burglary, receiving stolen property, obtaining property by threats, extortion by colour of office or franchise, false accounting by public officers, concealment of treasure trove and, except as regards offences relating to the public revenue, cheating; and

    (*b*) any offence under an enactment mentioned in Part I of Schedule 3 to this Act, to the extent to which the offence depends on any section or part of a section included in column 3 of that Schedule;

but so that the provisions in Schedule 1 to this Act (which preserve with modifications certain offences under the Larceny Act 1861 of taking or killing deer and taking or destroying fish) shall have effect as there set out.

(2) Except as regards offences committed before the commencement of this Act, and except in so far as the context otherwise requires,—

    (*a*) references in any enactment passed before this Act to an offence abolished by this Act shall, subject to any express amendment or repeal made by this Act, have effect as references to the corresponding offence under this Act, and in any such enactment the expression "receive" (when it relates to an offence of receiving) shall mean handle, and "receiver" shall be construed accordingly; and

    (*b*) without prejudice to paragraph (*a*) above, references in any enactment, whenever passed, to theft or stealing (including references to stolen goods), and references to robbery, blackmail, burglary, aggravated burglary or handling stolen goods, shall be construed in accordance with the provisions of this Act, including those of section 24.

33. Miscellaneous and consequential amendments and repeal

(1) The Post Office Act 1953 shall have effect subject to the amendments provided for by Part I of Schedule 2 to this Act and (except in so far as the contrary intention appears) those amendments shall have effect throughout the British postal area.

(2) The enactments mentioned in Parts II and III of Schedule 2 to this Act shall have effect subject to the amendments there provided for, and (subject to subsection (4) below) the amendments made by Part II to enactments extending beyond England and Wales shall have the like extent as the enactment amended.

(3) The enactments mentioned in Schedule 3 to this Act (which include in Part II certain enactments related to the subject matter of this Act but already obsolete or redundant apart from this Act) are hereby repealed to the extent specified in column 3 of that Schedule; and, notwithstanding that the foregoing sections of this Act do not extend to Scotland, where any enactment expressed to be repealed by Schedule 3 does so extend, the Schedule shall have effect to repeal it in its application to Scotland except in so far as the repeal is expressed not to extend to Scotland.

(4) No amendment or repeal made by this Act in Schedule 1 to the Extradition Act 1870 or in the Schedule to the Extradition Act 1873 shall affect the operation of that Schedule by reference to the law of a British possession; but the repeal made in Schedule 1 to the Extradition Act 1870 shall extend throughout the United Kingdom.

POST OFFICE ACT 1953
    25 Halsbury's Statutes (3rd ed.) 413.

EXTRADITION ACT 1870, SCHEDULE 1
    13 Halsbury's Statutes (3rd ed.) 266.

EXTRADITION ACT 1873, SCHEDULE
    13 Halsbury's Statutes (3rd ed.) 272.

SCHEDULE 3
    Schedule 3 is omitted in this edition, see 8 Halsbury's Statutes (3rd ed.) 806.

Supplementary

34. Interpretation

(1) Sections 4 (1) and 5 (1) of this Act shall apply generally for purposes of this Act as they apply for purposes of section 1.

(2) For purposes of this Act—

(a) "gain" and "loss" are to be construed as extending only to gain or loss in money or other property, but as extending to any such gain or loss whether temporary or permanent; and—

(i) "gain" includes a gain by keeping what one has, as well as a gain by getting what one has not; and

(ii) "loss" includes a loss by not getting what one might get as well as a loss by parting with what one has;

(b) "goods", except in so far as the context otherwise requires, includes money and every other description of property except land, and includes things severed from the land by stealing.

EFFECT OF SECTION
For the effect of this section, see above paras. [**312**]–[**322**] (subsection 2 (*a*)) and paras. [**380**]–[**383**] (Subsection 2 (*b*)).

35. Commencement and transitional provisions

(1) This Act shall come into force on the 1st January 1969 and, save as otherwise provided by this Act, shall have effect only in relation to offences wholly or partly committed on or after that date.

(2) Sections 27 and 28 of this Act apply in relation to proceedings for an offence committed before the commencement of this Act as they would apply in relation to proceedings for a corresponding offence under this Act, and shall so apply in place of any corresponding enactment repealed by this Act.

(3) Subject to subsection (2) above, no repeal or amendment by this Act of any enactment relating to procedure or evidence, or to the jurisdiction or powers of any court, or to the effect of a conviction, shall affect the operation of the enactment in relation to offences committed before the commencement of this Act or to proceedings for any such offence.

36. Short title, and general provisions as to Scotland and Northern Ireland

(1) This Act may be cited as the Theft Act 1968.

(2) [Repealed.]

(3) This Act does not extend to Scotland or, ... to Northern Ireland, except as regards any amendment or repeal which in accordance with section 33 above is to extend to Scotland or Northern Ireland.

REPEAL
Subsection (2) and a reference thereto in subsection (3) are repealed by the Northern Ireland Constitutional Act 1973, s. 41 (1), Sch. 6, Part I.

SCHEDULES

Section 32   SCHEDULE 1

OFFENCES OF TAKING, ETC. DEER OR FISH

Taking or killing deer

1.—(1) A person who unlawfully takes or kills, or attempts to take or kill, any deer in inclosed land where deer are usually kept shall on summary conviction be liable to a fine not exceeding fifty pounds, or, for an offence committed after a previous conviction of an offence under this paragraph, to imprisonment for a term not exceeding three months or to a fine not exceeding one hundred pounds or to both.

(2) Any person may arrest without warrant anyone who is, or whom he, with reasonable cause, suspects to be, committing an offence under this paragraph.

Taking or destroying fish

2.—(1) Subject to subparagraph (2) below, a person who unlawfully takes or destroys, or attempts to take or destroy, any fish in water which is private property or in which there is any private right of fishery shall on summary conviction be liable to a fine not exceeding fifty pounds or, for an offence committed after a previous conviction of an offence under this subparagraph, to imprisonment for a term not exceeding three months or to a fine not exceeding one hundred pounds or to both.

(2) Subparagraph (1) above shall not apply to taking or destroying fish by angling in the daytime (that is to say, in the period beginning one hour before sunrise and ending one hour after sunset); but a person who by angling in the daytime unlawfully takes or destroys, or attempts to take or destroy, any fish in water which is private property or in which there is any private right of fishery shall on summary conviction be liable to a fine not exceeding twenty pounds.

(3) The court by which a person is convicted of an offence under this paragraph may order the forfeiture of anything which, at the time of the offence, he had with him for use for taking or destroying fish.

(4) Any person may arrest without warrant anyone who is, or whom he, with reasonable cause, suspects to be, committing an offence under subparagraph (1) above, and may seize from any person who is, or whom he, with reasonable cause, suspects to be, committing any offence under this paragraph anything which on that person's conviction of the offence would be liable to be forfeited under subparagraph (3) above.

PREVIOUS CORRESPONDING OFFENCES
   This Schedule reproduces in a modified form offences under ss. 12 and 13 of the Larceny Act 1861 (5 Halsbury's Statutes (2nd ed.) 729, 730).

Section 33 (1), (2)   SCHEDULE 2

MISCELLANEOUS AND CONSEQUENTIAL AMENDMENTS

PART I

Amendments of Post Office Act 1953

1. The Post Office Act 1953 shall have effect subject to the amendments provided for by this Part of this Schedule (and, except in so far as the contrary intention appears, those amendments have effect throughout the British postal area).

2. Sections 22 and 23 shall be amended by substituting for the word "felony" in section 22 (1) and section 23 (2) the words "a misdemeanour", and by omitting the words "of this Act and" in section 23 (1).

3. In section 52, as it applies outside England and Wales, for the words from "be guilty" onwards there shall be substituted the words "be guilty of a misdemeanour and be liable to imprisonment for a term not exceeding ten years".

4. In section 53 for the words from "be guilty" onwards there shall be substituted the words "be guilty of a misdemeanour and be liable to imprisonment for a term not exceeding five years".

5. In section 54, as it applies outside England and Wales,—
   (a) there shall be omitted the words "taking, embezzling", and the words "taken, embezzled", where first occurring;
   (b) for the words "a felony" there shall be substituted the words "an offence" and the word "feloniously" shall be omitted;

(*c*) for the words from "be guilty" to "secreted it" there shall be substituted the words "be guilty of a misdemeanour and be liable to imprisonment for a term not exceeding fourteen years".

6. In sections 55 and 58 (1), after the word "imprisonment", there shall in each case be inserted the words "for a term not exceeding two years".

7. In section 57—
  (*a*) there shall be omitted the words "steals, or for any purpose whatever embezzles," and the words from "or if" onwards;
  (*b*) for the word "felony" there shall be substituted the words "a misdemeanour".

8. After section 65 there shall be inserted as a new section 65A—

"65A. Fraudulent use of public telephone or telex system

If any person dishonestly uses a public telephone or telex system with intent to avoid payment (including any such system provided, under licence, otherwise than by the Postmaster General), he shall be guilty of a misdemeanour and be liable on summary conviction to imprisonment for a term not exceeding three months or to a fine not exceeding one hundred pounds or to both, or on conviction on indictment to imprisonment for a term not exceeding two years."

9. Section 69 (2) shall be omitted.

10. For section 70 there shall be substituted the following section—

"70. Prosecution of certain offences in any jurisdiction of British postal area

(1) Where a person—
  (*a*) steals or attempts to steal any mail bag or postal packet in the course of transmission as such between places in different jurisdictions in the British postal area, or any of the contents of such a mail bag or postal packet;
  or
  (*b*) in stealing or with intent to steal any such mail bag or postal packet or any of its contents, commits any robbery, attempted robbery or assault with intent to rob;
  then, in whichever of those jurisdictions he does so, he shall by virtue of this section be guilty in each of the jurisdictions in which this subsection has effect of committing or attempting to commit the offence against section 52 of this Act, or the offence referred to in paragraph (*b*) of this subsection, as the case may be, as if he had done so in that jurisdiction, and he shall accordingly be liable to be prosecuted, tried and punished in that jurisdiction without proof that the offence was committed there.

(2) In subsection (1) above the reference to different jurisdictions in the British postal area is to be construed as referring to the several jurisdictions of England and Wales, of Scotland, of Northern Ireland, of the Isle of Man, and of the Channel Islands; and that subsection shall have effect in each of those jurisdictions except England and Wales."

11. In section 72 there shall be added as a new subsection (3)—

"(3) In any proceedings in England or Wales for an offence under section 53, 55, 56, 57 or 58 of this Act, section 27 (4) of the Theft Act 1968 shall apply as it is expressed to apply to proceedings for the theft of anything in the course of transmission by post; and in the case of proceedings under section 53 of this Act a statutory declaration made by any person that a vessel, vehicle or aircraft was at any time employed by or under the Post Office for the transmission of postal packets under contract shall be admissible as evidence of the facts stated in the declaration subject to the same conditions as under section 27 (4) (*a*) and (*b*) of the Theft Act 1968 apply to declarations admissible under section 27 (4)".

12. In section 87 (1), the definition of "valuable security" shall be omitted but, except in relation to England and Wales, there shall be substituted:—

" 'valuable security' means any document creating, transferring, surrendering or releasing any right to, in or over property, or authorising the payment of money or delivery of any property, or evidencing the creation, transfer, surrender or release of any such right, or the payment of money or delivery of any property, or the satisfaction of any obligation."

PART II

Other amendments extending beyond England and Wales

Act amended	Amendment
The Extradition Act 1873 (36 & 37 Vict. c. 60)	In the Schedule (additional list of extradition crimes) for the words "the Larceny Act 1861" there shall be substituted the words "the Theft Act 1968".
The Public Stores Act 1875 (38 & 39 Vict. c. 25)	For section 12 (incorporation of parts of Larceny Act 1861) there shall be substituted:— "(1) Any person may arrest without warrant anyone who is, or whom he, with reasonable cause, suspects to be, in the act of committing or attempting to commit an offence against section 5 or 8 of this Act. (2) If it is made to appear by information on oath before a justice of the peace that there is reasonable cause to believe that any person has in his custody or possession or on his premises any stores in respect of which an offence against section 5 of this Act has been committed, the justice may issue a warrant to a constable to search for and seize the stores as in the case of stolen goods, and the Police (Property) Act 1897 shall apply as if this subsection were among the enactments mentioned in section 1 (1) of that Act."
The Army Act 1955 (3 & 4 Eliz. 2. c. 18)	For section 44 (1) (*b*) there shall be substituted— "(*b*) handles any stolen goods, where the property stolen was public or service property, or". For section 45 (*b*) there shall be substituted— "(*b*) handles any stolen goods, where the property stolen belonged to a person subject to military law, or". In section 138 (1) for the words from "receiving" to "stolen" there shall be substituted the words "handling it". In section 225 (1) after the definition of "Governor" there shall be inserted— " 'handles' has the same meaning as in the Theft Act 1968"; and for the definition of "steals" there shall be substituted— " 'steals' has the same meaning as in the Theft Act 1968, and references to 'stolen goods' shall be construed as if contained in that Act".

Schedule 2

Act amended	Amendment
The Air Force Act 1955 (3 & 4 Eliz. 2. c. 19)	The same amendments shall be made in sections 138 and 223 as are above directed to be made in the corresponding sections of the Army Act 1955".
The Naval Discipline Act 1957 (5 & 6 Eliz. 2. c. 53)	In section 76 (1) for the words from "receiving" to "embezzling" there shall be substituted the word "handling". In section 135 (1) the same amendments shall be made as are above directed to be made in section 225 (1) of the Army Act 1955.
The Army and Air Force Act 1961 (9 & 10 Eliz. 2. c. 52)	Section 21 shall be omitted.

PART III

Amendments limited to England and Wales

The Gaming Act 1845 (8 & 9 Vict. c. 109)	In section 17 (punishment for cheating at play etc.) for the words "be deemed guilty of obtaining such money or valuable thing from such other person by a false pretence" and the following words there shall be substituted the words— "(a) on conviction on indictment be liable to imprisonment for a term not exceeding two years; or (b) on summary conviction be liable to imprisonment for a term not exceeding six months or to a fine not exceeding two hundred pounds or to both".

*   *   *   *   *

The Bankruptcy Act 1914 (4 & 5 Geo. 5. c. 59)	In section 166 (admissions on compulsory examination etc. not to be admissible as evidence in proceedings for certain offences) for the words following "against that person" there shall be substituted the words "or (unless they married after the making of the statement or admission) against the wife or husband of that person in any proceeding in respect of an offence under the Theft Act 1968".
The House to House Collections Act 1939 (2 & 3 Geo. 6. c. 44)	In the Schedule (offences for which a conviction is a ground for refusing or revoking a licence under the Act to promote a collection for charity) for the entry relating to the Larceny Act 1916 there shall be substituted:— "Robbery, burglary and blackmail".

*   *   *   *   *

The Visiting Forces Act 1952 (15 & 16 Geo. 6. & 1 Eliz. 2. c. 67)	In the Schedule there shall be inserted in paragraph 1 (a) after the word "buggery" the word "robbery", and in paragraph 3 there shall be added at the end— "(g) the Theft Act 1968, except section 8 (robbery)".

257

Act amended	*Amendment*
The Finance Act 1965 (1965 c. 25)	In Schedule 10 in the Table in paragraph 1, for the words "Sections 500 to 505" there shall be substituted the words "Sections 500 to 504".
The Finance Act 1966 (1966 c. 18)	In Schedule 6, in paragraph 13, for the words "Sections 500 to 505" there shall be substituted the words "Sections 500 to 504", and the words from "together with" to "the said section 505" shall be omitted.

* * * * *

The Firearms Act 1968 (1968 c. 27)	Schedule 1 (offences in connection with which possession of a firearm is an offence under section 17 (2)) shall be amended, except in relation to a person's apprehension for an offence committed before the commencement of this Act, by substituting for paragraph 4—

"4. Theft, burglary, blackmail and any offence under section 12 (1) (taking of motor vehicle or other conveyance without owner's consent) of the Theft Act 1968":

by omitting paragraph 7: and by substituting in paragraph 8 for the words "paragraphs 1 to 7" the words "paragraphs 1 to 6".

[Schedule 3 listed penal enactments superseded by this Act (s. 33 (3)). It is omitted from this edition].

THEFT ACT 1978

(1978 c. 31)

ARRANGEMENT OF SECTIONS

An Act to replace section 16 (2) (a) of the Theft Act 1968 with other provision against fraudulent conduct; and for connected purposes. [20th July 1978]

1. Obtaining services by deception

(1) A person who by any deception dishonestly obtains services from another shall be guilty of an offence.

(2) It is an obtaining of services where the other is induced to confer a benefit by doing some act, or causing or permitting some act to be done, on the understanding that the benefit has been or will be paid for.

EFFECT OF SECTION
   For the effect of this section see above, paras. [219]–[231].

PERSON
   This expression includes a body corporate by virtue of the Interpretation Act 1978, s. 5, Sch. I and special provision is made by the Theft Act 1968, s. 18, (para. [257]), *ante* as applied by s. 5 (1), *post*, concerning the liability of company officers for offences by the company.

DECEPTION
   For meaning, see s. 5 (1), *post* and paras. [154]–[181] above.

DISHONESTLY
   Note that the definition of "dishonestly" in s. 2 of the 1968 Act, (para. [109]), *ante*, does not apply here. See paras. [181]–[187], above.

SHALL BE GUILTY OF AN OFFENCE
   For punishments, see s. 4, *post*.

SUPPLEMENTARY
   See s. 5 (2)–(4), *post*.

2. Evasion of liability by deception

(1) Subject to subsection (2) below, where a person by any deception—

(a) dishonestly secures the remission of the whole or part of any existing liability to make a payment, whether his own liability or another's; or

(b) with intent to make permanent default in whole or in part on any existing liability to make a payment, or with intent to let another do so, dishonestly induces the creditor or any person claiming payment on behalf of the creditor to wait for payment (whether or not the due date for payment is deferred) or to forgo payment; or (*c*) dishonestly obtains any exemption from or abatement of liability to make a payment;

he shall be guilty of an offence.

(2) For purposes of this section "liability" means legally enforceable liability; and subsection (1) shall not apply in relation to a liability that has not been accepted or established to pay compensation for a wrongful act or omission.

(3) For purposes of subsection (1) (*b*) a person induced to take in payment a cheque or other security for money by way of conditional satisfaction of a pre-existing liability is to be treated not as being paid but as being induced to wait for payment.

(4) For purposes of subsection (1) (*c*) "obtains" includes obtaining for another or enabling another to obtain.

EFFECT OF SECTION
For the effect of this section see above, paras. [232]–[241].

PERSON; DECEPTION; DISHONESTLY
See the notes to s. 1, above.

WITH INTENT
As to proof of criminal intent, see the Criminal Justice Act 1967, s. 8, (8 Halsbury's Statutes (3rd ed.), 585).

3. Making off without payment

(1) Subject to subsection (3) below, a person who, knowing that payment on the spot for any goods supplied or service done is required or expected from him, dishonestly makes off without having paid as required or expected and with intent to avoid payment of the amount due shall be guilty of an offence.

(2) For purposes of this section "payment on the spot" includes payment at the time of collecting goods on which work has been done or in respect of which service has been provided.

(3) Subsection (1) above shall not apply where the supply of the goods or the doing of the service is contrary to law, or where the service done is such that payment is not legally enforceable.

(4) Any person may arrest without warrant anyone who is, or whom he, with reasonable cause, suspects to be, committing or attempting to commit an offence under this section.

EFFECT OF SECTION
For the effect of this section see above, paras. [242]–[249].

KNOWING
There is authority for saying that where a person deliberately refrains from making inquiries the results of which he might not care to have, this constitutes in law actual knowledge of the facts in question: see *Knox* v. *Boyd*, 1941 S.C.(J.) 82 at p. 86 and *Taylor's Central Garages (Exeter), Ltd.* v. *Roper* (1951), 115 J.P. 445 at pp. 449, 450, *per*, Devlin, J.; and see also in particular, *Mallon* v. *Allon,*[1964] 1 Q.B. 385; [1963] 3 All E.R. 843 at p. 394 and p. 847 respectively. Yet mere neglect to ascertain what could have been found out by making reasonable inquiries is not tantamount to knowledge; see *Taylor's Central Garages (Exeter), Ltd.* v. *Roper, ubi supra, per* Devlin, J.: and cf. *London Computator, Ltd.* v. *Seymour,* [1944] 2 All E.R. 11: but see also *Mallon* v. *Allon, ubi supra.*

DISHONESTLY
See the note to s. 1, above.

WITH INTENT
See the note to s. 2, above.

Section 5

SHALL BE GUILTY OF AN OFFENCE
  For punishments, see s. 4, *post.*

ARREST WITHOUT WARRANT
  As to arrest generally, see 11 Halsbury's Laws (4th ed.), paras. 99 *et seq.*

SUPPLEMENTARY PROVISIONS
  See s. 5 (2)–(4), *post.*

DEFINITIONS
  For "goods", see, by virtue of s. 5 (2), *post,* the Theft Act 1968, s. 34 (2) (*b*) p. 252, *ante.* Note as to "payment on the spot", sub-s. (2) above.

4. Punishments

(1) Offences under this Act shall be punishable either on conviction on indictment or on summary conviction.

(2) A person convicted on indictment shall be liable—

(*a*) for an offence under section 1 or section 2 of this Act, to imprisonment for a term not exceeding five years; and

(*b*) for an offence under section 3 of this Act, to imprisonment for a term not exceeding two years.

(3) A person convicted summarily of any offence under this Act shall be liable—

(*a*) to imprisonment for a term not exceeding six months; or

(*b*) to a fine not exceeding the prescribed sum for the purposes of section 28 of the Criminal Law Act 1977 (punishment on summary conviction of offences triable either way: £1,000 or other sum substituted by order under that Act),

or to both.

SHALL BE PUNISHABLE EITHER, ETC.
  For the new procedure for determining the mode of trial of offences triable either on indictment or summarily, see the Criminal Law Act 1977, ss. 19 *et seq,* (47 Halsbury's Statutes (3rd ed.), 700 *et seq*).

CONVICTION ON INDICTMENT
  All proceedings on indictment are to be brought before the Crown Court; see the Courts Act 1971, s. 6 (1), (41 Halsbury's Statutes (3rd ed.), 294).

SUMMARY CONVICTION
  Summary jurisdiction and procedure are mainly governed by the Magistrates' Courts Act 1952, (21 Halsbury's Statutes (3rd ed.), 181); the Magistrates' Courts Act 1957, (21 Halsbury's Statutes (3rd ed.), 316) and certain provision of the Criminal Justice Act 1967, (21 Halsbury's Statutes (3rd ed.), 363) and of the Criminal Law Act 1977 (47 Halsbury's Statutes (3rd ed.), 692).

IMPRISONMENT
  Under the Powers of Criminal Courts Act 1973, s. 30 (1), (43 Halsbury's Statutes (3rd ed.), 327) on conviction on indictment a fine (on which no statutory limit is placed) may be imposed in lieu of or in addition to imprisonment.

CRIMINAL LAW ACT 1977, S. 28.
  See 47 Halsbury's Statutes (3rd ed.), 709.

5. Supplementary

(1) For purposes of sections 1 and 2 above "deception" has the same meaning as in section 15 of the Theft Act 1968, that is to say, it means any deception (whether deliberate or reckless) by words or conduct as to fact or as to law, including a deception as to the present intentions of the person using the

261

deception or any other person; and section 18 of that Act (liability of company officers for offences by the company) shall apply in relation to sections 1 and 2 above as it applies in relation to section 15 of that Act.

(2) Sections 30 (1) (husband and wife), 31 (1) (effect on civil proceedings) and 34 (interpretation) of the Theft Act 1968, so far as they are applicable in relation to this Act, shall apply as they apply in relation to that Act.

(3) In the Schedule to the Extradition Act 1873 (additional list of extradition crimes), after "Theft Act 1968" there shall be inserted "or the Theft Act 1978"; and there shall be deemed to be included among the descriptions of offences set out in Schedule 1 to the Fugitive Offenders Act 1967 any offence under this Act.

(4) In the Visiting Forces Act 1952, in paragraph 3 of the Schedule (which defines for England and Wales "offence against property" for purposes of the exclusion in certain cases of the jurisdiction of United Kingdom courts) there shall be added at the end—

"(*j*) the Theft Act 1978".

(5) In the Theft Act 1968 section 16 (2) (*a*) is hereby repealed.

EXTRADITION ACT 1873, SCHEDULE
　See 13 Halsbury's Statutes (3rd ed.), 272.

FUGITIVE OFFENDERS ACT 1967, SCH. I
　See 13 Halsbury's Statutes (3rd ed.) 303.

VISITING FORCES ACT 1952, SCHEDULE
　See 29 Halsbury's Statutes (3rd ed.) 939.

6. Enactment of same provisions for Northern Ireland

An Order in Council under paragraph 1 (1) (*b*) of Schedule 1 to the Northern Ireland Act 1974 (legislation for Northern Ireland in the interim period) which contains a statement that it operates only so as to make for Northern Ireland provision corresponding to this Act—

(*a*) shall not be subject to paragraph 1 (4) and (5) of that Schedule (affirmative resolution of both Houses of Parliament); but

(*b*) shall be subject to annulment by resolution of either House.

ORDER IN COUNCIL ... WHICH CONTAINS A STATEMENT, ETC.
　The Order in Council in question is the Theft (Northern Ireland) Order 1978, s. I 1978 No. 1407.

SUBJECT TO ANNULMENT
　For provisions as to statutory instruments which are subject to annulment, see the Statutory Instruments Act 1946, ss. 5 (1), 7 (1), (32 Halsbury's Statutes (3rd ed.), 672, 673).

NORTHERN IRELAND ACT 1974, SCH. 1, PARA. 1
　See 44 Halsbury's Statutes (3rd ed.), 1012.

7. Short title commencement and extent

(1) This Act may be cited as the Theft Act 1978.

(2) This Act shall come into force at the expiration of three months beginning with the date on which it is passed.

(3) This Act except section 5 (3), shall not extend to Scotland; and except for that subsection, and subject also to section 6, it shall not extend to Northern Ireland.

Section 7

THREE MONTHS BEGINNING WITH...
This Act was passed (*i.e.*, received the Royal Assent) on 20th July 1978, and came into force on 20th October 1978.

INDEX

ABANDONED PROPERTY, 57–58

ABANDONMENT, 134

ABSTRACTING OF ELECTRICITY, 259 *et seq.*

ACCOUNTING
false, 250 *et seq.*; *see also* FALSE ACCOUNT-ING

ACTUS REUS
blackmail, 301 *et seq.*
burglary, 333 *et seq.*
false accounting, 251, 252
possession of housebreaking implements, 372–376
removal of articles from public places, 267–276
theft, of, 18 *et seq.*

AGGRAVATED BURGLARY, 364 *et seq.*
articles of aggravation, 365–367
"at the time" of burglary, 368
definition, 364
explosive, 367
firearm, 365
"has with him", 369
weapon of offence, 366

ANIMALS; *see* POACHING

ANNUITY CONTRACT
pecuniary advantage, and, 214

APPEAL
restitution order, against, 447–448

APPROPRIATION, 19 *et seq.*
act or omission, and, 51
civil law, authorised by, 105–106
co-owner, and, 63
consent, and, 28 *et seq.*; *see also* CONSENT
continuing act, as, 48 *et seq.*, 419
definition, 19–21
equitable interests, 61–62
estate agent, by, 67
handler of stolen goods, by, 45
insurance agent, by, 65
intention, and, 50
intimidation, and, 43–44
mistake, and, 74 *et seq.*
obligation, 65 *et seq.*
meaning of, 79–80
obligation to make restoration of property, 74 *et seq.*
partners, 63

APPROPRIATION—*continued*
possession, and, 23–27
property obtained by deception, and, 33–37
purchases in good faith of stolen goods, by, 46–47
right to rescind, and, 80–84
secret profit, and, 73
supermarkets, in, 39–42
things in action, 100–101
travel agent, by, 66
trustee, by, 63
unpaid seller, by, 106
voidable contract, and, 80–81

ARTICLE
definition, 372–373

ASSAULT
intent to rob, with, 137

ATTEMPT
conditional intention, and, 123–126
theft, and, 51–52

BAILMENT, 23–24
criminal deception, and, 206

BATTERY
abstraction of electricity from, 297

BICYCLE, 286

BLACKMAIL, 300 *et seq.*
actus reus, 301 *et seq.*
belief in right to gain, 315
claim of right, and, 182
definition, 300
demand, 302–304; *see also* DEMAND
gain—
debt, and, 316–317
gain by keeping, 321
intent to cause loss, 312–322
intention to return economic equivalent, 318
loss by not getting, 321
menaces, 305–309; *see also* MENACE
mens rea, 310 *et seq.*
protection of economic interests, 313
remoteness of gain, 322
robbery, and, 145, 149; *see also* ROBBERY
temporary gain, 319
temporary loss, 319
unwarranted demand, 323–330
view to gain, 312–322

BLOCK OF FLATS
building, and, 350–352

BORROWING
theft, and, 128–131

BUILDING, 345–356; *see also* BURGLARY
block of flats, 350–352
definition, 345
extent of, 350–353
inhabited vehicle, 354–356
inhabited vessel, 354–356
outbuilding, 346
part of, 347–349
terrace, 353

BURGLARY, 331 *et seq.*; *see also* POSSESSION
OF HOUSEBREAKING IMPLEMENTS
actus reus, 333 *et seq.*
aggravated; *see* AGGRAVATED BURGLARY
building, 345–356; *see also* BUILDING
conditional intention, and, 124, 359
definition, 332
entry, 333–335
entry for purpose alien to licence to enter, 340–341
entry under false pretences, 338–339
grievous bodily harm, and, 361
intention to enter as trespasser, 357
involuntary entry, 337
knowledge of having trespassed, 357
mens rea, 357 *et seq.*
rape, and, 362
shoplifting, and, 340–341
stealing, and, 360
tenant, from, 342
trespasser, entry as, 336–337
ulterior offence, 358
unlawful damage, and, 363
victim of, 342–344

CHARGE; *see* DEBT

CHEQUE
criminal deception, and, 166

CHEQUE CARDS, 157–158
making off without payment, and, 248

CLAIM OF RIGHT
blackmail, and, 182
deception, and, 181–183
forgery, and, 182

COLLECTION
definition, 263, 275

COMPANY DIRECTOR
false statements by, 259–261

COMPANY OFFICER
false accounting, and, 257–258

COMPENSATION
Police (Property) Act 1897, 451–454
Powers of Criminal Courts Act 1973, 450
powers to award, 450–455
third party, to, 442

CONDITIONAL INTENTION, 123 *et seq.*
assumption of ownership, and, 126
attempt, and, 123–126
burglary, and, 124, 359

CONSENT, 28 *et seq.*
appropriation, and, 30–32
dishonesty, and, 29
ownership, and, 30
taking conveyance, and, 287

CONTRACT
voidable; *see* VOIDABLE CONTRACT

CONTROL, 57–60
receiving, and, 409–411

CONVEYANCE, 279 *et seq.*
definition, 285–286
taken—
allowing oneself to be carried, 290–293
actus reus, 290–292
mens rea, 293
driving, 290–293
actus reus, 290–292
mens rea, 293

CONVICTION
restitution, and, 437

CO-OWNER, 63

COPYRIGHT, BREACH OF, 101

CORPORATION
false accounting, and, 257–258

CORPSE
theft, and, 54

COURTS
jurisdiction of, 433–434

CREDIT CARD
making off without payment, and, 248

CREDITOR
inducement to wait for or forgo payment, 237–238

CRIMINAL DAMAGE, 99
burglary, and, 363
husband and wife, 463–464

CRIMINAL DECEPTION, 153 *et seq.*; *see also* DECEPTION; OBTAINING BY DECEPTION; PECUNIARY ADVANTAGE
appropriation, and, 33–37
cheque cards, and, 157–158
intention to repay, and, 184–185
land, and, 199–204
lease, and, 201–203
machines, and, 159
mistake, and, 81
obtaining, 189–197
obtaining pecuniary advantage, 210 *et seq.*
property, and, 198 *et seq.*
services, 219 *et seq.*
things in action, 205

CROWN COURT
appeal against restitution order in, 447
jurisdiction of, 433

DAMAGE
criminal; *see* CRIMINAL DAMAGE

All references are to paragraph numbers

All references are to paragraph numbers

All references are to paragraph numbers